Introduction to management science

Introduction to management science

THOMAS M. COOK / ROBERT A. RUSSELL

The University of Tulsa

Prentice-Hall, Inc.

Englewood Cliffs, New Jersey

[Introduction to Management Science]
Thomas M. Cook/Robert A. Russell

10 9 8 7 6 5 4 3 2 1

Cook, Thomas M   (date)
  Introduction to management science.

  Includes bibliographies and index.
  1. Operations research.   2. Management—Mathematical models.   I. Russell, Robert A., (date)
joint author.   II. Title.
HD20.5.C655   658.4'034   76-54794
ISBN 0-13-486084-5

Designer: Betty Binns
Senior Production Editor: Joyce Fumia Perkins
Editorial Assistant: Mary Helen Fitzgerald
Cover and chapter-opening drawings: Douglas Florian

Prentice-Hall International, Inc., London   Prentice-Hall of Australia Pty.
Limited, Sydney   Prentice-Hall of Canada, Ltd., Toronto   Prentice-Hall
of India Private Limited, New Delhi   Prentice-Hall of Japan, Inc.,
Tokyo   Prentice-Hall of Southeast Asia Pte. Ltd., Singapore   Whitehall
Books Limited, Wellington, New Zealand

PRINTED IN THE UNITED STATES OF AMERICA

To our wives, Sandy and Sharon

$\left[\begin{array}{c} \text{Preface} \end{array}\right]$

Introduction to Management Science is intended to be used for a one-semester course that introduces the reader to the field of operations research/management science. The text presents a general introduction and, as such, can serve students from any discipline. However, the book is aimed at the business student who will most likely pursue a career in an organization requiring some managerial ability and decision-making skill. It can be successfully used at both the undergraduate and graduate levels.

Many schools require business students to take only one course in quantitative methods; so this text is planned for one-semester or two-quarter survey courses. Given this time constraint, one of our primary objectives was to select for the book those topics the student will actually use for real-world applications. In order to achieve this goal, we were guided by management science usage surveys conducted nationwide by ourselves and other researchers. As a result, *Introduction to Management Science* is specifically constructed to familiarize the student with those management science topics most used in real-world situations.

The mathematical level of the book is purposely kept low in order to make the material readable for both the business student and the layman. A course in college algebra or finite mathematics is sufficient prerequisite. Derivations that require calculus are placed in appendixes at the end of appropriate chapters. The student's ability to comprehend some of the material in the chapters on PERT, queuing, decision theory, and simulation would be enhanced by a course in statistics, but this is certainly not a necessity.

In order to help the student to learn the vocabulary of the discipline, important terms are italicized in the text line and set in color in the margin at the point of definition. Moreover, these definitions are identified by italic page references in the index.

At the end of chapters, two question sections reinforce new material and facilitate student recall. Questions in the first of these, *Review questions*, are specifically answered within the chapter text. The second set of questions, *Problems*, most often require the student to apply newly acquired procedures to realistic problem situations.

So that students can gauge their own comprehension, answers are given in a section at the back of the book for problems with problem numbers printed in color (for example, 2.9, 5.5, and 8.9, parts a, b, and c). Thus, upon completing an assignment, students can check a few answers for a reliable notion of their command of the topic. Those who need to can seek additional help before a new chapter presents new material to be learned.

Cases, too, are featured in appropriate chapters. They may be used as a basis for discussion of the chapter's management science technique, or they may be assigned as projects to be modeled and solved. With either approach, we hope they will help to motivate the student to apprehend the realistic function of management science techniques. Case discussions and solutions are provided in the instructor's guide.

Introduction to Management Science is organized into twelve chapters. Chapter 1 presents a brief history and a discussion of the nature and approach of management science. Several real-world applications and their specified benefits are also discussed in order to give the student a sense of the power and utility of the discipline. Chapter 2 is an elementary review of probability and probability distributions. Students who have taken probability courses will not need to study this chapter in depth, but it can serve as a valuable review for them. For students who have had no previous exposure, Chapter 2 is sufficient preparation for the probability demands of the rest of the text. Chapter 3 introduces decision making under uncertainty. An emphasis in this chapter is placed on structuring the decision problem and visualizing it as a decision tree.

The following five chapters deal with deterministic decision models. Chapters 4, 5, and 6 are a selfcontained package on linear programming. Chapter 4 stresses the formulation of LP models and their application and limitations. Chapter 5 addresses the graphical and simplex methods for solving LP problems. Sensitivity analysis of LP models is examined in Chapter 6. Chapters 7 and 8 are concerned with network models in management science. In Chapter 7 we present transportation and assignment models in terms of applications as well as solution procedures, and we discuss the advantages of special-purpose alogorithms. In the chapter on PERT, we return to stochastic decision problems. A discussion of work breakdown structures is also presented.

Several queuing models are discussed in Chapter 9. The assumptions of these analytic models are stressed, and many examples are solved. Chapter 10 on simulation serves as a tie-in between queuing and inventory, for both are amenable to analysis by simulation. Chapter 11 deals with classical EOQ models, their utility and their limitations as well. It also features an inventory problem solved by simulation.

Chapter 12 is the capstone for the entire text. In it we examine past and present trends in management science. Implementation problems that involve the management science specialist and management are highlighted. New directions and ways to enhance the continued growth of management science are summarized by some of the leading contributors to the field.

Several people have been extremely helpful to us at various stages of this project. We would especially like to thank the reviewers, whose comments and suggestions led to an improved manuscript: John J. Bernardo, University of Kentucky; Frank S. Budnick, University of Rhode Island; Gilbert R. Gordon, The City University of New York; Irwin Kruger, University of Miami; Mildred Massey, California State University at Los Angeles; John Neuhauser, Boston College; Richard Panicucci, Fairleigh Dickinson University; and Fred N. Silverman, The City University of New York.

We would like to thank the staff at Prentice-Hall for its assistance, particularly Business Management Editor Earl Kivett and Senior Production Editor Joyce Perkins, whose conscientious efforts undoubtedly led to a more readable text.

Our thanks also go to the typists who helped prepare this manuscript. We sincerely appreciate the contributions of Margaret Carpenter and her assistants, Mary Helen Domaracki and Liz Aivazian.

Finally, we should like to thank our families for their understanding and encouragement during the preparation of this manuscript.

THOMAS M. COOK
ROBERT A. RUSSELL

Contents

Contents

Introduction to management science

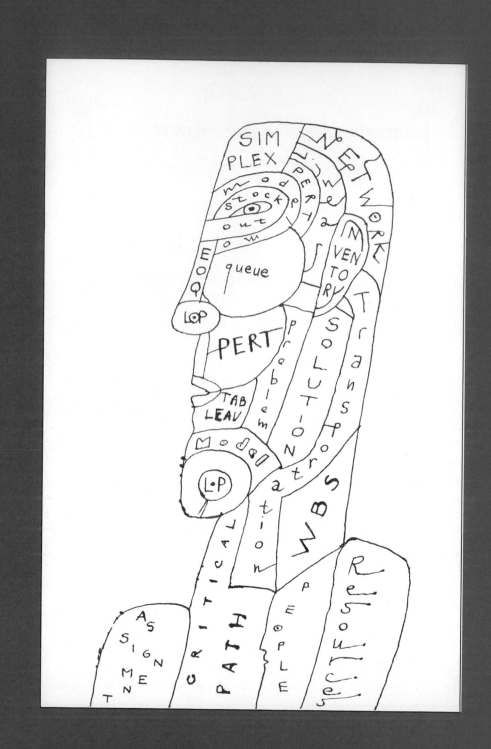

1

$$\Bigg[\ \ \text{Introduction to}$$
$$\text{management science}\ \ \Bigg]$$

Prior to the twentieth century, business and other organizations
functioned in a less complex environment than today's. Managers
of contemporary organizations must cope with a dynamic world
of increased population, inflation, recession, social consciousness,
and shortages of vital resources. Consequently, the decision-making
task of modern management is more demanding and more important
than ever.

Fortunately, we humans can use our ingenuity to find new ways
to handle the problems that confront us. Even though contemporary
institutions face an increasingly complex and uncertain environment,
they also have available innovative approaches to dealing with
decision problems. This book is concerned with some of the new
tools and technology that have been developed specifically to help
management in the decision-making process.

management
science

Management science is the discipline devoted to studying and
developing procedures to help in the process of making decisions.
It is also commonly called *operations research*. The two terms have
come to be used interchangeably, and we shall use both throughout
the text. The principal characteristic of operations research/man-
agement science (OR/MS) is its use of the scientific method for
decision making. Management can approach complex decision problems in several ways. Managers may resort to intuitive or observa-
tional approaches that depend on subjective analyses. Or, putting

operations
research

1

faith in "proven" procedures, they may simply repeat other managers' solutions. Such attempts at handling problems are sometimes called *seat-of-the-pants* approaches. They may not attack the problems in a systematic manner, and they do little to improve or advance the managerial decision process. On the other hand, a management science approach provides a rational, systematic way to handle decision problems. Using a systematic approach, the decision maker has a better chance to make a proper decision.

Our greatest technical accomplishments have been achieved by utilizing the scientific method. Only recently, however, have we begun to apply this methodology outside the laboratory environment of physics and chemistry. Even though these new environments are less controlled, the operations of organizations and their decision-making processes still lend themselves to analysis through scientific methodology.

How did scientific methodology come to be applied to decision problems? The answer to that question will further your comprehension of the field of management science.

[Historical overview]

Operations research / management science is an interdisciplinary field comprising elements of mathematics, economics, computer science, and engineering. Its specific content expanded enormously after the twentieth-century invention of electronic computers. Its fundamental philosophical principle, however—the use of scientific methodology to solve problems—was a recorded management technique much earlier. Venetian shipbuilders of the fifteenth century, for example, are known to have used an assembly line of sorts in outfitting ships.

Progress was not consistent until the Industrial Revolution, however. Based on his analysis of the manufacture of straight pins, Adam Smith proclaimed the merits of division of labor in 1776. Charles Babbage, an English mathematician and mechanical genius, wrote a seminal treatise titled *On Economy of Machines and*

Manufactures (1832). In it, Babbage discussed such issues relevant to management science as skill differential in wages and concepts of industrial engineering.

In the late nineteenth century, an American engineer, Frederick Taylor, formally advocated a scientific approach to the problems of manufacturing. Taylor, sometimes called the father of scientific management, was largely responsible for developing industrial engineering as a profession. It was his philosophy that there was one "best way" or most efficient way to accomplish a given task. He used time studies to evaluate worker performance and to analyze work methods.

Henry L. Gantt, a contemporary of Taylor's, refined the content of early scientific management by bringing into consideration the human aspect of management's attitude toward labor. He espoused the importance of the personnel department to the scientific approach to management. Perhaps his greatest contribution, however, was his scheduling system for loading jobs on machines. Basically a recording procedure, Gantt's system was devised to minimize job completion delays; it permitted machine-loadings to be planned months in advance.

The early scientific management era was an important stage of development for OR/MS. However, its progress was mostly limited to establishing or improving efficient performance of specific tasks in the lower levels of organizations. It may not be possible to pinpoint the first true application of management science, but several pioneers should be noted. As early as 1914 an Englishman named Frederick W. Lanchester attempted to predict the outcome of military battles based on the numerical strength of personnel and weaponry. Lanchester's predicting equation may represent the first attempt to model an organizational decision problem mathematically. In 1915 Ford W. Harris published a simple lot-size formula that constituted the basis for inventory control for several decades and still finds wide use today. Just as Harris helped to establish inventory control theory, a Danish mathematician, A. K. Erlang, founded modern waiting-line, or queuing, theory. He developed mathematical formulas to predict waiting times for callers using automatic telephone exchanges.

One of the first to apply sophisticated mathematical models to business problems in the United States was Horace C. Levinson, an astronomer by training. In the 1930s, Levinson studied such market-oriented applications as the relationship between advertising and sales and the effect of income and residential location upon customer purchases.

Despite such advances in the scientific approach to quantitative management problems before 1940, OR/MS did not emerge as a recognized discipline until World War II. In the late 1930s, the British assembled a team of specialists to investigate the effective use of radar. Subsequently, the British military establishment increasingly called upon the British scientific establishment to study such other problems as antisubmarine warfare, civilian defense, and the optimal deployment of convoy vessels to accompany supply ships.

This approach to military problem solving called upon experts from various areas of specialization. Perhaps the most famous British group was headed by the distinguished physicist P. M. S. Blackett. Blackett's Circus, so-called, consisted of three physiologists, two mathematical physicists, an Army officer, a surveyor, two mathematicians, an astrophysicist, and a general physicist. This multidiscipline team approach has become a characteristic of OR/MS. The highly successful British operational research was credited with helping to win the Battle of Britain and the Battle of the North Atlantic.

Such successes influenced the United States military establishment to include "operations analysis" groups on its staff. During World War II, the United States gathered mathematicians, statisticians, probability theorists, and computer experts to work on operations analysis. During the period, John von Neumann made immense contributions in the area of game theory and utility theory, and George Dantzig worked on the simplex method of linear programming.

After the war, the military establishment increased its research programs and retained some operations research personnel, but industry largely ignored the methodology of the discipline. Many operations research ideas naturally had a military orientation, and nonmilitary managers tended to regard the techniques either as irrelevant to their problems or impossible to implement. Two events helped to bring operations research to industry. In 1947, George

linear
programming

Dantzig developed *linear programming,* a technique that uses linear algebra to determine the optimal allocation of scarce resources. Obviously, such a method could be applied profitably to many business problems. Operations research began to be regarded as sometimes relevant to industry.

The second, and more important, occurrence to enhance the acceptability of nonmilitary operations research was the development and production of high-speed electronic computers. Some operations research techniques entailed long, complex calculations to solve real-world problems. Computers, capable of performing such calculations millions of times faster than people, were invaluable tools for the operations research profession. With the advent of electronic instruments to perform functions that were previously impossible or unprofitable, OR/MS could be perceived as valid to, and valuable for, business and industry. The dependence of OR/MS methodology on computers cannot be overemphasized. Even today, certain large-scale problems cannot be solved with current techniques and existing computer hardware. Research will undoubtedly improve the methodology; but it is ultimately the future generations of computers that will allow operations researchers and management scientists to extend the successful applications of their discipline.

Given the favorable climate engendered by industry's acceptance of OR/MS in the 1950s, the discipline developed rapidly. One measure of its formalization was the establishment of professional associations. Chief among these are: Operational Research Society (British, 1950); Operations Research Society of America (1952); The Institute of Management Science (United States, 1953); American Institute of Decision Sciences (1969).

Since 1950, OR/MS has progressed steadily, sometimes even explosively. More than 20,000 people are presently involved in applying, teaching, or researching the field. Most *Fortune 500* companies practice OR/MS. Smaller companies may not require full-time OR/MS programs and personnel, but they often hire management consultants for OR/MS projects. Given such exposure, business is finding increasingly desirable the employee who has

OR/MS training. As a result, many universities offer undergraduate and graduate degrees in the field, and most business schools have requirements in the subjects of operations research, management science, decision science, or quantitative methods.

[The nature of management science]

You have probably gained some insight into the nature of management science from the preceding brief historical overview. In this section we define the actual content of this discipline more specifically. Harvey Wagner, past president of The Institute of Management Sciences, has described OR/MS simply and yet precisely. Wagner states that operations research is a scientific approach to problem solving for executive management. The Operations Research Society of America amplifies this basic definition by calling operations research an experimental and applied science devoted to observing, understanding, and predicting the behavior of purposeful human/machine systems. It is logically applied, therefore, to the practical problems of government, business, and society.

As the foregoing definitions suggest, the fundamental characteristic of OR/MS is its scientific or systematic approach to decision making. But how can we apply the scientific method to the often uncontrollable and imprecise environment of the real world? In laboratory experiments, data are rejected unless they are demonstrably accurate, and all conditions are strictly controlled. In modern organizations, data are often imperfect, and the outside world exerts a significant influence on many of the variables under study. Factors relevant to a management science experiment are often impossible to manipulate. Furthermore, the functioning and profitability of the firm usually take precedence over artificial changes induced for the sake of experimentation. For example, a company would not temporarily close its warehouses in order to determine the exact shortage costs for its inventory.

Even though the management scientist usually cannot perform a "pure" scientific experiment, this does not prohibit using a scientific approach. The management scientist works in a situation analogous to an astronomer's: Each one has little control over a constantly changing universe and yet each performs scientific experiments and builds mathematical models to account for the observed phenomena.

THE SCIENTIFIC METHOD

In order to see how the management scientists may use a scientific approach, you must recall the basic steps of the scientific method. These are

1 Observation
2 Definition of the problem
3 Formulation of a hypothesis
4 Experimentation
5 Verification

As you would suppose, the first three steps of the scientific method can be carried out by the management scientist much as they would be by a chemist or a biologist. However, experimentation and verification can pose special problems in real-world applications.

Let us consider a hypothetical problem for the manager of a manufacturing firm to see how the scientific method can be applied to the analysis of a business problem. The first step of the scientific method requires the recognition of a particular phenomenon. Suppose that the manager of the manufacturing firm has observed a significant rise in inventory costs over the past year. This observation suggests the existence of a problem that can perhaps be treated, yielding benefits to the firm.

Thus, it is necessary to pinpoint the exact nature of the problem. The manager has observed rising costs. These may simply be due to inflation. Some observations may be directly related to the symptoms of the problem rather than to the problem itself. It is important that the decision maker formulate the problem precisely and address the truly relevant issues. Much time, effort, and money can be wasted looking at the wrong problem.

In our example, suppose that the manager has determined that inventory costs have risen even faster than the national rate of inflation. The manager suspects that a significant part of the increased cost is caused by the firm's current inventory policy and thus is potentially amenable to change. The manager's problem can now be clearly defined: It is necessary to determine a new inventory policy that will reduce inventory costs.

The inventory costs of the company are comprised primarily of inventory holding costs (costs of carrying and storing) and inventory replenishing costs (costs of ordering and restocking). A closer examination by the manager yields the fact that replenishing costs have increased more rapidly than holding costs. This is true primarily because transportation costs and the clerical costs of placing orders have risen sharply. The manager now has a hypothesis: Ordering larger quantities fewer times per year will decrease overall inventory costs. This new policy will increase holding costs somewhat, but it will lower replenishing costs at the same time.

Now the manager needs to determine how much larger the orders should be. A trial-and-error approach can be implemented by changing the order quantity and observing the effects on total inventory costs. Observations will then confirm or disprove the initial hypothesis. Another approach is to use a mathematical inventory model (Chapter 11) that "fits" the particular problem. This approach, if applicable, eliminates the need for trial and error, for the model determines the order quantity. A third approach is computer simulation (Chapter 10). In any of these situations, the manager ultimately determines whether the hypothesis is valid by comparing the cost of the new solution with the cost before experimentation. Higher costs may indicate that the original hypothesis is incorrect. In that case, further experiments are called for to try to develop a better hypothesis.

Verification of the conclusions of the experiment can be made in several ways. The most accurate, of course, is actually to implement the new solution within the company and then observe its effects. This procedure can be very dangerous in practice, and it may have far-reaching consequences throughout the organization. Usually, it is best to try to forecast the success of the new solution by applying it to hypothetical data or data that represent past transactions of the firm. However, since costs, prices, and demand are constantly changing, success on past data does not necessarily guarantee success in future inventory transactions for the company. Thus, complete verification in the real world is not always possible.

[A systems approach]

The scientific method is extremely useful for trying to solve certain very specific problems the management scientist encounters. It is usually applied, however, within a much broader context known as the *systems approach.* The word *system* is much used in our society. We hear of computer systems, solar systems, nervous systems, political systems, and systems we usually cannot beat. In this book, we shall refer to a system as a whole comprising interrelated parts intended to accomplish a specific objective. Thus, a computer system is made up of hardware components (such as the central processor unit, card reader, and disk and tape drives) and software components (such as the operating system software and various compilers). These components interact to accomplish the objective of processing computer jobs.

Organizations, too, conform to our definition of a system. One kind of organization that can use management science to its advantage—the kind with which we will be concerned primarily—is a human/machine system comprising components such as machinery, departments, divisions, and individual people. The main purpose of the management scientist is to aid in the achievement of the goals of the organization as a whole. Viewing the organization as a system permits us to consider the individual components in relation to the entire organization.

This perspective is essential, for the good of the whole may not necessarily derive from the greatest good for each of the parts. In other words, concentrating only on a particular component of the organizational system may result in *optimization,* or best achievement of goals, for that component but a less than optimal solution, or *suboptimization,* for the organization as a whole. Optimizing the organization's goals is sometimes accomplished by

system

optimizing its subsystems. In other cases, however, suboptimization of various components is necessary for the sake of the organization's greatest good. A systems approach best equips the decision maker to determine which alternatives actually will maximize the realization of the goals of the organization.

Just as a systems approach helps us to have a balanced perspective concerning an organization's components, it also helps us to view the organization as a component, or subsystem, of the environment in which it exists. Today's human/machine organizations operate under conditions of rapid change and ever-increasing complexity. Good decision making, therefore, requires that management take a broad view. Just as an inventory problem, for example, within a single component may affect an organization's production, finance, accounting, and personnel functions, so too the organization's inventory decisions can affect external supply, demand, and prices in the general market.

Usually, no single decision maker is sufficiently multitalented to understand the ramifications of proposed solutions on all aspects of the organization, including its internal and external environments. Often, a team of specialists is formed to attack quantitative management problems. The concept of the team approach to decision making is a key characteristic of the OR/MS approach. You may recall that one of the first operations research teams, Blackett's Circus, consisted of eleven different specialists. Depending on the type of application, an OR/MS team might include experts in mathematical programming, accounting, finance, marketing research, engineering, mathematics, behavioral science, statistics, computer programming, and other fields. This interdisciplinary approach tends to treat the individual phases of a problem most effectively; consequently, the success of the entire project is enhanced.

To summarize, management science applications include any approach to problem solving that incorporates all, or most of, the following characteristics:

1 Viewing the problem within a systems perspective
2 Applying the scientific method to develop the solution methodology
3 Using a team, or interdisciplinary, approach

4 Using a mathematical model

5 Using a high-speed electronic computer

We have not yet said much about the fourth essential characteristic of management science, model building. Your introduction to mathematical models is in the following section. Most of the topics you will encounter in this text involve some use of a mathematical model.

[Models in management science]

In general terms, a model is a representation or an abstraction of an object or a particular real-world phenomenon. A good model accurately displays the key properties of the entity it represents. Many different disciplines employ the use of models. For example, aeronautical engineers use scale-model airplanes in wind tunnels, and civil engineers may use scale models of bridges, buildings, or river systems. More abstract models are used by economists to predict future economic activity and by ecologists to estimate potential effects on the environment. In each of these applications, the model represents an abstraction of reality; and the purpose of the model is to gain specific information about, and general insight into, the phenomenon it represents. By using models, we may investigate certain cause-and-effect relationships and the interaction between key variables.

Many different models exist, but each may be classified as belonging to one of three types. An *iconic* model is a physical representation that actually looks like the model it represents. Examples of iconic models include model airplanes and cars, or photographs. An *analog* model substitutes one property for another; it can represent dynamic situations statically. For example, a slide rule is an analog model because it substitutes physical distances for numerical quantities. A frequency polygon is an analog model in statistics because it represents numerical data pictorially. Why is a flow chart an analog model in computer programming? The third class of model consists of *symbolic*, or *mathematical*, models.

iconic model

analog model

symbolic or mathematical model

This type of model is important to the management scientist. Mathematical models attempt to represent nonmathematical reality by means of equations and other mathematical statements. These models translate the essential features of a given situation into mathematical symbols. Then, the symbols can be manipulated in ways that the actual personnel, production, inventory, and so on, cannot. A mathematical model is thus a formal structure that creates a framework within which a problem can be analyzed.

Building useful models for management science applications requires a delicate balance between accuracy and simplicity. The model must be detailed enough to represent the essential realities of the problem and yet manageable in terms of computation and implementation. No mathematical model can capture all characteristics, properties, and uncertainties of a real situation. Attempting to build such a total model results in outright failure or in a model that is too cumbersome to use.

Some management science models involve relationships that cannot be expressed as a system of equations. An example is a model based on properties of mathematical group structures. (A group is a collection of elements having certain properties; matrices and real numbers are examples of groups.) However, most models created for management science applications do consist of a system of equations. A single equation, called the *objective function* is used to measure the effectiveness of proposed solutions. The remaining equations, called the *constraints*, ensure that the solution satisfies certain requirements dictated by the nature of the problem. To illustrate the nature of a mathematical model, let's consider a small mathematical model that has an objective function and only one constraint.

objective function

constraints

Our problem is well known in OR/MS literature. It is called the knapsack problem, or sometimes the cargo-loading problem, and it has many applications. Let's consider seven items that we would like to take on a camping trip. Table 1.1 lists the weight and the subjective value we have assigned to each item. We further assume that our knapsack has a 10-pound capacity, which means that we cannot take all seven items on the camping trip. The problem is to choose the items that maximize the sum of their values to us and yet do not exceed the 10-pound limit.

Table 1.1 Knapsack problem data

Item	Weight (lbs)	Value
1 Water	3	60
2 Tent	5	60
3 Food	4	40
4 Matches	1	10
5 Fishing tackle	4	20
6 Sleeping bag	3	10
7 Liquor	1	3

Before we create a mathematical model of this problem, we need to define some decision variables. Decision variables have two characteristics: They are the variables whose solution values actually indicate the solution to the problem and those variables over which the decision maker has control. Our problem is to decide which items to take on the trip. Therefore let

$$x_i = \begin{cases} 1 & \text{if we take item } i, \text{ for } i = 1, 2, \ldots, 7 \\ 0 & \text{otherwise} \end{cases}$$

Thus $x_4 = 1$ means that we take item 4 and $x_4 = 0$ means that we do not take item 4. Our measure of effectiveness is total value; therefore, our objective function is to maximize $60x_1 + 60x_2 + 40x_3 + 10x_4 + 20x_5 + 10x_6 + 3x_7$. Our only restraint is our weight capacity, which can be represented by $3x_1 + 5x_2 + 4x_3 + 1x_4 + 4x_5 + 3x_6 + 1x_7 \leq 10$. Our final mathematical model is thus

Maximize $60x_1 + 60x_2 + 40x_3 + 10x_4 + 20x_5 + 10x_6 + 3x_7$
subject to $3x_1 + 5x_2 + 4x_3 + 1x_4 + 4x_5 + 3x_6 + 1x_7 \leq 10$
where $x_i = 0$ or 1 for $i = 1, 2, \ldots, 7$

Solving the foregoing mathematical model is not so easy as deriving it, but this time the answer is given to you. The best solution is to take items 1, 2, 4, and 7, and the associated value is 133. This means that we would take water, a tent, matches, and liquor on the camping trip. Once the model and a solution procedure are established, we can investigate various properties of the problem if we want. For example, we can study the effect of capacity on maximum value by changing the capacity from 10 to other values (such as 9 or 11) and re-solving the model. In this way, a model can be manipulated to reveal various relationships among key variables in the problem.

Though model-building is an integral part of OR/MS procedures, it is still more an art than a science. Successful model-building comes with experience and practice at relating situations to mathematical equations. A few standard models have been created that can be used in certain commonly occurring problem situations. However, most quantitative problems are unique simply because every organization has its own restrictions, limitations, and goals. Most of the time, therefore, models have to be built from scratch.

No model is perfect, and no model can truly represent the situation it symbolizes. Thus, successful management science projects do not depend solely upon models and scientific techniques. As the discipline becomes more sophisticated, greater emphasis is being placed on human factors. There is awareness of the need to balance purely quantitative approaches with the experience, judgment, and insight provided by management. This is a progressive step.

The role models play in the OR/MS approach is shown in Figure 1.1, a diagram of an OR/MS study. Note that steps 2 through 4 suggest that the development of a satisfactory model may be progressive, requiring successive refinements at various stages. Steps 5 and 6 distinguish OR/MS from blue-sky, or unrealistic, procedures. No matter how sophisticated the procedures are, the OR/MS process is not useful unless the solution is amenable to control and can be successfully implemented. In the final analysis, success is measured by results.

Management science and the functional areas of business

Most of you reading this book are majoring in business and have interests in one of its primary functional areas. In this section, we relate management science to each of these areas. As you will see, these are basically two-way relationships: Management science needs information, policy, and other guidance from the functional

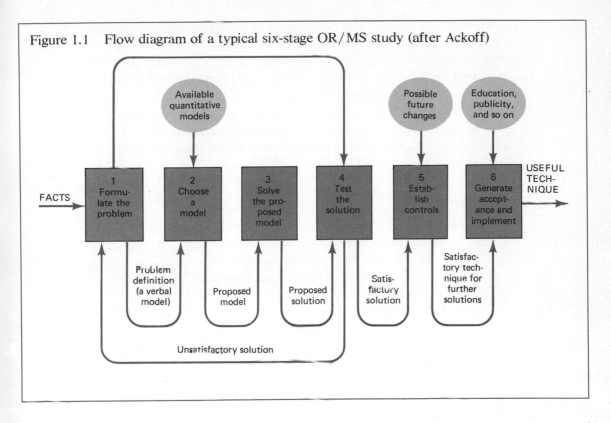

Figure 1.1   Flow diagram of a typical six-stage OR/MS study (after Ackoff)

areas, and each area has specific problems for which management science can help to generate solutions.

ACCOUNTING

Management science models and techniques are virtually useless without accurate data. An organization's accounting department can be vital in providing the necessary data. Woolsey and Swanson have advised the practicing management scientist to make friends with a cost accountant, who ". . . can be the greatest ally for which the up-and-coming OR man can hope."[1]

Management science, in return, can make significant contributions to the field of accounting. The study of management information

[1]R. E. D. Woolsey and H. S. Swanson, *Operations Research for Immediate Application: A Quick and Dirty Manual.* New York: Harper & Row Publishers, Inc., 1975, p. 168.

systems (MIS) has been applied to automate and improve various accounting procedures. An MIS is a formal system (usually computerized) for collecting, analyzing, and reporting information to managers. Statistical sampling theory has been used to improve the reliability and systematization of auditing procedures. Management science procedures have also been used to resolve transfer-pricing and byproduct-costing and to develop standard costs. Other applications include inventory control and forecasting future transactions.

FINANCE

The management scientist needs the financial analyst to provide input concerning cash-flow restrictions and policies. The OR/MS practitioner also needs data about the cost of capital and facts concerning long-range capital requirements. Successful management science applications in the financial realm include capital-budgeting, a procedure that assesses various projects requiring cash outlays in order to maximize net benefits in limited-budget situations. Computer simulation models have been used to build corporate financial-planning models. These simulation models are manipulated to answer various "what if" questions concerning the future of the firm. Management science has also been used to design investment portfolios. Portfolio selection procedures are used primarily to choose investment vehicles and mixes that will interact to minimize risk or maximize gain. Other financial applications include equipment-replacement analysis and determination of dividend policies.

MARKETING

Marketing-research applications are numerous. They include determination of product mix, product selection, and forecasting future demand. Advertising applications include the selection of media in order to maximize a product's effective exposure to a particular market segment at lowest cost. Management science techniques have also been used to assign salespeople to territories, to determine the appropriate number of accounts for them to serve, and to establish their travel routes in order to minimize the distances they must cover. Physical distribution problems are especially suited to resolution by management science techniques. Models have been developed to determine least-cost shipping patterns from plant to market. Location theory has been used to determine optimal locations and sizes for warehouses so that the cost of the distribution of goods is minimal. Other marketing applications include assessing competitive marketing strategies and analyzing packaging effectiveness.

MANAGEMENT

Management is a general term, and almost any application of management science can be viewed as an aid to management since one of management's primary functions is decision making. In some circles, management science and behavioral management are contrasted as quantitative and qualitative management, respectively. By behavioral management, we mean the body of knowledge devoted to understanding human and organizational behavior. Each mode, however, is less effective without the other. Behavioral scientists utilize quantitative techniques in order to draw conclusions concerning observed human or organizational behavior. Management science relies upon the fundamentals of behavioral management in order to solve real-world problems successfully. The solutions proposed by management scientists almost always require some changes within the organization. These changes often have behavioral ramifications. In fact, it is entirely accurate to describe the management scientist as an agent of change.[2]

Management science exists ultimately for people. As a collection of techniques and models isolated from a human context, the discipline is meaningless. If management science is to be implemented successfully, human factors and behavioral aspects must receive careful consideration. After all, what good is an optimally balanced assembly line if the workers are poorly motivated or on strike?

[Management science in action]

There are obviously multitudes of management science applications, ranging from traditional military and production concerns to more contemporary ones in the fields of environmental engineering, the

---

[2] M. Radnor and R. Neal, "The Progress of Management-Science Activities in Large U.S. Industrial Corporations," *Operations Research*, 21 (March–April 1973), 427–450.

social sciences, and even sports. In this section, we will discuss four specific applications of management science in which concrete results were achieved.

VEHICLE-ROUTING PROBLEM

Many organizations are faced with the problem of how to route a fleet of vehicles efficiently. This problem is particularly common among wholesale and retail distributers (who schedule deliveries), refuse collection companies (which schedule collections), and the U.S. Postal Service (which does both).

Let's consider the actual industrial refuse collection problem experienced by a private firm in a large southwestern city.[3] The firm had roughly 740 scheduled pickups during a 6-day work week. The accounts were scattered throughout an entire city and its outlying areas, situated within a 20-mile radius from the central truck depot. Between 120 and 160 accounts were serviced daily Monday through Friday, and certain accounts were serviced 2, 3, or 6 times a week. The firm used four large hoist-compactor trucks to collect the refuse. These large trucks are quite uneconomical to operate; management estimated that it cost $25 per hour to operate each of them.

The problem was to sequence these four trucks. Each morning, the trucks would leave the depot, collect the refuse at the various accounts, visit dump sites whenever necessary, and ultimately return to the depot. Management's approach to sequencing the trucks had been basically intuitive rather than scientific and methodical. As a result, fuel costs were high, and the drivers often earned overtime pay by working late to finish their rounds.

This problem is generically related to the classical traveling salesman problem in operations research literature. Basically, how can a single salesman, vehicle, or other entity be sequenced among n points, visting each one only once so as to minimize total distance traveled? The complexity of the problem will be clearer if you consider how many possible sequences there are. In general, for n points to be visited, there are $(n - 1)!$ possible sequences. Thus, for $n = 11$ there are 3,628,800 possible sequences, but for $n = 21$

---

[3]R. Russell, "Efficient Truck Routing for Industrial Refuse Collection," paper presented at the ORSA/TIMS meeting, San Juan, Puerto Rico, October, 1974.

there are 2,432,900,000,000,000,000 possible sequences. Can you imagine how many sequences there are for $n = 160$?

The management science approach to this problem does not attempt to find the one best (optimal) sequence. Technology does not yet exist to consistently find the optimal solution to sequencing problems with more than 150 points in the sequence. In addition, this vehicle-routing problem has complicating factors such as the need to have all four truck routes reasonably evenly balanced with respect to workload and the fact that some accounts have time constraints. (That is, several of the accounts must be serviced at specified times of the day.)

In order to develop a more efficient routing system, a systematic solution procedure, more often called an *algorithm*, was developed algorithm and coded for use on a computer. Solutions were generated that attempted to minimize the distance traveled while meeting time constraints and balancing the routes. The computerized procedure generated four well-balanced routes with significant improvements in the distances traveled. The new routes were implemented by management, and the drivers then made a few refinements in the routes that had been generated by computer. After implementing the new routes, each truck's travel time was reduced by roughly 2 hours each day. The reduction in distance traveled per day by the four trucks averaged 25 percent.

In a very similar application to school bus routing in Tennessee, a management science approach enabled a school district to save approximately $250,000 annually. The number of buses needed dropped from 13 to 9, and the total distance traveled by the buses was reduced by 50 percent.[4]

AMBULANCE DEPOT LOCATION

Facility location problems comprise a significant portion of the OR/MS literature. In this case, we examine the effective location of ambulance facilities in New York City.[5] The city of New York

[4] P. Krolak, "Empirical and Theoretical Bounds on Generalized Vehicle Scheduling," paper presented at the ORSA/TIMS meeting, Las Vegas, Nevada, November 1975.

[5] E. S. Savas, "Simulation and Cost-Effectiveness Analysis of New York's Emergency Ambulance Service," *Management Science*, 15 (August 1969), B-608–B-627.

decided to undertake a management science study to improve ambulance service and, in particular, to reduce the response time (from receipt of call to arrival at the scene).

The city's policy had been to station 109 ambulances at a total of 49 hospitals. Each hospital was in a designated district and sent out ambulances in response to requests only from within that district. The city had several ideas about how to improve the ambulance service: The first was to locate some ambulances at satellite garages located at demand centers within the already established hospital districts. A method to compare the proposed satellite system with the old system, however, was needed. Any model or procedure to be used had to consider where ambulance satellite garages should be located, the locations of hospitals, the geographic distribution and frequency of calls within each district, and, finally, the number of ambulances.

The problem is too complex to be solved optimally by analytical methods. The city decided to use a computer simulation model to evaluate various proposed systems. Once constructed, the simulation model would estimate actual response times and performance given any specified number of ambulances and their locations. The city decided to simulate 175,000 calls for the Kings County Hospital district in Brooklyn. The average response time with the old system (housing ambulances at the hospital) was 13.5 minutes. Various new systems were tried, and the analysis indicated that moving ambulances from hospitals to satellite garages could reduce the response time slightly. Basing all seven ambulances at satellite garages reduced the average response time from 13.5 to 12.0 minutes.

Further "what if" questions were then considered by means of the simulation model. Three more ambulances were worked into the model, and it was found that the best strategy was to house six ambulances at the hospital and four at satellite garages. With this strategy, the model predicted an average response time of 10.9 minutes.

It was then decided to simulate an entirely new approach in which hospital districts were ignored. That is, the model was adapted to predict the outcome if ambulances were to be stationed at patient demand centers without regard to hospital locations. An ambulance would simply proceed to the nearest available hospital after picking up a patient. This procedure would require a central dispatching facility to coordinate the status of requests with each ambulance and hospital. When this strategy was simulated, it produced the best results. If ten ambulances were located at demand centers in the Kings County district, response time was shown to drop 30 percent. Even greater improvement might be attainable with the development of an integrated computer-based information system for dispatching ambulances.

INVENTORY CONTROL SYSTEM

Now, let's consider a computer-oriented inventory control system that was successfully applied to the centralized control of inventory in several branch warehouses.[6] The purpose of the branch, or satellite, warehouses was to increase the firm's competitive advantage by offering quick delivery times to customers. The satellite warehouses were managed by a centralized inventory control group whose objective was to maintain adequate levels of inventories to provide good customer service at least cost.

Prior to a management science approach (in 1968), the inventory manager's policy was to restock each major warehouse once a week. The manager reviewed each inventory item daily and ordered approximately a 2-month supply of any product for which the current level was below one month's estimated sales. In an effort to improve upon the manual inventory system, the company decided to computerize certain tasks such as inventory forms and, at the same time, to investigate other possible changes.

Other improvements in inventory policy were slow to evolve, however, because management was basically skeptical about radically innovative management science techniques. One of the first changes was the development of a more accurate procedure for forecasting each satellite warehouse's transactions. An exponential smoothing procedure was used to forecast sales; then, based on these sales, forecasts, new reorder points, and order quantities were calculated by means of inventory control models. Daily ordering

[6] J. Bishop, Jr., "Experience with a Successful System for Forecasting and Inventory Control," *Operations Research*, 22 (Nov.-Dec. 1974), 1224-1231.

reports were generated by the computer, which provided relevant data for each product. Included in the report were suggested order quantities. However, the report had a unique feature: It allowed management to override the computer on any items whose inventory levels were below the reorder point. Thus, management had the option of accepting the computerized order quantities or of suggesting order quantities of its own. This manual override feature turned out to be the key to implementing the management science approach successfully. It gave management an awareness of its participation in, and essential control over, decision-making processes. Initially, management was reluctant to accept the computer output, and it countermanded 80 percent of the computer's decisions. Confidence was gained, and overridden output had dropped to 10 percent a year later.

Several other reports were generated for the firm, including a monthly out-of-stock analysis and a final report that summarized the month's transactions and the status of satellite warehouse operations. The management science approach was successful in that manual errors were reduced by 75 percent, inventories by 30 percent, and out-of-stock situations by 25 percent. The first-year return on investment was approximately 150 percent, all development costs included.

The experience was so positive that the firm undertook further systematic investigations. The second phase included a computer simulation model of the inventory system. With the aid of the simulation model, the firm studied different inventory policies, review periods, and levels of the production-planning horizon. The practice of management science has become an ongoing function in this firm.

PRODUCTION PLANNING AND DISTRIBUTION

The final application we will examine concerns the minimization of combined production and distribution costs. This case differs from the previous three in that the mathematical model is solved so that it yields the best possible solution; that is, an *optimal* solution is sought.

The complex problem was encountered by General Motors

Corporation in the production and distribution of automobiles.[7] The problem involves the determination of the number and type of each model of car to produce at each plant and then the determination of the distribution center to which each model should be shipped. Production costs vary at each plant, as do transportation costs from plant to distribution center. Bounded capacities are associated with each plant and indicate the minimum and maximum number of cars that can be produced. Bounds also exist on how many of each different model can be produced at each plant. Each distribution center has a specific number of each model for which there is customer demand.

The problem can be mathematically modeled as a particular type of linear programming problem. (We'll discuss this topic in Chapter 4.) A typical application for the Pontiac or Buick division involves a mathematical model with 1,200 equations and 4,000 variables. Recently developed OR/MS techniques enable a system of this size to be solved on a computer in less than 10 seconds. (It should be noted here, however, that the entire solution process is *not* a 10-second procedure. Much time is spent setting up the problem, collecting data, and readying the data for computer usage.)

The speed of computation encouraged the company to develop an on-line computer capability. The mathematical model is linked to a graphics display terminal and an English-language input processor. Thus, one need not be an OR/MS expert to use the system. Management can feed in relevant data using the English language and within seconds observe the optimal solution on the display terminal. The system is currently being used by the executive division for planning purposes.

[Summary]

You have been introduced to operations research/management science in this chapter. As an interdisciplinary field, OR/MS has existed only a little more than 30 years, but its body of knowledge

---

[7] F. Glover and D. Klingman, "Network Application in Industry and Government," Research Report CCS247, University of Texas, Austin, Texas, 1975.

draws upon related fields as old as human communication. Earliest formal OR/MS activities were military applications by the British during World War II. The field has grown greatly since the early 1940s, and OR/MS is now widely practiced in business and government.

In principle, OR/MS is the application of scientific or systematic methods to improve the decision-making process. The OR/MS approach assumes a systems viewpoint from which scientific procedures can be applied to various aspects of an entire problem. The advantage of the systems approach is that it allows the optimization of an organization's overall goals, not just those of isolated departments or components of the human/machine system.

The characteristic most distinguishing the OR/MS approach is its use of mathematical models. Mathematical models attempt to translate the essential qualities of real-world situations into systems of equations. Manipulating or solving the mathematical models can engender effective strategies or courses of action for the decision maker.

The real-world applications of OR/MS are numerous. In this chapter, we presented four applications in which specific improvements over previous operations were achieved. OR/MS procedures are distinguished from other theoretical scientific endeavors in that they must ultimately be useful or implementable in the real world. OR/MS must eventually serve the end to which it is directed— namely, human needs.

[Looking ahead]

In the chapters to follow we shall examine certain basic OR/MS methods. These methods include some of the most widely used OR/MS techniques today. That is the main reason for your exposure to them in an introductory text.

All OR/MS procedures belong in one of three categories. These three categories are defined according to the nature of the environment in which a decision must be made. The environment or the data for a problem can be either

1 Deterministic

2 Stochastic

3 Uncertain

deterministic problems *Deterministic problems* are those in which data are known with certainty. For example, the knapsack problem we examined earlier is a deterministic problem since all values, weights, and capacities were known exactly. *Stochastic problems* are those in which the data are not known with certainty, but a probability distribution is known. For example, consider an inventory problem in which the customer demand for a product each month is not known exactly. However, past records for the company indicate a reliable frequency distribution for this stable product. Thus, we can specify the probability that future demand will exceed a specified amount. Problems that must be dealt with when data are *uncertain* are the most difficult of all. An example of this type of problem is the determination of a bid in a competitive bidding situation. In bidding for a contract, the uncertainty hinges around the bids to be submitted by the compeititon. Future demand or future sales are often uncertain quantities, too.

stochastic problems

uncertain problems

In subsequent chapters we first look at decision theory—the analysis of decisions under relative uncertainty. We then consider some deterministic models such as linear programming, transportation and assignment models, and some inventory models. Stochastic problems to be studied include some inventory models, PERT for project scheduling, queuing models or the analysis of waiting lines, and computer simulation. Cases follow these topics to illustrate the environments in which real-world problems exist and to encourage you to usc these newly acquired techniques to develop appropriate solutions or make responsible decisions.

[Bibliography]

Ackoff, Russell L., and Patrick Rivett, *Manager's Guide to Operations Research.* New York: John Wiley & Sons, Inc., 1963.

———, and Maurice W. Sasieni, *Fundamentals of Operations Research.* New York: John Wiley & Sons, Inc., 1968.

Anderson, D. R., D. J. Sweeney, and T. A. Williams, *An Introduction to Management Science: Quantitative Approaches to Decision Making.* St. Paul, Minn.: West Publishing Company, 1976.

Churchman, C. West, Russell L. Ackoff, and E. L. Arnoff, *Introduction to Operations Research.* New York: John Wiley & Sons, Inc., 1957.

Eck R. D., *Operations Research for Business.* Belmont, California: Wadsworth Publishing Company, Inc., 1976.

Hillier, F. S., and Gerald J. Lieberman, *Introduction to Operations Research.* San Francisco: Holden-Day, Inc., 1974.

Levin, Richard I., and Charles A. Kirkpatrick, *Quantitative Approaches to Management* (3rd ed.). New York: McGraw-Hill Book Company, 1975.

Miller, David W., and Martin K. Starr, *Executive Decisions and Operations Research* (2nd ed.). Englewood Cliffs, N.J.: Prentice-Hall, Inc., 1969.

Thierauf, Robert J., and R. C. Klekamp, *Decision Making through Operations Research.* New York: John Wiley & Sons, Inc., 1975.

Waddington, C. H., *OR in World War II: Operational Research Against the U-Boat.* London, England: Paul Elek Ltd., 1973.

[Review questions]

1 Management science attempts to apply scientific methodology in solving decision problems. How does this methodology differ from the scientific method used in the physical science laboratory?

2 What characteristics distinguish the OR/MS approach to problem solving?

3 In what ways does management science contribute to the functional areas of business? In what ways does it borrow from these areas?

4 What are the advantages of adopting a systems perspective in making decisions for an organization?

5 Several applications of management science are mentioned in this chapter. List as many others as you can.

6 In the context of decision making, explain the difference in the terms *deterministic, stochastic,* and *uncertain.*

7 In order for management science applications to be successful in the real world, more than just a good mathematical model is necessary. What else is needed?

8 What are some of the factors responsible for the rapid growth of OR/MS after 1950?

9 Does management science benefit all levels of management? Explain.

10 Pick some organization with which you are familiar and describe the organization as a whole and its related components.

11 What are some advantages of using mathematical models? What are some potential pitfalls?

12 An appliance manufacturer has developed a small mathematical model that forecasts potential sales given price and advertising expenditures. Let y represent sales and x_1 and x_2 represent advertising expenditures and price, respectively. Then the model predicts that $y = 8.14 + 66x_1 - .17x_2$. Determine the sales forecast if the price is $250 and advertising expenditures are $40,000. Comment on the possible accuracy or inaccuracy of the model. What variables or relationships may have been omitted?

13 Three OR/MS applications are listed as follows. In each case, state the variables relevant to the problem, the data that are required, and what form the output, or answer to the problem, should take.
  a Scheduling commercial airlines between major U.S. cities
  b Determining the location and size of regional warehouses for a retail manufacturer
  c Selecting an investment portfolio for an insurance company

2

[Probability concepts and distributions]

In the first chapter, you learned that there are three states in which decisions are made: certainty, in which all relevant information is known; stochastic, or risk, conditions, in which limited information (usually in terms of probabilities) is available; and total uncertainty, in which little or nothing is known. Decisions under certainty are, of course, the easiest to make. When information is certain, a systematic analysis of even large-scale decision problems can usually be made. However, most real-world decision problems are made under conditions that are neither completely certain nor completely uncertain. The decision maker usually has some information to work with but is uncertain to a degree about what will happen after the decision is made.

The use of probability theory can be of great help in making decisions under risk conditions. By organizing relevant information, assessing the likelihood of various alternatives, and systematically analyzing the problem, the decision maker can usually reach a more effective decision than by the seat-of-the-pants, or intuitive, approach. Overall goals or objectives can best be met when probabilistic information is considered in a systems context. For example, probability theory can be useful in helping a contractor decide whether or not to bid on a $100,000 contract that costs $5,000 in bidding expenses. Or, a production manager might use probability theory to decide how much inventory to stock in order to avoid large stock-outs and provide an adequate level of service to the customer.

Founded in mathematics, probability theory is rigorous and well defined. In this chapter, we shall develop only the aspects you will need for the material in the rest of this book. In effect, then, this is a brief and specialized review. If you have not studied probability theory before, you will find an elementary introduction to the subject here.

In simple terms, a probability is a measure of the likelihood that an event will occur. If we reach into a deck of cards, we can say that the likelihood of getting a card that is a club is $^{13}/_{52}$, or .25. The .25 is a quantification of the likelihood that we will draw a club. Thus, a probability is actually a measure of chance. Probability is the mathematical expression of uncertainty; modern probability has its foundations in mathematical measure theory.

We shall be concerned with probabilities as they pertain to decision making. Probabilities of two types are used in decision making. *objective probability* *Objective probabilities* are those for which there is definitive historical information or rigorous analysis to support the assignment of probabilities. For instance, the .25 probability of drawing a club from a deck of cards is an objective probability. The probability of getting a head in tossing a fair coin is .50 and is an objective probability. Past experience has shown that this statement of likelihood is true, and it can easily be argued mathematically.

Frequently, a decision maker is confronted with a situation in which an exact objective probability is not available. For example, the exact probability of receiving a contract is not known, or the probability of next month's sales exceeding $50,000 is not known *subjective probability* with certainty. A *subjective probability* is based on the personal experience of the decision maker. It may rely in part on previous records or outside information, but it represents the decision maker's degree of belief that a particular event will occur. The odds a bookie gives for major sports events are subjective probabilities, but they are based also on past records, outside information, and so on. A retail clothing buyer's sales estimates also qualify as subjective probabilities. The buyer must consider the desirability of various lines and then subjectively estimate potential sales. In deciding how much to order, the buyer may subjectively assess the probabilities that sales will be at or below different volumes.

Subjective probabilities are essentially educated guesses, and some people feel that subjective probabilities should not be included as input to formal analysis of a decision problem. These objectivists feel that subjective input should be considered only after a formal analysis is accomplished with the available objective information. Subjectivists, on the other hand, believe in using subjective estimates and probabilities in analyzing a decision problem. They argue that people who run businesses and others who make consequential decisions do so based on their experience, intuition, and hunches. Subjectivists feel that the decision process is more likely to be correct if subjective estimates and probabilities are used in a formal or systematic analysis.

[Basic concepts]

In probability applications, we often want to determine the likelihood of a particular random phenomenon or occurrence. In probability theory, we call a specified outcome of a random phenomenon an event *event*. If we perform a statistical experiment in coin tossing, we may ask what the probability is of the event *getting two heads in a row*. An inventory manager may want to determine the probability of the event *incurring a stock-out next month*.

Events may be classified as simple or compound. A *simple event* simple event consists of a single possible outcome of a random phenomenon. For example, suppose we toss three coins and consider the event *getting three heads*, or *HHH*. This is a simple event. A *compound* compound *event*, on the other hand, consists of two or more simple events. event The event of getting two heads when we toss three coins is a compound event since it consists of the three simple events *HHT*, *THH*, and *HTH*.

In assessing probabilities for a particular problem, it is necessary to specify the universe of all possible outcomes. A simple event sample is called a *sample point*, and the collection of all possible sample point points is called the *sample space*. We denote the sample space sample by the letter *S*. Thus, in the example of tossing three coins, the space sample space *S* consists of all possible outcomes. In this case *S* = {*HHH, HHT, HTH, THH, TTH, HTT, THT, TTT*}. Assuming the coins are fair, then each of the sample points in S is equally likely to occur; thus, the probability of each sample point is $1/8$.

Let's consider another random experiment in which a single die is cast. The six-sided cube will show from one to six dots. If we let the simple events be defined by the number of dots showing, then $S = \{1, 2, 3, 4, 5, 6\}$. In Figure 2.1 we represent S with a Venn diagram. Consider the event E_1, which is defined as getting a one or a two. E_1 is the outlined area in Figure 2.1. Event E_1 is a compound event, and its probability is equal to the probability of the simple events of which it is composed. If we denote $P(E_1)$ as the probability of E_1, we have $P(E_1) = 1/6 + 1/6 = 1/3$.

For every event E there exists a *complementary event* $\bar{E}$. The complement $\bar{E}$ consists of all the sample points in S that are not in E. Thus, in Figure 2.1, $\bar{E}_1 = \{3, 4, 5, 6\}$. Together, an event and its complement must comprise the entire sample space. By knowing the probability of each individual sample point, we can calculate the probability of each event in S. Thus $P(\bar{E}_1) = 1/6 + 1/6 + 1/6 + 1/6 = 2/3$. However, this counting process is not convenient for large or infinite sample spaces. Fortunately, basic probability laws can be used to help determine probability in more general situations.

complemen-
tary event

PROBABILITY AXIOMS

Certain properties of probability are fundamental to the understanding and application of probability theory. For example, the probability of any event being between 0 and 1 is a fundamental property. Let E_i represent any event in the sample space S; then we have the following three axioms.

Nonnegativity The probability of any event in S is greater than or equal to 0 and less than or equal to 1.

$$0 \leq P(E_i) \leq 1 \qquad \text{for any } E_i \text{ in } S$$

Additivity If two events E_i and E_j are both in S but have no sample points in common, the probability that at least one of these events occurs is the sum of $P(E_i)$ and $P(E_j)$.

$$P(E_i \text{ or } E_j) = P(E_i) + P(E_j)$$

Figure 2.1　The sample space S

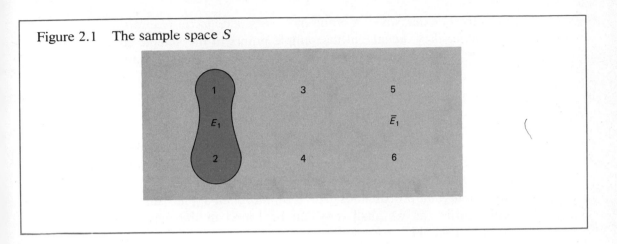

Completeness of sample space　The probability of the entire sample space is 1.

$P(S) = 1$

The additivity property of the second axiom refers to events that are mutually exclusive. *Mutually exclusive events* cannot occur at the same time and are characterized by not having any sample points in common. Figure 2.2 graphically illustrates two mutually exclusive events E_i and E_j. In Figure 2.1, E_1 and $\bar{E}_1$ are also mutually exclusive events. An event and its complement are always mutually exclusive. But an event and its complement are also

mutually exclusive events

Figure 2.2　Mutually exclusive events E_i and E_j

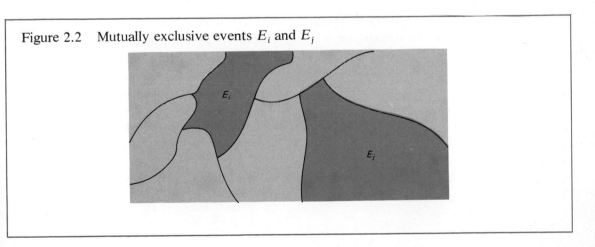

collectively exhaustive. A group of events is *collectively exhaustive* if together they include all the sample points in the sample space. Thus $E_1 = \{1, 2\}$ and $\bar{E}_1 = \{3, 4, 5, 6\}$ are collectively exhaustive in $S = \{1, 2, 3, 4, 5, 6\}$.

collectively exhaustive events

MARGINAL, CONDITIONAL, AND JOINT PROBABILITIES

So far, we have only considered the probabilities of events that are unaffected by the outcome of other events. Unconditional probabilities that do not depend on other events are sometimes called *marginal* probabilities. The term *marginal* applies since these probabilities (as we shall see) can be found in the margin of a probability table.

marginal probability

If we roll a die and ask what the probability of a five is, then we are asking for a marginal probability since it does not depend on other events or outside information. For a fair die, the probability of a five is $1/6$. But suppose we consider another event that constitutes additional information concerning the outcome of the die. Suppose you cannot see the die at first and someone tells you that it does not show a three. Now what is the probability of a five? The probability is now $1/5$ rather than $1/6$ since one of the six possibilities has been eliminated. This is an example of a *conditional probability*, a probability that depends on the outcome of another event.

conditional probability

Conditional probabilities are important in the business world, for there are many instances in which decisions under uncertainty depend on the outcome of other factors. For instance, we might want to know the probability of small car sales given new government fuel efficiency regulations, or we might want to estimate the chances of success for a new product given a nationwide advertising effort.

We denote conditional probability as $P(A|B)$, which is read, "the probability of A, given B." If we roll a die and let A equal the event of getting a five, and B the event a three or four does not show, then we have $P(A) = 1/6$ but $P(A|B) = 1/4$. If we let C equal the event that a four or five does not show, then $P(A|C) = 0$.

We determined the foregoing probabilities by logical reasoning, but there exists a formula for conditional probability:

$$P(A\,|\,B) = \frac{P(A \text{ and } B)}{P(B)} \qquad \text{provided that } P(B) > 0 \qquad\qquad [2.1]$$

We only consider conditional probabilities when $P(B) > 0$ anyway, because it makes little sense to consider the probability of A given B if B never occurs. By $P(A \text{ and } B)$, we mean the probability that both A and B occur. In order to understand this and the concept of conditional probability, consider the Venn diagram in Figure 2.3. Notice that the shaded area A and B is the intersection of event A and event B. We can intuitively explain formula 2.1 for conditional probability by assuming that the areas A, B, and A and B corresponds to actual probabilities. Thus, if a sample point falls in B, the probability that it also falls in A is equal to the ratio of the area of A and B to the area of B. Thus we get $P(A\,|\,B)$ = $[P(A \text{ and } B)]/[P(B)]$.

The probability of two or more events occurring is called a *joint probability*. Thus $P(A \text{ and } B)$ is a joint probability.

joint
probability

[Example] Let's illustrate some of these conditional and joint probabilities with an example. For a graduate thesis, a student is attempting to determine the relationship between the success of OR/MS projects and the formalization of OR/MS procedures within the company. To gather information, 100 companies are surveyed

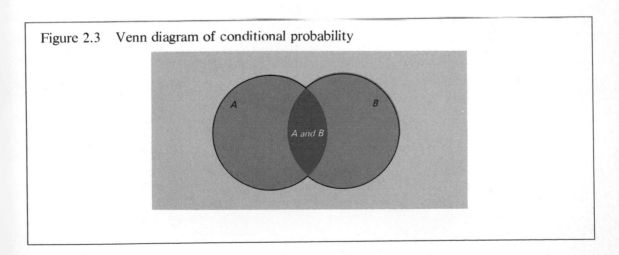

Figure 2.3   Venn diagram of conditional probability

about their OR/MS operations. The student finds that 70 of the companies report that their OR/MS projects are successful, and 50 report formalization of OR/MS procedures. Let's define four different events:

A = company reports success
B = company reports failure
C = company has formalized OR/MS procedures
D = company does not have formalized OR/MS procedures

Based on the 100-company sample, the student calculated the probabilities shown in Table 2.1. We shall use these data for insight into the nature of various probabilities by posing some pertinent questions, then showing you how to find the answers.

Regardless of whether the company formalized procedures or not, what is the probability that the company had successful OR/MS applications? The required probability is $P(A)$, which is an unconditional or marginal probability found in the margin of Table 2.1. There you see that $P(A) = .70$.

If you were to pick one of the companies surveyed at random, what is the probability that it would report both formalized procedures and project success? This probability is a joint probability involving both events A and C. From the table we can see that the graduate student has calculated $P(A$ and $C)$ and found it to be .40.

What is the probability that a company surveyed had not formalized OR/MS procedures? This is another marginal probability, this time

Table 2.1 Probabilities revealed by 100-company survey

		Formalized	Not formalized	
	Event	C	D	Marginal probability
Success	A	.40	.30	.10
Failure	B	.10	.20	.30
	Marginal probability	.50	.50	

represented by $P(D)$. We can read that $P(D) = .50$ from the bottom margin of the table.

What is the probability that a company reported OR/MS success given that it had formalized procedures? This question requires a conditional probability. Specifically, we seek $P(A|C)$. From formula 2.1 we have $P(A|C) = [P(A \text{ and } C)]/[P(C)] = {}^{.40}/{}_{.50} = .80$.

What is the probability that a company reported OR/MS success given that it had not formalized procedures? Again we seek a conditional probability, $P(A|D) = [P(A \text{ and } D)]/[P(D)] = {}^{.30}/{}_{.50} = .60$.

Notice the probabilities of success of .80 and .60, respectively, given formalized and nonformalized procedures. If the foregoing survey were actual and had been carefully performed, these probabilities would lead you to some reasonable conclusions about formalized versus nonformalized OR/MS procedures. You could then make decisions that would significantly improve the probability of project success. And that is what this book is all about.

THE ADDITIVE AND MULTIPLICATIVE LAWS

In addition to the axioms of probability, two other rules are helpful in calculating probabilities. The *additive law* pertains to the union of two events; we read $P(A \text{ or } B)$ as the probability that either A or B occurs. The additive law states that

additive law

$$P(A \text{ or } B) = P(A) + P(B) - P(A \text{ and } B) \qquad [2.2]$$

This formula makes sense intuitively if you look again at Figure 2.3. The sum $P(A) + P(B)$ includes $P(A \text{ and } B)$ twice. Thus $P(A \text{ or } B) = P(A) + P(B) - P(A \text{ and } B)$. In the special case where A and B are mutually exclusive events, the additive rule is equivalent to the additivity axiom, yielding $P(A \text{ or } B) = P(A) + P(B) - 0 = P(A) + (B)$.

multiplicative law The *multiplicative law* pertains to the intersection of events; it can be derived directly from the conditional probability formula 2.1. In fact, the multiplicative law is merely another statement of the definition of conditional probability. The multiplicative law states that

$$P(A \text{ and } B) = P(A) \cdot P(B|A) \qquad [2.3]$$

The multiplicative and additive rules are useful in determining probabilities of compound events. Compound events, you will recall, consist of two or more simple events. Let's explore some examples.

[Example]   The Bugle Company (newspaper publishers) conducted a survey to determine the readership of the various newspapers within the city. The company publishes both a morning and an evening paper. The survey indicated that 60 percent of subscribers to any newspaper read the morning *Bugle*, 30 percent read the evening *Bugle*, and 10 percent read both.

What is the probability that a subscriber in the city received either the morning or the evening paper from the Bugle Company? We define two events. Let

A = a subscriber reads the morning *Bugle*
B = a subscriber reads the evening *Bugle*

The desired probability is $P(A \text{ or } B)$. From the additive law, we have $P(A \text{ or } B) = P(A) + P(B) - P(A \text{ and } B)$. Since $P(A$ and $B)$ is given in the problem as .10, we have $P(A \text{ or } B) = .60 + .30 - .10 = .80$.

What is the probability that a subscriber receives neither a morning nor an evening paper from the Bugle Company? This probability is the complement of $(A$ or $B)$ that we found in the preceding question. Thus, the probability that a subscriber takes neither paper is $1 - P(A \text{ or } B) = 1 - .80 = .20$. Clearly, the Bugle Company has a lion's share of the market.

[Example]   The Medalist Golf Ball Company sells its products in boxes of a dozen balls. Quality control consists of testing two balls taken randomly from each box. The box is rejected only if both balls tested prove to be defective. Suppose that a box actually has two defective balls. What is the probability that it will be rejected? First, define the events:

A = the first ball is defective
B = the second ball is defective

Then, we want $P(A$ and $B)$. From the multiplicative law we have that $P(A$ and $B) = P(A) \cdot P(B|A)$. $P(A) = 2/12$ since there are 2 defectives out of 12 balls. However, $P(B|A) = 1/11$ since if A

occurs there are only 11 balls in the box and only 1 is defective. Thus $P(A \text{ and } B) = (2/12)(1/11) = 2/132 = .0164$. The probability that the box would be rejected is quite small.

INDEPENDENT AND DEPENDENT EVENTS

We have already defined three relationships between events; we have discussed complementary, mutually exclusive, and completely exhaustive events. The meaning of independent events is easy to perceive. Two events A and B are independent if the outcome of one has no affect on the probability of the outcome of the other. More formally, events A and B are *independent* if

$$P(A|B) = P(A) \text{ or } P(B|A) = P(B)$$

If these conditions do not hold, then the events are *dependent*.

Imagine flipping a coin in your left hand and another in your right hand. Does the outcome of one coin affect the outcome of the other? It does not. The probability of a head is $1/2$ for each hand regardless of the outcome in the other hand. In the golf balls example, however, we had a case of dependence. The probability of drawing a defective golf ball on the second draw did depend on the outcome of the first draw.

For independent events, the multiplicative law simplifies since $P(A|B) = P(A)$. Thus, for independent events we have

$$P(A \text{ and } B) = P(A) \cdot P(B) \tag{2.4}$$

Formula 2.4 extends to more than two events, as the following example illustrates.

[Example] Consider a coin tossing experiment in which we toss a fair coin five times.

If a head has appeared four times in a row, what is the probability of a head on the fifth trial? Since each trial is an independent event, the probability of a head on the fifth trial is still $1/2$.

What is the probability of tossing five straight heads? Each trial is an independent event, but in this case we are asking for the probability that all five events will happen. Thus, the multiplicative law yields the probability $(1/2)(1/2)(1/2)(1/2)(1/2) = 1/32$.

[Example] Consider a playing card problem in which we have an ordinary deck of 52 cards composed of four suits of 13 cards each. Suppose we randomly draw 1 card and then another without replacing the first.

What is the probability that both cards are clubs? Define the events:

A = first card is a club
B = second card is a club

Then, it is straightforward to find that $P(A \text{ and } B) = P(A) \cdot P(B \mid A)$ = $^{13}/_{52} (^{12}/_{51}) = ^{156}/_{2,652} = .059$. In this case, the second draw is dependent on the first.

What is the probability of drawing two clubs if the first is replaced? Since the events are now independent we have $P(A \text{ and } B) = P(A) P(B) = ^{13}/_{52} (^{13}/_{52}) = ^{169}/_{2,704} = .063$.

[Probability distributions]

In this section, we shall define a random variable and examine the concepts of a probability distribution. In addition, we shall describe several discrete probability distributions and several continuous probability distributions.

You learned earlier that an event is a specified outcome of an experiment or a random phenomenon. An example is the toss of a coin. The outcomes associated with the experiment are the displays of a head or of a tail. Now, if a numerical value, such as 0 or 1, is attached to each of the two possible outcomes, then the elementary, or individual, outcomes of the experiment can be termed a random variable. More specifically, a *random variable* is a function whose numerical value depends on the outcome of some experiment. For example, the roll of one die can be thought of as an experiment with the outcomes being the spots on the face of the die. The random variable could then be defined as the number of spots on the face of the die or any other similar function, such as those described in Table 2.2. Remember, a random variable is a function

random variable

Table 2.2   Random variables

Number of spots on face of the die	A possible value of the random variable	A possible value of the random variable
1	1	25
2	2	50
3	3	75
4	4	100
5	5	200
6	6	25

that assigns a numerical value to an elementary outcome of an experiment.

probability distribution   A *probability distribution* relates a probability to the values a random variable can take on. These values of the random variable represent an exhaustive and mutually exclusive set of values. Consequently, the probabilities of a probability distribution must add to 1.

DISCRETE PROBABILITY DISTRIBUTIONS

Discrete probability distributions are probability distributions in which the random variables are discrete. That is, the random variable takes on specific and discontinuous values. In other words, there are gaps between values that the random variable can take on. In a continuous probability distribution, on the other hand, the random variable can take on the value of any real number between the limits of the distribution. An example of a discrete probability distribution is a simple toss of a coin where a head is assigned the value of 0 and a tail is assigned the value of 1. Table 2.3 defines this probability distribution.

If the example is expanded to the toss of four coins and the random variable is defined as the number of heads, then the probability distribution in Table 2.4 is defined. You can verify the probability reflected in Table 2.4 by listing all the possible outcomes and adding those outcomes that yield a specific number of heads.

Table 2.3   Probability distribution of a coin toss

Random variable	Probability
0	.50
1	.50
	1.00

There are 2^4, or 16, possible outcomes. The probability distribution in Table 2.4 is graphed in Figure 2.4.

cumulative probability distribution   A *cumulative probability distribution* is a function of some random variable that defines the probability of the random variable's being less than or equal to a specific value of the random variable. In other words,

$$F(x) = P(X \leq x)$$ [2.5]

where X = random variable
         x = value of the random variable

In the discrete case,

$$F(x) = \sum_{x_i \leq x} P(x_i)$$ [2.6]

Given our previous example of four coin tosses, the cumulative probability function is shown in Table 2.5 and Figure 2.5.

Table 2.4   Discrete probability distribution

Random variable	Probability
0	1/16
1	4/16
2	6/16
3	4/16
4	1/16

Figure 2.4   Discrete probability distribution for number of heads in four tosses
of a fair coin

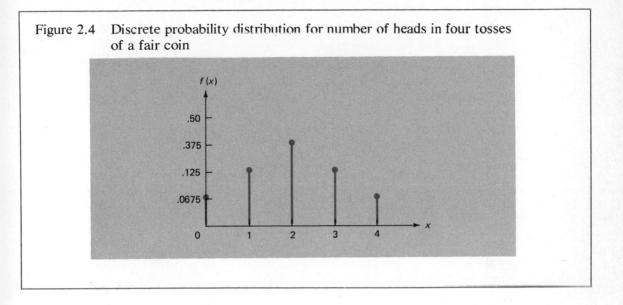

Binomial distribution   One of the most common discrete probability distributions is the binomial distribution. In order for you
to make sense of the binomial distribution, you must first understand
what is meant by a Bernoulli trial. A *Bernoulli trial*, sometimes   Bernoulli
called a Bernoulli *process*, is a random phenomenon involving two   trial
mutually exclusive and exhaustive events. A flip of a coin is a
Bernoulli trial. An acceptance or rejection of a shipment of parts
is a Bernoulli trial. Typically, the two events are referred to as
success and failure. The probability of a success is denoted by

Table 2.5   Cumulative probability distribution for four coin tosses

x	Probability	Cumulative probability
0	$^1/_{16}$	$^1/_{16}$
1	$^4/_{16}$	$^5/_{16}$
2	$^6/_{16}$	$^{11}/_{16}$
3	$^4/_{16}$	$^{15}/_{16}$
4	$^1/_{16}$	1.0

Figure 2.5 Cumulative probability distribution for four coin tosses

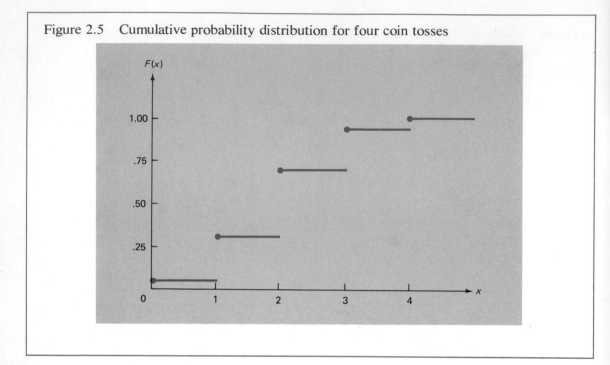

p and the probability of a failure is $1 - p$, which is denoted by q. Suppose there are 100 balls in an urn, 5 gold and 95 silver. We draw 1 ball from the urn at random. If a gold ball is considered a successful draw and a silver ball is considered a failure, $p = .05$ and $q = .95$.

The random variable of a binomial distribution is the number of successes in n *independent* Bernoulli trials where the probability of a success remains constant. In the case of drawing balls from an urn, the ball must be placed back in the urn for independence to be maintained. Let us return to our example of tossing a coin four times. The random variable is the number of heads. What we have is four independent Bernoulli trials with a head defined as a success and a tail defined as a failure. In this case, p is equal to .50 and q is equal to .50. If the random variable is the number of heads in four tosses, then that random variable is binomially distributed, as shown in Table 2.6.

Table 2.6   Binomial distribution with $p = .5$, $n = 4$

X	P(x)
0	.0625
1	.25
2	.375
3	.25
4	.0625

In order to assess probabilities for binomial random variables with any number of Bernoulli trials and any probability of success, the following probability function can be used.

$$P(y) = (nCy)(p^y q^{n-y}) \qquad [2.7]$$

where y = number of successes
        nCy = number of combinations of n things taken y at a time
        p = probability of success
        q = probability of failure
$nCy = n!/[y!(n-y)!]$
where $n! = (n)(n-1)(n-2) \ldots (1)$
        $0! = 1$

To illustrate the use of this function, consider the following problem. A shipment of 20 light bulbs has just been received. Historically, 10 percent of the light bulbs received from the supplier have been defective. If each bulb is tested and a defective bulb is designated as a success, then the probability distribution of the number of defective bulbs in a random shipment of 20 is as shown in Table 2.7. As you can see from Table 2.7, the probability that there would be more than 9 defective bulbs is virtually zero.

Let's illustrate the use of the probability function to calculate one of these discrete probabilities.

$$
\begin{aligned}
P(y = 2) &= [20/2!\,(20-2)!]\,(.1)^2(.9)^{18} \\
&= (20 \cdot 19/2)\,(.1)^2(.9)^{18} \\
&= (190)(.01)(.1502) \\
&\cong .2852
\end{aligned}
$$

Table 2.7   Binomial distribution with $P = .1$, $n = 20$

Number of defective bulbs	Probability
0	.1216
1	.2702
2	.2852
3	.1901
4	.0898
5	.0319
6	.0089
7	.0020
8	.0004
9	.0001
10	.0000
11	.0000
⋮	⋮
20	

As you can easily see, the computation of binomial probabilities can get very laborious, even using an electronic calculator. For this reason, binomial tables are included at the end of the book. You should verify the values in Table 2.7 by using the binomial tables.

Poisson distribution   The other discrete probability distribution we shall discuss in this chapter is the Poisson distribution, derived by Siméon Poisson in 1837. We examine the Poisson distribution because of its significant application in queuing theory (the subject of Chapter 9). Let's define a random variable as the number of events that occur during a certain interval of time or space. The random variable could be the number of telephone calls in an hour, the number of arrivals to a toll gate in 15 minutes, or the number of customers to shop at a store in a day. If the following three conditions are present, the random variable is said to be Poisson distributed.

1 During some interval Δt, the probability of an occurrence of an event (such as an arrival) is constant, regardless of when Δt starts.

2 The occurrence of an event is independent of any other occurrence of the event.

3 If Δt is chosen such that the probability of the occurrence of an event within Δt is small, then the probability that the event will occur is approximately proportional to the width of the interval. For example, let $\Delta t = 1$ second. If P(occurrence in Δt) = .005, then P(occurrence in $2\Delta t$) = .01.

If a random variable is distributed in a Poisson manner, the probability that the random variable will take on any value k is given in equation 2.8. This function is called a *probability mass function.*

probability mass function

$$P(X = k) = e^{-m}m^k/k! \quad \text{for } m > 0; k = 0, 1, 2, \ldots \quad [2.8]$$
where e = the base of natural logarithms with a value approximately equal to 2.71828

m = mean number of events occurring in a given time interval

k = number of events

Consider the following example. An average of three cars per minute arrives to a toll gate according to a Poisson process. The probability distribution of the number of cars arriving to the toll gate per minute is contained in Table 2.8.

Table 2.8   Poisson distribution with $m = 3$

Arrivals to toll gate in 1 minute	Probability
0	.0498
1	.1494
2	.2240
3	.2240
4	.1680
5	.1008
6	.0504
7	.0216
8	.0081
9	.0027
10	.0008
11	.0002
12	.0001

To illustrate how these probabilities are calculated, let's find the probability of four cars arriving during 1 minute.

$$
\begin{aligned}
P(X = 4) &= e^{-3}3^4/4! \\
&= 3^4/[(2.71828^3)(4)(3)(2)(1)] \\
&= 81/[(20.0837)(24)] \\
&= .1680
\end{aligned}
$$

Poisson tables are included at the end of the book so that you won't have to work probability calculations out for yourself.

CONTINUOUS PROBABILITY DISTRIBUTIONS

Continuous probability distributions are analogous to discrete probability distributions. The only difference is in the nature of the random variable. If a random variable can take on all values of the real number system between two limits, then it is said to be *continuous*. For example, the number of customers arriving to a supermarket is a discrete random variable, but the time between customer arrivals is continuous because time can be measured on a continuous scale.

Continuous probability distributions can be hard to understand if you have not been exposed to the integral calculus because these probabilities can no longer be calculated by a simple counting procedure. With continuous random variables, it is not appropriate to define the probability of the random variable taking on some specific value. The probability that the random variable equals some value k is zero, or, in notation, $P(X = k) = 0$. It is only appropriate to ascertain the probability that the random variable will fall within some range of values. For example, the probability that a randomly selected 35-year-old man will weigh between 175 and 200 pounds can be calculated given certain assumptions about the probability distribution of the weight of 35-year-old men. The probability of a man weighing 175 pounds exactly, and not the most minute fraction more or less, is theoretically zero. A *probability density function* (pdf) describes a continuous probability distribution. On a graph, the pdf is represented by a curve. The total area under the curve defined by the pdf is equal to 1.

probability density function (pdf)

This all becomes easier to understand if you look at Figure 2.6. The probability that the random variable x falls between 0 and

Figure 2.6 Probability density function (pdf)

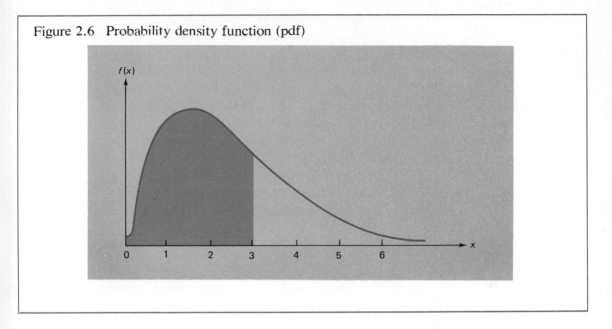

3 equals the ratio of the area under the curve between 0 and 3 to the total area under the curve, which, by definition, must equal 1. By merely looking at the graph in Figure 2.6, you might estimate that the probability that x will fall between 0 and 3 is approximately .60. To calculate $P(0 < x < 3)$ exactly, the calculus must be used. Fortunately, tables at the end of the book relieve you of the necessity of calculating probabilities directly. In actuality, the exact probability is found by taking the definite integral from 0 to 3 of $f(x)[\int_0^3 f(x)\,dx]$. In the following sections, we are going to examine the two continuous probability distributions most commonly used in management science.

Uniform distribution The probability density function for the uniform distribution is the simplest of pdfs. If b is the upper limit that the random variable x can take on and a is the lower limit, then the pdf for the uniform distribution is

$$f(x) = 1/(b - a) \quad \text{for } a \leq x \leq b \qquad [2.9]$$
0 elsewhere

The graph of the pdf in equation 2.9 is shown in Figure 2.7.

The key to understanding the uniform distribution is this: You must realize that the probability of a uniformly distributed random variable's falling within a certain range is merely the ratio of the width of that interval to the entire width of the uniform distribution. For example, suppose a random variable x is uniformly distributed between 2 and 10. The pdf for this distribution is $f(x) = 1/(10 - 2)$ for $2 \leq x \leq 10$, and zero elsewhere; so the $P(2 \leq x \leq 4)$ is merely $2/8$, or .25. Figure 2.8 shows graphically that the area under the curve from 2 to 4 is 25 percent of the area under the curve.

The cumulative probability distribution function is expressed below:

$$F(x) = \begin{cases} 0 & \text{for } x < a \\ \dfrac{x - a}{b - a} & \text{for } a \leq x \leq b \\ 1 & \text{for } x > b \end{cases}$$

Where $F(x) = P(y \leq x)$
y = random variable

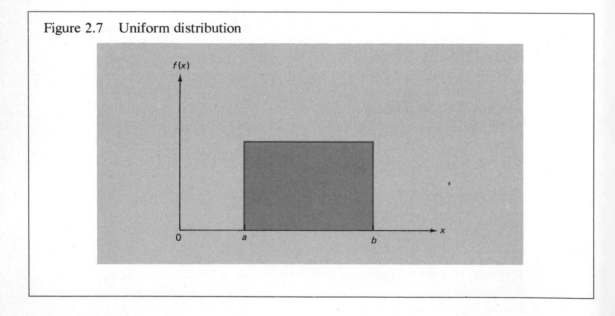

Figure 2.7   Uniform distribution

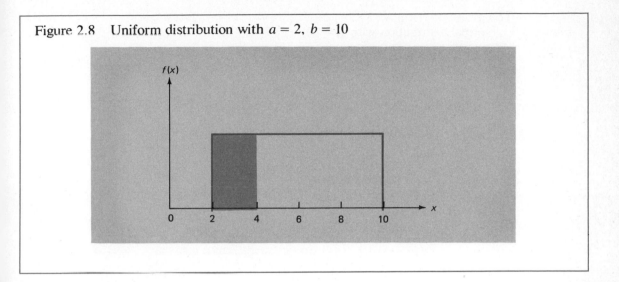

Figure 2.8 Uniform distribution with $a = 2$, $b = 10$

If we apply it to the preceding example, the probability that x will be ≤ 6 is $F(6) = (6 - 2)/(10 - 2) = {}^{4}/_{8} = .50$.

Normal distribution Perhaps the most useful of the continuous probability distributions is the normal, also referred to as the *Gaussian*, distribution. Reasons for the normal distribution's utility include the following:

1 The normal can be used under certain conditions to approximate both the binomial distribution and the Poisson distribution.

2 Many random phenomena behave according to a normal distribution, including such examples as height of adult females, IQ scores, classroom performances of students, and so on.

3 Due to the central limit theorem, if x is a random variable with mean μ and variance σ^2, then the mean of random samples of size n is normally distributed with mean μ and variance σ^2/n, irrespective of the distribution of the random variable.

The pdf of the normal distribution is

$$f(x) = \left(\frac{1}{\sigma \sqrt{2\pi}} \right) e^{-(x-\mu)^2/2\sigma^2} \qquad \text{for } -\infty < x < \infty \qquad [2.10]$$

Figure 2.9   Normal distribution with μ = 10, σ = 2

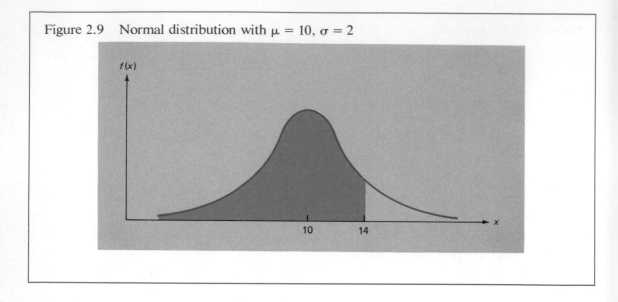

where   μ = mean
            σ = standard deviation

Because the foregoing function (equation 2.10) cannot be integrated directly, probabilities associated with the normal distribution are calculated by using a table of probabilities for a standard normal distribution with a mean of zero and a standard deviation of one. In order to use this table for a normal distribution with mean μ and variance σ^2, the following transformation is necessary:

$$Z = (x - \mu)/\sigma \qquad\qquad [2.11]$$

where Z = a normally distributed random variable with mean 0 and standard deviation 1

Once Z is calculated, it is easy to look the probability up in the normal tables at the end of the book.

To illustrate the use of the normal tables, let's assume a random variable is normally distributed with mean 10 and standard deviation 2. What is the probability that random variable x is less than 14? First, when we calculate Z we get $Z = (14 - 10)/2 = 2$. The normal

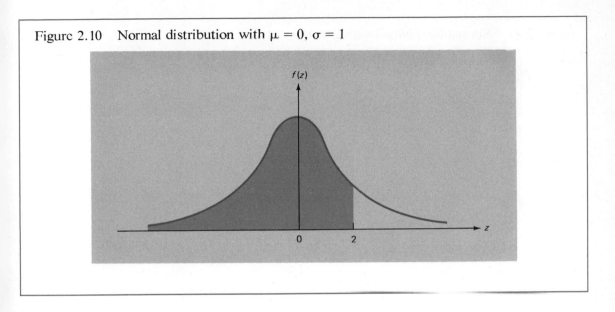

Figure 2.10   Normal distribution with $\mu = 0$, $\sigma = 1$

table at the end of the book gives the probability that the random variable Z is less than or equal to some specific value z_i, $P(Z \le z_i)$; in other words, the table gives the area under the standard normal curve from $-\infty$ to z_i.

To find $P(x \le 14)$, which is the shaded area in Figure 2.9, we merely look in the normal table for $P(Z \le 2)$, which is the shaded area in Figure 2.10, because $P(x \le 14) = P(Z \le 2)$.

The standard normal table gives the probability that the random variable Z will be less than or equal to some specific value. If it is necessary to find $P(a \le x \le b)$ or $P(x \ge b)$, you must use the symmetry properties of the normal distribution. For example, suppose you had $P(10 \le x \le 14) = P(0 < Z < 2)$. (See Figure 2.11.) We know that half the distribution lies to the left of $Z = 0$; therefore $P(0 \le Z \le 2) = .97725 - .5 = .47725$. Similarly

$$
\begin{aligned}
P(X > 14) &= 1 - P(x < 14) \\
&= 1 - .97725 \\
&= .02275
\end{aligned}
$$

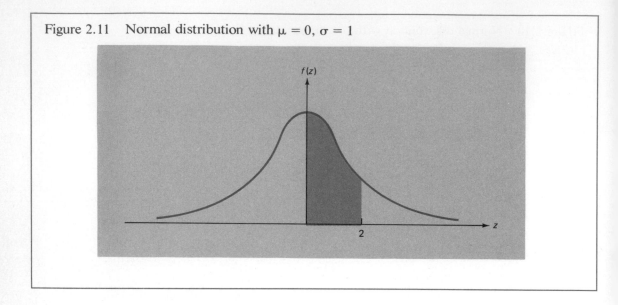

Figure 2.11   Normal distribution with $\mu = 0$, $\sigma = 1$

One final example: What is the probability that x will fall between 12 and 14? Looking at Figure 2.12, it is easy to see that $(12 < x < 14)$ $= P(x \le 14) - P(x \le 12)$. Remember that

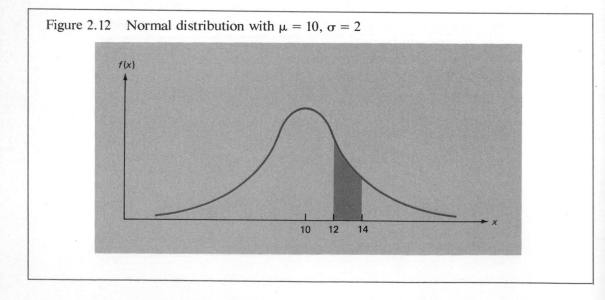

Figure 2.12   Normal distribution with $\mu = 10$, $\sigma = 2$

$$P(x \leq 14) = P[Z \leq (14 - 10)/2]$$
$$= P(Z \leq 2)$$
$$= .97725$$
$$P(x \leq 12) = P[Z \leq (12 - 10)/2]$$
$$= P(Z \leq 1)$$
$$= .8413$$

Therefore, $P(12 \leq x \leq 14) = .97725 - .8413 = .1359$.

[Bibliography]

Breiman, Leo, *Probability.* Reading, Mass.: Addison-Wesley Publishing Co., Inc., 1968.

Burr, Irving W., *Applied Statistical Methods.* New York: Academic Press, Inc., 1974.

Chao, L. L., *Statistics: Methods and Analyses.* New York: McGraw-Hill Book Company, 1969.

Feller, William, *An Introduction to Probability Theory and Its Applications.* vol. I (2nd ed.), 1957; vol. II (3rd ed.), 1968, New York: John Wiley & Sons, Inc.

Mendenhall, William, and James E. Reinmuth, *Statistics for Management and Economics.* North Scituate, Mass.: Duxbury Press, 1971.

Richmond, Samuel B., *Operations Research for Management Decisions.* New York: The Ronald Press Company, 1968.

————, *Statistical Analysis* (2nd ed.). New York: The Ronald Press Company, 1964.

Stockton, John R., and Charles T. Clark, *Introduction to Business and Economic Statistics* (5th ed.). Cincinnati, Ohio: South-Western Publishing Company, 1975.

Trueman, Richard E., *An Introduction to Quantitative Methods for Decision Making.* New York: Holt, Rinehart and Winston, Inc., 1974.

[Review questions]

1 Why is an understanding of probability important for making business decisions?

2 Explain the difference between objective and subjective probabilities. Give an example of each.

3 An event and its complement have no points in common. Are they independent or dependent? Explain.

4 What is conditional probability?

5 Distinguish between mutually exclusive events and independent events.

6 If a collection of events is mutually exclusive and collectively exhaustive, what is the sum of their probabilities?

7 Define and give an example of a random variable.

8 What is a probability distribution?

9 Distinguish between a discrete probability distribution and a continuous probability distribution.

10 Define and give an example of a cumulative probability distribution.

11 What is a Bernoulli trial? Give an example.

12 Why is the Poisson distribution important to management science?

[Problems]

2.1 Suppose you flip a fair coin four times:
    a What is the probability that you will obtain the outcome *HTHT?*
    b What is the probability of getting four heads in a row?
    c What is the probability of getting a tail on the fourth trial given that the results the first three times were heads?

2.2 Consider an urn that has six black and four white balls:
    a Suppose that after each ball is drawn it is replaced. What is the probability of drawing a white ball?
    b What is the probability of drawing three white balls in a row?

c Suppose now that the balls are not replaced after drawing. What is the probability of drawing a white on the second trial given that the first trial resulted in a black ball?

2.3 If you flip a fair coin five times, what is the probability of getting at least three heads?

2.4 A project manager is currently supervising four projects. The probabilities that each one will be completed on time are .70, .90, .80, and .60, respectively. Assuming that the project times are independent, what is the probability that all four projects will be completed on time?

2.5 Consider two urns: The first urn has six black and four white balls, and the second urn has seven white and three black balls. An urn is selected at random, and then a ball is selected at random from the urn. What is the probability that a white ball is selected? Suppose that the selection process is biased so that there is a 60 percent chance of choosing the first urn: What is the probability of choosing a white ball now?

2.6 A production manager has studied past daily demand for widgets and has arrived at the following probability distribution for demand:

Demand	Probability
0	.10
1	.20
2	.30
3	.25
4	.15

What is the probability of two or more units of demand during any day?

2.7 An accountant has to audit 20 accounts of a firm. Fifteen of these accounts are high volume and 5 are low volume. If the accountant randomly selects 4 accounts, what is the probability that none are low-volume accounts?

2.8 A market survey conducted in four cities pertained to preference for Flagrant soap. The responses are shown by city in the table following:

	Los Angeles	Chicago	Boston	Miami
Yes	47	50	63	45
No	33	50	30	48
No opinion	10	8	7	7

a What is the probability that a consumer selected at random preferred Flagrant?

b What is the probability that a consumer preferred Flagrant and was from Chicago?

c What is the probability that a consumer preferred Flagrant given that he was from Chicago?

d Given that a consumer preferred Flagrant, what is the probability she was from Miami?

2.9 An insurance broker estimates that there is a 30 percent chance of a sale upon initial contact with a client. However, on a call-back there is a 60 percent chance of a sale. If the broker is limited to one call-back per prospective customer, what is the probability that any prospect will buy?

2.10 Suppose that the failure rate for candidates initially sitting for the C.P.A. exam is 70 percent. If four candidates sit for the exam for the first time, what is the probability that three will pass?

2.11 Sturdy Construction has submitted a bid for project. If Sturdy's leading competitor submits a bid, then the management at Sturdy feels its chance of getting the contract is .50. However, if the leading competitor does not submit a bid, Sturdy's chances increase to .80. If there is a .90 chance that the leading competitor will submit a bid, what are Sturdy's chances of receiving the contract?

2.12 A new procedure has been developed to test for the presence of a rare disease. The procedure is accurate 95 percent of the time in diagnosing a patient who has the disease. The procedure is accurate 90 percent of the time in diagnosing a patient who does not have the disease. Given a positive test result, what is the actual probability that the patient has the disease? Assume that roughly 20 percent of those who take the test have the disease.

2.13 An M.B.A. class has 35 students, whose ages are distributed as follows:

Age	Number of students
21	15
22	5
23	5
24	4
25	3
28	2
40	1

a Define the probability distribution of the age of the student.

b Define the cumulative probability distribution of the age of the student.

c If a student is picked out of the class at random, what is the probability the student will be less than 24 years old?

d What is the probability that a student randomly chosen will be 22 or 23 years old?

2.14 A door-to-door salesman has a 10 percent chance of making a sale at any one house.

a If he makes 10 calls during 1 day, what is the probability of making 2 sales?

b If he makes 15 calls during 1 day, what is the probability of making 2 sales?

c If he makes 10 calls, what is the probability of making more than 3 sales?

d If he makes 12 calls during the day, define the probability distribution of the number of sales during the day.

2.15 A prestigious university accepts approximately 25 percent of applicants applying for admission to its Ph.D. program in English. The program is quite small and this year had only 25 applicants.

a What is the probability that the first-year Ph.D. class in English will exceed 10 students?

b What is the probability of fewer than 2 students being admitted to the program?

2.16 Upon receiving a shipment of valves, a company inspects a random sample of 15 valves. Historically, 10 percent of the inspected valves have been defective. If management has decided that the entire shipment should be rejected if 2 or more bad valves are found in the sample, what is the probability that the shipment will be accepted?

2.17 Demand at a TV store for the 25-inch color TV has been about 2 sets per week.

   a What is the probability that 10 sets will be sold in the next 4 weeks?

   b What is the probability that fewer than 10 sets will be sold in the next 4 weeks?

   c What is the probability that between 7 and 14 sets will be sold in the next 4 weeks?

2.18 A professional football team has a firm policy of drafting defensive linemen that have certain attributes. One attribute is height. If a college prospect is less than 6 feet, 3 inches tall, the policy states he cannot be drafted. The height of college defensive linemen is normally distributed, with a mean of 6 feet, 5 inches and a standard deviation of 3 inches.

   a What proportion of defensive linemen will be rejected due to height?

   b What is the probability that a college defensive lineman will be between 6 feet, 2 inches tall and 6 feet, 9 inches?

2.19 A local dairy has a machine that fills gallon cartons of milk automatically. State regulations allow a tolerance of ±1 ounce for a gallon of milk. The amount the machine automatically puts in the carton is normally distributed, with a mean of 128 ounces and a standard deviation of .5 ounces.

   a What percentage of the gallon cartons are in violation of state regulations?

   b What is the probability that a carton chosen at random will contain less than 126 ounces?

   c What is the probability that a carton chosen at random will contain between 126 and 130 ounces?

2.20 Assume IQ scores are normally distributed, with a mean of 100 and a standard deviation of 10.

a What is the minimum score that would put a person in the top 10 percent?

b What is the probability of a person's scoring between 90 and 110?

c If people scoring over 140 are classified as geniuses, what percent of the population is in this category?

3
[Decision theory]

In the first chapter, we said that management science is a rational methodology for making management decisions. Decision theory fits the same generic definition; but, actually, decision theory constitutes a particular branch of management science. Most complex executive decisions are decisions that must be made in an environment of uncertainty. For example, capital expansion decisions must be made even though such important factors as product demand, cost of materials, and cost of labor are not known with certainty. Often, the manager must choose between several different courses of action in an attempt to optimize his decision process. Decision theory helps the decision maker to address the problem of making complex choices under uncertain conditions. It must be noted that decision theory does not generate alternative courses of action; it merely provides a rational way of choosing among several alternative strategies.

For example, a marketing vice-president of a cosmetic firm may need to make the decision to introduce or not to introduce a particular new product. What does this decision depend on? The potential payoff or profit generated from the new product would have to be considered. This payoff would depend on a number of factors, such as demand for the product, the actions of competitors, price, and promotional strategy. Obviously, the "simple" product development problem is much more complicated than it appears on the surface. It is further complicated by the uncertain nature of factors such as levels of demand and actions of competitors. Some risk or uncertainty might be reduced by spending money on market research. (Whether to do so involves another potentially difficult decision.) Decision theory can be very helpful in confronting a multifaceted decision such as this.

Decision theory can be used for a wide range of problems. These problems generally involve discrete choices and probabilistic events that have a bearing on the desirability of the various actions the decision maker can take. The following applications indicate the flexibility of decision theory.

1 *Natural resources development* Should an oil or gas well be drilled? What set of seismic experiments should be run? What is the expected payoff of the investment in exploration?

2 *Agricultural applications* What crops should be planted? Should excess acreage be planted? What actions should be taken to fight pests?

3 *Financial applications* What is the proper investment portfolio? What capital investments should be made this year?

4 *Marketing applications* Which new product should be introduced? What is the best distribution channel to use? What is the best inventory strategy?

5 *Production applications* Which of several different types of machine should be purchased? What maintenance schedules should be used?

6 *Personal decisions* What college should you go to? What should you major in? Should you go to graduate school or to work? If to work, which job offer should you accept? Should you get married?

[A basic decision problem]

Consider the following problem. There are 100 opaque urns, each filled with 10 balls. There are two different kinds of urn. Type I urn holds 5 black balls and 5 white balls. Type II urn has 8 black balls and 2 white balls. There are 70 type I urns and 30 type II urns. An urn is picked at random from the 100 urns, and you are asked to guess whether it is type I or type II. If you guess that it is a type I urn and it is, you win $500; if it is a

Table 3.1 Payoff table for urn problem

	Expected value ($)			
State of nature	A_1	A_2	A_3	Probability of state of nature
Θ_1	500	−150	0	.7
Θ_2	−200	1,000	0	.3

type II urn, you lose $200. If you guess that it is an urn of type II and it is, you win $1,000; but if it is a type I urn, you lose $150. Remember that the urn in front of you, the decision maker, is either a type I or type II urn. In other words, there are two states of nature, Θ_1 and Θ_2, corresponding to the urns of type I and type II. You have three alternatives: You can guess either type I or type II or refuse to take the gamble. Which action would you take? What could you expect to gain or lose from your decision? These are the kinds of questions decision theory can answer.

The facts of this decision problem are summarized in Table 3.1. If you know the expected value of each of the three alternative actions, you can simply choose the alternative with the highest expected value. The *expected monetary value* (EMV) of A_1 (the first alternative, namely, guessing that the urn is type I), is simply *expected monetary value (EMV)*

$$EMV = \sum_{i=1}^{2} p(\Theta_i) x_i$$

where $p(\Theta_i)$ = probability that the true state of nature is Θ_i
x_i = payoff for the alternative action, given Θ_i is the true state of nature

Hence,

$$EMV[A_1] = (.7)(500) + (.3)(-200)$$
$$= 350 - 60$$
$$= \$290$$
$$EMV[A_2] = (.7)(-150) + (.3)(1,000)$$
$$= -105 + 300$$
$$= \$195$$
$$EMV[A_3] = (.7)(0) + (.3)(0)$$
$$= 0$$

Therefore, if your objective is to maximize the expected monetary value of the urn decision problem, you would guess that the urn in front of you is type I. You can feel confident that if you were allowed to take this gamble a large number of times, on the average you could expect to gain $290. However, if you are allowed only one chance to guess, you stand a good chance of losing $200.

DECISION TREES

A *decision tree* presents another way to visualize the typical decision theory problem. Figure 3.1, for example, shows an unevaluated decision tree for the urn problem. There are four didactic, or instructive, parts to a decision tree: decision nodes (shown as squares in the illustrations); chance nodes (shown as circles); alternative

Figure 3.1   Decision tree for the basic urn problem

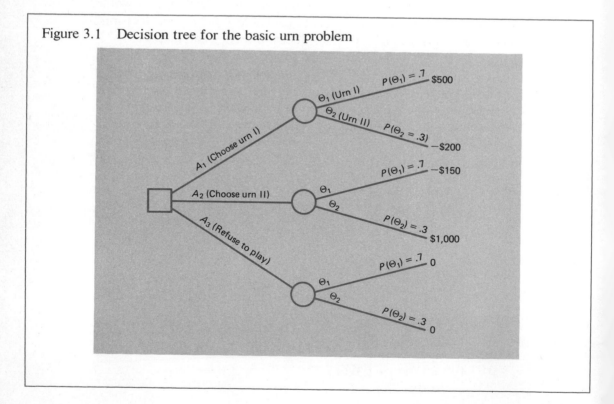

branches (straight lines that state alternatives); and probabilistic branches (straight lines that state probabilities).

decision node

A *decision node* represents the choice between alternatives. From it come *alternative branches* that show, or name, the choices. These alternative branch

chance node

branches lead to *chance nodes*, which represent factors in the decision situation over which the decision maker has no control. From these chance nodes come *probabilistic branches* that state the actual or probabilistic branch estimated numerical likelihood of various chances. Since the events, or states of nature, are mutually exclusive and exhaustive, the probabilities associated with each event must add to 1.

Can you see that a decision tree is an analog of a particular kind of problem? A decision must be made among several alternatives. One or more alternatives is associated with chance factors. These chances, however, can be assessed probabilistically. On the basis of evaluation at several stages, therefore, the decision maker can regard the alternatives rationally and choose the one most compatible with ultimate goals.

HOW TO EVALUATE DECISION TREES

In order to evaluate a decision tree, it is necessary to evaluate each chance node and each decision node. These two types of node are evaluated differently. Chance nodes are evaluated using the expected value, and the value of a decision node is the expected value of the most desirable alternative action. Nodes 2, 3, and 4 in the decision tree in Figure 3.2 are chance nodes, and consequently their values are equal to the expected values calculated earlier. Node 1 is a decision node where the decision maker is asked to choose between A_1, A_2 and A_3. Since the highest EMV of the alternative actions is \$290, the value of node 1 is \$290. Given that the decision maker wishes to maximize EMV, A_1 is the appropriate choice, rather than A_2 or A_3.

In the urn problem, the probabilities associated with the two states of nature were known because the total number of each type of urn was known and the urn was chosen randomly (each urn had an equal chance of being chosen). In real problems, these probabilities are rarely known with certainty, and usually the decision maker is forced to estimate the various probabilities subjectively.

Figure 3.2   Evaluated decision tree for the urn problem

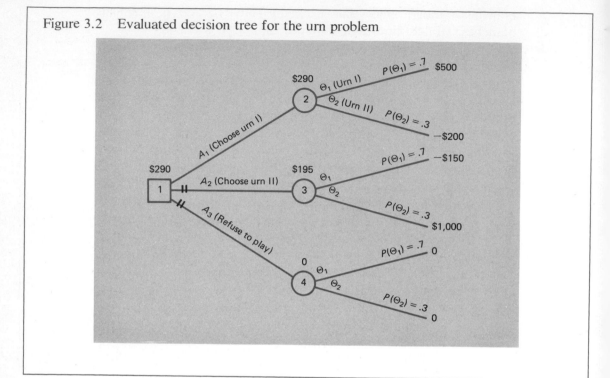

The quality of the decision, therefore, can depend greatly upon reliable subjective probabilities.

[Example]   Fred Fudd is graduating from high school this year and must decide first what college to attend and then what course of study to pursue. Because of parental pressure, Fred must go to college, but he is free to select which college to attend. He has narrowed his choice to two very dissimilar schools. He has been accepted at State University and his home town college, Wood. In addition to choosing between schools, Fred must decide whether to major in engineering or business. Because of the nature of the two schools, Fred has a different probability of success (that is, of graduating) depending on which college he attends and which field he majors in.

1 If he goes to State University and chooses business, his probability of graduating is .60.

2 If he chooses State University and chooses engineering, his probability of success is .70.

3 If he goes to Wood and chooses business, his probability of success is .90.

4 If he goes to Wood and chooses engineering, his probability of success is .95.

5 A State University graduate in business averages $25,000 per year for the first 5 years of full-time employment.

6 A State University graduate in engineering averages $20,000 per year for the first 5 years of full-time employment.

7 A Wood graduate in business averges $14,000 per year for the first 5 years of full-time employment.

8 A Wood graduate in engineering averages $15,000 per year for the first 5 years of full-time employment.

9 If Fred doesn't graduate, he will average $8,000 per year for the first 5 years of full-time employment.

In approaching Fred's problem, let's assume that his sole criterion for making a decision is to maximize average expected income over the first 5 years of his career. Having made that assumption, it is fairly easy to solve Fred's problem using decision theory. What decisions must Fred make? First, he must decide which university to attend; then, he must decide what to major in. So he has two decisions to make. What are the states of nature associated with the alternatives? No matter what school or discipline Fred chooses, he will either graduate or flunk out.

Let Θ_1 = graduate from State University Business School
Θ_2 = fail to graduate from State University Business School
Θ_3 = graduate from State University Engineering School
Θ_4 = fail to graduate from State University Engineering School
Θ_5 = graduate from Wood Business School
Θ_6 = fail to graduate from Wood Business School
Θ_7 = graduate from Wood Engineering School
Θ_8 = fail to graduate from Wood Engineering School
A_1 = choose to go to State University

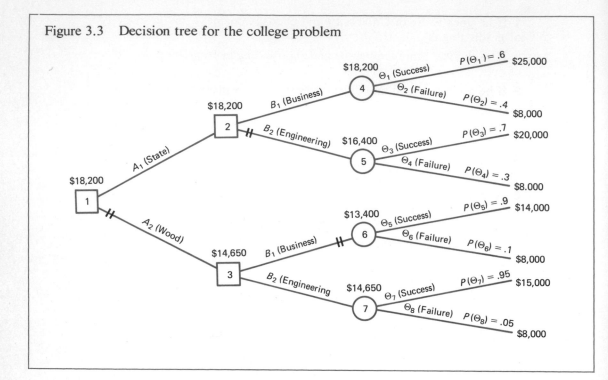

Figure 3.3   Decision tree for the college problem

A_2 = choose to go to Wood College
B_1 = choose to major in business
B_2 = choose to major in engineering

Figure 3.3 shows the decision tree presenting Fred's problem. In order to show more clearly how to evaluate a decision tree, let's evaluate each node in Figure 3.3 individually. Nodes 4 to 7 are chance nodes and are, therefore, evaluated by finding the expected value. Nodes 1 to 3 are decision nodes whose value is the expected value of the most desirable alternative action.

Node 7 N_7 = (.95)(15,000) + (.05)(8,000)
= $14,650
Node 6 N_6 = (.9)(+14,000) + (.1)(8,000)
= $13,400
Node 5 N_5 = (.7)(20,000) + (.3)(8,000)
= $16,400

Node 4 $N_4 = (.6)(25,000) + (.4)(8,000)$
           $= \$18,200$

Node 3   Since $N_7 > N_6$, $N_3 = N_7$ and action B_2 is preferable to B_1,
           $N_3 = \$14,650$

Node 2   Since $N_4 > N_5$, $N_2 = N_4$ and action B_1 is preferable to B_2,
           $N_2 = \$18,200$

Node 1   Since $N_2 > N_3$, $N_1 = N_2$ and action A_1 is preferable to A_2,
           $N_1 = \$18,200$

You should verify each number on the decision tree and work through the process of arriving at the decision. Go over it until you're sure you understand this example thoroughly.

$$\boxed{\begin{array}{c}\text{The decision problem with an opportunity}\\ \text{to obtain additional information}\end{array}}$$

So far, we have considered the most basic, and least complex, decision theory problem. Actually, however, real-world problems are seldom so simple. Now, we will complicate the basic decision problem so that you will see how more realistic problems can be solved.

Often, the decision maker has an opportunity to gather or purchase additional information that may have a bearing on the decision process. Most decision problems in the real world include the option of obtaining additional information. For example, as the urn-chooser in our first problem, it would certainly be beneficial if you had the opportunity to sample a ball from the urn in front of you in order to better guess the real state of nature. The question is, how does the additional information change the basic decision problem? The answer is that the *probabilities* of the various states of nature are actually changed. If the probabilities are changed, then obviously the EMVs of the various actions are also changed. What might have been the optimal decision before the additional information was obtained might now be least desirable.

Let's change the original urn problem by allowing you, as the decision maker, to draw one ball out of the urn. Let's further assume

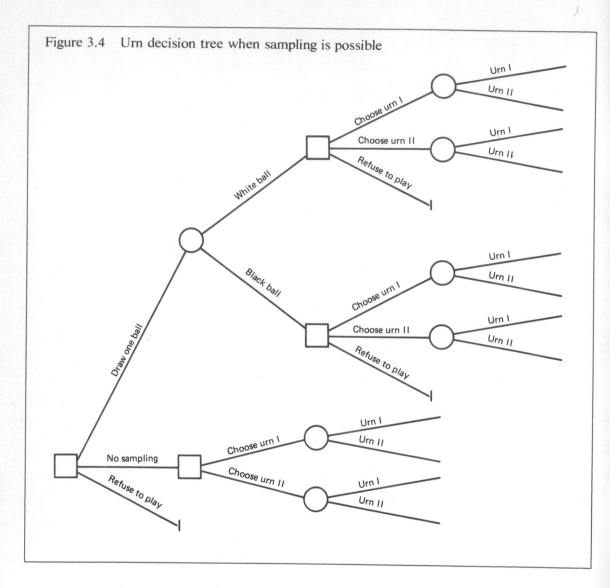

Figure 3.4   Urn decision tree when sampling is possible

that the cost of drawing the ball from the urn is $50. You now have two decisions to make: First, you must decide whether or not to buy the information; and second, you must guess which type of urn has been placed in front of you. If you elect to pay for the opportunity to sample from the urn, either of two outcomes is possible: You will select a white ball or a black ball. Based on this limited information, you must decide on the type of urn.

A decision tree helps to clarify the decision process when additional information is obtainable. Notice that the lower part of the decision tree in Figure 3.4 has not changed from the original problem. However, if you choose to pay $50 to sample a ball from the urn, the decision tree becomes considerably larger; that is, the changing situation is reflected by new branches. To evaluate the top of the decision tree, we must assess new probabilities, such as the probability of Θ_1 given that a white ball is chosen from the urn $[P(\Theta_1|W)]$. There are basically two types of chance node in the Figure 3.4 decision tree. Chance determines what color ball is drawn, and chance determines which kind of urn is on the table. Therefore, it is necessary to assess the following probabilities:

$P(\Theta_1|W)$ = the probability of urn type I given that a white ball is drawn

$P(\Theta_1|B)$ = the probability of urn type I given that a black ball is drawn

$P(\Theta_2|W)$ = the probability of urn of type II given that a white ball is drawn

$P(\Theta_2|B)$ = the probability of urn of type II given that a black ball is drawn

$P(W)$ = the probability of drawing a white ball

$P(B)$ = the probability of drawing a black ball

REVISING PRIOR PROBABILITIES

In order to determine the foregoing probabilities, it is necessary to use *Bayes' theorem.* Bayes' theorem allows us to revise the probabilities of the states of nature given new information. Bayes' theorem states:

Bayes'
theorem

$$P(A|B) = \frac{P(B|A)\,P(A)}{P(B|A)\,P(A) + P(B|\bar{A})\,P(\bar{A})} \qquad [3.1]$$

(See the appendix at the end of this chapter for the derivation of equation 3.1.)

If we apply Bayes' theorem to our example, we have

$$P(\Theta_1|W) = \frac{P(W|\Theta_1)\,P(\Theta_1)}{P(W|\Theta_1)\,P(\Theta_1) + P(W|\Theta_2)\,P(\Theta_2)} \qquad [3.2]$$

We know how many balls of each color are in both types of urn and the distribution of types of urn. We know all the probabilities on the right side of equation 3.2. Therefore, it is a simple matter of arithmetic to calculate $P(\Theta_1|W)$:

$$
\begin{aligned}
P(\Theta_1|W) &= [(.5)(.7)]/[(.5)(.7) + (.2)(.3)] \\
&= .35/.41 \\
&= .854
\end{aligned}
$$

Similarly,

$$
\begin{aligned}
P(\Theta_2|W) &= [P(W|\Theta_2)\,P(\Theta_2)]/[P(W|\Theta_2)\,P(\Theta_2) + P(W|\Theta_1)\cdot P(\Theta_1)] \\
&= [(.2)(.3)]/[(.2)(.3) + (.5)(.7)] \\
&= .06/.41 \\
&= .146
\end{aligned}
$$

$$
\begin{aligned}
P(\Theta_1|B) &= [P(B|\Theta_1)P(\Theta_1)]/[P(B|\Theta_1)\cdot P(\Theta_1) + P(B|\Theta_2)\,P(\Theta_2)] \\
&= [(.5)(.7)]/[(.5)(.7) + (.8)(.3)] \\
&= .35/.59 \\
&= .593
\end{aligned}
$$

$$
\begin{aligned}
P(\Theta_2|B) &= [P(B|\Theta_2)\,P(\Theta_2)]/[P(B|\Theta_1)\,P(\Theta_1) + P(B|\Theta_2)\cdot P(\Theta_2)] \\
&= [(.8)(.3)]/.59 \\
&= .24/.59 \\
&= .407
\end{aligned}
$$

These conditional probabilities are called *a posteriori probabilities* because they cannot be established exclusive of some other property of the problem. In this example, we cannot determine the a posteriori probabilities until after the sampling is completed. Since Θ_1 and Θ_2 are mutually exclusive and exhaustive, $P(W$ and $\Theta_1) + P(W$ and $\Theta_2) = 1$; and since $P(W$ and $\Theta_1) = P(W|\Theta_1)P(\Theta_1)$, then

a posteriori probabilities

$$
\begin{aligned}
P(W) &= P(W|\Theta_1)P(\Theta_1) + P(W|\Theta_2)P(\Theta_2) \\
&= (.5)(.7) + (.2)(.3) \\
&= .41
\end{aligned}
$$

Similarly

$$P(B) = P(B|\Theta_1)P(\Theta_1) + P(B|\Theta_2)P(\Theta_2)$$
$$= (.5)(.7) + (.8)(.3)$$
$$= .59$$

Obviously, since the ball that is drawn in the sample must be either a white or a black ball, $P(W) + P(B)$ must equal 1. Remember, the probabilities at any chance node must add to 1. Now that we have calculated the necessary probabilities, it is a fairly mechanical procedure to evaluate the tree. Notice in Figure 3.5 that the cost of the additional information is subtracted from each applicable payoff at the ends of the decision tree. The same adjustment can be achieved if we leave the payoffs the same and charge a tariff of \$50 at branch A_1.

Let's evaluate the decision tree in Figure 3.5 node by node:

Node 14 $N_{14} = (.593)(-50) + (.407)(-50)$
$$= -\$50$$

Node 13 $N_{13} = (.593)(-200) + (.407)(950)$
$$= -118.60 + 386.65$$
$$= \$268.05$$

Node 12 $N_{12} = (.593)(450) + (.407)(-250)$
$$= 266.85 \quad 101.75$$
$$= \$165.10$$

Node 11 $N_{11} = (.854)(-50) + (.146)(-50)$
$$= -\$50$$

Node 10 $N_{10} = (.854)(-200) + (.146)(950)$
$$= 170.80 + 138.70$$
$$= -\$32.10$$

Node 9 $N_9 = (.854)(450) + (.140)(-250)$
$$= 384.30 - 36.50$$
$$= \$347.80$$

Node 8 $N_8 = (.7)(-150) + (.3)(1,000)$
$$= -105 + 300$$
$$= \$195$$

Node 7 $N_7 = (.7)(500) + (.3)(-200)$
$$= 350 - 60$$
$$= \$290$$

Node 6   Since $N_{13} > N_{12} > N_{14}$, A_2 is the most attractive alternative and $N_6 = \$268.05$

Node 5   Since $N_9 > N_{10} > N_{11}$, A_1 is the best alternative and $N_5 = \$347.80$

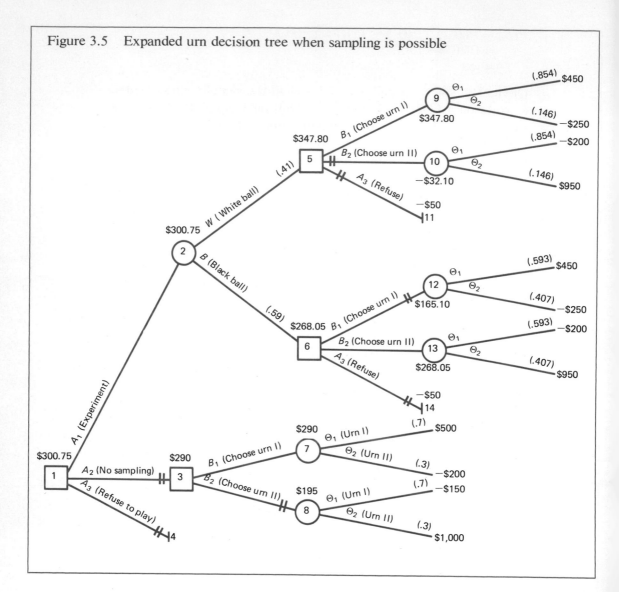

Figure 3.5   Expanded urn decision tree when sampling is possible

Node 4 $N_4 = (.7)(0) + (.3)(0)$
            $= 0$

Node 3   Since $N_7 > N_8$, A_1 is the best alternative and $N_3 = \$290$

Node 2 $N_2 = (.41)(347.80) + (.59)(268.05)$
            $= 142.60 + 158.15$
            $= \$300.75$

Node 1 Since $N_2 > N_3 > N_4$, it seems wise to experiment and $N_1 =$ $300.75

According to our evaluation of this decision tree, the *optimal strategy* (sometimes referred to as the Bayesian strategy) would be to sample one ball and if it is white, guess that the urn is type I. If the sampled ball is black, then you should guess that the urn is type II. The expected monetary value of the urn decision is $300.75. optimal, or Bayesian, strategy

THE VALUE OF INFORMATION

In order to make the decision whether or not to buy additional information, it is often helpful to ascertain the expected value of sample information (EVSI) and the expected value of perfect information (EVPI). Clearly, most information is imperfect; hence, the upper bound on the amount you would be willing to pay for information is the expected value of perfect information. The *expected value of sample information* is merely the EMV with the information minus the EMV without any information. Therefore, in our urn example, the EVSI = $350.75 − $290, or $60.75. expected value of sample information (EVSI)

The value of perfect information is a legitimate issue when you are deciding whether or not to buy information. Clearly, if the expected value of a market research project is $10,000, it would be foolish to pay $15,000 for the study. The *expected value of perfect information* can be calculated by subtracting the EMV without information from the EMV with perfect information. expected value of perfect information (EVPI)

Let's take the urn example (see Figure 3.6). The EMV without information is $290. The EMV with perfect information is

$$\sum_{i=1}^{N} P(\Theta_i) \, P_i$$

where $P(\Theta_i)$ = probability that Θ_i is the true state of nature

P_i = the optimal payoff if Θ_i is the true state of nature

N = number of states of nature

Therefore,

$$\begin{aligned}
\text{EMV with perfect information} &= (.7)(500) + (.3)(1,000) \\
&= 350 + 300 \\
&= \$650
\end{aligned}$$

Figure 3.6 Urn decision tree when perfect information is not available

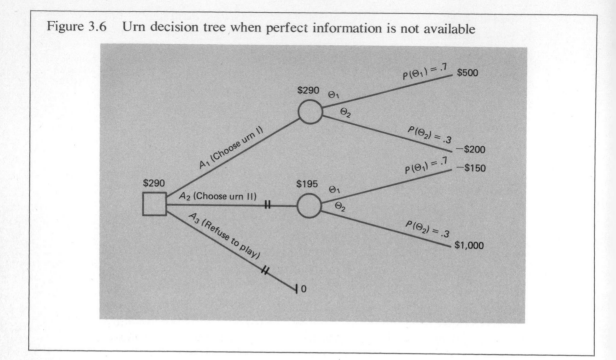

EVPI = 650 − 290
    = $360

If you are one who makes decisions by maximizing EMV (an *EMVer*), then you would pay up to $360 for perfect knowledge of the type of urn that is sitting on the table.

[Example]   A contractor has been invited to bid on a construction job. The value of the contract depends on the length of time it takes to complete the project. If the project is finished on time, there is profit of $50,000. If the contractor is late finishing the project, he will lose $10,000. Weather is the sole determinant of whether the project will be late. If the weather is good, the project will be completed on time; if it is bad, the project will not be completed on schedule. Based on his past experience the contractor's subjective probability of good weather is 20 percent. The contractor, however, has the opportunity to buy a long-range forecast from an independent weather-forecasting company. The weather-forecasting company has a fairly good track record for these long-range forecasts. Its files indicate that 70 percent of the time it successfully predicted good weather, and 80 percent of the time it was able to predict bad weather. In other words,

$P(O_1|\Theta_1) = .7 \ P(O_1|\Theta_2) = .20$
$P(O_2|\Theta_1) = .3 \ P(O_2|\Theta_2) = .80$
where O_1 = prediction of good weather
$\quad\quad O_2$ = prediction of bad weather
$\quad\quad \Theta_1$ = good weather
$\quad\quad \Theta_2$ = bad weather

The cost of the weather-forecasting service is $5,000.

In developing the decision tree for the contractor's problem, it is helpful to identify what decisions the contractor must make and in what sequence those decisions must be made. First, he must make the decision whether to buy the weather forecast information. If the decision is made to buy the information, the contractor must make the bid decision based on the forecast. The decision tree in Figure 3.7 is fairly straightforward.

To evaluate the decision tree in Figure 3.7, it is necessary to calculate the a posteriori probabilities.

$$\begin{aligned}
P(\Theta_1|O_1) &= [P(O_1|\Theta_1)P(\Theta_1)]/[P(O_1|\Theta_1)P(\Theta_1) + P(O_1|\Theta_2)P(\Theta_2)] \\
&= [(.7)(.2)]/[(.7)(.2) + (.2)(.8)] \\
&= .14/(.14 + .16) \\
&= .14/.30 \\
&= .467
\end{aligned}$$

$$\begin{aligned}
P(\Theta_2|O_1) &= [(.2)(.8)]/.30 \\
&= .16/.30 \\
&= .533
\end{aligned}$$

$$\begin{aligned}
P(\Theta_1|O_2) &= [(.3)(.7)]/[(.3)(.2) + (.8)(.8)] \\
&= .06/.70 \\
&= .087
\end{aligned}$$

$$\begin{aligned}
P(\Theta_2|O_2) &= [(.8)(.8)]/.7 \\
&= .64/.70 \\
&= .913
\end{aligned}$$

Figure 3.7   Contract bid decision tree

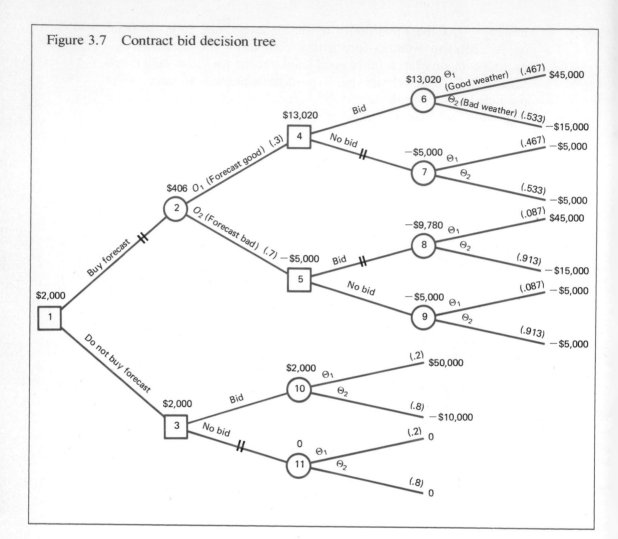

$$P(O_1) = P(O_1|\Theta_1)\,P(\Theta_1) + P(O_1|\Theta_2)\,P(\Theta_2)$$
$$= (.7)(.2) + (.2)(.8)$$
$$= .30$$
$$P(O_2) = .70$$

Once the probabilities have been calculated, the tree is evaluated by assessing the value of each chance node and each decision node.

Node 11 $N_{11} = (0)(.2) + (0)(.8)$
$$= 0$$

Node 10 $N_{10} = (.2)(50,000) + (.8)(-10,000)$
                $= 10,000 - 8,000$
                $= \$2,000$

Node 9 $N_9 = (.087)(-5,000) + (.913)(-5,000)$
              $= -\$5,000$

Node 8 $N_8 = (.087)(45,000) + (.913)(-15,000)$
              $= 3,915 - 13,695$
              $= -\$9,780$

Node 7 $N_7 = (.467)(-5,000) + (.533)(-5,000)$
              $= -\$5,000$

Node 6 $N_6 = (.467)(45,000) + (.533)(-15,000)$
              $= 21,015 - 7,995$
              $= \$13,020$

Node 5   Since $N_9 > N_8$, the value of node 5 is $-\$5,000$

Node 4   Since $N_6 > N_7$, the value of node 4 is $\$13,020$

Node 3   Since $N_{10} > N_{11}$, the value of node 3 is $\$2,000$

Node 2 $N_2 = (.3)(13,020) + (.7)(-5,000)$
              $= \$406$

Node 1   Since $N_2 < N_3$, the value of node 1 is $\$2,000$

Therefore, the Bayesian, or optimal, strategy is to bid on the project without buying the forecast.

The expected value of sample information is EMV with information minus EMV without. Therefore, EVSI is $\$406 + \$5,000 - \$2,000 = \$3,406$. Since we subtracted $\$5,000$ from payoffs in the upper part of the decision tree, it is necessary to add back this $\$5,000$ when computing the EVSI.

The EVPI is calculated in the following manner: EMV with perfect information is $(.2)(\$50,000) + (.8)(0) = \$10,000$. The EMV without perfect information is $\$2,000$. Therefore, the EVPI is $\$10,000 - \$2,000 = \$8,000$. Consequently, the upper bound on the value of a weather forecast is $\$8,000$.

[Decision problem for nonEMVers]

Decision makers can be classified in three categories:

1 Risk takers

2 EMVers

3 Risk averters

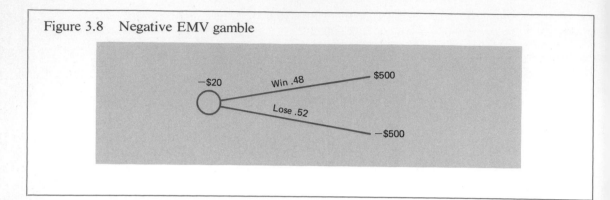

Figure 3.8   Negative EMV gamble

A risk taker might choose a gamble that has a negative EMV.
People who gamble in Nevada know that the expected value of
their gamble is negative, but because they enjoy the excitement
or the thrill of winning they are willing to play against the odds.
A risk taker might take the gamble pictured in Figure 3.8 even
though the EMV is −$20.

People who take action strictly on the basis of the EMV of the
decision probably constitute the smallest category of decision maker.
Later in this section, we shall discuss methodology to deal with
decisions under uncertainty for the nonEMVer.

The last category of decision maker is that of risk avoiders, or
risk averters. Most people fit into this category when they are

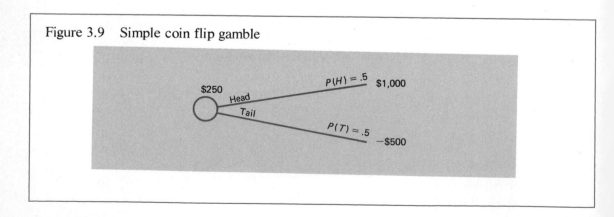

Figure 3.9   Simple coin flip gamble

Figure 3.10　Simple gamble

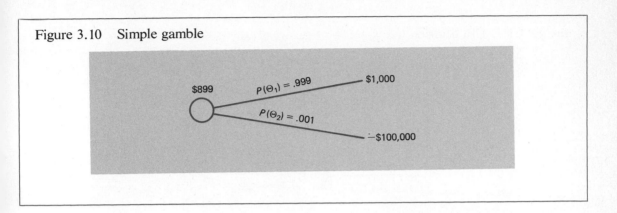

confronted with decisions that entail significant monetary payoffs. Would you pay $250 to be allowed to gamble on the flip of a coin that has a payoff of $1,000 if you win and −$500 if you lose? If not, what would you pay for the chance pictured in Figure 3.9? If you would not pay $250 or more for the gamble, you are a risk avoider. If you would pay more than $250 for the chance to play the coin flip gamble, you are a risk taker.

　　If you have decided you would pay up to $250 for the Figure 3.9 gamble, what about the gamble pictured in Figure 3.10? An EMVer would be willing to pay up to $899 to take this gamble. Would you? Would you take the gamble for nothing? By now, you probably realize that at least for some ranges of monetary payoffs, many people are not EMVers.

　　Let's reconsider the urn problem without any experimental options. One way to proceed is to determine the value of each chance node subjectively instead of computing the expected value. This value is known as the *certainty equivalent* of a gamble. In other words, ask yourself the question, What is the gamble at node 2 in Figure 3.11 worth? If, after some deliberation, you determine that you would pay $100 for the gamble, assign a value of $100 to node 2. Similarly, suppose you decide the certainty equivalent of the node 3 gamble is $25; then you would choose urn I. If you had an extreme aversion to risk, you might not assign positive values to nodes 2 and 3. That is, someone might have to pay you to take either of these gambles.

certainty
equivalent

Figure 3.11   Urn decision tree

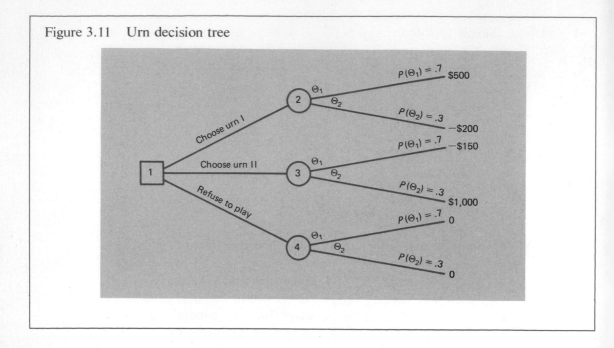

It becomes less feasible to assign a certainty equivalent to each chance node in a decision process as the number and complexity of the chance nodes increase. In other words, what if the chance node has more than two or three states of nature and its probabilities are difficult to assess subjectively? For example, what would your certainty equivalent be for the gamble pictured in Figure 3.12?

Fortunately, there is a procedure for dealing with the psychology of the nonEMVer. The basic idea is to measure the decision maker's attitude toward risk and then to substitute payoffs modified by the decision maker's risk attitude for the original monetary payoffs. The substitute payoffs can be thought of as specially designed lottery tickets[1] that entitle the owner to a p chance at winning W and a $1 - p$ chance at winning L. (Usually, L is a negative dollar amount.) The only requirements are that W be clearly preferable to L and that the decision maker be a rational person. If W and L are monetary

[1] Raiffa, Howard, *Decision Analysis: Introductory Lectures on Choices Under Uncertainty* (Reading, Mass.: Addison-Wesley Publishing Co., Inc., 1968), p. 57.

Figure 3.12　Complex gamble

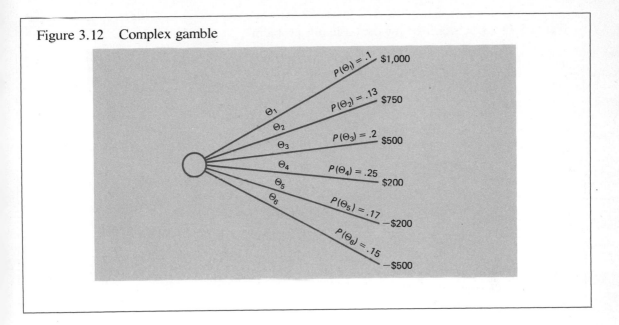

valucs, then the monetary value of a lottery ticket with $p - 1$ is W, and a lottery ticket with $p = 0$ has a dollar value of L. Since attitudes toward risk differ among individuals, these are probably the only two points that a group of decision makers can agree upon. If W and L are sufficiently wide apart to encompass all the payoffs of a decision problem, then intermediate points relating relevant dollar values to lottery tickets can be determined.

Let's return to the urn problem to illustrate how to adjust for nonEMVers. Figure 3.13 shows the original decision tree. In the urn problem thus depicted, W can be set equal to $1,000 and L to $-200. We can then measure the decision maker's attitude toward risk by asking a series of questions such as the following: What would you pay for a 50–50 chance at winning $1,000 or losing $200? What would you pay for a 75 percent chance at winning $1,000 and a 25 percent chance at losing $200? What would you pay for a 25 percent chance at winning $1,000 and a 75 percent chance at losing $200? If someone would have to pay you to take a specific lottery ticket, how much would they have to pay you? (Remember, lottery tickets represent various gamble parameters.)

Figure 3.13 Decision tree for the basic urn problem

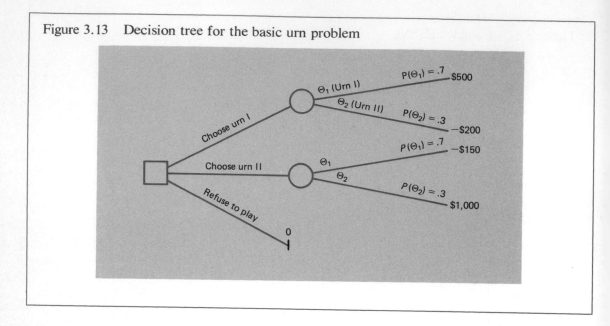

Let's assume that a decision maker has answered a series of these kinds of questions and the answers are summarized in Table 3.2. These values can plotted and a smooth, concave curve fitted to them. (We have done so in Figure 3.14.) This curve represents the locus of points where a particular decision maker professes indifference between the choices of taking a precisely defined gamble and a certain amount of money. You will note that the illustration contrasts the nonEMVer's indifference curve with an EMVer's.

Table 3.2 Lottery ticket dollar equivalence

p	Certainty equivalent ($ value)
0	−200
.25	−50
.50	50
.75	200
1.00	1,000

Figure 3.14 NonEMVer's indifference curve contrasted with EMVer's

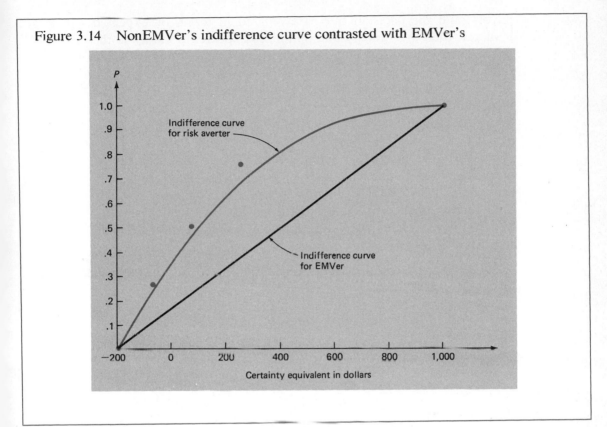

Certainty equivalent in dollars

Once the indifference curve has been drawn, it is easy to use the decision theory developed thus far in this chapter to solve decision problems in terms of the individual decision maker's attitude toward risk. The simple procedure is based upon one very reasonable principle: If a gamble is modified by substituting a different payoff and if the decision maker is indifferent between the original payoff and the new payoff, then that same decision maker should be indifferent between the original gamble and the modified gamble if all else remains unchanged.

Therefore, if a decision maker is indifferent between x dollars and a lottery ticket with a specific value for p, it is reasonable to substitute the lottery ticket for the monetary payoff. If lottery tickets with different values of p are substituted for each monetary payoff, and the decision tree is evaluated in terms of expected p values, then the strategy that optimizes expected p values is the optimal strategy for that decision maker's particular attitude toward risk. Obviously, this optimal strategy may differ from the optimal strategy of an EMVer or even of another risk averter. To further understand the use of decision theory for a nonEMVer, consider the next example.

[Example] An editor of a large publishing company has just received a prospectus and four chapters of a manuscript. After reviewing the material, the editor's intuition is that the proposed book has a 40 percent chance to be successful and a 60 percent chance to fail. If it is successful, the publishing company can expect to make a profit of $100,000 over a period of 5 years. If the book is a

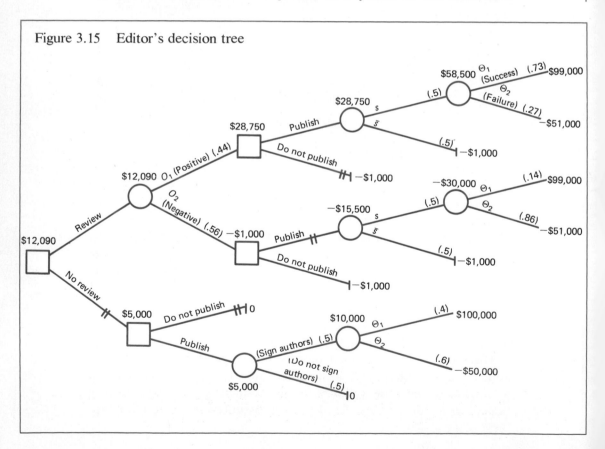

Figure 3.15   Editor's decision tree

Table 3.3   Indifference table

p	Certainty equivalent ($ value)
0	−51,000
.10	−45,000
.25	−35,000
.50	−10,000
.75	15,000
.90	55,000
1.00	100,000

failure, the company will lose $50,000. If the editor decides to publish the book, there is only a 50–50 chance of convincing the authors to sign a contract with the editor's publishing company. The manuscript can be sent off for review by outside experts for a cost of $1,000. In the past, this review process has successfully predicted the success or failure of a book 80 percent of the time; that is, P(predicted success and the book was successful) = .80 and P(predicted failure and the book failed) = .80. An EMVer's decision tree for this problem is depicted in Figure 3.15.

If the editor were an EMVer, the manuscript should be sent out for review and the project signed if the reviews are positive or abandoned if the reviews are negative. This particular editor, however, has an aversion to risk and wonders whether the strategy of an EMVer is consistent with this attitude toward risk. Using $100,000 as W and −$50,000 as L, the editor has decided after considerable deliberation that the indifference parameters are established by p chance at winning $99,000 and $1 - p$ chance at losing $51,000 (the publishing company's money) and the dollar amounts shown in Table 3.3.

Figure 3.16 fits an indifference curve to the points in Table 3.3. With the function graphed in Figure 3.16, it is now possible to substitute (from the indifference curve) lottery tickets with specific p values for monetary payoffs in the editor's original decision tree (Figure 3.15). Once the substitution is made, it is simply a mechanical procedure to evaluate the tree in terms of p values and thus find the optimal strategy for the editor's individual attitude toward risk. This is done in Figure 3.17.

Figure 3.16 Editor's indifference curve

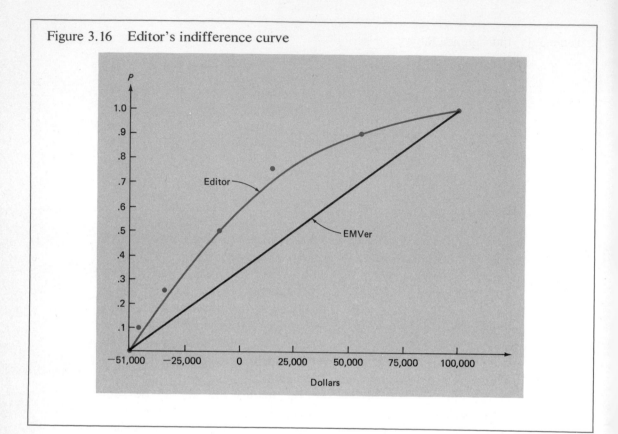

As you can see by comparing Figure 3.15 and 3.17, an EMVer would not act differently from an individual with an attitude toward risk similar to the editor's as graphed in Figure 3.16. Why?

[Summary]

A great many decision problems exist in which a decision must be made among several alternative actions. The consequences of those alternatives devolve from the existence of one or more states of nature, each of which has some probability of being the true state of nature. Critics of decision theory contend, however, that because the probability estimate is subjective in nature, the theory is of little practical value. The fact that subjective probabilities

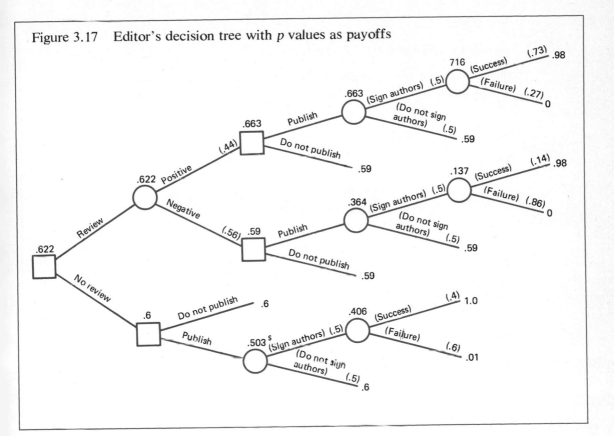

Figure 3.17   Editor's decision tree with *p* values as payoffs

are imperfect should make you cautious in your use of decision theory, but it should not prevent you from using it. A decision maker should, however, be aware of the sensitivity of a basic decision made under decision theory to plausible changes in the probabilities. These can be considered by perturbing the various probabilities and reevaluating the decision tree.

[Bayes' theorem appendix]

By the general law of multiplication

$$P(A \text{ and } B) = P(A \,|\, B) \cdot P(B)$$
$$= P(B \,|\, A) \cdot P(A)$$

Therefore,

$$P(A|B) = [P(A \text{ and } B)] / P(B)$$

Since A and $\bar{A}$ are mutually exclusive and are the only events that jointly occur with B,

$$P(B) = P(A \text{ and } B) + P(\bar{A} \text{ and } B)$$
$$= P(B|A)P(A) + P(B|\bar{A})P(\bar{A})$$

Therefore,

$$P(A|B) = \frac{P(A \text{ and } B)}{P(B|A)P(A) + P(B|\bar{A})P(\bar{A})}$$
$$= \frac{P(B|A)P(A)}{P(B|A)P(A) + P(B|\bar{A})P(\bar{A})}$$

It can be shown that the expression above can be generalized to yield

$$\frac{P(A_i)P(B|A_i)}{\sum_{j=1}^{k} P(A_j)P(B|A_j)}$$

where A_j denotes mutually exclusive events.

[Bibliography]

Hadley, George, *Introduction to Probability and Statistical Decision Theory.* San Francisco: Holden-Day, Inc., 1967.

Jedamus, P. and R. Frame, *Business Decision Theory.* New York: McGraw-Hill Book Company, 1969.

Pratt, J. W., Howard Raiffa, and R. Schlaifer, *Introduction to Statistical Decision Theory.* New York: McGraw-Hill, Book Company, 1965.

Raiffa, Howard, *Decision Analysis: Introductory Lectures on Choices Under Uncertainty.* Reading, Mass.: Addison-Wesley Publishing Co., Inc., 1968.

Schlaifer, R., *Analysis of Decisions Under Uncertainty.* New York: McGraw-Hill Book Company, 1969.

Trueman, Richard E., *An Introduction to Quantitative Methods for Decision Making.* New York: Holt, Rinehart and Winston, Inc., 1974.

Winkler, R. L., *Introduction to Bayesian Inference and Decision*. New York: Holt, Rinehart, and Winston, Inc., 1972.

[Review questions]

1 Define *decision theory*.

2 Distinguish between subjective probabilities and objective probabilities.

3 What does EMV stand for? How is EMV calculated?

4 In your own words, how is a decision tree evaluated?

5 What does EVSI stand for? How is EVSI calculated?

6 Why is it sometimes important to know the expected value of perfect information?

7 In your own words, how is EVPI calculated?

8 What does Bayes' theorem contribute to decision theory?

9 State Bayes' theorem algebraically.

10 Distinguish between EMVers and risk averters.

11 What are the major criticisms of decision theory?

[Problems]

3.1 The Ace Construction Company has been asked to make a sealed bid on building 40 lighted tennis courts for State University. It costs $10,000 to build each court, and just to bid costs $5,000. The company is considering five bids; and, based on previous experience, each bid has a different subjective probability of being the winning bid. The bids and probabilities are summarized below:

Bid number	Amount of bid	Probability of winning
1	Cost + 5%	.90
2	Cost + 10%	.75
3	Cost + 15%	.60
4	Cost + 20%	.40
5	Cost + 25%	.10

a Draw the decision tree for this problem.
b Assuming Ace Construction Company wants to maximize the EMV, what bid should it submit to State University?

3.2 You have a trip to make next week, and you are trying to decide whether to make the trip by air, automobile, or train. The weather is the primary determinant of your enjoyment of the trip. The weather bureau has forecast an 80 percent chance of good weather next week. Your trip enjoyment in case of good and bad weather are measured in utiles in the table.

Weather	Airplane	Auto	Train
Good	100	65	50
Bad	0	20	50

a Draw the decision tree for this problem, labeling all branches, states of nature, payoffs, and probabilities.
b If you wished to maximize expected utiles, which mode of transportation would you choose?

3.3 You are the owner of a local sporting goods shop, and you have an opportunity to buy leather soccer balls at a special price if you buy the balls sometime before July 31. You must, however, buy in even dozens. If you buy early, you can buy the balls for $10 each. If you buy during the soccer season, the balls will cost $12 each. If you overstock and must sell the balls after the soccer season, you feel you will have to sell them for $8 each. The balls retail for $18 and the level of demand shown in the following table is predicted. Notice that sales are also in even dozens.

Demand (doz.)	Probability
2	.25
3	.30
4	.30
5	.15

a Draw the decision tree, labeling properly.
b Evaluate the tree.
c How many soccer balls would an EMVer order early?

3.4 You are an engineering student and are trying to decide whether, upon graduation, to go to work as an engineer or spend another year in school getting an M.B.A. Since you are an EMVer, all you really care about is your expected income. Presently, the market for engineers is depressed, and the probability of getting an engineering job is only .50. Your subjective probability of getting a job requiring an M.B.A. in 1 year is .70. However, you can do some research into expected strength of the market for M.B.A.s. You feel that this research will be correct with a probability of .70. The states of nature are that you will be able to get a job utilizing your education or you will not; that is, $P(O_1|\Theta_1) = .7$. The average M.B.A. earns $14,000 per year to start, and the average engineering student makes $12,000 at the start. If you can't get a job utilizing your education, you can always drive a taxi for $9,000 per year.

   a Draw the decision tree and label it.
   b What is the optimal strategy of an EMVer?
   c What is the optimal EMV?
   d What is the expected value of sample information?

3.5 You are a betting person and wish to bet on the State University varsity/alumni game. You have no information on the odds for either team's winning. The only information you have is that the varsity has won 12 and the alumni have won 8. Ties are broken by sudden death playoffs. You have an opportunity to do some research into the strengths and weaknesses of the two teams; the outcome of this research will indicate a winner. The only bet you can make is an even $100.

O_1 = research indicates varsity will win
O_2 = research indicates the alumni will win
Θ_1 = varsity will win
Θ_2 = alumni will win
$P(O_1|\Theta_1) = .70$
$P(O_2|\Theta_1) = .30$
$P(O_1|\Theta_2) = .40$
$P(O_2|\Theta_2) = .60$

   a Draw the decision tree.
   b Indicate the optimal strategy for an EMVer.
   c Interpret the decision tree in your own words.
   d Would your decision strategy be the same as an EMVer's strategy? Explain.

3.6 An oil company is trying to decide on its bidding policy for the purchase of some offshore drilling rights. Based on the history of other areas of similar characteristics, the management of the oil company thinks that there are three possible levels of oil in the offshore area in question, with the probabilities reflected in the following table.

Strategy	Payoff	Probability
1	Not enough recoverable oil to cover drilling and production costs (i.e., total loss of $25 million)	.40
2	Total oil production of 50 million barrels	.50
3	Total oil production of 100 million barrels	.10

Drilling costs and production costs are estimated at $100 million for the life of the area. The current market price of oil is $11 per barrel. The problem is that management doesn't know whether or not to bid or how much to bid for the oil rights. Its policy is that management should select one of the three bidding strategies and bid $2, $3, or $4 per expected barrel of oil based on its supposition of what the competition will bid. Management's subjective probabilities on this aspect of the problem of getting the drilling rights are summarized in the following table.

Bid ($)	Probability of outbidding the competition
2	.10
3	.30
4	.60

a Draw the decision tree and label it properly.
b Evaluate the decision tree from the point of view of an EMVer.
c What is the optimal strategy, and what is the EMV of the oil company's drilling rights problem?

3.7 A small firm has developed a new machine to manufacture printed circuit boards. The machine is a considerable improvement over machines currently on the market. If management decides to manufacture this new machine, it is almost certain that the larger firms in the industry will copy the design and take the majority of the market through price competition. Therefore, management feels that the decision of whether or not to manufacture depends solely on expected profit in the first year of production. The costs of setting up the production lines and marketing the new machine are estimated to be $250,000. The variable cost of the machine is about $10,000 per machine, and the firm plans to sell the machine for $15,000. To simplify the problem, let's assume that the market demand will be either 50 or 75 machines. Assume that demand and production are evenly distributed throughout the year. Management believes that these two levels of demand are equally likely. Market research can be done at a cost of $10,000. In the past, this market research has successfully predicted demand level 75 percent of the time; that is, P(research indicates demand will be for 50 machines and the demand is for 50 machines) = .75.

  a Draw and label the decision tree.
  b Evaluate the decision tree.
  c What is the optimal strategy of an EMVer?
  d Interpret the decision tree.
  e What is the expected value of sample information?
  f What is the expected value of perfect information?

3.8 An oil company must decide whether or not to drill an oil well in a particular area. The decision maker believes that the area could be dry, reasonably good, or a bonanza, with the respective probabilities of .40, .40, and .20. If the well is dry, no revenue is generated. If the well is reasonably good, the expected profit is $75,000. If the well is a bonanza, the expected profit is $200,000. In any case, the cost of drilling the well is $40,000. At a cost of $15,000, the company can take a series of seismic soundings that usually help determine the underlying geological structure at the site. These experiments will disclose whether there is no structure, open structure, or closed structure. Let's denote these experimental outcomes as O_1, O_2, and O_3, respectively. Let

Θ_1 = dry hole
Θ_2 = reasonably good potential
Θ_3 = bonanza

Past experience has indicated the following conditional probabilities:

$P(O_1|\Theta_1) = .60 \qquad P(O_1|\Theta_2) = .40 \qquad P(O_1|\Theta_3) = .10$
$P(O_2|\Theta_1) = .30 \qquad P(O_2|\Theta_2) = .40 \qquad P(O_2|\Theta_3) = .40$
$P(O_3|\Theta_1) = .10 \qquad P(O_3|\Theta_2) = .20 \qquad P(O_3|\Theta_3) = .50$

  a Draw and label the decision tree for this problem.
  b Evaluate the decision tree.

c What is the optimal strategy for an EMVer?
d What is the EMV of the optimal strategy?
e What is the EVSI?
f What is the EVPI?

3.9 Design a series of questions and try to find a friend's indifference curve for various levels of dollar investment.

3.10 Assume you are the president of Ace Construction Company in problem 3.1. What would your optimal strategy be, given your personal attitude toward risk?

3.11 Measure your personal attitude toward the risk involved in problem 3.8. Substitute p values for monetary payoffs, and then find your optimal strategy. Discuss and interpret your answer.

[Edgartown fisheries case]

On a rainy day in March 1969, Lars Dyson, M.B.A. '48, businessman and adventurer, president of Edgartown Fisheries, faces a difficult and perplexing decision problem.

Edgartown Fisheries is in the shark-fishing business and operates one fishing boat especially equipped for sharking in the North and Middle Atlantic. The Company was formed in order to exploit a technique which had previously been little used for shark fishing, a technique called "long-line" fishing, in which arrays of long, baited lines are suspended from buoys. Dyson has now had a few years' experience using this technique, and he and his crew feel that they have acquired a substantial skill in catching shark this way. Nevertheless, he feels anxious about Edgartown Fisheries' future, largely because of uncertainties about the size of the catch and the price which the fish will command.

On this particular rainy day, Dyson has just received a letter from an Italian shark importer who offers to make a one-season contract with Edgartown Fisheries for 300,000 pounds of shark at 55 cents a pound, delivered in Italy. The shark is to be delivered by October 10, 1969, but Edgartown Fisheries may, under the terms of the proposed contract, divide the 300,000 pounds into partial shipments in any way it desires. Dyson has to decide whether or not to accept the contract within the next few days, and he has assembled the following information to help him with his decision.

Shark Production and Market The Atlantic sharking season runs from April 1 through October 31. However Edgartown Fisheries ordinarily obtains only about 120 days of active fishing, the other 90 days being spent either in port or traveling to and from the fishing grounds. (The travel and port time is somewhat affected by various factors, particularly the weather.) There are two distinct types of season. In a good season, Edgartown Fisheries can catch about 600,000 pounds of shark; in a bad season, about 480,000 pounds. The variation in the size of the catch from day to day is small enough to be ignored, so that Dyson is willing to think of his catch as being a constant 5,000 pounds per fishing day if the season is good or 4,000 pounds per fishing day if the season is bad. Thus it is possible to determine, after the first few weeks of the season have passed, whether the season will be good or bad. Unfortunately, it is impossible to tell ahead of the start of the season what kind of a season it will be.

Shark is caught not only in the Atlantic but also in the Pacific, primarily by the Japanese. The price for Atlantic shark, therefore, depends not only on whether the Atlantic catch is large or small, but also on the size of the catch in the Pacific. Table 1 shows the price

Table 1   Anticipated price per pound of shark landed in New Bedford

Pacific catch	Atlantic catch	
	Large	Small
Large	30¢	35¢
Small	40¢	45¢

per pound which Dyson expects for shark landed in New Bedford (his home port) under each of the four conditions that may occur. For example, if Dyson encounters a large catch (5,000 pounds per day) and the Pacific catch turns out small, Dyson expects to receive 40 cents per pound landed in New Bedford.

As with the Atlantic catch, it is impossible to tell before the start of the season whether the Pacific catch will be large or small. However, after the first few weeks of the season have passed, the size of the Pacific catch to date provides a reliable indication of the rest of the season. Dyson's wife can obtain this information and radio it to him.

As he looks forward to the season, the four possible conditions that may occur all seem equally likely to Dyson, so he assigns them the probabilities given in Table 2.

Table 2 Probabilities of various catch sizes

Pacific catch	Atlantic catch	
	Large	Small
Large	.25	.25
Small	.25	.25

Shipping to Italy Dyson can store shark already caught in a cold-storage warehouse for as long as one season at essentially no cost. He is therefore not constrained to ship the fish to Italy as soon as they are caught. He can ship fish from New Bedford to Italy at a cost of 19 cents per pound by a standard freighter service offering weekly departures. Any one freighter will take all or any part of the 300,000-pound order.

Alternatively, Dyson could ship the 300,000 pounds by sending his own vessel to Italy. His boat can carry only 150,000 pounds of shark packed in ice, so that two trips of his own boat would be required to deliver the entire shipment of 300,000 pounds. In each round trip to Italy, his boat would lose the equivalent of about 20 fishing days. (Note that the 300,000 pounds must be delivered before the end of the season.) In comparing the cost of operating his boat for fishing with the cost of operating his boat for transporting fish to Italy, Dyson finds that the additional fuel required to transport the fish just about balances the cost of the bait that would have been used in the corresponding time spent fishing. Use of the boat to transport the fish will actually reduce the cost of tackle, since no tackle will be used in a transport operation whereas tackle is regularly lost while fishing.

Costs and Assets On April 1, 1969, at the start of the season, Dyson will have assets which, besides his boat and some office equipment, include $20,000 cash and 40 miles of ready-to-use tackle. Excluding tackle, his total costs for the entire fishing season (interest payment on boat mortgage, crew's wages, office rent, etc., and fuel and bait) will be about $160,000. Regarding tackle, in his normal fishing operations Dyson carries 20 miles of tackle on board his boat; the other 20 miles he has are stock he carries for replacement purposes. Loss of tackle turns out to depend directly not on the number of days of fishing, but rather on the number of pounds of shark caught. Based on past experience, Dyson knows that he will have to replace about one mile of tackle for every 50,000 pounds of shark caught. The cost of ready-to-use tackle (including hooks, buoys, radar reflectors, etc.) from Dyson's regular supplier is $1,000 per mile. However, 30 miles of Dyson's present tackle were purchased used from the estate of another shark fisherman in New Bedford at a cost of $22,500. This is the only instance that Dyson has ever encountered of used tackle being for sale, and he considers future availability of used tackle to be a virtual impossibility.

[Case problems]

1 What basic decisions does Mr. Dyson have to make?

2 Construct and evaluate the decision tree for Mr. Dyson's problem.

3 Assuming Mr. Dyson is an EMVer, what is his optimal strategy?

4 How much money can Mr. Dyson expect to make during the coming season?

[Consolidated Construction, Inc. case]

Consolidated Construction, Inc., located in Flint, Michigan is a manufacturer and distributor of building supplies. Its product line was originally restricted to hardware attachments such as window locks and cabinet latches, but with the purchase of a woodworking plant in central Michigan the line was expanded to include plastic-surfaced cabinets for bathroom and kitchen use. This woodworking capability eventually brought about a decision to manufacture doors and windows. Success in the window market is dependent upon finding design characteristics which make installation of window units by carpenters easier and cheaper.

For the past six weeks Consolidated personnel have been negotiating with Fairview Machine Company of Saginaw, Michigan, concerning a new device for counterbalancing twin-sash windows. Fairview is a small company founded by two brothers to capitalize on their skill in mechanical innovation. They have been successful in designing and building such items as semi-automatic feed mechanisms and hoppers with shakers to drop parts appropriately placed for machining. In addition, they are skillful in modifying general-purpose machining equipment to increase its productivity in particular applications.

James Fairley, the younger of the two brothers who had founded Fairview, started thinking about the window counterbalance only after an accident in the Company's plant. A window frame had been damaged beyond repair when it was hit by an electric motor that was being moved across the plant by an overhead crane. Mr. Fairley thought, as he watched the carpenter replace the window frame, that the installation process would be more efficient and the counterbalance would have better mechanical characteristics, if the counterbalance were embedded in the frame rather than being visible in the window track.

In the next few days he worked out a new design for counterbalancing double-hung windows of such novelty that his patent attorney felt confident that he could secure a patent on the device.

Mr. Fairley had no intention of involving the Fairview Machine Company in marketing domestic building supplies and thought he could exploit his new idea better if he sold the rights to some firm that could market the device. For this reason he approached Consolidated Construction.

During the negotiations, it became clear to Fairley that he would have to design production equipment also, and the negotiations reached the stage where Fairview would give Consolidated exclusive rights to the patent for five years and would supply production equipment for that period. James Fairley had come up with two design proposals for the production equipment and would guarantee that, whichever of the two Consolidated chose, it would be delivered and working at Consolidated's plant by the end of the current year. It was agreed that Consolidated would pay a fixed amount of $450,000 for the five-year rights and an additional amount for royalties and for rental of the equipment. At first, Fairley wanted a royalty on each window sold, but it was soon agreed that the cost of collection in such a scheme would be large, and it was finally agreed that Consolidated pay a flat rental and royalty whatever the volume. For the first design they agreed on $500,000 per year, and for the second $340,000. Consolidated's production manager did an analysis of the internal production costs and estimated that the variable manufacturing cost would be $4.30 per unit with the production equipment renting for $500,000 per year and $5.50 per unit for the equipment renting for $340,000 per year.

The choice between machines meant that the volume of business was crucial, and the discussion at Consolidated was focused for several days on the market acceptability of the product. First a price was established at $10.00 per sash; this seemed to be the only reasonable choice based on a study of competing products and their prices. Although the total market consists both of domestic and industrial windows, Consolidated Construction sold almost exclusively in the domestic market. The distribution channels for industrial windows were entirely different and Consolidated had never tried to penetrate that market.

There are two styles of domestic double-hung windows. They are differentiated by the structure of the exterior frame and are known as Eastern and Western style windows. The counterblancing device James Fairley had developed allowed the insertion of the Eastern style window into the house frame to be accomplished much more easily than it was with the weight or spring-loaded counterbalances currently in use. For Western style window frames it did not appear to offer such a pronounced advantage over designs currently in use.

With these facts in mind, they were certain that they could achieve a sales level of 100,000 units a year in the market for Eastern style windows. They were considerably less sure about the Western market. If this market could be penetrated at all, sales level was expected to be 50,000 units annually, and the odds of this occurring were assessed at 50–50.

The marketing and distribution for either or both domestic window types was through regular channels and Consolidated's marketing manager stated that the incremental marketing and distribution costs would be 50¢ per unit.

They did not expect the sales level to grow or fluctuate significantly from year to year after a market segment was developed.

Thus it appeared to the management of Consolidated that the reasonable choice to make, if they bought the rights, was to install the equipment with lower rental cost if only they could find out that they would sell to the Eastern style market and not to the Western style market but to opt for the equipment with the higher rental cost if they could know they would penetrate both markets.

So the discussion led to the realization that information which would help them re-assess the 50–50 odds on penetration of both markets

Introduction to management science

would be worth considering. Craig Wentworth, Vice President of Marketing, seized the opportunity to tell them about success stories he had been hearing about a market survey firm in Detroit. The firm and its successes had even been the subject of an article in the latest issue of the building suppliers' trade association journal. He suggested Consolidated could try out the firm to help them here. Since time was short the cost might be low. And so the market research firm was contacted about surveying the Western market. In a day spent at the offices of the firm, it was learned that for $10,000 a series of demonstrations to some of Consolidated's outlets would be made. On the basis of the analysis of the responses to the demonstrations, the firm would report to Consolidated that the market potential for the window was either favorable or unfavorable, and that was all they would be willing to assert.

They pointed out, of course, that their reporting as a result of their tests that the odds favored Consolidation's penetration into the Western style market was not to be taken as a guarantee that Consolidated would. Their tests did not provide 100% reliable results, but they were good. They had had considerable follow-up on their testing procedures and were willing to supply statements about the accuracy they had achieved. Translated into the current circumstances, the survey firm's statistician said: "If you penetrate the market for Western style windows and if we were to have done a survey the odds are 9 to 1 that the survey report would have been favorable. On the other hand we are not quite as good in the opposite direction. If you try and fail to penetrate the market and if we had done a survey the odds are 7 to 3 that we would have reported the odds as unfavorable."

With these numbers and the 50–50 odds on penetration currently held at Consolidated the statistician did the calculations leading to the probabilities in Table 1. Craig Wentworth shook his head. "Didn't it say there," he said, "that if the survey were run and a favorable report received the odds went from 50–50 to 3 to 1 for, whereas if the report were unfavorable they became 7 to 1 against? Wasn't the

Table 1   Probability calculations done by the market research statistician

Outcome	Its probability
Current ones	
Market	
Eastern only	.50
Western as well	.50
Test accuracy	
Report favorable when penetration	.90
Report unfavorable when not	.70
Calculations	
Report favorable and penetration of Western	.45
Report unfavorable but penetration	.05
Report unfavorable and not penetration	.35
Report unfavorable but penetration	.15
New probabilities	
Survey	
Survey says favorable	.60
Survey says unfavorable	.40
Market	
If Survey says favorable	
Eastern market only	.25
Western as well	.75
If Survey says unfavorable	
Eastern market only	.875
Western as well	.125

statistician more sure of himself when he said favorable? Wasn't he saying Consolidated should be more sure of itself when he said unfavorable?''

When Consolidated's marketing personnel left the survey firm's office, they promised they would decide within the week whether or not they would use the market survey.

The next morning at their offices in Flint, they reviewed the situation. The first decision was whether or not Consolidated should purchase the patent rights from Fairview. That alone involved an investment of $450,000. But even though the payment would be made this year, there were tax benefits available if it were amortized over the 5-year life of the contract.

The next part of the decision was the choice of equipment and clearly that depended on how well they might do in the market for Western style windows. So they called James Fairley to see whether they could put off the decision for two weeks or so. But he showed so much irritation when asked for this delay that Consolidated promised to inform him within a day whether they would purchase the rights although they needed more time before they could decide on the equipment. For that choice they asked for and got two weeks.

[Case problems]

1 What basic decisions must be made by Consolidated Construction Inc.?

2 Verify the probabilities given in Table 1.

3 Construct and evaluate the decision tree for this problem.

4 What is the optimal strategy for Consolidated Construction Inc? (Assume that the objective is to maximize EMV.)

5 What is the expected value of the market research information?

6 How much profit can Consolidated Construction expect to make from the patented window counterbalance during the next 5 years?

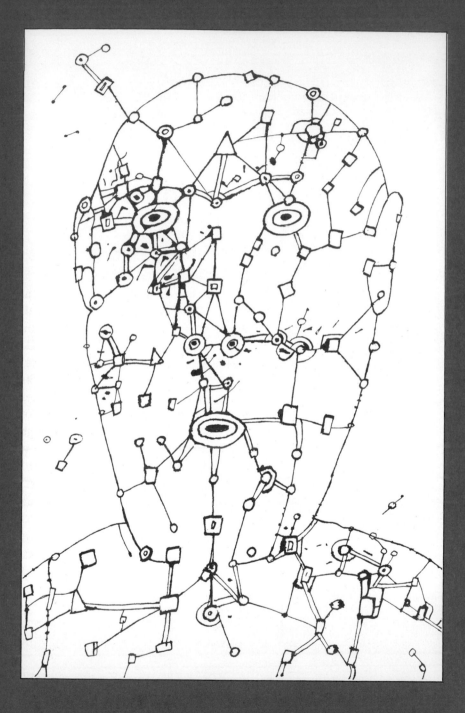

4

$$\left[\begin{array}{c} \text{Linear programming} \\ \text{and modeling} \end{array}\right]$$

Of all the available techniques and decision tools in management science, linear programming (LP) is one of the most widely used. It is primarily concerned with the determination of the best allocation of scarce resources. Usually, a firm's scarce resources include capital, labor, raw materials, finished goods, or time. For instance, a marketing department may suggest several new products that its firm can sell successfully. However, each new product contributes a different amount to profit and requires a different amount of each of the scarce resources. Furthermore, there are not enough resources to produce all the new products suggested. Which new products and how much of each one should the firm produce? Linear programming can be used to aid in this decision process. In this case, it would probably be used to show what profit mix will maximize profits but not exceed the available resources.

mathematical programming
Linear programming is a component of the more general technique of *mathematical programming*. Mathematical programming is concerned with the development of modeling and solution procedures for the purpose of maximizing the extent to which the goals and objectives of the decision maker are realized. Very special conditions must hold before a general mathematical programming problem is actually an LP problem. These special linearity conditions will be described later in the chapter.

Despite the implication of its name, LP has little to do with computer programming. In LP, the word *programming* is related to planning. Specifically, it refers to modeling a problem and subsequently solving it by mathematical techniques. As we shall see, LP is very similar to setting up and solving a system of linear equations.

Even though LP is quite different from computer programming, computer development has played an integral part in the successful application of LP. Real-world LP problems often involve hundreds of variables and equations. These problems would be impossible to solve without a high-speed computer.

Historically, significant contributions to LP were Leontief's input-output analysis in 1936 and the publication, in 1947, of George Dantzig's technique for, and mathematical proof of, the simplex solution procedure. Today, LP is one of the most widely used mathematical programming and optimization techniques. In surveying *Fortune 500* companies, the authors found that of those responding 95 percent claimed to use LP at least to some extent. More specifically, 37.5 percent claimed to use it very frequently, 32.5 percent used it frequently, 25 percent used it rarely, and only 5 percent never used it. Undoubtedly, smaller companies use LP less. In some cases, it is simply not needed; in other cases, managers may not understand LP nor realize its potential. In appropriate situations, LP can be a very powerful tool.

[General areas of application]

As you can imagine, LP has many business applications. But LP is also often used as a tool for developing economic theory and for the systematic analysis of problems both in the physical and social sciences. When a problem can be looked at as a matter of effectively allocating scarce resources, LP can often be used in its solution.

Industrial, agricultural, and military applications of LP are the most extensive. Some of these include scheduling military and industrial oil tanker fleets, dietary planning, agricultural land use and farm management, urban traffic control, oil refinery operation, scheduling blast furnace operations, and minimizing trim losses in paper mills.

Each of the functional areas of business has its own relationship to LP. In accounting, this relationship is multifaceted. In an LP analysis, the accountant supplies required data. Some public accounting firms employ teams of management consultants as advisors to clients. These consultants sometimes use LP to help solve clients' problems. Moreover, certain LP applications are directed to the accounting function itself. These are usually in the areas of budgeting and financial planning. One particularly interesting example is an accounting system in the petroleum industry that is structured on an LP model.[1] Applications in finance include portfolio selection models and financial mix strategies in which LP is used to select the best means for financing company projects.

Marketing applications of LP are numerous and include effective media selection for advertising strategies, development of least-cost distribution patterns, warehouse location, and optimal allocation of sales forces. Management applications of LP include production scheduling, human resource planning, and other kinds of resource allocation.

The list of applications is continually growing as more decision makers are becoming aware of the utility of LP and the availability of computers increases. The development of more powerful computers will also pave the way for applications that are currently beyond the capability of existing hardware.

[Problems LP can be used on]

In this section, we discuss some of the general problem situations to which LP can be applied. The following five areas represent the kinds of problems for which LP is now widely used. Can you think of other examples, perhaps innovative ones?

[1]J. Demski, "An Accounting System Structured on a Linear Programming Model," *The Accounting Review*, 42 (October 1967), 701–712.

Blending In blending problems, several raw ingredients are mixed into a final product that must fulfil certain specifications. Each of the raw ingredients contributes certain properties to the final product and entails a given cost. Examples of blending problems are blending petroleum products, mixing cattle feed, mixing meats to make sausage, and mixing paint. Many different combinations of these ingredients will result in satisfactory end products; the objective is to determine the blend of ingredients that does not exceed available supply, meets all technical specifications, and minimizes costs.

Determining product mix In these problems, it is necessary to determine the kinds and quantities of products to be manufactured in order to maximize profits. A firm can almost always manufacture several different products; each of these requires the use of limited production resources and contributes a certain amount toward profit. The final product mix must take into consideration the limited resources, expected demand for each product, and various management policies.

Physical distribution and assignment In physical distribution problems it is necessary to ship goods from supply points or production facilities to warehouses or centers of customer demand. Each supply point has a specified capacity, and each point of demand has a specified level of demand. Furthermore, shipping and/or production costs vary for the different plant-to-market alternatives. The problem is to determine the shipping pattern that minimizes shipping costs, meets all demand, and does not exceed available supply. In assignment problems, the objective is to assign facilities or people to specified jobs in order to maximize performance or minimize costs or time.

Production scheduling and inventory planning Many firms produce products that are subject to fluctuations in demand. Widely varying production rates have proven to be very costly. The problem is basically to determine a production schedule that meets anticipated demand and yet maintains reasonable inventory levels and minimizes the overall costs of production and carrying inventory.

Purchasing Linear programming can be used to help confront the kind of purchasing decisions in which products are available at different quantities, qualities, and prices. The objective is profit maximization, and the purchase decision must take into consideration the output requirements and specifications as well as budget limitations. Linear programming can also be used in "make-or-buy" situations. In these cases the problem is whether to produce a product or purchase it from an outside source.

[The LP model]

Linear programming is a mathematical technique that will maximize or minimize a linear function subject to a system of linear constraints. This linear function, together with the system of linear constraints, forms what is called the *linear programming model*. The canonical form of an LP model is as follows:

linear programming model

Maximize $c_1 x_1 + c_2 x_2 + ... + c_n x_n$ [4.1]
subject to the restrictions $a_{11} x_1 + a_{12} x_2 + ... + a_{1n} x_n \leq b_1$ [4.2]
$$a_{21} x_1 + a_{22} x_2 + ... + a_{2n} x_n \leq b_2$$
$$\vdots$$
$$a_{m1} x_1 + a_{m2} x_2 + ... + a_{mn} x_n \leq b_m$$
and $x_1 \geq 0, x_2 \geq 0, ..., x_n \geq 0$ [4.3]

Any problem whose mathematical formulation fits this general model is an LP problem.

An LP model consists of two basic parts—an objective function and a set of constraints. The function, 4.1, being maximized, $c_1 x_1 + c_2 x_2 + ... + c_n x_n$, is called the *objective function*. It is simply a mathematical expression that measures the effectiveness of a particular solution for the LP problem. The restrictions, 4.2, in the foregoing model are called *constraints*. These mathematical statements specify such elements of the problem as the limitations of available resources or the demand that must be met. Conditions, 4.3, are called the *nonnegativity conditions*.

objective function

constraints

nonnegativity conditions

The x_j variables are *decision variables*; that is, they are the variables

decision variables

whose value is determined when the LP model is solved. Their values provide the answers that are being sought in the LP analysis. In order to determine the values of the decision variables, the LP model needs data. The input data constants are often referred to parameters as *parameters*. The a_{ij}, c_j, and b_i in the general model are all parameters of the model.

Not all valid LP models fit the exact form of the standard model. Variations include an objective function that is to be minimized and constraints that are equations rather than inequalities.

FORMULATING LP MODELS

There are many different types of models. You may be familiar with econometric models, civil-engineering prototype models, iconic and analog models, even models of the world. In this section, we shall deal with mathematical models. Before any problem can be solved by LP analysis, it must be formulated as a mathematical model that fits the general form set forth in the preceding section. In any mathematical model, the decision maker is attempting to represent the essence of some problem in terms of relationships between symbols. In LP formulations, the real-world problem is translated into mathematical equations.

Model building is more an art than a science; thus, formulating successful models depends greatly upon the decision maker's own ingenuity and experience. Formulation can often be the most difficult part of an LP analysis. It is also the most important, for once the problem has been formulated correctly, it can be solved on a computer by an LP computer code. We shall state several business problems and show how to formulate them as LP models. In this way, you will begin to gain a feeling for how to approach the formulation of an LP model.

[Product mix example] The Faze Linear Company is a small manufacturer of high-fidelity components for the discriminating audiophile. It currently manufactures power amplifiers and preamplifiers; it has the facilities to produce only power amps, only preamps, or a combination of both. Production resources are limited, and it is critical that the firm produce the appropriate number of power amps and/or preamps in order to maximize profit. Currently, the power amp is selling for $799.95 and is contributing $200 toward profit. The preamp sells for $1,000 and contributes $500 to profit.

We shall assume that the firm can sell all the components that it can produce and that plant equipment and labor skills are interchangeable between the power amps and preamps.

Constructing the objective function Given its limited production capacities, Faze Linear would like to produce the exact number of power amps and/or preamps each day that maximize its profits. The objective function of the LP model must evaluate the profit potential of any proposed product mix. The first step in the construction of the objective function is the determination of the appropriate decision variables. What is the manufacturer trying to decide? Specifically, the answer to the question, How many power amps and how many preamps should I produce each day? Thus, let the decision variable x_1 equal the number of power amps to be produced each day, and let x_2 equal the number of preamps to be produced each day. Since x_1 and x_2 contribute $200 and $500, respectively, to profit, we may state the objective function as: Maximize $200x_1 + 500x_2$. Preamps contribute more to profit; so it may seem that only preamps should be produced. However, this may not be true since preamps also require more production resources.

Constructing the constraints In this simplified example, we shall assume that there are only three production resources. The production process is limited by scarcity of high-quality transistors for the preamps, assembly worker hours, and inspection and testing worker hours. Due to a shortage of high-quality transistors, at most 40 preamps can be manufactured on a daily basis; all other electronic components are in adequate supply. There are only 240 hours of assembly worker time available each day. Furthermore, each power amp requires 1.2 hours for assembly and each preamp requires 4 hours. Finally, there are 81 worker hours available for inspection and testing each day, and the two components require .5 and 1 hour respectively.

Since power amps do not require the transistor that is in short supply, the limited availability of these transistors will directly affect only the number of preamps produced each day. This constraint may be expressed as $x_2 \leq 40$.

Both components require assembly time; thus, the assembly time constraint must insure that the combined assembly time of both components must not exceed 240 hours. This may be expressed as $1.2x_1 + 4x_2 \leq 240$. For inspection and testing time, the constraint is $.50x_1 + 1x_2 \leq 81$. Since it is impossible to produce a negative number of components, we impose the nonnegativity conditions $x_1, x_2 \geq 0$.

The final LP formulation is thus

Maximize $\quad 200x_1 + 500x_2$
subject to $\quad x_2 \leq \quad 40$
$\quad 1.2x_1 + 4x_2 \leq 240$
$\quad .50x_1 + 1x_2 \leq \quad 81$
$x_1, x_2 \geq 0$

This problem is simple, and LP is not necessary to solve it. However, product mix problems involving hundreds of products and constraints are impossible to solve intuitively, and the use of LP is necessary. As an exercise, try to solve the Faze Linear problem intuitively. How high is your profit? Later on, we shall determine the optimum product mix by LP.

GUIDELINES FOR CONSTRUCTING LP MODELS

In order to formulate an LP model successfully, the decision maker must:

1 Understand the problem

2 Identify the decision variables

3 Choose a numerical measure of effectiveness for the objective function

4 Represent this measure of effectiveness as a linear expression involving the decision variables

5 Identify and represent all constraints as linear expressions involving the decision variables

6 Collect data or make appropriate estimations for all parameters of the model

It is not possible to give a magic formula for success in LP model formulation, but the following suggestions can help.

Understand the problem   Make sure that you understand the problem fully. Is the objective clear? Is the problem a maximization or a minimization?

Determine variables   Decide what the decision variables should be. What, precisely, is being sought in the problem? Is it a production schedule, a resource allocation, a shipping pattern, or something else? Remember that the optimum values of the decision variables must provide the answers to the problem. The most common error beginning students make is defining decision variables incorrectly and thus developing invalid models.

Identify and represent all constraints   A constraint must be constructed for each limited resource. Be certain each decision variable that affects the given resource is included in the constraint. Formulate constraints for all technical specifications or requirements, such as usage or production in fixed proportions. Finally, check for other types of constraint, such as management policies, demand, or other pertinent conditions.

Collect relevant data   All parameters of the model must be defined as numerical constraints. Are all relevant data available? In LP analysis, the collection and estimation of relevant data is often the most time-consuming part of the project.

[Diet problem example]   In this example, we present a simplification of the classical diet problem. This is a minimization, rather than a maximization, problem. The objective is to determine the type and amount of foods to include in a daily diet in order to meet certain nutritional requirements at minimum cost. The foods we include are tuna fish, milk, spinach, and whole-wheat bread; the only nutrients we consider are vitamins A, C, and D, and iron. We are given the nutritional and cost data shown in Table 4.1.

The decision to be made is simply to determine the amount of each type of food to include in the daily diet. Thus, let x_1 = number

Table 4.1　Nutrition and cost data for diet problem

Nutrient	Gallon of milk	Pound of tuna fish	Loaf of bread	Pound of spinach	Recommended daily allowance
Vitamin A	6,400	237	0	34,000	5,000 IU
Vitamin C	40	0	0	71	75 mg
Vitamin D	540	0	0	0	400 IU
Iron	28	7	13	8	12 mg
Cost	$1.60	$1.00	$.65	$.30	

of gallons of milk, x_2 = number of pounds of tuna fish, x_3 = number of loaves of bread, and x_4 = number of pounds of spinach. The objective function, therefore, is to minimize $1.60x_1 + 1.00x_2 + .65x_3 + .30x_4$.

The constraints must insure that the RDA for each vitamin is met. For vitamin A, each gallon of milk contains 6,400 IU, each pound of tuna fish contains 237 IU, bread contains none, and each pound of spinach contains 34,000 IU. Hence, the RDA constraint for vitamin A is written $6,400x_1 + 237x_2 + 0x_3 + 34,000x_4 \geq 5,000$.

The other three constraints and nonnegativity conditions are written:

$$40x_1 + 0x_2 + 0x_3 + 71x_4 \geq 75$$
$$540x_1 + 0x_2 + 0x_3 + 0x_4 \geq 400$$
$$28x_1 + 7x_2 + 13x_3 + 8x_4 \geq 12$$
$$x_1, x_2, x_3, x_4 \geq 0$$

[Production/distribution example]　In this example, two production plants located in different parts of the country must produce and distribute a product to three regional warehouses. The three warehouses have demands of 500, 2,000, and 900, respectively. The cost of shipping, based primarily on distance, is given in Table 4.2. The labor and power costs are less at plant 1; each unit is produced at a cost of $1.50. Each unit at plant 2 is produced at a cost of $2.

The objective in this problem is to meet all demand and minimize the combined cost of production and distribution. The decision to

Table 4.2   Cost ($) of shipping one unit

From plant	To warehouse		
	1	2	3
1	.30	.90	.80
2	.70	.20	.40

be made concerns how much should be shipped from each plant to each warehouse.

It is more meaningful (though not essential) to represent these decision variables as variables with two subscripts. Let

x_{ij} − amount shipped from plant i to warehouse j
where $i = 1, 2$
          $j = 1, 2, 3$

Since each unit that is shipped must first be produced, we develop an objective function to minimize $(1.50 + .30)x_{11} + (1.50 + .90)x_{12} + (1.50 + .80)x_{13} + (2 + .70)x_{21} + (2 + .20)x_{22} + (2 + .40)x_{23}$.

The only restriction in this model is that demand must be met. In order to meet the demand at warehouse 1, all the shipments sent to warehouse 1 must sum to 500. Thus, the first constraint is $x_{11} + x_{21} = 500$. The other two demand constraints are $x_{12} + x_{22} = 2,000$ and $x_{13} + x_{23} = 900$. The nonnegativity condition is $x_{ij} \geq 0$ for all i and j. The complete formulation of the model is thus

Minimize $1.80x_{11} + 2.40x_{12} + 2.30x_{13} + 2.70x_{21} + 2.20x_{22} + 2.40x_{23}$
subject to $x_{11} + x_{21} = 500$
                $x_{12} + x_{22} = 2,000$
                $x_{13} + x_{23} = 900$
$x_{ij} \geq 0$ for all i and j

[Blending example]   The Green Turf Lawn and Garden Store is trying to sell its own brand of lawn fertilizer this year. It plans to sell two types of fertilizer, one high in nitrogen content and the other an all-purpose fertilizer. The fertilizers are mixed from two different components that contribute nitrogen and phosphorus

Table 4.3   Cost and composition of fertilizer components

Mixing component	Cost ($)	Nitrogen (%)	Phosphorus (%)
1	.20	60	10
2	.30	10	40

in different amounts. The composition of each component and cost per pound is given in Table 4.3.

This season's demand is estimated to be 5,000 25-pound bags of high-nitrogen fertilizer and 7,000 25-pound bags of all-purpose fertilizer. The fertilizer high in nitrogen is to contain between 40 and 50 percent nitrogen, and the all-purpose fertilizer is to contain, at most, 20 percent phosphorus. How many pounds of each mixing component should Green Turf purchase in order to satisfy estimated demand at minimum cost?

Let x_1 and x_2 be the number of pounds of mixing component 1 that are purchased for the high-nitrogen and all-purpose fertilizers, respectively. Similarly, let y_1 and y_2 be the number of pounds of mixing component 2 that are obtained for the high-nitrogen and all-purpose fertilizers. The objective function is then formulated to minimize $.20x_1 + .30y_1 + .20x_2 + .30y_2$.

Assuming that Green Turf wants at least to meet its estimated demand, we can specify the demand on high-nitrogen fertilizer by $x_1 + y_1 \geq 25 \, (5,000)$. Similarly, the demand for all-purpose fertilizer is specified by $x_2 + y_2 \geq 25 \, (7,000)$.

Since the different mixing components contribute different amounts of nitrogen and phosphorus, we must calculate a weighted average to represent the content of a particular blend. The high-nitrogen fertilizer must contain at least 40 percent nitrogen. Thus $(.60x_1 + .10y_1)/(x_1 + y_1) \geq .40$. This constraint is not a linear expression, but it can be turned into one by eliminating the fraction thus:

$.60x_1 + .10y_1 \geq .40 \, (x_1 + y_1)$
$.20x_1 - .30y_1 \geq 0$

The upper limit of 50 percent nitrogen can be written $(.60x_1 + .10y_1)/(x_1 + y_1) \leq .50$, or $.10x_1 - .40y_1 \leq 0$.

Finally, the 20 percent phosphorus restriction on the all-purpose fertilizer is represented $(.10x_2 + .40y_2)/(x_2 + y_2) \leq .20$, or $-.10x_2 + .20y_2 \leq 0$.

The final LP model, then, is stated:

Minimize $.20x_1 + .30y_1 + .20x_2 + .30y_2$
subject to $x_1 + y_1 \geq 125,000$
$\qquad x_2 + y_2 \geq 175,000$
$\quad .20x_1 - .30y_1 \geq 0$
$\quad .10x_1 - .40y_1 \leq 0$
$\quad -.10x_2 + .20y_2 \leq 0$
$x_1, x_2, y_1, y_2 \geq 0$

[Machine loading example] Nickleson Machine Shop wants to develop a math model to help decide which jobs should be processed on which machines so as to minimize total cost. Initially, the manager wants to try LP on a small example to see if the results are satisfactory. The first consideration, then, is loading three jobs; two machines are available for processing. The jobs correspond to producing three, seven, and four units, respectively, for products 1, 2, and 3. Machine 1 has 8 hours available during each day, but machine 2 has only 6. Table 4.4 gives relevant cost and production time data.

If we let x_{ij} = the amount of product j to be allocated for production to machine i, then we can formulate the objective function to

Table 4.4   Machine loading cost and production time data

Machine	Product	Cost of producing one unit of product j on machine i (\$)			Time required to produce one unit of product j on machine i(hr)		
		1	2	3	1	2	3
1		13	9	10	.4	1.1	.9
2		11	12	8	.5	1.2	1.3

minimize $13x_{11} + 9x_{12} + 10x_{13} + 11x_{21} + 12x_{22} + 8x_{23}$. The time constraints on machine availability are

Machine 1 $.4x_{11} + 1.1x_{12} + .9x_{13} \leq 8$
Machine 2 $.5x_{21} + 1.2x_{22} + 1.3x_{23} \leq 6$

The production requirements specify that the appropriate number of units be produced for each product. These constraints are

Product 1 $x_{11} + x_{21} = 3$
Product 2 $x_{12} + x_{22} = 7$
Product 3 $x_{13} + x_{23} = 5$

The final LP model is

Minimize $13x_{11} + 9x_{12} + 10x_{13} + 11x_{21} + 12x_{22} + 8x_{23}$
subject to $.4x_{11} + 1.1x_{12} + .9x_{13} \leq 8$
$.5x_{21} + 1.2x_{22} + 1.3x_{23} \leq 6$
$x_{11} + x_{21} = 3$
$x_{12} + x_{22} = 7$
$x_{13} + x_{23} = 4$
$x_{ij} \geq 0; i = 1, 2; j = 1, 2, 3$

[Mathematical assumptions and limitations of LP]

Now that you are more familiar with LP, we can discuss the requirements for an LP model. It is tacitly assumed that there is a single goal we can represent by a linear objective function and that all restrictions are linear in nature. Given these prior conditions, any LP model has two basic properties: certainty and linearity.

certainty   *Certainty* requires that all parameters of the model be known. In the realm of decision-making problems, LP falls into the class of decision making under certainty. In other words, the objective function coefficients, c_j, the coefficients of the constraints, a_{ij}, and the right-hand-side numbers, b_i, must all be known constants. When a decision maker cannot determine exact values for some of these parameters, specific numerical values must be estimated and assigned, nonetheless, in order to use LP. This requirement bears repeating: Specific numerical values are necessary in order to solve an LP model. By using sensitivity analysis (a technique discussed in Chapter 6), the decision maker can explore the effects of changing some parameters over a range of values. This capability is particularly important when some parameters have been estimated or are known to change over time.

linearity   *Linearity* is a property of mathematical functions. The term denotes the stable relationship between dependent and independent variables that are graphically expressed by straight lines. Suppose y is a variable whose value depends on the value of an independent variable x. If y is linearly related to x, then the graph of y versus x results in a straight line.

In LP, we generally use more than two variables. Suppose we have n variables $x_1, x_2, ..., x_n$. Then a linear expression in terms of these variables is of the form $a_1 x_1 + a_2 x_2 + ... + a_n x_n$. Note that in a linear expression the coefficients are constants, all variables have an exponent of 1, and no variables are multiplied together.

The linearity assumption of LP means that it is necessary for the objective function and the left-hand side of every constraint to be a linear expression. For example, $8x_1 + 17x_2$ is a linear expression, but $8x_1^2 + 17x_2 x_3$ is nonlinear since x_1 has an exponent of 2, and x_2 and x_3 form a product.

Three properties of linearity help to clarify the implications of linearity. These properties are proportionality, additivity, and divisibility.

proportion-   *Proportionality* requires that the amount of each resource used
ality   must be proportional to the value of the decision variable. This must be true over the entire range of values for the decision variable. Thus, there can be no special costs that raise a decision variable's value above zero, such as a fixed, or start-up, charge associated with beginning an activity. In the objective function, the contribution to profit must also be proportional to the value of the decision variable. For example, in an objective function to maximize $3x_1 + 7x_2$, each unit of x_1 contributes \$3 (a proportional amount) to the value of the objective function.

additivity   *Additivity* postulates that the value of the objective function and the amount of resource used is equal to the sum of the contributions of all decision variables. Using the same objective function, maximize $3x_1 + 7x_2$, suppose that $x_1 = 1$ and $x_2 = 1$. Additivity asserts that the contributions of 3 and 7 respectively must add together to form a sum of 10.

divisibility   *Divisibility* simply means that the decision variables are allowed to assume a continuous range of values. Thus the decision variable values may be fractional or any decimal value. The point here is that LP generally will not provide integer, or whole number, solutions. Of course, we know that it is impossible to manufacture a fractional number of automobiles. In problems where integer solutions are required, LP may be used to provide approximate answers by rounding off the solution to integers. However, doing so may cause significant departure from optimality. If optimal integer solutions are required, you must resort to another, more difficult, branch of mathematical programming known as *integer programming.*

integer programming

Obviously, then, conditions compatible with linear expression must exist before LP can be used. Many mathematical programming models are nonlinear, and other techniques must be used to solve these types of problem. In some cases, however, LP is used to get approximate solutions to nonlinear problems. This is done since LP is generally much faster and can solve much larger problems than the nonlinear techniques.

[Bibliography]

Charnes, Abraham and W. W. Cooper, *Management Models and Industrial Applications of Linear Programming.* New York: John Wiley & Sons, Inc., 1961.

Daellenbach, Hans G., and Earl J. Bell, *User's Guide to Linear Programming.* Englewood Cliffs, N.J.: Prentice-Hall, Inc., 1970.

Dano, Sven, *Linear Programming in Industry: Theory and Applications,* 2nd ed. Vienna: Springer-Verlag, OHG, 1965.

Dantzig, George B., *Linear Programming and Extensions.* Princeton, N.J.: Princeton University Press, 1963.

Driebeek, Norman J., *Applied Linear Programming.* Reading, Mass.: Addison-Wesley Publishing Co., Inc., 1969.

Gass, Saul I., *Illustrated Guide to Linear Programming.* New York: McGraw-Hill Book Company, 1970.

Hadley, George, *Linear Programming*. Reading Mass.: Addison-Wesley Publishing Co., Inc., 1962.

Haley, K. B., *Mathematical Programming for Business and Industry*. New York: St. Martin's Press, Inc., 1967.

Hamilton, William F., et al., *Linear Programming for Management*. Newburyport, Mass.: Entelek, 1969.

Henderson, A., and R. Schlaifer, "Mathematical Programming: Better Information for Better Decision Making," *Harvard Business Review*, 32 (May–June, 1954), 73–100.

Hillier, Frederick and Gerald J. Lieberman, *Introduction to Operations Research*. San Francisco: Holden-Day, Inc., 1974.

Kwak, No Kyoon *Mathematical Programming with Business Applications*. New York: McGraw-Hill Book Company, 1973.

Naylor, Thomas H., Eugene T. Byrne, and John M. Vernon, *Introduction to Linear Programming: Methods and Cases*. Belmont, Calif.: Wadsworth Publishing Company, Inc., 1971.

Orchard-Hays, William, *Advanced Linear Programming Computing Techniques*. New York: McGraw-Hill Book Company, 1968.

Stockton, R. Stansbury, *Introduction to Linear Programming*. Homewood, Ill.: Richard D. Irwin, Inc., 1971.

Strum, Jay E., *Introduction to Linear Programming*. San Francisco: Holden-Day, Inc., 1972.

Taha, H. A., *Operations Research: An Introduction*. New York: The Macmillan Company, 1971.

Teichroew, Daniel, *An Introduction to Management Science: Deterministic Models*. New York: John Wiley & Sons, Inc., 1964.

Wagner, Harvey M., *Principles of Management Science with Applications to Executive Decisions*. Englewood Cliffs, N.J.: Prentice-Hall, Inc., 1970.

[Review questions]

1 How does LP differ from just solving a system of equations?

2 Interpret the difference between an equality, and an inequality, constraint.

3 The nonnegativity conditions are not always imposed in every LP model. Give some situations in which they might not be enforced.

4 What does linearity mean?

5 Can you think of any LP applications other than those discussed in the chapter?

6 What are three properties of linearity?

7 Explain what is meant by the phrase, "Model building is more an art than a science."

8 What assumptions must be satisfied in order for a problem to be solved by LP?

[Problems]

4.1 The Ace Manufacturing Company produces two lines of its product, the super and the regular. Resource requirements for production are given in the table. There are 1,600 hours of assembly worker hours

Product line	Profit contribution ($)	Assembly time (hr)	Paint time (hr)	Inspection time (hr)
Regular	50	1.2	.8	.2
Super	75	1.6	.9	.2

available per week, 700 hours of paint time, and 300 hours of inspection time. Regular customers will demand at least 150 units of the regular line and 90 of the super. Formulate an LP model that will determine the optimal product mix on a weekly basis.

4.2 The Crazy Nut Company wishes to market two special nut mixes during the holiday season. Mix 1 contains $1/2$ pound of peanuts and $1/2$ pound of cashews. Mix 2 contains $3/5$ pound of peanuts, $1/4$ pound of cashews, and $3/20$ pound of almonds. Mix 1 sells for $1.49 per pound, and mix 2 sells for $1.69 per pound. The data pertinent to the raw

Ingredient	Amount available (lb)	Cost per lb ($)
Peanuts	30,000	.35
Cashews	12,000	.50
Almonds	9,000	.60

ingredients appear in the table. Assuming that Crazy can sell all cans of either mix that it produces, formulate an LP model to determine how much of mixes 1 and 2 to produce.

4.3 The Viscus Oil Company must decide how to allocate its budget from windfall profits. The government grants certain tax breaks if the company invests funds in research concerned with energy conservation. However, the government stipulates that at least 60 percent of the funds must be funneled into research for automobile efficiency. Viscus has a $1 million budget for energy research and development this year; the research proposal data are shown in the table. Assum-

Project	Management policy on upper limit of expenditures ($)	Forecast return on investment (%)
Methanol fuel research	300,000	4.0
Electrically operated cars	100,000	0.1
Emission reduction	300,000	3.0
Solar cells	200,000	2.0
Windmills	100,000	1.0

ing Viscus wants to maximize return on its investments and receive the government tax break, how should the budget be allocated? Formulate as an LP model.

4.4 The Leiz Manufacturing Company produces small chips for use in pocket calculators. Leiz has two plants that produce the chips and then distribute to five different wholesalers. The cost of production at plants 1 and 2 is $2.19 and $2.38, respectively. Forecast demand indicates that shipments will have to be 2,000 to wholesaler 1; 3,000 to wholesaler 2; 1,000 to wholesaler 3; 5,000 to wholesaler 4; and 4,000 to wholesaler 5. The distribution costs of shipping a chip from plant to wholesaler are shown in the table. Production capacity at

From plant	To wholesaler				
	1	2	3	4	5
1	.03	.02	.05	.04	.02
2	.06	.04	.02	.03	.05

each plant is 8,000 units. Formulate an LP model to determine how many chips each plant supplies each wholesaler.

4.5 Mydlend Mortgage Company makes four types of loan, as listed in the table. The company is trying to decide how to allocate $5 million

Type of loan	Yield (%)	Risk (%)
First mortgage	7	3.5
Remodeling	1	2.0
Auto	8	3.8
Signature	14	4.0

in funds. The company president has decided that the average risk must not exceed 3.7 percent. Formulate an LP model to maximize yield in allocating the $5 million.

4.6 An agriculture student wants to determine what quantities of various grains to feed cattle in order to meet minimum nutritional requirements at lowest cost. The student is considering the use of corn, barley, oats, and wheat. The table relates the relevant dietary information

Nutrient	Corn	Barley	Oats	Wheat	Recommended daily allowance
Protein	10	9	11	8	20 mg
Calcium	50	45	58	50	70 mg
Iron	9	8	7	10	12 mg
Calories	1,000	800	850	9,000	4,000
Cost per lb	$.55	$.47	$.45	$.52	

per pound of grain. Formulate an LP model to determine the dietary mix that minimizes cost.

4.7 A manufacturer of tennis rackets would like to introduce its new line of poly-play rackets. The firm may advertise in leading tennis magazines or on television during the World Championship Tennis pro tour and major international tournaments. The feeling is that those players whose annual income exceeds $15,000 will be 1.8 times more likely to buy this new racket. The objective in the advertising scheme is to maximize potential sales. One unit of TV advertising costs $35,000 and reaches approximately 2 million people, half of whom make more than $15,000 annually. One unit of advertising in tennis magazine 1 costs $25,000 and reaches 1 million people, three-quarters of whom are in the higher income bracket. One unit of advertising in tennis magazine 2 costs $15,000 and reaches 600,000 people, two-thirds of whom have incomes exceeding $15,000. The total advertising budget is $250,000. Formulate the problem as an LP model.

4.8 The Normal Distribution Company supplies five major metropolitan areas from three of its regionally located warehouses. It would like to minimize the transportation cost of shipping from warehouse to market. Transportation costs are shown in the table. Formulate an

From warehouse	To city					Supply
	1	2	3	4	5	
1	7	5	12	11	9	500
2	13	12	6	3	8	300
3	7	6	5	4	14	350
Demand	150	200	100	300	400	

LP model to meet all demand at minimum transportation cost.

4.9 A manufacturer of office equipment would like to optimize the company's product mix. Currently, the firm produces desks, chairs, tables, and filing cabinets. Each product's resource requirements are given in the table. The desks, chairs, tables, and cabinets contribute

Product	Wood (board ft)	Plastic (sq ft)	Steel alloy (lb)	Administrative worker hours
Desks	0	6	9	2.5
Chairs	3	1	1	1.2
Tables	5	2	2	2.2
Cabinets	0	0	15	1.9
Availability	1,000	1,200	1,000	1,500

$150, $45, $100, and $40 to profit, respectively. The minimum monthly demand requirements are 75 desks, 120 chairs, 100 tables, and 50 filing cabinets. Additionally, management does not want the number of filing cabinets to exceed 10 percent of the total number of items produced. Formulate as an LP model.

4.10 The Smelly Oil Company produces all three major types of gasoline, regular, premium, and unleaded. Its gasoline is produced by blending two petroleum components and a high-octane lead additive. Minimum octane ratings must be met as provided in the following table of data:

Gasoline	Minimum octane	Selling price per gal. ($)
Regular	89	.50
Premium	94	.54
Unleaded	87	.49

Cost and availability data for the ingredients in the blends are shown in the next table:

Blending ingredients	Octane	Cost per gal. ($)	Availability per month (gal.)
Component 1	130	.24	76,000
Component 2	75	.18	95,000
Lead additive	1,100	1.50	60,000

Formulate an LP problem to determine the blends that maximize profits and meet all technical specifications. Assume that octane values mix linearly.

4.11 The Coldman Company has a production planning problem. Management wants to plan production for the ensuing year so as to minimize the combined cost of production and inventory storage costs. In each quarter of the year, demand is anticipated to be 65, 80, 135, and 75, respectively. The product can be manufactured during regular time at a cost of $16 per unit produced, or during overtime at a cost of $20 per unit. The table gives data pertinent to production capacities.

	Capacities in units		
Quarter	Regular time	Over-time	Quarterly demand
1	80	10	65
2	90	10	80
3	95	20	135
4	70	10	75

The cost of carrying one unit in inventory per quarter is $2. The inventory level at the beginning of the first quarter is zero. Formulate an LP model to minimize the production plus storage costs for the year.

4.12 Jiffy Job Shop would like to try a quantitative approach to its machine loading problem. There are three machines in the shop, and they are used to produce five different products. Each machine has

Machine	Product	Cost of producing one unit of product j on machine i ($)					Time required to produce one unit of product j on machine i (hr)				
		1	2	3	4	5	1	2	3	4	5
1		12	10	13	9	8	1	.8	1.5	.5	.6
2		7	6	12	11	9	1.5	.9	.7	.4	.9
3		14	8	5	3	2	1.2	1.1	.9	.8	.5

an 8-hour time availability each working day. Today, the demand is 6, 3, 2, 1, and 5 for products 1 through 5, respectively. The table gives relevant cost and production time data. Formulate an LP model to determine the amount of product j to be allocated for production on machine i.

4.13 Ma-Bell Corporation has a scheduling problem. Operators are needed according to the schedule shown in the table. Operators work

Time period	Operators needed
Midnight to 4 A.M.	4
4 A.M. to 8 A.M.	6
8 A.M. to noon	90
Noon to 4 P.M.	85
4 P.M. to 8 P.M.	55
8 P.M. to midnight	20

8-hour shifts and can begin work at either midnight, 4 A.M., 8 A.M., noon, 4 P.M., or 8 P.M. Let x_j equal the number of operators beginning work in time period j, $j = 1, 2, ..., 6$. Formulate an LP model to hire the minimum number of operators the company needs.

4.14 The Akron Tire Company currently produces four lines of tires, the economy, glass-belted, snow tire, and the steel radial. Recent recessionary trends have caused a decline in demand, and the company is laying off workers and discontinuing its third shift.

The problem it faces is that of rescheduling production during the first and second shifts for the remaining quarter of the year. The production process primarily involves the use of vulcanization, fabrication, and plastometer machines. However, the limiting resource in production is the availability of machine hours on the vulcanization machines. The economy, glass-belted, snow tire, and steel radial require 4, 5, 5, and 7 hours, respectively, of vulcanizing time.

The sales manager has forecast the expected sales for each of the four tires in the last quarter of the year. These estimates are shown in the following table:

	Forecast sales			
Month	Economy	Glass-belted	Snow tire	Steel radial
October	8,000	19,000	4,000	7,000
November	7,000	19,000	15,000	7,000
December	6,000	18,000	17,000	7,000

The production capacity in terms of vulcanizing hours available is expressed by month and shift in the next table:

Month	Vulcanizing hours available	
	Shift 1	Shift 2
October	110,000	100,000
November	130,000	120,000
December	115,000	116,000

The labor cost of operating the vulcanizing machines is $10 per hour during the first shift. The shift differential requires that the wages be $12 per hour during the second shift. The other relevant cost is storage: It costs $4 per month to store a tire, regardless of its type. Note that it will be necessary to store some tires in the problem, as there is not enough labor available during December to meet December demand.

Assuming that the company wishes to produce exactly as many tires as the sales manager has forecast, formulate an LP model to determine a production schedule that will meet demand at minimum total cost.

4.15 Agricultural applications of LP are numerous. The optimal use of agricultural land resources is becoming increasingly important in order to feed the world's people. This case is based on an actual model used to allocate land optimally given a set of agronomic and institutional constraints specific to the foreign country.

We consider a group of 11 possible crops and 8 agricultural regions in which the crops may be cultivated. Each region is currently supporting a certain acreage of one or more of the 11 crops. However, a reallocation of the land may result in more efficient utilization, and also a higher net revenue per acre of crop, in each region.

The 11 crops are catagorized as follows:

Winter crops	Summer crops
1 Wheat	5 Cotton variety 1
2 Barley	6 Cotton variety 2
3 Broad beans	7 Rice
4 Lentils	8 Corn
	9 Millet
	10 Sesame
	11 Sugar cane

The following variables are relevent to the model:

i = region number (8)

j = crop number (11)

r_{ij} = net revenue factor per acre of crop j in region i

x_{ij} = acreage to be assigned to crop j in region i

y_{ij} = actual current acreage of crop j in province i

w_i = total area in winter crops in region i

s_i = total area in summer crops in region i

y_i = total cultivated area in region i (note that $w_i < y_i$ and $s_i < y_i$)

$y_{i\ 11}$ = actual acreage of sugar cane in region i

The objective function of the model defines net revenue in terms of crop yield, a_{ij}, crop price, p_j, and cultivation costs, c_{ij}. Thus $r_{ij} = a_{ij} p_j - c_{ij}$. Assuming that all parameters a_{ij}, p_j, and c_{ij} are known, we can then calculate the r_{ij} for the objective function.

The constraints relate to the following restrictions:

The total acreage of winter crops must equal w_i.

The total acreage of summer crops must equal s_i.

The total acreage of cotton crops in each region i must not exceed one-third of the total cultivated area in region i.

Even though the objective is to maximize net revenue, there exists a constraint that the new acreage of the staple crops wheat, broad beans, and corn must be at least .3, .3, and .85, respectively, as large as the current acreage of these three crops.

Each region must cultivate the exact same amount of sugar cane as is currently being cropped.

Formulate an LP model to maximize the net revenue, subject to the foregoing constraints.

5

[Solving LP problems: graphical and simplex methods]

In the previous chapter, we examined some of the mathematical assumptions of LP, how to formulate LP problems, and typical areas of application. In this chapter, we shall investigate how these formulated LP models can be solved. We will look first at the graphical method of solution; it yields insight into the nature of an LP problem. The graphical method is limited to problems with no more than three variables since we cannot draw graphs in more than three dimensions. Therefore, our second subject, the simplex method, is the technique used for solving most real-world LP problems. It is a relatively efficient solution procedure, and with the aid of a computer, it enables us to solve LP problems that have many variables and constraints.

[The graphical method]

The graphical method of LP solution simply involves plotting each of a problem's constraints to form a region of possible solutions. We then examine this region to select the best alternative. To illustrate the graphical method, let's return to the Faze Linear product mix example of Chapter 4. Recall that the objective is to produce the appropriate number of power amplifiers and preamplifiers in order to maximize profit. The two components contribute $200 and $500, respectively, to profit. The model we derived is

Maximize $200x_1 + 500x_2$ (profit)
subject to $x_2 \leq 40$ (transistor availability)
  $1.2x_1 + 4x_2 \leq 240$ (assembly time)
  $.5x_1 + 1x_2 \leq 81$ (inspection/testing time)
$x_1, x_2 \geq 0$

The next step in the graphical method is to plot the constraints on a graph. Since the constraints are inequalities rather than equations, their graphs are regions rather than lines. However, the easiest way to graph an inequality is first to graph it as an equality, then simply shade in the appropriate area.

The first constraint $x_2 \leq 40$ can be located on the graph by first locating its x_1 and x_2 intercepts on the x_1 and x_2 axes, respectively. Since the first constraint does not involve x_1, it does not have an x_1 intercept. The x_2 intercept is determined by treating the constraint as an equation yielding $x_2 = 40$. The graph of $x_2 = 40$ is shown in Figure 5.1.

Figure 5.1   Graph of $x_2 = 40$

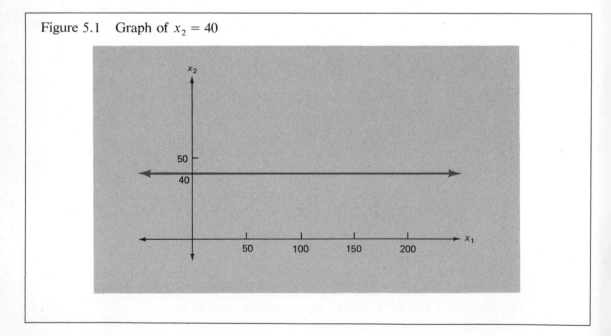

Figure 5.2   Graph of $x_2 \le 40$

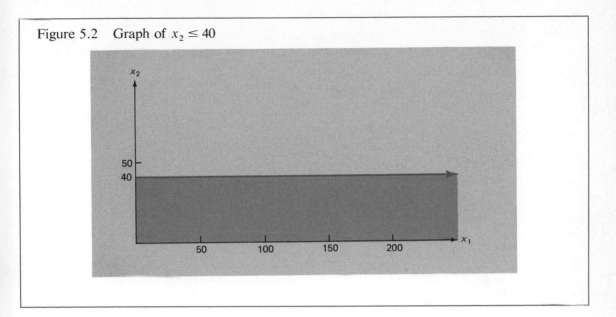

The inequality $x_2 \le 40$ is graphed from $x_2 = 40$ (as shown in Figure 5.1) by simply observing on which side of the line the origin is located. Substituting $x_1 = 0$ and $x_2 = 0$ into the inequality $x_2 \le 40$, we find that 0 is smaller than 40, and the origin is thus included in the inequality. Thus the graph of $x_2 \le 40$ is the region established by the line $x_2 = 40$, and it contains the origin. The graph of $x_2 \le 40$ is shown in Figure 5.2. Notice that the shaded area is bounded by the x_1 and x_2 axes as a result of the nonnegativity conditions. That is, the conditions $x_1, x_2 \ge 0$ restrict the expression of the constraint to the first quadrant of the plane.

In the second constraint, we determine the x_1 intercept by letting $x_2 = 0$ and solving $1.2x_1 + 4(0) = 240$, from which we obtain $x_1 = 200$. Setting $x_1 = 0$, we obtain the x_2 intercept by solving $1.2(0) + 4x_2 = 240$; thus we have $x_2 = 60$. Plotting the second constraint with the first, we obtain the graph in Figure 5.3. The third constraint is plotted in the same way, and finally we have established the region of possible solutions as indicated in Figure 5.4.

Any proposed solution to the Faze Linear problem is possible only if it falls within the shaded region. Called the *feasible* region,

Figure 5.3   Graph of $x_2 \le 40$ and $1.2x_1 + 4x_2 \le 240$

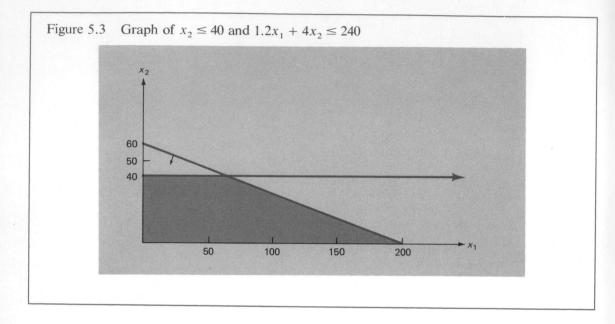

Figure 5.4   Graph of Faze Linear constraints

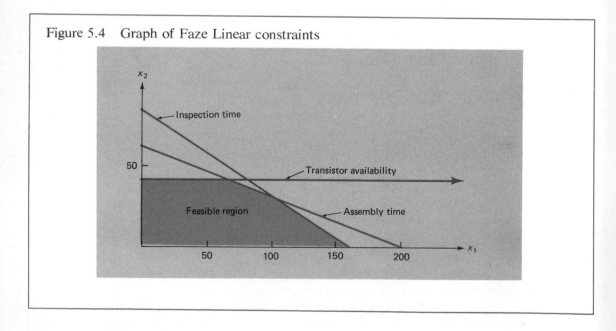

this area encompasses all points that satisfy all constraints and the nonnegativity conditions. Any solution that satisfies all con- feasible and infeasible solutions straints is said to be feasible, and a solution that violates any one of the constraints is *infeasible*. For example, Faze Linear may want to produce $x_1 = 100$ power amps and $x_2 = 20$ preamps. Such a solution is feasible (as you can see in Figure 5.5). However, if the company wants to produce $x_1 = 100$ power amps and $x_2 = 50$ preamps, this is not feasible since it violates the third constraint. To calculate this, substitute $x_1 = 100$ and $x_2 = 50$ into the third constraint; then, you have $.5(100) + 1(50) = 50 + 50 = 100 > 81$. The production of 100 power amps and 50 preamps daily requires 100 hours of inspection and testing time daily, and only 81 hours are available. From Figure 5.5, you can see that the point (100, 50) does not fall in the feasible region.

optimal solutions An *optimal* solution is a solution that is not only feasible but achieves the *best possible* value for the objective function. If we are trying to increase profit, an optimal solution is a feasible solution that maximizes profit. Similarly, if we are minimizing, an optimal

Figure 5.5   Graph of Faze Linear feasible, infeasible, and extreme points

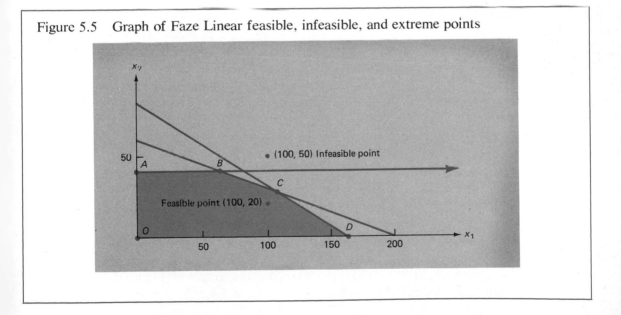

solution is a feasible solution that minimizes whatever criterion of effectiveness the objective function measures. The goal of LP is to determine an optimal solution. Therefore, let's proceed to find the optimal solution to the Faze Linear problem.

At first, the determination of an optimal solution may seem to be almost impossible. You see that the feasible region in Figure 5.5 encompasses an infinite number of feasible solutions. How, then, can we find the one or ones that are optimal? Fortunately, LP provides a result that allows us to exclude all but a finite number of feasible points.

In Figure 5.5, notice that the feasible region contains five vertices. These vertices, or corner points, are called *extreme points* of the feasible region. They play an integral part in the simplex method, as the fundamental theorem of LP describes. The *extreme point theorem* states: If an optimal solution to a linear programming problem exists, then at least one such optimal solution must be an extreme point solution.

extreme points

extreme point theorem

The importance of the extreme point theorem is that it restricts our search for an optimal solution from an infinite number of possibilities to a finite number of extreme points, no matter how large the problem. Of course, really large LP problems have an astronomical (though finite) number of extreme points.

In our small example with the Faze Linear Company, we have only five extreme points. One of these includes the origin (0,0). One approach to determining the optimal solution is to find the coordinates of the other four extreme points and then simply find the profit associated with each of these. The point with the highest profit is the optimal solution to the Faze Linear problem.

Finding the coordinates of all five extreme points, however, is laborious and unnecessary. The following procedure can be used to single out an extreme point that is the optimum. The objective function is the measuring device we use to determine the relative worth of any proposed solution. Let P = profit; then we wish to maximize $P = 200x_1 + 500x_2$. The objective function is now in the form of a linear equation. If we let $P = \$20,000$, we can then plot the graph of $20,000 = 200x_1 + 500x_2$ on the graph of Figure 5.5. Doing this, we get the result shown in Figure 5.6.

Any point on the line $20,000 = 200x_1 + 500x_2$ within the feasible

Figure 5.6   Graph of Faze Linear profit lines and optimal solution

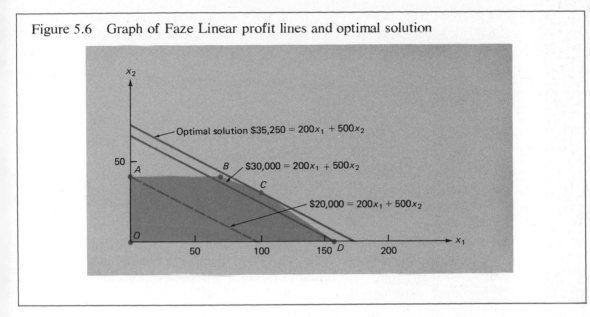

region is feasible and will yield a profit of $20,000. If we convert the objective function to slope-intercept form, we obtain $x_2 = -.4x_1 + .0020P$. Thus the slope of the objective function is $-.4$ regardless of the profit P. Letting $P = \$30,000$ we again plot a profit line shown in Figure 5.6. Any point on the line and in the feasible region will yield a profit of $30,000. We can see that moving the profit line with slope $-.4$ away from the origin toward the northeast increases profit. We must move the line as far as we can and still have at least one point on the line be in the feasible region. Clearly, this is accomplished at the extreme point C. Thus the point C is the optimum solution to the Faze Linear problem.

Precisely how does point C yield the optimum solution? The point C consists of an x_1 coordinate and an x_2 coordinate. Evaluating these two coordinates then yields a production level for x_1 and x_2, that is, the optimal number of power amps and preamps to produce each day. In order to determine the coordinates of the point C, we notice that the point C occurs at the intersection of the two lines $1.2x_1 + 4x_2 = 240$ and $.5x_1 + 1x_2 = 81$. Thus the coordinates can be determined by solving these two equations simultaneously.

$$1.2x_1 + 4x_2 = 240$$
$$\underline{-2.0x_1 - 4x_2 = -324}$$
$$-.8x_1 \qquad = -84$$
$$x_1 \qquad = 105$$

Substituting 105 for x_1 in the first equation, we obtain $x_2 = [240 - 1.2(105)]/4 = 28.5$. Thus, optimal product mix is to produce 105 power amps and 28.5 preamps each day. The profit associated with the optimal solution is found by substituting into the objective function to yield $200(105) + 500(28.5) = \$35,250$.

Did you notice that the LP solution suggests the production of 28.5 preamps daily? As we have said before, LP does not necessarily generate integer solutions. It is impossible to manufacture 28.5 preamps per day unless a unit is half-completed one day and then finished the next day, and so on. If whole number solutions are sought, what is wrong with trying to produce 105 power amps and 29 preamps? Alternatively, we could round off the LP optimal solution and produce 105 and 28, respectively, for a profit of \$35,000 per day. This solution, however, might not be the optimal integer solution.

[The simplex method]

As you can probably imagine now, it is impossible to use the graphical method of solution on problems that are at all complex. The greatest importance of the graphical method is as an aid to understanding the simplex method. We will discuss the simplex method in its basic form here. For large-scale, real-world applications of LP, more sophisticated variants of the simplex method are actually used; however, the principles are essentially the same.

The simplex method is similar to solving a system of linear equations. In fact, the simplex method does solve a system of equations, and the solution derived not only solves the equations but also optimizes an objective function. In this sense, the simplex method is a straightforward generalization of various methods for solving a system of equations with which you may be familiar, such as Gauss-Jordan elimination.

Solving linear programming problems

Figure 5.7   Faze Linear feasible region and associated extreme points

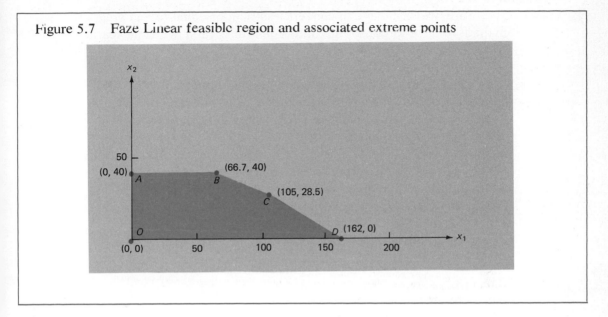

The simplex method is an *iterative technique.* That is, it establishes an initial feasible solution, then repeats the solution process, making successive improvements, until the optimal solution is found. It is sometimes referred to as an *adjacent extreme point solution procedure* because it generally begins at a feasible extreme point, then successively evaluates adjacent extreme points until the one representing the optimal solution is found. Recall from the extreme point theorem that an optimum (if it exists) may always be found at an extreme point. This can be illustrated by considering the feasible region of the Faze Linear problem we previously solved by the graphical method. Figure 5.7 shows the five extreme points and their respective coordinates. When we solve the Faze Linear problem by the simplex method, we shall find that the simplex method starts at the origin $(0,0)$, proceeds to the adjacent extreme point $(0,40)$, goes to $(66.7,40)$, and finally arrives at the next adjacent extreme point $(105,28.5)$, which is the optimal solution.

iterative technique

adjacent extreme point solution procedure

SIMPLEX PROCEDURES

In order to use the simplex method, it is necessary to state all the constraints as equations rather than inequalities. Mathematically, it is easier to solve systems of equations than systems of inequalities.

Introduction to management science

Therefore, we shall have to convert less-than-or-equal-to and greater-than-or-equal-to constraints into equations. First we shall learn how to convert $\leq$ constraints.

Suppose we have the constraint $x_1 + x_2 \leq 5$. We may convert this inequality to an equation by adding an additional variable, called a *slack variable*. Thus we have $x_1 + x_2 + s_1 = 5$, where $s_1 \geq 0$. A slack variable, as the name implies, represents unused resources. In the foregoing equation, if $x_1 = 2$ and $x_2 = 1$, then s_1 must equal 2. Thus $x_1 + x_2 < 5$ and s_1 represents two units of the right-hand-side resource that are left over.

slack variable

Notationally, we distinguish between slack and decision variables. The x_i represent decision varibles and refer to actual activities; the s_i denote slack variables that represent unused capacity.

Now to convert the LP formulation of the Faze Linear problem to standard form by adding a slack variable for each $\leq$ constraint:

Maximize $\quad 200x_1 + 400x_2$
subject to $\quad x_2 + s_1 = 40$
$\qquad 1.2x_1 + 4x_2 + s_2 = 240$
$\qquad .5x_1 + 1x_2 + s_3 = 81$
$x_1, x_2, s_1, s_2, s_3 \geq 0$

We have thus transformed a system of inequalities into a system of equations ready to be solved by the simplex method. Notice that even though the slack variables are added to the constraints, they do not appear in the objective function. This is equivalent to giving each slack a coefficient of zero in the objective function.

The simplex method is only concerned with solutions that correspond to extreme points of the feasible region. These extreme point solutions are also called *basic feasible solutions*. In general, an LP problem in standard form has more variables than constraints. For instance, let $n =$ the number of decision variables and $m =$ the number of inequality constraints; then m slack variables must be added to convert the inequality constraints to equations in standard form. Thus, we generally have $m + n$ variables and m constraints. This actually gives us n *degrees of freedom* (choices) in solving the $m \times (m + n)$ system of equations. That is, we may set n particular variables equal to zero and then solve the m equations in terms of the remaining m variables. To illustrate, let us take a small 2×3 example. Suppose we wish to solve

basic feasible solutions

$$2x_1 + 3x_2 + 8x_3 = 11$$
$$4x_1 + 6x_2 + 7x_3 = 13$$

We have one degree of freedom in the foregoing 2×3 system since we have one more variable than equation. Actually, the number of solutions to the system is infinite, since we can set x_1 equal to any number and solve in terms of x_2 and x_3. For example, x_1 can be set equal to zero, in which case we get $x_2 = 1$ and $x_3 = 1$ as the solution. However, we can set $x_2 = 0$ and we get $x_1 = \frac{3}{2}$ and $x_3 = 1$. We can even set $x_3 = 0$, but if we do in this system, we get no solution at all.

In general, the variables set to zero are called *nonbasic variables* and those that are nonzero are called *basic variables*. In the example above, one solution is $x_1 = 0$, $x_2 = 1$, and $x_3 = 1$; in this case, x_1 is a nonbasic variable and x_2 and x_3 are basic variables. In the simplex method, with $m + n$ variables and m constraints, there will be, at most, m variables not equal to zero. A solution derived by setting a certain n of the variables equal to zero is a *basic solution*. If all nonzero variables are also nonnegative, the basic solution is also feasible and thus corresponds to an extreme point.

There are potentially $\binom{m + n}{m} = (m + n)! / m! n!$ basic solutions to an LP problem. For large m and n, then, you can see that the number of possible solutions becomes astronomical. Fortunately, the simplex method only examines basic feasible solutions. In the Faze Linear problem, we have five variables and three constraints. There are potentially $5!/(3!2!) = 10$ basic solutions to this problem. However, only five of these are basic feasible. To illustrate the solution values of all five variables associated with each extreme point, look at Table 5.1. Notice that the values of all the variables, including the slack, are nonnegative.

BASIC STEPS IN THE SIMPLEX PROCEDURE

Now that you have some idea how the simplex method works, let us look closer at the details of the procedure. In successively examining adjacent extreme points, the simplex method continually finds improved solutions. That is, it only examines points that are not only feasible but yield at least as good a value in the objective

Table 5.1 Basic feasible solutions for the Faze Linear problem

Extreme point (in Figure 5.6)	Power amps x_1	Preamps x_2	Transistor slack s_1	Assembly slack (hr) s_2	Inspection slack (hr) s_3	Profit ($)
A	0	40.0	0	80.0	41.0	20,000
B	66.7	40.0	0	0	7.7	33,333
C	105.0	28.5	11.5	0	0	35,250
D	162.0	0	40.0	45.6	0	32,400
O	0	0	40.0	240.0	81.0	0

function as the previous point. In short, the simplex method encompasses the following basic steps:

1 An initial basic feasible solution is established.

2 An optimality check is next performed to determine whether the solution is yet optimal. If the solution is optimal, stop, for no further calculations are needed. However, if the solution is not optimal, a new variable must be found that will improve the solution. This new *entering variable* is always a nonbasic variable whose value is currently zero.

_{entering variable}

3 The value of the entering variable is increased until the value of some basic variable is forced down to zero. This basic variable is called the *leaving variable*.

_{leaving variable}

4 The entering variable now takes the place of the leaving variable; at any iteration there are only *m* variables that are in the solution. The next step is to update all relevant information required in the simplex procedure. This updating process is called *pivoting*. After updating, the procedure returns to step 2.

_{pivoting}

THE SIMPLEX TABLEAU

Each repetition of steps 2 through 4 is called an *iteration* in the simplex method. The computer can execute such iterations by merely storing the appropriate information and then operating on it whenever it is needed. When you execute the simplex method by hand, the calculations are more conveniently dealt with in tabular form. This

_{iteration}

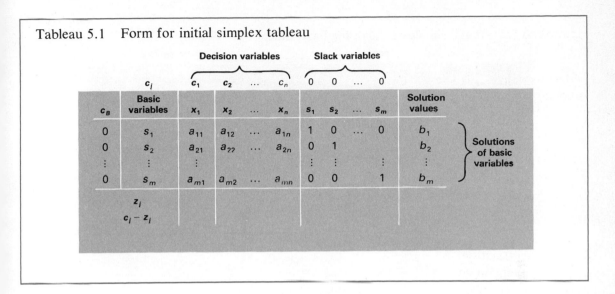

Tableau 5.1 Form for initial simplex tableau

c_B	Basic variables	Decision variables c_1	c_2	...	c_n	Slack variables 0	0	...	0	Solution values
	c_j	x_1	x_2	...	x_n	s_1	s_2	...	s_m	
0	s_1	a_{11}	a_{12}	...	a_{1n}	1	0	...	0	b_1
0	s_2	a_{21}	a_{22}	...	a_{2n}	0	1			b_2
⋮	⋮	⋮				⋮	⋮	⋮		⋮
0	s_m	a_{m1}	a_{m2}	...	a_{mn}	0	0		1	b_m
	z_j									
	$c_j - z_j$									

Solutions of basic variables

simplex tableau table is called a *simplex tableau*; the form of a starting tableau is shown in Tableau 5.1.

The c_j row at the top of the tableau is the coefficients of the respective variables in the objective function. The variables in the *Basic variables* column are those m variables currently in the solution. All other variables are assumed to be zero. The solution value for these basic variables is found under the *Solution values* column at the far right. The c_B column at the far left is those c_j coefficients associated with the basic variables. The a_{ij} terms correspond to the coefficients in the original set of constraints. The bottom row of the tableau is very important, for this row indicates whether the solution is optimal. These $c_j - z_j$ numbers under each column indicate the per-unit increase in the value of the objective function for every unit of x_j brought into solution. The z_j numbers represent the amount of profit that is lost for each unit of variable x_j that is brought into solution. These $c_j - z_j$ indicators are often called *opportunity* *opportunity*, or *relative*, *costs*.
costs

To further illustrate the simplex tableau and the simplex calculations, let us return to the Faze Linear problem. In this problem

Tableau 5.2   Initial simplex tableau for Faze Linear

c_B	c_j	200	500	0	0	0	
	Basic variable	x_1	x_2	s_1	s_2	s_3	Solution
0	s_1	0	①	1	0	0	40
0	s_2	1.2	4	0	1	0	240
0	s_3	.5	1	0	0	1	81
	z_j	0	0	0	0	0	
	$c_j - z_j$	200	500	0	0	0	0

we have two decision variables, three constraints, and three slack variables. The initial tableau for this problem is found in Tableau 5.2. Notice that the numbers under the columns headed by the variables (such as x_1, x_2, s_3) are simply the columns of the constraint coefficients we established in the original model in standard form. Similarly, the solution column is simply the original right-hand side.

THE BASIC STEPS APPLIED

Step 1: Establish initial basic feasible solution   To complete the initial tableau requires no calculation (except possibly the z_j values). The tableau always contains as many basic variables as there are constraints. To determine which variables are in the initial solution, we scan the original column of coefficients of the constraints in standard form and pick those variables that have a +1 coefficient and all other coefficients of 0. These starting variables are always either slack variables or *artificial variables*, which we shall discuss later in the chapter. Setting up the initial tableau completes the first step of the simplex method.

Step 2: Check solution for optimality   In the lower right-hand side of the initial Faze Linear tableau (Tableau 5.2), the profit of the current solution is 0. This is because only slack variables are in solution. The *Solution* column indicates that $s_3 = 81$—that is, we have 81 hours of inspection time left over—and s_1 and s_2 are equal to 40 and 240, respectively. In the tableau, the decision variables x_1 and x_2 are nonbasic and equal to zero; thus, we are producing nothing and, consequently, making zero profit. This basic feasible solution corresponds to extreme point O in Figure 5.7.

The $c_j - z_j$ opportunity costs indicate whether the current solution is optimal or not. In this case, they indicate that it is not optimal because they are not all less than, or equal to, zero.

The z_js represent the amount of profit that is given up for each unit of variable x_j that enters the solution. The c_js indicate the amount of profit gained for each unit of x_j brought into solution. The $c_j - z_j$, then, represents the net profit for bringing x_j into solution. Thus, we can improve our profit by bringing in either x_1 or x_2. Normally, you will choose the variable whose $c_j - z_j$ is largest. This choice of entering variable gives the fastest rate of improvement, though not necessarily the greatest degree of improvement. Hence, x_2 is chosen as the entering variable.

The z_js can be calculated by observing how much of each of the current basic variables must be given up in order for x_j to have its value increased and enter the solution. The coefficients in the column of the tableau that are directly under any variable substitution x_j are called *substitution rates* or *substitution coefficients*. They rates or indicate how much of the current solution must be changed for coefficients every unit of x_j brought into solution. Thus, from Tableau 5.2, we can see that if 1 unit of x_2 enters the solution (that is, if one preamp is produced), then we must give up 1 unit of transistor slack, 4 units of assembly slack, and 1 unit of inspection slack time. Furthermore, each of the three basic variables s_1, s_2, and s_3 is worth zero, zero, and zero, respectively. It costs nothing to give them up! Thus, each $z_j = 0$. Each $c_j - z_j$ for the nonbasic variables is calculated

$$c_1 - z_1 = 200 - [0(0) + 0(1.2) + 0(.5)] = 200$$
$$c_2 - z_2 = 500 - [0(1) + 0(4) + 0(1)] = 500$$

The $c_j - z_j$ for all basic variables is always zero.

For every unit of x_1 brought into solution, we can increase profits by 200; for every unit of x_2, we can increase profits by 500. Therefore, because when we are maximizing, we normally bring in the nonbasic variable that has the largest $c_j - z_j$ value, x_2 now enters the solution.

Step 3: Increase value of entering variable until some basic variable reaches zero Since only m variables can be basic (in this case $m = 3$), we must now determine a variable to leave the basis. Our resources are limited; so increasing the value of x_2 forces at least some of the other basic variables to decrease in value. We must be careful not to increase x_2 so much that some basic variable becomes negative. Happily, there is a simple test to determine which variable should leave the solution and how much of x_2 should enter. This *ratio test* consists of dividing each number in the *Solution* column by its associated coefficient in the column under x_2. This ratio is formed only for those rows in which the coefficient under x_2 is positive. Negative and zero coefficients are excluded. Hence, for row 1 we form the ratio $^{40}/_1$; for row 2, $^{240}/_4$; for row 3, $^{81}/_1$. We get 40, 60, and 81, respectively. The row that has the smallest ratio shows the variable to leave the solution. Since row 1 has the smallest ratio, s_1 leaves the solution. The value of the minimum ratio gives the amount of x_2 that enters the solution. On the basis of these operations, we are now in business producing 40 preamps a day!

ratio test

If you view the simplex tableau as a representation of a system of equations, it is easier to understand why the ratio test determines the maximum amount of x_2 that can enter the solution. Rewriting the elements in Tableau 5.1 as coefficients, we have

$$0x_1 + 1x_2 + 1s_1 + 0s_2 + 0s_3 = 40$$
$$1.2x_1 + 4x_2 + 0s_1 + 1s_2 + 0s_3 = 240$$
$$.5x_1 + 1x_2 + 0s_1 + 0s_2 + 1s_3 = 81$$

Since x_1 and x_2 are nonbasic in the initial tableau, their values are zero. However, as we consider increasing the value of x_2, we can express the basic variables s_1, s_2, and s_3 in terms of the value of x_2 as

$s_1 = 40 - x_2$
$s_2 = 240 - 4x_2$
$s_3 = 81 - x_2$

From the three foregoing equations, we can see that increasing the value of x_2 to a sufficiently high value causes some slack variable to become negative. We want to find the largest possible value for x_2 so that a basic variable becomes zero but not negative. We could solve the three inequalities for x_2 so that

$40 - x_2 \geq 0$
$240 - 4x_2 \geq 0$
$81 - x_2 \geq 0$

However, these simply imply that $x_2 \geq {}^{40}/_1$, $x_2 \geq {}^{249}/_4$, and $x_2 \geq {}^{81}/_1$. Thus, the largest possible value for x_2 is 40, and the ratio test is a shortcut for determining this value.

Step 4. Bring new variable into solution and revise tableau for new iteration In the last basic step of the simplex method, we must bring x_2 into the solution and revise all the numbers in the tableau so that we may return to step 2 and begin a new iteration. The procedure used to do this is pivoting. All rows in the tableau, including the $c_j - z_j$, are updated by this procedure. After the initial tableau, we shall dispense with the z_j row at the bottom of the tableau. There are two steps to the pivoting process. In one step, pivot row we update the *pivot row*; this is the row in which the minimum ratio occurred. In the other step, we update all remaining rows.

The number in the tableau that occurs at the intersection of the leaving row and entering column is called the *pivot element*. In pivot element Tableau 5.2, the circled number is the pivot element, and the arrows indicate the entering column and leaving row. The entire pivot row is updated by dividing all entries in the pivot row by the pivot element. Thus, we divide the pivot row by 1, yielding $({}^0/_1 \quad {}^1/_1 \quad {}^1/_1 \quad {}^0/_1 \quad {}^0/_1 \quad {}^{40}/_1)$. Tableau 5.3 shows the partially completed tableau. The pivot row did not change, for the pivot element was 1. Naturally, for any pivot element other than 1, the row changes.

Tableau 5.3 First iteration with pivot row updated

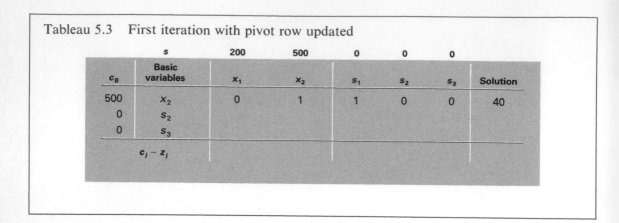

| c_B | Basic variables | s | 200 | 500 | 0 | 0 | 0 | |
		x_1	x_2	s_1	s_2	s_3	Solution
500	x_2	0	1	1	0	0	40
0	s_2						
0	s_3						
	$c_j - z_j$						

For every row other than the pivot row, we can update by using the formula:

New row = old row − pivot intersection number × new pivot row

pivot intersection number where the *pivot intersection number* is the number in the row that is in the pivot column. To demonstrate the formula, let's update the remaining rows in the tableau:

New row 2

$$
\begin{array}{rrrrrr}
(1.2 & 4 & 0 & 1 & 0 & 240) \\
-(4)(0 & 1 & 1 & 0 & 0 & 40) \\
\hline
1.2 & 0 & -4 & 1 & 0 & 80
\end{array}
$$

New row 3

$$
\begin{array}{rrrrrr}
(.5 & 1 & 0 & 0 & 1 & 81) \\
-(1)(0 & 1 & 1 & 0 & 0 & 40) \\
\hline
.5 & 0 & -1 & 0 & 1 & 41
\end{array}
$$

New $c_j - z_j$ row

$$
\begin{array}{rrrrr}
(200 & 500 & 0 & 0 & 0) \\
-(500)(0 & 1 & 1 & 0 & 0) \\
\hline
200 & 0 & -500 & 0 & 0
\end{array}
$$

In Tableau 5.4, the completed tableau for the second solution is presented.

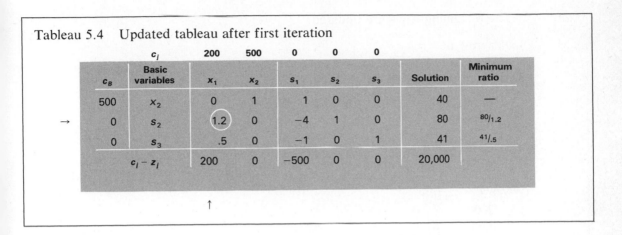

Tableau 5.4   Updated tableau after first iteration

c_B	Basic variables	c_j 200 x_1	500 x_2	0 s_1	0 s_2	0 s_3	Solution	Minimum ratio
500	x_2	0	1	1	0	0	40	—
0	s_2	1.2	0	−4	1	0	80	$80/1.2$
0	s_3	.5	0	−1	0	1	41	$41/.5$
	$c_j - z_j$	200	0	−500	0	0	20,000	

The solution corresponds to extreme point A in Figure 5.7. The current solution value in the lower right-hand side of the tableau is calculated by taking the c_B column times the *Solution* column to yield: Profit = 500(40) + 0(80) + 0(41) = 20,000.

The pivoting process merely involves multiplying one equation by a constant and adding it to another equation. However, certain rules involving elementary row operations are observed so that the solution to the updated system of equations is the same as the original LP model. Thus, the rows in the tableau of Tableau 5.4 still represent equations.

Returning to our calculations, we can see that the second solution in Tableau 5.4 is not optimal since $c_1 - z_1 = 200$. Thus, x_1 will be the entering variable, and the leaving variable is calculated by forming the minimum ratios $80/1.2$ and $41/.5$. No ratio is formed for row 1 since it has a zero in the x_1 column. Row 2 yields the minimum ratio, and s_2 becomes the leaving variable. Thus, 1.2 becomes the pivot element.

In updating the rows of the tableau, we first calculate the new pivot row:

$$(1.2/1.2 \quad 0/1.2 \quad -4/1.2 \quad 1/1.2 \quad 0/1.2 \quad 80/1.2)$$
$$= (1 \quad 0 \quad -10/3 \quad 5/6 \quad 0 \quad 66^2/3)$$

The remaining rows are updated:

New row 1

$$\begin{array}{cccccc}
(0 & 1 & 1 & 0 & 0 & 40) \\
-0(1 & 0 & -10/3 & 5/6 & 0 & 66\,2/3) \\
\hline
0 & 1 & 1 & 0 & 0 & 40
\end{array}$$

New row 3

$$\begin{array}{cccccc}
(.5 & 0 & -1 & 0 & 1 & 41) \\
-(.5)(1 & 0 & -10/3 & 5/6 & 0 & 66\,2/3) \\
\hline
0 & 0 & 2/3 & -5/12 & 1 & 7\,2/3)
\end{array}$$

New $c_j - z_j$ row

$$\begin{array}{ccccc}
(200 & 0 & -500 & 0 & 0) \\
(-200)(1 & 0 & -10/3 & 5/6 & 0) \\
\hline
0 & 0 & 166\,2/3 & -166\,2/3 & 0
\end{array}$$

The new solution value is $500(40) + 200(66\,2/3) + 0(7\,2/3) = 33,333\,1/3$. This basic feasible solution corresponds to extreme point B in Figure 5.7. The updated tableau is shown in Tableau 5.5.

One more iteration is required before optimality is reached. The next, and final, solution is presented in Tableau 5.6. This solution corresponds to the optimal extreme point C in Figure 5.7. The tableau indicates optimality since all solution values are nonnegative and all $c_j - z_j$ are less than, or equal to, zero, which indicates

Tableau 5.5   Updated tableau after second iteration

| c_B | Basic variables | c_j | 200 | 500 | 0 | 0 | 0 | |
			x_1	x_2	s_1	s_2	s_3	Solution
500	x_2		0	1	1	0	0	40
200	x_1		1	0	-10/3	5/6	0	66 2/3
0	s_3		0	0	2/3	-5/12	1	7 2/3
	$c_j - z_j$		0	0	166 2/3	-166 2/3	0	33,333 1/3

Tableau 5.6   Optimal tableau for Faze Linear problem

c_B	Basic variables	c_j						
		200	500	0	0	0		
		x_1	x_2	s_1	s_2	s_3	Solution
500	x_2	0	1	0	$5/8$	$-3/2$	$28\frac{1}{2}$
200	x_1	1	0	0	$-5/4$	5	105
0	s_1	0	0	1	$-5/8$	$3/2$	$11\frac{1}{2}$
	$c_j - z_j$	0	0	0	$-62\frac{1}{2}$	-250	35,250

that no higher profit can be achieved. The feasibility of the solution may be checked by substituting this tableau's values back into the original constraints of the model.

From Tableau 5.6, we can see that variables x_2, x_1, and s_1 are in the final solution at values 28.5, 105, and 11.5, respectively. This corresponds to real conditions of producing 28.5 preamps and 105 amps and having 11.5 surplus transistors. The optimal profit is found in the lower right-hand corner at a value of $35,250. This solution is precisely the same solution as determined by the graphical method.

Which of the three resources are being fully utilized? From the optimal tableau, we can see that slack variables s_2 and s_3 are nonbasic and therefore have value zero. Consequently, there is no surplus assembly or inspection time, and these two resources are being fully utilized.

MINIMIZATION PROBLEMS AND OTHER TYPES OF CONSTRAINTS

In the previous section, we examined the maximization of an *LP* problem with only $\leq$ constraints. In this section, we consider minimization and equality as well as $\geq$ constraints.

There are two approaches to solving a minimization problem. First, we can simply formulate the minimization problem, then change the signs of all coefficients in the objective function and solve the problem as a maximization problem. The resulting values of the decision variables will be correct, and multiplying the final objective function value by -1 yields the correct minimum value. Many computer codes only maximize (or minimize), and the decision maker must sometimes use this reversing trick to solve an *LP* problem on the computer.

Another approach to minimization involves changing the simplex solution procedure. Again, the alteration is simple; it involves only a change in the selection criterion for the entering variable. Instead of picking the variable with the most positive $c_j - z_j$ to enter the solution, we simply pick the variable with the most negative $c_j - z_j$. Such a selection lowers rather than raises the value of the objective function. The minimization procedure terminates when all $c_j - z_j \geq 0$. Before we illustrate this minimization procedure, however, you must learn how to handle equality and $\geq$ constraints. These constraints often occur in maximation problems; they are not restricted to minimization problems.

Consider the constraint $7x_1 + 5x_2 = 10$. This equality constraint is already an equation, and it appears to be ready for the simplex method. However, it is not clear what the starting value of x_1 and x_2 should be in the initial solution. To answer this would require solving the system of constraints. We can avoid having to solve the system if we add a dummy variable, called an *artificial variable.* Thus we convert the initial equality to $7x_1 + 5x_2 + A_1 = 10$. In the initial solution, we shall let $A_1 = 10$. Unlike slack variables, artificial variables are not allowed to assume a nonzero value in the optimal solution. For example, if A_1 were to equal 2 in the preceding equation, then $7x_1 + 5x_2$ would equal 8 rather than 10.

Artificial variables are used only to obtain a starting (*pseudofeasible*) solution for the simplex method and must eventually be forced out of the solution. We shall do this by assigning artificial variables extremely low objective function coefficients in maximization problems and extremely high objective function coefficients in minimization problems.

In a $\geq$ constraint, the idea is to add an artificial and subtract a slack. If we have the constraint $7x_1 + 5x_2 \geq 10$, we convert this to an equation by subtracting a slack to yield $7x_1 + 5x_2 -$

artificial variable

$s_1 = 10$. In order to obtain a starting feasible solution, we then add an artificial to obtain $7x_1 + 5x_2 - s_1 + A_1 = 10$. In this case, A_1 allows us to determine a starting solution easily, and s_1 allows the value of $7x_1 + 5x_2$ to exceed 10.

In the following minimization example, you will encounter constraints of all three types.

[Example] Consider an oil company that produces a petroleum product requiring the input of crude oil A and crude oil B. Each barrel of the final product contains 50 gallons. Of this 50 gallons, at least 20 gallons must be crude oil A and, at most, 30 gallons can be crude oil B. Crude oil B costs $6 per barrel, and crude oil A costs $8 per barrel. How many gallons of crude A and B should be in each barrel of the petroleum product in order to meet specifications and minimize costs?

If we let x_1 equal the number of gallons of crude B in a barrel of final product and x_2 the number of gallons of crude A, then the problem is formulated thus:

Minimize $.12x_1 + .16x_2$
subject to $x_1 + x_2 = 50$
$$x_1 \leq 30$$
$$x_2 \geq 20$$

$x_1, x_2 \geq 0$

Converting the constraints to standard form, we have

$$x_1 + x_2 + A_1 = 50$$
$$x_1 + s_2 = 30$$
$$x_2 - s_3 + A_3 = 20$$

The subscripts of the slacks and artificials are chosen to correspond to the number of the constraint in which they appear.

In the objective function, we must penalize the artificial variables so that they will not appear in the final solution. Assigning the artificials an arbitrarily high cost accomplishes this. If we let M represent a very large number (say 999,999,999 on the computer) then we can write the objective function as: Minimize $.12x_1 + .16x_2 + 0s_2 + 0s_3 + MA_1 + MA_3$. The problem is now in standard form and can be solved by the simplex method. The big M is simply

Figure 5.8 Graphical solution of oil company's minimization problem

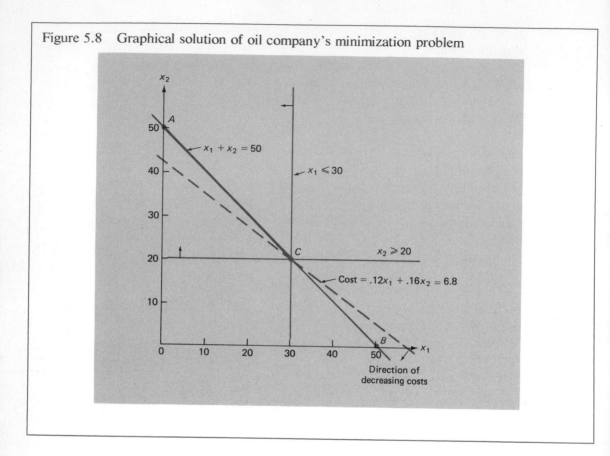

treated as a number; thus, the basic simplex procedure does not change.

To help you visualize the nature of the minimization problem, let's consider a brief graphical analysis. In Figure 5.8, the oil company's minimization problem is graphed. The constraints $x_1 \leq 30$ and $x_2 \geq 20$ each define a half-space in the plane, but since the constraint $x_1 + x_2 = 50$ is an equation, it defines the line AB in Figure 5.8. The set of points that satisfy all three constraints is line segment AC. Thus, the feasible region in this case is simply a line segment rather than a two-dimensional region.

The objective function, cost $= .12x_1 + .16x_2$, is represented by the dotted line in Figure 5.8. Points A and C are the only extreme

Solving linear programming problems

points of the feasible region. The direction of decreasing costs is toward the southwest; thus point $C = (30,20)$ is the optimal extreme point. The associated solution is to mix 30 gallons of crude B and 20 gallons of crude A per barrel for a minimum cost of $6.80.

Now let's solve the same problem with the simplex method. Since some variables that have coefficients of zero are not shown in each constraint, we rewrite the initial *LP* model in order to demonstrate the existence of each variable in each constraint. The problem is thus restated

Minimize $.12x_1 + .16x_2 + 0s_2 + 0s_3 + MA_1 + MA_3$
subject to $1x_1 + 1x_2 + 1A_1 + 0s_2 + 0s_3 + 0A_3 = 50$
                $1x_1 + 0x_2 + 0A_1 + 1s_2 + 0s_3 + 0A_3 = 30$
                $0x_1 + 1x_2 + 0A_1 + 0s_2 - 1s_3 + 1A_3 = 20$
$x_1, x_2, A_1, s_2, s_3, A_3 \geq 0$

In developing the initial tableau, it is important to remember that those variables with a coefficient of $+1$ in one row and 0 in all other rows will be in the initial solution. Hence A_1, s_2, and A_3 are the initial basic variables. All this is shown in Tableau 5.7.

As far as procedure goes, the only change from our maximization example is that we pick the variable with the most negative $c_j - z_j$ to enter the solution. In this case, $.16 - 2M$ is more negative

Tableau 5.7   Initial tableau for minimization problem

	c_j	.12	.16	0	M	0	M	
c_B	Basic variables	x_1	x_2	s_3	A_1	s_2	A_3	Solution
M	A_1	1	1	0	1	0	0	50
0	s_2	1	0	0	0	1	0	30
M	A_3	0	1	-1	0	0	1	20
	z_j	M	2M	-M	M	0	M	70M
	$c_j - z_j$	$.12 - M$	$.16 - 2M$	M	0	0	0	

$\rightarrow$ (at A_3 row)

$\uparrow$

than $.12 - M$; thus x_2 is the entering variable. The minimum ratios of $^{50}/_1$ and $^{20}/_1$ are calculated for rows 1 and 3, respectively. Since $20 < 50$, we find that A_3 will leave the solution.

From Tableau 5.7, we can see that the pivot element is 1; thus the updated pivot row becomes

$$(^0/_1 \quad ^1/_1 \quad -^1/_1 \quad ^0/_1 \quad ^0/_1 \quad ^1/_1 \quad ^{20}/_1)$$
$$= (0 \quad 1 \quad -1 \quad 0 \quad 0 \quad 1 \quad 20)$$

The other rows are updated thus:

New row 1

$$
\begin{array}{rrrrrrr}
(1 & 1 & 0 & 1 & 0 & 0 & 50) \\
-(1)(0 & 1 & -1 & 0 & 0 & 1 & 20) \\
\hline
1 & 0 & 1 & 1 & 0 & -1 & 30
\end{array}
$$

New row 2

$$
\begin{array}{rrrrrrr}
(1 & 0 & 0 & 0 & 1 & 0 & 30) \\
-(0)(0 & +1 & -1 & 0 & 0 & 1 & 20) \\
\hline
1 & 0 & 0 & 0 & 1 & 0 & 30
\end{array}
$$

New $c_j - z_j$ row

$$
\begin{array}{rrrrrr}
(.12 - M & .16 - 2M & M & 0 & 0 & 0) \\
-(.16 - 2M)(0 & 1 & -1 & 0 & 0 & 1) \\
\hline
.12 - M \quad 0 & .16 - M & 0 & 0 & -.16 + 2M
\end{array}
$$

Tableau 5.8   Tableau after first iteration for minimization problem

	c_j	.12	.16	0	M	0	M	
c_B	Basic variables	x_1	x_2	s_3	A_1	s_2	A_3	Solution
M	A_1	①	0	1	1	0	−1	30
0	s_2	1	0	0	0	1	0	30
.16	x_2	0	1	−1	0	0	1	20
	$c_j - z_j$	$.12 - M$	0	$.16 - M$	0	0	$-.16 + 2M$	$30M + 3.2$

The completed tableau is shown in Tableau 5.8. Note that we have succeeded in driving one of the artificials from the solution. We have also dispensed with the z_j row, for you will recall that it is useful only in the initial tableau.

In the next iteration, x_1 has the most negative $c_j - z_j$. Its $c_j - z_j$ value is $.12 - M$, meaning that for every unit of x_1 brought into solution, we can increase our cost by $.12 - M$; actually, this is a decrease since $.12 - M < 0$. The minimum ratio test provides an interesting situation. We have ratios of $^{30}/_1$ and $^{30}/_1$ in rows 1 and 2. Why isn't a ratio for row 3 calculated? The fact that both ratios for rows 1 and 2 are the same means that either A_1 or s_2 may be chosen as the leaving variable. This tie also means that one of the basic variables will assume a zero value in the updated tableau. This situation is referred to as *degeneracy*. We shall discuss it later in the chapter. For the moment, we chose A_1 as the leaving variable. The pivot element is 1, and the updated pivot row is (1 0 1 1 0 −1 30). The other rows are

New row 2

$$
\begin{array}{rrrrrrr}
(1 & 0 & 0 & 0 & 1 & 0 & 30) \\
-(1)(1 & 0 & 1 & 1 & 0 & -1 & 30) \\
\hline
(0 & 0 & -1 & -1 & 0 & 1 & 0)
\end{array}
$$

New row 3

$$
\begin{array}{rrrrrrr}
(0 & 1 & -1 & 0 & 0 & 1 & 20) \\
-(0)(1 & 0 & 1 & 1 & 0 & -1 & 30) \\
\hline
(0 & 1 & -1 & 0 & 0 & 1 & 20)
\end{array}
$$

New $c_j - z_j$ row

$$
\begin{array}{rrrrrr}
(.12 - M & 0 & .16 - M & 0 & 0 & -.16 + 2M) \\
-(.12 - M)(\quad 1 & 0 & 1 & 1 & 0 & -1) \\
\hline
0 & 0 & .04 - .12 + M & 0 & -.04 + M
\end{array}
$$

In Tableau 5.9 we find the updated, and optimal, tableau. All the $c_j - z_j$ values are greater than or equal to zero, all basic variable values are nonnegative, and the constraints are satisfied; the solution is optimal. The solution indicates that we should mix 30 gallons of crude oil A and 20 gallons of crude oil B in each 50-gallon barrel of the petroleum product. The total cost per barrel is $6.80. In this example, all artificials have been driven from the solution.

degeneracy

Tableau 5.9 Optimal tableau for minimization problem

c_B	c_j Basic variables	.12 x_1	.16 x_2	0 s_3	M A_1	0 s_2	M A_3	Solution
.12	x_1	1	0	1	1	0	−1	30
0	s_2	0	0	−1	−1	1	1	0
.16	x_2	0	1	−1	0	0	1	20
	$c_j - z_j$	0	0	.04	$-.12 + M$	0	$-.04 + M$	6.8

If any artificials remain at nonzero value in a final solution, they indicate that the original problem does not have a feasible solution.

[Summary of simplex procedure]

The following steps summarize the procedures we have discussed for solving LP problems by the simplex method.

1 Assuming that the LP model has been correctly formulated, it must first be converted to standard form.

2 Convert ≤ constraints to standard form by adding a slack variable, equality constraints by adding an artificial variable, and ≥ constraints by adding an artificial, and subtracting a slack, variable.

3 Choose the initial basic feasible solution by placing in solution those slack and/or artificial variables that have a +1 coefficient in the original column of constraints in standard form.

4 Fill in the initial tableau by simply entering the constraint equations as they appear in standard form. Calculate the $c_j - z_j$ values for the solution.

5 Check the $c_j - z_j$ values for the solution. If the problem is a maximization and all $c_j - z_j$ values are ≤ 0, *stop*, for the solution is optimal. (If the problem is a minimization and all $c_j - z_j$ values are ≥ 0, *stop*, for the solution is optimal.)

6 Otherwise, determine the entering variable by selecting the variable whose $c_j - z_j$ value is most positive (or most negative in a minimization).

7 Determine the variable to leave the solution by forming the ratios between the entries in the solution column and associated positive entries in the column of the variable entering the solution. The row in which the minimum ratio occurs designates the basic variable that is to leave the solution.

8 Bring the entering variable into solution and update the tableau by pivoting. Divide the pivot row by the pivot element and update all other rows by the formula on page 154. Go to step 5.

[Special cases in the simplex method]

In most applications of LP, a unique optimal solution is obtained. However, variations do exist. We shall now show you how to approach certain of these special cases.

UNBOUNDED SOLUTION

It is possible for an LP problem to have a nonempty set of feasible solutions and yet have no finite optimal solution. This can occur whenever the feasible region extends infinitely in the direction of improvement for the objective function. Consider the example

Maximize $x_1 + x_2$
subject to $5x_1 - x_2 \geq 10$
$\qquad\qquad 3x_1 - 2x_2 \leq 9$
$x_1, x_2 \geq 0$

The graph of this problem is shown in Figure 5.9.

As you can see, the feasible region is unbounded. We can pick arbitrarily large values of x_1 and x_2 in order to make the objective function as high as desired. Thus, there exists no finite optimum. Note however, that an infinite feasible region does not imply an unbounded solution. In this example, if we were minimizing the same objective function, the finite optimum would occur at $x_1 = 2$ and $x_2 = 0$.

Figure 5.9   Unbounded feasible region

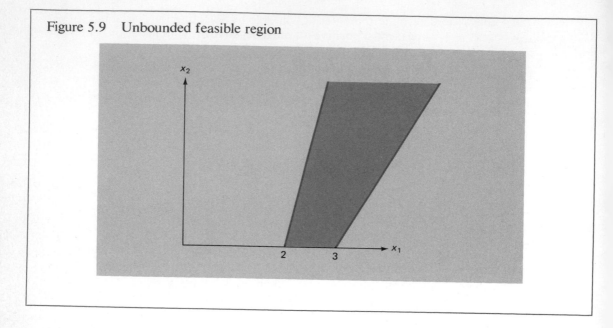

The simplex method can detect the existence of an unbounded solution during the process of selecting the entering variable. If a variable with a promising $c_j - z_j$ opportunity cost has been chosen, the next step is to calculate the minimum ratio in order to determine the leaving variable. However, if no entries in the pivot column are positive, no ratio can be formed and the problem is identified as unbounded. To visualize this situation, look at the second simplex tableau in standard form as shown in Tableau 5.10. At this iteration, it would pay $6/5$ for every unit of x_2 brought into solution, but the solution is unbounded since the entries $-1/5$ and $-7/5$ are both negative in the potential pivot column under x_2.

The detection of unbounded solutions in the simplex tableau can be explained by reinterpreting the meaning of tableau elements in a given column. We have called these elements substitution coefficients, for they represent the per-unit decrease of the solution values for every unit of the associated variable brought into solution. For example, the $-1/5$ and $-7/5$ under variable x_2 in Table 5.11 represent

Tableau 5.10   Unbounded solution

c_B	Basic variables	c_j 1 x_1	1 x_2	0 s_1	$-M$ A_1	0 s_2	Solution
1	x_1	1	$-1/5$	$-1/5$	$1/5$	0	2
0	s_2	0	$-7/5$	$3/5$	$-3/5$	0	3
	$c_j - z_j$	0	$6/5$	$1/5$	$-M - 1/5$	0	2

the reduction in the solution values 2 and 3 for every unit of x_2 brought into solution. Since $-1/5$ and $-7/5$ are negative, this means that the solution values 2 and 3 will actually increase by $1/5$ and $7/5$, respectively, for every unit of x_2 brought into solution. Thus, no matter how much of x_2 is brought into solution, the solution values of the basic variables will never become negative or infeasible. Therefore, an unlimited amount of x_2 can enter the solution, causing the problem to be unbounded.

Tableau 5.11   Modified Faze Linear problem at optimality

c_B	Basic variables	x_1	x_2	s_1	s_2	s_3	Solution
400	x_2	0	1	0	$5/8$	$-3/2$	28.5
200	x_1	1	0	0	$-5/4$	5	105
0	s_1	0	0	1	$-5/8$	$3/2$	11.5
	$c_j - z_j$	0	0	0	0	-400	32,400

Unbounded solutions usually mean that the LP model has been formulated incorrectly. No meaningful real-world LP problems exist in which the decision variables can assume infinite values.

NO FEASIBLE SOLUTION

It is also possible to have an LP problem in which no feasible solution exists. This situation corresponds to a problem that is formulated incorrectly or has conflicting restrictions within the constraint set. Consider the example

Minimize $x_1 + x_2$
subject to $\quad x_1 - x_2 \geq 1$
$\qquad -x_1 + x_2 \geq 1$
$x_1, x_2 \geq 0$

It is obvious from inspecting the model that the two constraints are inconsistent. The graph in Figure 5.10 shows the nature of the inconsistency. No point satisfies both constraints simultaneously.

Figure 5.10   No feasible region

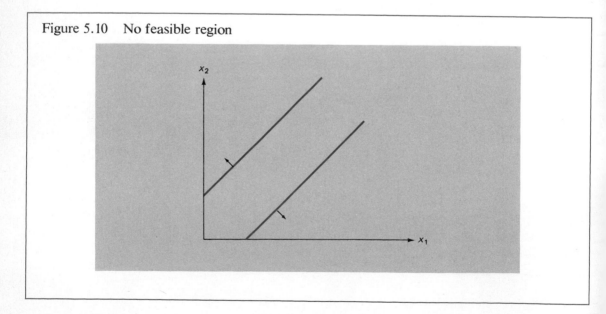

Solving linear programming problems

In the simplex method, an infeasible problem is indicated whenever the final solution contains an artificial variable at nonzero value.

DEGENERACY

We have already run across the notion of degeneracy in the minimization example. In a nondegenerate solution, the nonbasic variables have zero values and the m basic variables in solution have positive values. In a degenerate solution, at least one basic variable has a zero value. This does not really pose a problem. If you check back to Tableau 5.9, you'll see that the basic variable s_2 has a zero value, and therefore the solution is degenerate. All this means is that there is no slack in the second constraint.

Theoretically, degeneracy does pose a potential problem. Early researchers were afraid that *cycling* could occur in a degenerate solution. In cycling, a degenerate basic variable is removed from the solution at zero value only to return at a later iteration with no improvement, thereby creating a cycle and an infinite loop. Techniques were established to assure that cycling would never occur. Practically speaking, remedies are virtually unnecessary, for cycling almost never occurs in real-world applications.

ALTERNATIVE OPTIMA

The optimal solution to an LP problem is not necessarily unique. It is possible that an adjacent extreme point will yield the same profit (or cost). Graphically, this happens whenever the slope of the objective function equals the slope of a constraint equation that passes through an optimal extreme point. In Figure 5.11, we show a modified version of the Faze Linear problem. The problem was modified by changing the profit of x_2 (preamps) to 400 rather than 500. With this modification, both the points (105,28.5) and (162,0) yield a profit of $32,400, which is optimal. In Figure 5.11, if the dotted line representing the objective function were moved toward the feasible region it would eventually intersect the entire line segment between points (105,28.5) and (162,0) rather than at a single extreme point.

Figure 5.11   Faze Linear problem with alternative optima

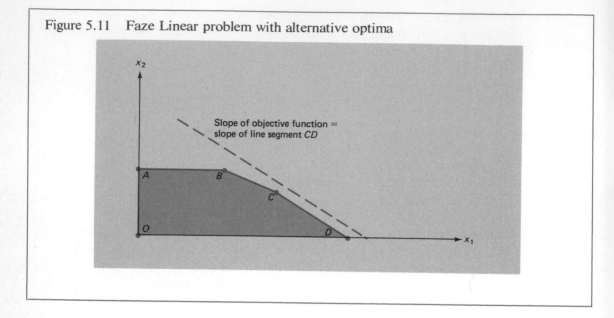

Alternative optima are also easy to detect in the simplex tableau. Let us consider the modified Faze Linear problem in Tableau 5.11. The solution remains unchanged from Tableau 5.6; only the $c_j - z_j$ values have changed. The $c_j - z_j$ row indicates that the solution is still optimal. But since the $c_j - z_j$ for s_2 is zero, we may pivot in s_2 for x_2 and change the profit by zero. The resulting solution also yields a profit of \$32,400 and thus is an alternate optimum.

In general, if a nonbasic variable has a $c_j - z_j$ of zero at optimality, it indicates an alternative optimal solution exists and can be obtained by simply bringing this nonbasic variable into the solution.

[Computers and linear programming]

Applications of LP in the real world inevitably involve the use of electronic digital computers. In these cases, extensive information, data manipulation, and numerical computation require high-speed computers.

Major computer manufacturers can usually provide computer software packages that perform LP on their machines. For example, IBM, Control Data Corporation, Univac, and Honeywell, among others, have standard LP packages. However, it is not necessary to have your own computer in order to use LP. Commercial computer time-sharing companies with available software packages have made it rather easy to use a computer without having to own one.

Performing LP analysis can be relatively cost-effective. For example, an LP problem with 62 variables and 32 constraints was run on a Xerox Sigma 6 computer, and the total cost of the job was around $1. This cost is based on computer execution time, core memory required, and other factors. Of course, really large industrial applications cost considerably more, but it has been shown, for example, that a medium-size oil refinery saves approximately $2,000 daily after its operation has been analyzed with LP.[1]

Naturally, LP analysis requires resources other than computer hardware and software. Two other necessary ingredients are a source of reliable data (which is harder to come by than you might realize!), and personnel who know how to model the problem, load it on the computer, and interpret the computer output. The interpretation of computer output is sometimes facilitated by using report generators to summarize the information that is to be conveyed to management. This step alone requires personnel who are adept at LP and, possibly, computer programming.

[Summary]

In solving LP problems, the graphical method, because it can solve problems with only three or fewer variables, is useful only for illustrative purposes. The simplex method, or a variation of it, is actually used in real applications. On a computer, the simplex method

---

[1] Harvey M. Wagner, *Principles of Management Science* (Englewood Cliffs, N.J.: Prentice-Hall, Inc., 1975), p. 585.

is capable of solving problems that have hundreds of decision variables and constraints. Though real problems are never solved by hand, you should have gained an understanding of how the simplex method works from this chapter. Iterative procedures are common among the many techniques used in OR/MS.

Understanding the principles of the simplex method will also enhance your understanding of post-optimality analysis. In the next chapter, we look at some of the questions that can be answered once the optimal solution has been obtained.

[Review questions]

1 Under what conditions can you use the graphical method to solve an LP problem?

2 What does every basic feasible solution correspond to, geometrically?

3 What characterizes an iterative procedure?

4 Why are slack variables added to $\leq$ constraints? What is the purpose of artificial variables?

5 Given an LP problem with $m + n$ variables and n constraints, how many basic variables (variables in solution) will there always be?

6 What is the meaning of a $c_j - z_j$, and what is the rationale for picking the nonbasic variable with the largest positive $c_j - z_j$ to enter the solution when maximizing?

7 Why are slacks and/or artificial variables used in the starting solution?

8 What is the purpose of the minimum ratio test in the simplex method?

9 How does the simplex method detect when the optimal solution has been achieved?

10 What is the difference between a degenerate and a nondegenerate solution?

11 Can there be more than one optimal solution to an LP problem?

12 How does the simplex method detect an unbounded solution?

13 Why are some nonlinear problems solved approximately by the use of LP?

[Problems]

5.1 Solve the following problem graphically.

Maximize $6x_1 + 8x_2$
subject to $\quad x_1 \leq 12$
$\qquad\qquad x_2 \leq 10$
$\qquad 2x_1 + 3x_2 \leq 36$
$x_1, x_2 \geq 0$

5.2 Solve the following minimization problem by the graphical method.

Minimize $\quad x_1 + x_2$
subject to $\quad x_2 \geq 2$
$\qquad 2x_1 - x_2 \geq 0$
$\qquad 3x_1 + 2x_2 \leq 12$
$x_1, x_2 \geq 0$

5.3 Consider the problem

Maximize $\quad 2x_1 + 6x_2 + 5x_3$
subject to $\quad x_1 + x_2 + x_3 = 3$
$\qquad x_1 + 2x_2 + 3x_3 \leq 10$
$\qquad 2x_1 + 6x_2 + 1x_3 \geq 5$
$x_1, x_2, x_3 \geq 0$

a Convert this system to standard form.

b What is the maximum number of possible basic solutions?

5.4 Solve by the simplex method.

Maximize $\quad 8x_1 + 7x_2$
subject to $\quad 3x_1 + 4x_2 \leq 15$
$\qquad 7x_1 + 5x_2 \leq 20$
$x_1, x_2 \geq 0$

5.5 Solve the following minimization by the simplex method.

Minimize $\quad 12x_1 + 18x_2$
subject to $\quad 2x_1 + 3x_2 \geq 6$
$\qquad 5x_1 + x_2 \geq 10$
$x_1, x_2 \geq 0$

5.6 Determine the optimal solution to the following problem.

Maximize $3x_1 + 2x_2 + 5x_3$

subject to
$$5x_1 + 4x_2 + x_3 \le 40$$
$$11x_1 - 4x_2 = 0$$
$$-4x_1 + 5x_2 + 3x_3 \ge 10$$

$x_1, x_2, x_3 \ge 0$

5.7 Use the simplex method to determine the optimal solution to the problem in the production-distribution example in Chapter 3.

5.8 Consider the following problem with only one constraint:

Maximize $5x_1 + 2x_2 + 3x_3 + x_4$

subject to $4x_1 + 3x_2 + 3x_3 + x_4 \le 7$

$x_i \ge 0$ for all i

a How many variables will be in any basic solution?
b Find the optimal solution by inspection.
c Verify your results with criteria from the simplex method.

5.9 Consider the LP problem

Maximize $2x_1 + 3x_2 + 5x_3 + 1x_4$

subject to
$$3x_1 + 1x_2 + 1x_3 + 3x_4 = 5$$
$$2x_1 - 1x_2 + 1x_3 + 1x_4 = 3$$
$$5x_1 + 2x_3 + 3x_4 \le 8$$

$x_1, x_2, x_3, x_4 \ge 0$

After the model has been converted to standard form, the optimal tableau is:

c_B	c_j Basic variables	2 x_1	3 x_2	5 x_3	1 x_4	$-M$ A_1	$-M$ A_2	0 S_3	Solution
1	x_4	0	0	0	1	1	1	−1	0
5	x_3	2.5	0	1	0	−1.5	−1.5	2	4
3	x_2	.5	1	0	0	−.5	−1.5	1	1
	$c_j - z_j$	−12	0	0	0	$8 - M$	$11 - M$	−12	23

a What is the optimal solution?
b Is it degenerate?
c Are there any alternative optima?
d Is the solution unbounded?

5.10 The Slik Oil Company produces two lines of motor oil and a special engine additive called *Motor Honey*. All three products are produced by blending two components. These components contribute various properties, including viscosity. The viscosity in the product is proportional to the viscosities of the blending components. The pertinent data appear in the tables below: Assuming no limitation on the demand, determine how many barrels of each oil product Slik should produce each week?

Blending Component	Viscosity	Cost per barrel ($)	Availability per week (bbl)
1	20	6.50	10,000
2	60	11.00	4,000

Product	Viscosity required	Profit contribution per barrel ($)
30W oil	30	8
40W oil	40	9
Motor Honey	50	12

5.11 A stereo mail-order warehouse has 8,000 feet available for storage of loudspeakers. The jumbo speakers cost $295 each and require 4 square feet of space; the mid-size speakers cost $110 and require 3 square feet of space; and the economy speakers cost $58 and require 1 square foot of space. The demand for the jumbo speakers is, at most, 20 per month. The wholesaler has $10,000 to invest in loudspeakers this month. Assuming the jumbo speakers contribute $105 to profit, the mid-size contribute $50, and the economy contribute $28, how many units of each type should the wholesaler buy and stock?

5.12 The Green Country Lumber Company produces two wood products, interior wood paneling and plywood. The resource requirements for each product are provided in the following table: Assuming that production time is limited to 4,000 hours per week, use the simplex method to maximize Green Country's profit.

Wood product	Production time (per sq yd)	Demand	Profit contribution (per sq yd)
Plywood	.025 hr	At least 6,000 sq yd per week	.30
Paneling	.040 hr	At most 4,000 sq yd per week	.45

Introduction to management science

5.13 Assuming that you have formulated the LP model for problem 4.14 about the Akron Tire Company, solve the model by the use of an LP computer code. What is the optimum production schedule and its associated minimum quarterly cost?

5.14 Using an LP computer code, find the optimum land allocation for problem 4.15 based on the data in the two tables that follow.

Area presently cropped (*in* 1,000s of acres)

Region	Wheat	Barley	Broad beans	Lentils	Cotton type 1	Cotton type 2	Rice	Corn	Millet	Sesame	Sugar cane
	Winter Crops						**Summer crops**				
1	201		17		230		216	103			
2	94	10	4				138	76			
3	106		9		143		201	41			
4	8		38			55		42		27	
5	15		76			89		13	133		
6	21	98	8			108		15			
7	30		51	80		58		97			
8	105		13					13	123	6	62

Net revenue factor (r_{ij})

Region	Wheat	Barley	Broad beans	Lentils	Cotton type 1	Cotton type 2	Rice	Corn	Millet	Sesame	Sugar cane
					Crop						
1	1.4	2.9	2.8	4.1	.2	.7	1.0	2.3	.7	1.7	.8
2	1.1	2.7	2.9	3.9	.1	.8	1.1	2.1	.6	1.8	.9
3	1.3	2.8	3.0	2.8	.1	.6	.9	2.2	.5	2.0	1.1
4	1.5	2.6	2.9	4.3	.1	.8	1.2	2.3	1.0	2.7	1.2
5	1.1	2.9	3.1	4.4	.2	.8	.8	2.0	1.3	2.2	.8
6	1.2	3.0	2.8	4.4	.1	.9	.7	2.0	1.2	2.5	1.7
7	1.3	2.6	2.7	5.0	.1	.8	.9	2.1	.7	2.6	1.0
8	1.1	2.6	2.6	4.5	.2	.8	.8	1.9	.9	2.1	1.9

[The Ward advertising case]

Professor Scott Ward, a professor of marketing at a leading business school, decided to put into practice some of the scientific methods that he was teaching his students. He firmly believed that advertising was an area where his know-how in operations research methods would pay off. Ward's impression was that most advertising decisions were made on the basis of rules of thumb, or rough judgments. Hence, he believed that he would be deluged by prospective clients if he could demonstrate the value of the modern management science approach to a few large advertisers.

Professor Ward's first opportunity came as a result of a lecture he gave to a group of beer marketing executives. After the talk, John Parrish of Schultz Brewery told Ward of some difficulties that Schultz was having in planning their advertising campaigns. Specifically, Mr. Parrish and some of the other members of the Schultz management felt that the company was not getting the maximum effectiveness from their advertising expenditures. However, Mr. Parrish continued, they did not know how they might improve the situation. Ward then outlined his ideas to Mr. Parrish and was immediately retained to prepare a proposal for a Schultz advertising campaign. Ward's role would be to recommend an allocation of advertising expenditures among various media, yet he would not be involved in the actual content of the advertising.

Schultz, a national brewer, distributed beer in 42 large cities. Since Schultz beer was regarded as a premium beer, it appealed to only a particular class of beer drinkers. Thus, it was believed to be important to consider not only the *total* audience reached by a medium, but also the *composition* of the audience (that is, the percentage of males and females, income classes, age classes, and so forth).

Professor Ward also stressed two other factors that should be taken

From *Introduction to Linear Programming: Methods and Cases* by Thomas H. Naylor, Eugene T. Byrne, and John M. Vernon. © 1971 by Wadsworth Publishing Company, Inc., Belmont, California 94002. Reprinted by permission of the publisher.

Introduction to management science

into account in evaluating media: (1) the percentage of the relevant audience that would probably be exposed to an ad—for example, not all of the potential Schultz beer consumers who read a magazine also read a particular ad in that magazine—and (2) the estimated quality of the ad in terms of its expected effectiveness—for example, a page in magazine A might be expected to have a greater effect on sales than a page in magazine B.

Thus, Ward decided to construct an index of "effective exposure," or EE, for each alternative type of advertising. Of course, in constructing the index he relied heavily on the experience and judgment of the members of Mr. Parrish's staff.

To explain the EE index to Mr. Parrish, Ward selected a full page advertisement in magazine A as an example. The total audience was estimated to be 6 million. However, after considering the composition of the total audience, it was estimated that 4 million was a better figure to represent potential Schultz customers. Next, Ward applied two other factors to further reduce the number of potential customers. It was estimated that only about 35 percent of the 4 million would actually read the ad in magazine A, or $(0.35)(4,000,000) = 1,400,000$. Second, the qualitative index of magazine A was adjudged to be 0.7 relative to other media (on a scale ranging from 0 to 1.0). Thus, the EE index for a page in magazine A was computed as $(0.7)(1,400,000)$, or 980,000. . . . [See the table for Schultz's advertising options.]

Mr. Parrish . . . remarked to Ward, however, that there were a number of other things that had to be considered, and it would not be possible simply to choose those alternatives that yielded the highest effective exposure per dollar of cost. For example, the Schultz management believed it essential to place at least one full-page ad in at least one issue of both magazines A and C over a six-month period. Furthermore, management had firm beliefs about the need to allocate at least half of the advertising budget to magazine advertising, and to sponsor at least one baseball game on television.

Ward assured Mr. Parrish that such considerations could be handled easily within a linear programming framework. He then gave Mr. Parrish a brief explanation of the principle of linear programming, explaining

Alternative types of advertising available to Schultz

Type	Cost per unit ($)	Effective exposure per unit (EE)
Magazines		
A (weekly) page; ¹/₂-page	60,000; 35,000	980,000; 512,000
B (weekly) page	20,000	230,000
C (monthly) page	12,000	140,000
D (weekly) page; ¹/₂-page	13,000; 8,500	215,000; 112,000
E (monthly) page; ¹/₂-page	10,000; 6,000	110,000; 96,000
F (weekly) page	5,500	78,000
Newspapers		
1,000-line ads in 42 cities (per wk)	33,000	570,000
Television		
Network ball-game sponsorship	125,000	1,185,000
Spot (2 commercials in 42 cities per wk)	18,000	238,000

that the objective was to maximize the total effective exposure subject to various restraints. He pointed out that the restraints could be judgmental, budgetary, or otherwise. For example, since his proposal was to be for a six-month period, restraints would be needed to prevent physical impossibilities—such as a solution calling for 30 full-page ads in magazine A when there could only be 26 issues in the period (Schultz never advertised on more than one page in any single issue).

[Case problems]

1 Given a six-month advertising budget of $525,000, what are some systematic ways of selecting the best advertising program for Schultz?

2 Are all the assumptions of LP satisfied in the Schultz problem? Is it possible to buy a noninteger number of ads?

3 Use LP as a tool to develop a solution that is an effective, but not necessarily optimal, integer solution.

6

$$\Big[\ \text{Sensitivity analysis}\ \Big]$$

In the two preceding chapters, we have studied how to model an LP problem and how to calculate an optimal solution by using the simplex method. These two phases, however, generally do not complete an LP analysis; a third phase, called *sensitivity analysis* or *postoptimality analysis*, is usually undertaken. In this chapter we discuss sensitivity analysis and the kinds of questions it allows the decision maker to answer. We look first at an LP model called the *dual problem* to learn what information it can provide concerning the value of our limited resources. Then, we examine some basic procedures in sensitivity analysis and explore the sensitivity of an optimal LP solution to changes in the data or parameters of the model.

[The nature of sensitivity analysis]

If all the parameters for LP models were perfectly accurate or never changed over time, there would be little need for sensitivity analysis. However, the parameters (the c_j, a_{ij}, and b_i) used in real-world LP models are often only estimates. These parameters are often arrived at by means of subjective estimates, limited sampling, or observations subject to human error. Even if the parameters are accurately measured or predicted at a particular time, they may be subject to change. Businesses operate in a dynamic environment, and data pertaining to demand, prices, or resource availability may change significantly in short periods of time. Thus, management and the quantitative decision maker should not consider the original, computer-generated simplex solutions to be final or sacred in any sense. A problem's "optimal" solution is only as accurate as the original data from which it is derived. Thus, it is important to be able to investigate the possible effects on the optimal solution as the various a_{ij}, b_i, and c_j parameters change.

Some LP models may be relatively insensitive to changes in the parameters. In these cases, the original solution may remain optimal even as the parameters are varied over a wide range of values. On the other hand, some models are acutely sensitive to even minor changes in a single parameter. For these models, it is very important to identify the critical parameters so that special care may be taken in estimating their values and investigating their total effect on the optimal solution.

Through the use of sensitivity analysis, new insights can be obtained from the LP model without its having to be re-solved. For example, management may ask, "If the net profit on our deluxe product were to drop 20 percent in the next year, would our current production schedule remain optimal, and, if so, by how much would our total profit change?" Or, a firm may want to know by how much it can reduce the availability of a particular resource before endangering its ability to meet next month's demand. Or, the manager of a product development division might ask, "Given our current limited resources, if we were to introduce a new product, how much must it contribute to profit and overhead in order to make it worthwhile to produce?"

Answers to these questions and many others can be investigated through sensitivity analysis. Management should be aware of the types of question it can pose and reasonably expect to answer through sensitivity analysis. It is more important for you to understand the nature of sensitivity analysis than to be able to work through the calculations of the simplex method in this respect: Once the model is established, the simplex method is completely computerized in real-world applications. Sensitivity analysis, however, is valueless unless you understand what kinds of insight it can yield. With such understanding, you can perceive decision problems in terms of questions sensitivity analysis can answer.

[Duality]

Every LP problem has a counterpart problem called the *dual*. We shall discuss the dual problem and duality primarily as they apply to *shadow prices*, which tell us something about the value of limited resources. But you should be aware that the notion of duality is central to optimization theory, not only for LP but for all mathematical programming. Duality provides the theoretical basis for many sophisticated solution procedures and algorithms for solving special classes of mathematical programming problems. Indeed, duality provides the foundation for sensitivity analysis.

In the next section, you will learn how the dual is formed from the original, or *primal*, LP problem. You will also discover that solving the original LP model yields the optimal solution to the dual problem, and vice versa. Thus, in solving any LP problem, we can solve either the primal or the dual, whichever is computationally easier. (Generally, the problem with fewer constraints is easier to solve.)

THE DUAL PROBLEM

Let's explore the dual problem for an LP problem that has all inequality constraints. Consider the primal problem

Primal
Maximize $5x_1 + 4x_2 + 9x_3$
subject to $7x_1 + 6x_2 + 3x_3 \leq 20$
$1x_1 + 4x_2 + 8x_3 \leq 15$
$x_1, x_2, x_3 \geq 0$

The associated dual is stated

Dual
Minimize $20y_1 + 15y_2$
subject to $7y_1 + 1y_2 \geq 5$
$6y_1 + 4y_2 \geq 4$
$3y_1 + 8y_2 \geq 9$
$y_1, y_2 \geq 0$

Can you determine how the dual was formed from the primal problem? All the coefficients in the dual are derived from the primal. Actually, the dual constitutes something of a flip-flopped version of the primal. In order to take the dual of a primal problem that has all inequalities in the same direction, we follow these steps:

1 Form the dual objective function from the primal right-hand-side coefficients.

2 Form the *i*th dual constraints from the *i*th column of coefficients in the primal constraints.

3 Form the dual right-hand-side coefficients from the primal objective function coefficients.

4 If the primal is a maximization, form the dual as a minimization (and vice versa), and reverse the direction of the inequalities in the constraints.

We associate a dual variable y_i with the *i*th primal constraint. Thus, the number of variables in the dual problem depends upon the number of primal constraints, not of primal variables. The one-to-one correspondence between entries in the dual problem and those in the primal is further illuminated by Table 6.1.

Table 6.1 Relationship between primal and dual coefficients

Primal		Dual
*i*th primal constraint	$\longleftrightarrow$	*i*th dual variable y_i
Objective function coefficient c_j	$\longleftrightarrow$	Right-hand-side coefficient for *j*th dual constraint

Sensitivity analysis

Let's take the dual of the Faze Linear example of previous chapters. Its primal problem is

Maximize $200x_1 + 500x_2$
subject to $x_2 \leq 40$ (transistors)
$1.2x_1 + 4x_2 \leq 240$ (assembly hours)
$.5x_1 + x_2 \leq 81$ (inspection hours)
$x_1, x_2 \geq 0$

The dual problem is

Minimize $40y_1 + 240y_2 + 81y_3$
subject to $1.2y_2 + .5y_3 \geq 200$
$y_1 + 4y_2 + y_3 \geq 500$
$y_1, y_2, y_3 \geq 0$

If you understand the economic situations represented by the primal and dual problems, you will better understand the conceptual relationship between the two. Recall that x_1 represents the number of power amps, and x_2 the number of preamps, to produce each day. The y_i variables of the dual represent the marginal value of primal resource i. Thus, y_1 represents the amount by which profit in the primal objective function can be increased per *additional* unit of transistors made available. Likewise, y_2 measures the potential contribution of an additional assembly hour, and y_3 measures the potential contribution of each additional inspection hour. In the primal problem, the objective function maximizes the total contribution to profit. In the dual problem, the objective function minimizes the total marginal value of all resources.

Similarly, a primal constraint insures that the availability of a primal resource is not exceeded, and a dual constraint insures that the marginal value of the required resources for each product must be at least that of the product's profit contribution. For example, in the first dual constraint to the Faze Linear problem, we have $0y_1 + 1.2y_2 + .5y_3 \geq 200$. This constraint specifies that the number of transistors required to produce a power amp (zero) times the marginal value of a transistor (y_1) plus the time required to assemble a power amp (1.2) times the marginal value of assembly hours (y_2) plus the time required to inspect a power amp (.5) times the marginal value of inspection hours (y_3) must be greater than or equal to

Introduction to management science

200, which is the profit contribution of a power amp. The second dual constraint is interpreted in a similar manner.

SHADOW PRICES

Earlier in the chapter, we stated that it is possible to solve an LP problem in either its primal or dual form. As a matter of fact, an optimal simplex tableau contains the solution to both the primal and its associated dual. To see this, refer to the optimal tableau for the Faze Linear problem that is reconstructed in Tableau 6.1. The optimal primal solution is found in the *Solution* column; the optimal values of x_2, x_1, and s_1 are 28.5, 105, and 11.5, respectively. But where is the optimal dual solution? If you enjoy working puzzles, you may want to explore Tableau 6.1 a bit before reading further.

Recall that there are as many dual variables as there are primal constraints. If there are m primal constraints, we seek m dual variable values. In Tableau 6.1, there are three primal constraints, and we seek the values of the dual variables y_1, y_2, and y_3. You will always find the optimal dual variable values in the $c_j - z_j$ row corresponding to m particular variables. These variables are precisely those m variables that are in solution in the initial tableau. In this example, s_1, s_2, and s_3 were initially in solution. In order to determine the optimal value of y_1, y_2, and y_3, we simply change the signs of the $c_j - z_j$ values associated with s_1, s_2, and s_3. Thus $y_1 = 0$, $y_2 = 62.5$, and $y_3 = 250$. You can check the feasibility of these values by substituting them into the dual constraints.

Tableau 6.1　Optimal tableau for Faze Linear problem

| c_B | Basic variables | c_j | 200 | 500 | 0 | 0 | 0 | |
			x_1	x_2	s_1	s_2	s_3	Solution
500	x_2		0	1	0	$5/8$	$-3/2$	$28 1/2$
200	x_1		1	0	0	$-5/4$	5	105
0	s_1		0	0	1	$-5/8$	$3/2$	$11 1/2$
	$c_j - z_j$		0	0	0	$-62 1/2$	-250	35,250

Whenever an artificial variable is in the initial solution, an M coefficient may appear in the $c_j - z_j$ row. For example, suppose an artificial has a $c_j - z_j$ value of $-1.6 - 3M$ in the final tableau. In order to obtain the optimal dual variable associated with the constraint in which the artificial appears, we simply change the sign and ignore the M coefficient. Thus, the associated dual variable is 1.6. In Chapter 5, Tableau 5.9 contains two artificial variables and depicts the optimal solution to the primal. The associated dual solutions are $y_1 = .12$, $y_2 = 0$, and $y_3 = .04$.

shadow
prices The values of the optimal dual variables are quite important; they are called *shadow prices*. At optimality, the ith shadow price (y_i) measures the per-unit contribution of the ith primal resource to the value of the objective function as long as the current basis remains optimal. The ith shadow price y_i is meaningful only so long as changes in the availability of primal resources do not cause some current basic variable to be pivoted out of solution. To illustrate, let us return to Tableau 6.1. We have already found that $y_1 = 0$, $y_2 = 62.5$, and $y_3 = 250$. Thus, an additional unit of assembly time is worth \$62.50 to the value of the objective function. The manager, however, must be aware that a shadow price measures gross contribution, not net contribution. The net value of assembly time also has to reflect the cost of procuring that additional hour. Assuming that you were production manager at Faze Linear and that additional assembly and inspection hours cost roughly the same, which department would you choose to expand? Why?

To answer that question knowledgeably, you would require an analysis to determine how much each department could be expanded before the basis would change and the shadow prices become meaningless. Such an investigation is called sensitivity analysis, and it is the topic to which we now turn.

[Sensitivity analysis]

Now that you have some idea of the kinds of information conveyed by the primal and dual aspects of an LP problem, let us explore how the optimal solution changes with respect to changes in the various parameters of the model. We have already seen how useful shadow prices can be in giving insight into the economic aspects of the LP model. Using sensitivity analysis, we can determine the range over which shadow prices remain valid as well as answer many other meaningful questions.

Specifically, we address three types of basic sensitivity analysis:

1 Right-hand-side ranging

2 Adding a new variable

3 Changes in the objective function coefficients

Other kinds of analysis, which we shall not address in this introductory text include changes in the constraint coefficients and adding another constraint.

RIGHT-HAND-SIDE RANGING

The objective of right-hand-side ranging analysis is to determine how much the right-hand side of a particular constraint can be increased or decreased; thus, we establish the range over which the associated shadow price is valid. The analysis is relatively straightforward if the effect of slack in a constraint is understood.

Consider the constraint $x_1 + x_2 \leq 10$. If we introduce a slack variable s_1, we obtain $x_1 + x_2 + s_1 = 10$. If $s_1 = 0$, then $x_1 + x_2$ must sum to 10. On the other hand, if $s_1 = 2$, then the sum of $x_1 + x_2$ is 8, and, effectively, their sum has been reduced. The point to be made is that introducing positive slack in a constraint is tantamount to decreasing the right-hand side. Likewise, introducing negative slack is equivalent to increasing the right-hand side. In particular, if $s_1 = -3$, then $x_1 + x_2$ must sum to 13 in the foregoing equation.

Given the fact that introducing positive or negative slack is equivalent to decreasing or increasing the right-hand side, then right-hand-side ranging for a particular constraint simply boils down to determining the maximum amount of positive and negative slack that can be introduced. To see how to do this, refer to Tableau 6.1, the optimal simplex tableau associated with the Faze Linear problem.

The right-hand side of the second constraint in the original primal model is 240, indicating that 240 hours of assembly time is available.

Tableau 6.2   Short version of Faze Linear optimal tableau

c_B	Basic variables	s_2	Solution	Minimum ratio
500	x_2	$5/8$	$28 1/2$	$28 1/2 \div 5/8 = 45.6$
200	x_1	$-5/4$	105	—
0	s_1	$-5/8$	$11 1/2$	—

Let us investigate how much the 240 can be decreased before some variable currently basic is pivoted out of the basis. As we have said, this amounts to determining how much positive slack can be brought into the second constraint.

In Tableau 6.1, the second slack s_2 is associated with the second constraint. How much of positive s_2 can be introduced in the second constraint without changing the basis? The maximum amount is easily determined in exactly the same manner that we determined how much of the entering variable could be brought into solution in the simplex procedures of Chapter 5. To do so, we must simply perform the minimum ratio test!

Consider Tableau 6.2, which is a shortened version of Tableau 6.1. The maximum amount of s_2 we can introduce is found by determining the minimum ratio between the entries in the *Solution* column and their associated positive entries in the s_2 column. Since $5/8$ is the only positive entry, the minimum ratio, by default, is $28 1/2 \div 5/8 = 45 3/5$. Hence, we. may decrease the right-hand side by a maximum of $45 3/5$; any larger decrease causes basic variable x_2 to be pivoted out of solution. In terms of the Faze Linear problem, this means that the 240 assembly hours can be reduced to $194 2/5$ before the basis changes and the shadow price y_2 becomes invalid.

To determine how much the right-hand-side entry of 240 can be increased, we consider introducing $-s_2$ into the solution (see Tableau 6.3). You should be aware that the variable $-s_2$ is not actually a part of the simplex tableau; it is introduced at this point

Tableau 6.3   Tableau with $-s_2$ introduced for right-hand-side ranging

c_B	Basic variables	$-s_2$	Solution	Minimum ratio
500	x_2	$-5/8$	$28 1/2$	—
200	x_1	$5/4$	105	$105 \div 5/4 = 84$
0	s_1	$5/8$	$11 1/2$	$11 1/2 \div 5/8 = 18.4$

only as a means of performing right-hand-side ranging. Notice that the signs on the entries in the s_2 column have also been changed. The minimum ratio is clearly $11 1/2 \div 5/8 = 18 2/5$. Thus, we may increase the right-hand side of 240 by $18 2/5$ before the basis changes. In terms of the Faze Linear problem, this means that the assembly hours can be increased to $258 2/5$ before s_1 is pivoted out of solution.

We have now determined the total range over which the shadow price $y_2 = 62.5$ is valid. As long as the amount of assembly hours is between $194 2/5$ and $258 2/5$, the y_2, or marginal value of assembly hours, is \$62.50 per unit.

We can also perform right-hand-side ranging for the other two constraints in the Faze Linear problem. For the first constraint, the analysis is even simpler. The decrease is determined by $11 1/2$

Table 6.2   Analysis of right-hand-side ranging summarized

Resource	Original right-hand-side value	Shadow price ($)	Range Minimum	Range Maximum
Transistors	40	0	$28 1/2$	No limit
Assembly time	240	62.50	$194 2/5$	$258 2/5$
Inspection time	81	250.00	$73 1/3$	100

$\div$ 1 − 11½. The amount of increase is unbounded since no minimum ratio can be formed with nonpositive entries from the s_1 column. This makes sense intuitively, for slack s_1 is already in solution; that is, we already have 11½ transistors left over. It should not affect the current solution no matter how many transistors might be made available; they would only be surplus. For the third constraint, the range or inspection time over which the shadow price remains valid is 73⅓ to 100. Table 6.2 summarizes our right-hand-side ranging analysis.

ADDING A NEW VARIABLE

It is not unusual to want to introduce a new variable into an existing LP model. It is very helpful to know whether such a variable (or product) will be active in the solution or what its objective function coefficient must be in order for it to be in solution. Given the new variable's resource requirements, it is possible to determine such information without having to re-solve the problem.

Since the shadow prices give us the marginal value of each scarce resource, we may use them to calculate the opportunity cost of bringing a new variable into solution. That is, we can use the shadow prices to calculate the total value in terms of resources that must be given up in order to bring each unit of the new variable into solution.

Let us return to the Faze Linear example and introduce a new, high-quality digital tuner that is sure to tickle the fancy of many an audiophile. Suppose that, in addition to the power amp (x_1) and the preamp (x_2), the management at Faze Linear is also considering the production of a new tuner (x_3). In terms of the scarce resources, the new tuner would require 1 high-quality transistor, 5 hours of assembly, and 2 hours of inspection. The marketing department forecasts that this tuner should enter the market with a price of approximately $1,500. If mark-up is 100 percent—that is, profit contribution is $750—should Faze Linear produce this product?

The opportunity cost of producing the tuner can be calculated by multiplying the shadow price of each scarce resource times the amount of the resource required by the production of the tuner.

Table 6.3   New product analysis

Resource	Shadow price($)	Amount of resource required	Opportunity cost ($)
Transistors	0	1	0
Assembly hours	62.5	5	312.50
Inspection hours	250.0	2	500.00
Total opportunity cost (z_3)			812.50

Summing these opportunity costs gives us the amount of profit that must be forfeited in order to produce the tuner. This is equivalent to the z_j we used in the simplex calculations. The analysis is not completed until the c_j, or the amount of profit gained, is also considered.

For the tuner, we have an opportunity cost of 0(1) + 62.5 (5) + 250 (2) = \$812.50. If the profit contribution is only \$750, then the $c_j - z_j$ for the tuner is 750 − 812.50 = −62.50, and it should not be produced and sold at this price. Table 6.3 summarizes the analysis. It is clear from Table 6.3 that if Faze Linear wants to produce the tuner, its profit contribution must be raised from \$750 to over \$812.50. This can be accomplished by cutting corners on production costs or raising the selling price.

CHANGES IN THE OBJECTIVE FUNCTION COEFFICIENTS

The objective function coefficients (usually profits or costs) may change over time, or they may originally have been rough estimates. In either case, it may be necessary for management to investigate the effects that changes in the objective function coefficients have on the optimal solution. Unlike changes in the right-hand side, changes in the objective function coefficients do not change the values of the basic variables so long as the basis does not change. Thus, changes in the objective function coefficients can only affect the optimality of the current solution and the objective function value itself. Changes in optimality are signaled by the $c_j - z_j$ values.

We will separate this analysis into two parts: First, we shall deal with nonbasic objective function coefficients; and then, we shall approach basic objective function coefficients.

Nonbasic objective function coefficient   Such a coefficient is one whose associated decision variable is nonbasic and not in solution. Thus, the decision variable associated with a nonbasic objective function coefficient is automatically zero; and its $c_j - z_j \leq 0$ if we are maximizing or $c_j - z_j \geq 0$ if we are minimizing. This must be true, for otherwise we could pivot the decision variable into solution and improve the objective function value.

Changing a nonbasic objective function coefficient, then, affects the value of the $c_j - z_j$ indicator. The basis does not change unless $c_j - z_j$ becomes greater than zero if maximizing and less than zero if minimizing. The amount that c_j can change is governed by the current $c_j - z_j$ value. Thus, we have the following rules:

1 If you are maximizing, you may decrease the value of any nonbasic c_j to minus infinity. You may increase c_j up to the value of z_j.

2 If you are minimizing, you may increase the value of any nonbasic c_j to infinity. You may decrease c_j down to the value of z_j.

To illustrate these rules, refer again to Tableau 6.1. The only nonbasic variables are s_2 and s_3. Currently, the objective function coefficients of s_2 and s_3 are both zero. Let us denote the objective function coefficients as c_{s_2} and c_{s_3}, respectively. Then, the first rule specifies that c_{s_2} may decrease to $-\infty$ and may increase to 62.5. If c_{s_2} were to increase to, say, 63, then its associated $c_j - z_j$ would become $+.5$, and s_2 would be brought into solution, thus changing the current basis. Likewise, we may decrease c_{s_3} to $-\infty$ and increase c_{s_3} to 250.

Basic objective function coefficient   If we consider changing an objective function coefficient whose associated decision variable is basic, the same principles apply as in the case of a nonbasic. However, changing a basic objective function coefficient can affect the $c_j - z_j$ of all nonbasic variables. Thus, a more lengthy analysis is required when the objective function coefficient is basic. To begin with, let us consider changing the profit contribution of power amps in the Faze Linear example. Presently, the objective function

Tableau 6.4   Changed power amp profit contribution

c_B	Basic variables	c_j 200 x_1	$500 + \Delta$ x_2	0 s_1	0 s_2	0 s_3	Solution
$500 + \Delta$	x_2	0	1	0	$5/8$	$-3/2$	$28\,1/2$
200	x_1	1	0	0	$-5/4$	5	105
0	s_1	0	0	1	$-5/8$	$3/2$	$11\,1/2$
	$c_j - z_j$	0	0	0	$-62\,1/2 -$ $5/8\,\Delta$	$-250 +$ $3/2\,\Delta$	$35{,}250 +$ $28\,1/2\,\Delta$

coefficient $c_2 = 500$. Let us denote the change in c_2 by Δ. Incorporating this change into Tableau 6.1, we establish the values of Tableau 6.4.

In Tableau 6.4, notice the new $c_j - z_j$ values for the nonbasic variables s_2 and s_3. These new values are determined by calculating a new z_j value in precisely the same manner that we did in Chapter 5 in the section headed, *The basic steps applied.*

The value of Δ may vary so long as no $c_j - z_j$ for a nonbasic variable remains greater than zero. Thus, we need to solve for Δ such that

$$-62\,1/2 - 5/8\,\Delta \leq 0$$
$$-250 + 3/2\,\Delta \leq 0$$

The first inequality yields $\Delta \geq -100$, and the second one requires that $\Delta \leq 166\,2/3$. Thus, the allowable range on Δ is $-100 \leq \Delta \leq 166\,2/3$. The c_2 coefficient that was originally 500 may vary from 400 to $666\,2/3$ before the basis changes.

If there were many nonbasic variables, the foregoing analysis would become tedious. Fortunately, there is an equivalent shortcut procedure. This procedure refers to the optimal tableau and simply forms ratios between the $c_j - z_j$ row and the tableau entries in the row associated with the current basic variable whose objective function coefficient is being analyzed. Suppose that we are considering changes in a basic objective function coefficient c_j. Let i denote

Table 6.4 Sensitivity analysis for basic objective function coefficients

	Basic variables	
	Power amps, x_1	Preamps, x_2
Tableau row i	2	1
Original c_j	200	500
Min $(c_j - z_j)/a_{ij} > 0$	50	166 2/3
Upper limit for c_j	250	666 2/3
Min $|(c_j - z_j)/a_{ij} < 0|$	50	100
Lower limit for c_j	150	400
Range for c_j	150 to 250	400 to 666 2/3

the tableau row in which the associated basic variable x_j appears. Let a_{ij} denote the entries in the tableau. Then for i fixed, we find

Minimum $(c_j - z_j)/a_{ij} > 0$ for the maximum positive change

and

Minimum $|(c_j - z_j)/a_{ij} < 0|$ for the maximum negative change

Thus, in the previous example where we considered changing c_2, we find the maximum positive change to be minimum $^{-250}/_{-3/2}$ = 166 2/3 and the maximum negative change to be minimum $^{-62.5}/_{5/8}$ = -100.

In Table 6.4, this analysis, along with an analysis on basic objective function coefficient c_1, is summarized. When you are sure you understand the analysis for c_2, work through the analysis for c_1 = 200 to see if your results agree with those in Table 6.4.

[Summary]

In this chapter, we have examined the closely related topics of the dual problem and sensitivity analysis. In more advanced topics, duality plays a very important role in the development of optimization techniques. We studied the dual problem primarily as a means for understanding shadow prices better. Shadow prices provide valuable information about the marginal value of scarce resources.

Sensitivity analysis allows us to determine the range over which these shadow prices are valid. A sensitivity analysis can actually be more useful to management than the optimal LP solution itself. It can help management make better decisions regarding such problems as capacity expansion, adding new products, changes in resource availabilities, and price fluctuations. In general, it is a technique that helps management to better relate the economics of the firm to the LP model being analyzed.

In right-hand-side ranging, we determined the range over which a right-hand side can be varied without causing the basis to change. In adding a new variable, we determined whether the variable is worthwhile to introduce to the solution or what its objective function must be in order to make it worthwhile. The final kind of sensitivity analysis involved a ranging analysis on the objective function coefficients. In two separate procedures, we determined the range over which nonbasic and basic objective function coefficients can change before the basis changes.

Right-hand-side ranging and objective coefficient analysis are often times standard output of available LP computer codes. The addition of a new product, however, generally requires individual analysis.

[Review questions]

1 What is a shadow price?

2 Explain why a shadow price is valid only for a specified range of values of the right-hand side.

3 If a primal LP model has m constraints and n variables, how many constraints and variables will its dual have?

4 In what ways can sensitivity analysis be more valuable to management than the optimal solution alone?

5 For any nonbasic variable in an optimal LP solution, how much would its objective function coefficient have to change in order for it to enter the solution?

6 Explain whether each kind of change in a, b, and c, below, prior to a change of basis can affect (1) solution, (2) solution value, (3) $c_j - z_j$ values, or (4) other entries in the tableau.
a Changes in the right-hand side
b Changes in the objective function coefficients
c Adding a new variable

[Problems]

6.1 Formulate the dual problem for the linear programming model below.
Maximize $16x_1 + 10x_2 + 9x_3$
subject to $3x_1 - 4x_2 + 8x_3 \le 52$
$14x_1 + 7x_2 + 4x_3 \le 40$
$x_1, x_2, x_3 \ge 0$

6.2 The LP problem following is the dual to a problem. Find the primal problem to which it corresponds.
Minimize $3x_1 + x_2 + 5x_2$
subject to $x_1 + x_2 + x_3 \ge 40$
$2x_1 + 3x_2 \ge 50$
$3x_1 + 2x_2 + 4x_3 \ge 20$
$x_1, x_2, x_3 \ge 0$

6.3 Given the primal problem
Minimize $15x_1 + 40x_2$
subject to $x_1 \ge 13$
$x_2 \ge 10$
$3x_1 + 4x_2 \ge 15$
$-5x_1 + 17x_2 \ge 19$
$x_1, x_2 \ge 0$
From a computational point of view, would you rather solve this primal or its associated dual? Why?

6.4 You are given the following product mix problem:
Maximize $4x_1 + 5x_2$
subject to $x_1 + 2x_2 \le 8$ (machine A hours)
$3x_1 + 2x_2 \le 12$ (machine B hours)
$x_1, x_2 \ge 0$
a Write the dual of this problem.
b Solve the primal and the dual.
c Interpret the primal and the dual.

6.5 Solve the following primal problem graphically, and solve its associated dual by inspection.

Maximize $4x_1 + 8x_2$
subject to $8x_1 + 4x_2 \leq 8$
$x_1, x_2 \geq 0$

6.6 The following primal problem has two variables and three constraints. Solve it indirectly by solving the dual problem by the simplex method.

Maximize $2x_1 + x_2$
subject to $x_2 \leq 10$
$2x_1 + 5x_2 \leq 60$
$2x_1 + 2x_2 \leq 18$
$x_1, x_2 \geq 0$

6.7 The optimal simplex tableau for a maximization problem with all $\leq$ constraints is shown following:

c_B	c_j Basic variable	4 x_1	2 x_2	0 s_1	0 s_2	0 s_3	Solution
2	x_2	0	1	1	-1	0	4
4	x_1	1	0	$-1/4$	$3/4$	0	3
0	s_3	0	0	2	-4	1	8
	$c_j - z_j$	0	0	-1	-1	0	20

a Which of the three resources are being fully utilized?
b Suppose that the resources could be obtained at no cost. Which right-hand side would you recommend for expansion, and why?
c How much can each right-hand-side coefficient be increased before the basis changes?
d Find the new solution when the first right-hand-side coefficient is increased by 6.

6.8 Try to give an economic interpretation of the dual to the example concerning production distribution in Chapter 4.

6.9 Consider the diet problem example in Chapter 4. Try to give a possible economic interpretation of its dual. *Hint:* The dual variables can be thought of as values or "prices" associated with each nutrient.

6.10 Below you will find the optimal tableau of the diet problem example in Chapter 4.

c_B	Basic variables	c_j 1.60 x_1	1.00 x_2	.65 x_3	.30 x_4	0 s_1	0 s_2	0 s_3	0 s_4	M A_1	M A_2	M A_3	M A_4	Solution
1.60	x_1	1	0	0	0	0	0	.0018	0	0	0	.0018	0	.7407
0	s_1	0	−237	0	0	1	−47.89	23.62	0	−1	47.89	−23.62	0	28200.48
.30	x_4	0	0	0	1	0	−.014	.0010	0	0	.014	−.001	0	.6390
0	s_4	0	−7	−13	0	0	−.112	−.0435	1	0	.112	.0435	−1	13.8516
	$c_j - z_j$	0	1.00	.65	0	0	.0042	.0026	0	M	M − .0042	M − .0026	M	$1.39

a What is the optimal solution? Is it palatable to you? How much does it cost to feed each individual on a daily basis? Do you think the constraints covered everything that should be considered in a daily diet?

b Which nutritional requirements are being met exactly? Which nutrients are being given in overdoses?

c Determine the range over which the vitamin C requirement can vary before the basis changes.

d For all four foods, determine the range over which their prices can vary without changing the basis.

6.11 Refer to Tableau 5.9, which is the optimal tableau for the minimization problem solved in Chapter 5.

a What are the shadow prices?

b What is the new minimum cost if the cost per gallon of crude oil is dropped by $.02?

c How much can the right-hand-side restriction of 20 on crude oil A change before the basis changes?

d Over what range can the cost for crude oil A vary without changing the basis?

6.12 The Southeastern Textile Mill produces four different styles of cotton cloth. The four basic materials are a bleached style, a printed style, and two dyed styles, red and blue. The profit contributions of these four products are, respectively, $.80, $1.20, $1.50, and $1.60 per square yard. The company is committed to produce at least 6,000 square yards of the printed style for next week. The maximum possible sales for the bleached style is 100,000 square yards.

c_B	Basic variables	c_j →	.80 x_1	1.20 x_2	1.50 x_3	1.60 x_4	0 s_7	0 s_1	0 s_2	0 s_3	0 s_4	0 s_5	0 s_6	$-M$ A_7	Solution
1.60	x_4		-.60	0	0	1	2.38	.78	-.06	0	0	0	0	-2.38	1792837
1.50	x_3		1.64	0	1	0	-1.14	-.71	.07	0	0	0	0	1.14	6862
0	s_3		0	0	0	0	33.00	0	0	1	0	0	0	-33.00	179802000
0	s_4		-2.38	0	0	0	-4.10	-.48	.01	0	1	0	0	4.10	9783616
0	s_5		-.86	0	0	0	-.11	-.06	-.03	0	0	1	0	.11	39759680
0	s_6		1	0	0	0	0	0	0	0	0	0	1	0	100000
1.20	x_2		0	1	0	0	-1	0	0	0	0	0	0	1	6000
	$c_j - z_j$		-.71	0	0	0	-.92	-.18	-.001	0	0	0	0	$-M + .92$	2886032

Southeastern's production involves five basic processes. These processes and their available capacity in millions of process hours are: desizing, 15; bleaching, 150; printing, 180; dyeing, 15; and calendering, 45. The resource requirements of each of the four products are stipulated in Southeastern's LP model. Let

x_1 = number of square yards of bleached material produced
x_2 = number of square yards of printed material produced
x_3 = number of square yards of red dyed material produced
x_4 = number of square yards of blue dyed material produced

Maximize $.80x_1 + 1.20x_2 + 1.50x_3 + 1.60x_4$
subject to

$$7.7x_1 + 11.1x_2 + 7.7x_3 + 8.3x_4 \leq 15,000,000$$
$$100.x_1 + 95.x_2 + 91.x_3 + 83.x_4 \leq 150,000,000$$
$$33.x_2 \leq 180,000,000$$
$$2.5x_3 + 2.9x_4 \leq 15,000,000$$
$$2.5x_1 + 3.3x_2 + 3.1x_3 + 2.9x_4 \leq 45,000,000$$
$$x_1 \leq 100,000$$
$$x_2 \geq 6,000$$

$x_1, x_2, x_3, x_4 \geq 0$

After adding the required slack and artificial variables, the optimal simplex tableau is as presented on the opposite page.

a What is the optimal solution and the total profit?

b Is the solution degenerate? Are there alternative optima?

c Which of the five departments appears to be most promising in terms of expansion? What else would you have to take into consideration?

d What is the incremental profit associated with adding one more process hour of bleaching capacity? Over what range is this valid?

e Consider another new printed style x_5 which requires 9.1 hours of printing and 4.0 hours of calendering. What does its profit contribution have to be in order for it to be profitably produced?

f Suppose that an additional 10 hours of bleaching capacity is made available. What are the new values for x_1, x_2, x_3, and x_4? *Hint:* Use the appropriate substitution coefficients in the optimal tableau.

6.13 Consider the 2×2 example in problem 6.4. Find three feasible solutions for the primal problem and three feasible solutions for the dual problem. Plug these feasible solutions into their respective objective functions and observe their respective solution values. Are the values of the objective function of the maximization problem (this is often called the *max* objective function) always less than or equal to those of the minimization (the *min*)? Observe their two optimal values.

A fundamental result in duality theory is the *dual theorem*. It states that if both the primal and dual are feasible, then the solution value of any feasible solution of the max problem is always less than or equal to any feasible solution of the min problem. Furthermore, the optimal solution values of the two problems are equal.

dual theorem

6.14 Another fundamental property in duality theory is called *complementary slackness*. Basically, this is a statement of the fact that if a constraint in an LP problem is not tight, its associated shadow price must be zero. A constraint is tight if the solution variable values equal the right-hand side when they are substituted into the constraint. Thus, a nontight constraint is simply one in which some slack exists. Consider the optimal solution to the Faze Linear problem (Tableau 6.1). Which constraints are tight? Which shadow prices are zero?

complementary slackness

Complementary slackness is intuitively reasonable, for if a constraint is not tight, some of the associated resource is left over and should have a marginal value (shadow price) of zero.

[Red Brand Canners case]

On Monday, September 13, 1965, Mr. Mitchell Gordon, Vice-President of Operations, asked the Controller, the Sales Manager, and the Production Manager to meet with him to discuss the amount of tomato products to pack that season. The tomato crop, which had been purchased at planting, was beginning to arrive at the cannery, and packing operations would have to be started by the following Monday. Red Brand Canners was a medium-size company which canned and distributed a variety of fruit and vegetable products under private brands in the western states.

Mr. William Cooper, the Controller, and Mr. Charles Myers, the Sales Manager, were the first to arrive in Mr. Gordon's office. Dan Tucker, the Production Manager, came in a few minutes later and said that he had picked up Produce Inspection's latest estimate of the quality of the incoming tomatoes. According to their report, about 20 percent of the crop was Grade "A" quality and the remaining portion of the 3,000,000-pound crop was Grade "B."

Gordon asked Myers about the demand for tomato products for the coming year. Myers replied that they could sell all of the whole canned tomatoes they could produce. The expected demand for tomato juice and tomato paste, on the other hand, was limited. The Sales Manager then passed around the latest demand forecast, which is shown in Table 1. He reminded the group that the selling prices had been set in light of the long-term marketing strategy of the company, and potential sales had been forecasted at these prices.

Bill Cooper, after looking at Myer's estimates of demand, said that it looked like the company "should do quite well (on the tomato crop) this year." With the new accounting system that had been set up, he had been able to compute the contribution for each product, and

[1] Reprinted from *Stanford Business Cases 1965* with the permission of the publishers, Stanford University Graduate School of Business. Copyright © 1965 by the Board of Trustees of the Leland Stanford Junior University.

Table 1 Demand forecasts

Product	Selling price per case ($)	Demand forecast (cases)
24–2½ whole tomatoes	4.00	800,000
24–2½ choice peach halves	5.40	10,000
24–2½ peach nectar	4.60	5,000
24–2½ tomato juice	4.50	50,000
24–2½ cooking apples	4.90	15,000
24–2½ tomato paste	3.80	80,000

according to his analysis the incremental profit on the whole tomatoes was greater than for any other tomato product. In May, after Red Brand had signed contracts agreeing to purchase the grower's production at an average delivered price of 6 cents per pound, Cooper had computed the tomato products' contributions (see Table 2).

Dan Tucker brought to Cooper's attention that, although there was ample production capacity, it was impossible to produce all whole tomatoes as too small a portion of the tomato crop was "A" quality. Red Brand used a numerical scale to record the quality of both raw produce and prepared products. This scale ran from zero to ten, the higher number representing better quality. Rating tomatoes according to this scale, "A" tomatoes averaged nine points per pound and "B" tomatoes averaged five points per pound. Tucker noted that the minimum average input quality for canned whole tomatoes was eight, and for juice it was six points per pound. Paste could be made entirely from "B" grade tomatoes. This meant that whole tomato production was limited to 800,000 pounds.

Gordon stated that this was not a real limitation. He had been recently solicited to purchase 80,000 pounds of Grade "A" tomatoes at 8½ cents per pound and at that time had turned down the offer. He felt, however, that the tomatoes were still available.

Myers, who had been doing some calculations, said that although he agreed that the Company "should do quite well this year," it would

Table 2   Product item profitability

Costs ($)	Product					
	24–2¹/₂ Whole tomatoes	24–2¹/₂ Choice Peach halves	24–2¹/₂ Peach nectar	24–2¹/₂ Tomato juice	24–2¹/₂ Cooking apples	24–2¹/₂ Tomato paste
Selling price	4.00	5.40	4.60	4.50	4.90	3.80
Variable costs						
Direct labor	1.18	1.40	1.27	1.32	.70	.54
Variable overhead	.24	.32	.23	.36	.22	.26
Variable selling	.40	.30	.40	.85	.28	.38
Packaging material	.70	.56	.60	.65	.70	.77
Fruit*	1.08	1.80	1.70	1.20	.90	1.50
Total variable costs	3.60	4.30	4.20	4.38	2.80	3.45
Contribution	.40	1.02	.40	.12	1.10	.35
Less allocated overhead	.28	.70	.52	.21	.75	.23
Net profit	.12	.32	(.12)	(.09	.35	.12

*Product usage is as given below

Product	Pounds per case
Whole tomatoes	18
Peach halves	18
Peach nectar	17
Tomato juice	20
Cooking apples	27

not be by canning whole tomatoes. It seemed to him that the tomato cost should be allocated on the basis of quality and quantity rather than by quantity only, as Cooper had done. Therefore, he had recomputed the marginal profit on this basis (see Table 3), and from his results, Red Brand should use 2 million pounds of the "B" tomatoes for paste, and the remaining 400,000 pounds of "B" tomatoes and all of the "A" tomatoes for juice. If the demand expectations were realized, a contribution of $48,000 would be made on this year's tomato crop.

Table 3 Marginal analysis of tomato products

Costs ($)	Canned whole tomatoes	Tomato juice	Tomato paste
Selling price	4.00	4.50	3.80
Variable cost (excluding tomato costs)	2.52	3.18	1.95
	1.48	1.32	1.85
Tomato cost	1.49	1.24	1.30
Marginal profit	.01	.08	.55

Z = cost per pound of "A" tomatoes in cents

Y = cost per pound of "B" tomatoes in cents

(1) (600,000 lbs. $\times$ Z) + (2,400,000 lbs. $\times$ Y) = (3,000,000 lbs. $\times$ 6)

(2) $\dfrac{Z}{9} = \dfrac{Y}{5}$

Z = 9.32 cents per pound

Y = 5.18 cents per pound

[Case problems]

1 Before any systematic analysis can be performed on the Red Brand Cannery problem, the issue of relevant data must be resolved. With which cost-and-profit data do you agree, Table 2 or Table 3? Does the fact that Red Brand has already purchased the 3-million-pound crop at planting affect your answer?

2 Do you think that the allocated overhead should be subtracted from the profit contribution per case as shown in Table 2?

3 Propose a systematic procedure for developing a good solution for the production of tomato products. Be sure to include an analysis of whether or not Red Brand should purchase the additional 80,000 pounds of grade "A" tomatoes. You may or may not want to use sensitivity analysis.

4 Determine an optimal solution to the Red Brand Canners problem.

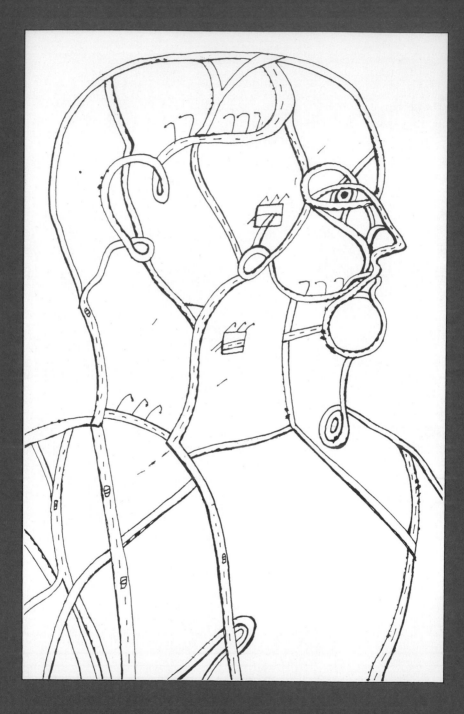

7

[Transportation and assignment problems]

[Network models in management science]

In this chapter, we explore two very special LP models. Transportation and assignment models fall into the category of *network models* in management science (as does PERT, a program evaluation and review technique we discuss in the next chapter). Network models arise frequently in management science applications. A *network* is network a collection of nodes or points connected by links. (Figure 7.2 depicts a simple network.) Networks may represent not only abstract problems but also physical systems, such as pipeline, electrical-wiring, or river systems.

Networks have long been used in electrical-engineering applications, and more applications are being found in other fields. Network models generally are used in such areas as communications networks, transportation systems, water systems analysis, information theory, cybernetics, and project planning and control. In addition to their widespread applicability, network models constitute one of the few categories of management science model that is amenable to really large-scale analysis. Network models involving hundreds, or even thousands, of variables can be solved using some of the larger computers. Practitioners often try to model, or even approximate, a problem as a network problem in order to gain computational efficiency.

[Rationale for special-purpose algorithms]

The transportation and assignment models we shall examine in this chapter are two of the more common network models. They have many applications, both directly and as subproblems of even larger problems. They are both LP models and thus can be solved by using a general-purpose LP computer code. However, transportation and assignment models have a special mathematical structure that can be exploited to yield streamlined versions of the general simplex method. Taking advantage of special network structure can yield not only cost savings in terms of computation but also solutions to large-scale problems that are otherwise too large to be solved on contemporary computers by the general simplex method. These streamlined versions of the simplex method are special-purpose algorithm algorithms. An *algorithm* is a systematic procedure for arriving at a solution for a problem. The primary benefits of these special-purpose algorithms for transportation and assignment problems are as follows:

1 Computations are generally 100 to 150 times faster than the general simplex method.

2 Significantly less computer memory is required, thus permitting even larger problems to be solved.

3 Transportation and assignment problems that have integer (whole-number) data yield integer solutions when solved by special-purpose algorithms.

This third factor is particularly important. Many real-world applications require whole-number solutions. For example, it is hard to ship half a car from Detroit or to build one-third of an airplane. Furthermore, general LP can yield noninteger solutions that deviate significantly from optimality when they are rounded off. Other general management science techniques that guarantee an integer solution, moreover, are usually inefficient and unable to solve large-scale problems.

[Advantages and disadvantages of heuristics]

In this chapter, we shall develop special-purpose algorithms to solve the transportation and assignment models. In the case of the transportation problem, we shall also consider *heuristic* solution approaches. heuristic

A *heuristic* is a rule-of-thumb procedure that determines a good, but not necessarily optimal, solution to a problem. The simplex method, for example, is not heuristic since it is an optimization technique that guarantees the optimal solution, provided one exists. Heuristic solutions are usually obtained much faster and thus at lower cost. These simple rules of thumb can also be performed by hand sometimes, thus eliminating the need to use a computer. On the other hand, heuristics cannot be considered so accurate as optimization techniques since an optimal solution is not guaranteed. A good heuristic is generally within 10 percent of optimality, but the great disadvantage of using a heuristic is that the amount of error is not known. That is, if you use a heuristic that has not been thoroughly tested, you do not know whether your answer is 5, 10, or even 30 percent from the optimal solution.

Management science techniques have made significant progress in helping to solve medium and large-scale operational problems. Sometimes, however, it is said that little has been done to help management with the small or daily problems of operation. It is in this area that heuristics can be most beneficial. Their simplicity and ease of calculation make it possible for management to use these decision rules on a short-term basis without having to undertake extensive preparations.

Do not gain too simple a notion of heuristics, however. Sophisticated heuristics have been developed for certain very difficult problems for which there are no effective optimization techniques.

For these problems, heuristics are not a convenience but a necessity. Among problems of this type are warehouse location models, vehicle-routing problems, airline scheduling, job shop scheduling, network design problems, and others.

[The transportation problem]

The particular model we address in this section is called the *Hitchcock-Koopmans transportation problem* after its two formulators. As you have probably guessed, the model can be used to determine optimal shipping patterns. The model has many other applications, however; it is sometimes called the distribution problem.

Figure 7.1   Location of plants and warehouses for Faze Linear

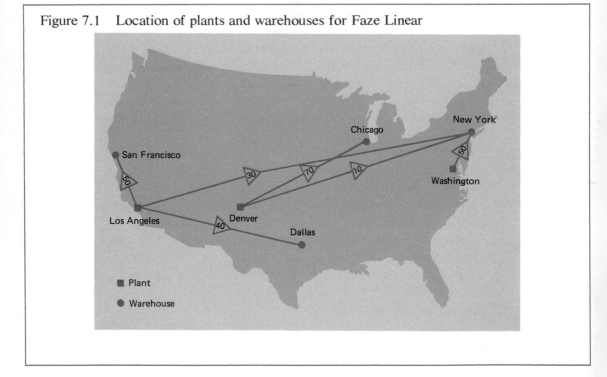

Table 7.1   Data for Faze Linear distribution problem

Shipping costs ($)

From plant	To warehouse				Supply
	New York	Chicago	Dallas	San Francisco	
Washington, D.C.	8	9	11	16	50
Denver	12	7	5	8	80
Los Angeles	14	10	6	7	120
Demand	90	70	40	50	

[Example]   The Faze Linear Company is very progressive and has already used LP to determine its optimal product mix (see Chapter 5). The company is now faced with the problem of how to distribute its electrical components from plants to regional warehouses. Faze Linear has plants located in Washington, D.C., Denver, and Los Angeles; regional warehouses are located in New York, Chicago, Dallas, and San Francisco (see Figure 7.1). This month, the company has available 50 units at Washington, 80 units at Denver, and 120 units at Los Angeles. In order to meet predicted demand, Faze Linear must ship 90 units to New York, 70 to Chicago, 40 to Dallas, and 50 to San Francisco. Relevant per-unit transportation costs for each component as well as demand-and-supply data are given in Table 7.1. Faze Linear wants to determine the shipping pattern that meets all demand at minimum transportation cost.

The Faze Linear distribution problem is actually an LP problem. To formulate it, let x_{ij} denote the amount to be shipped from plant i to warehouse j where $i = 1, 2, 3$ and $j = 1, 2, 3, 4$. In this notation, x_{23} represents the number of units to be shipped from Denver to Dallas. Notice that the first subscript refers to the row (plant) in Table 7.1 and the second subscript refers to the column (warehouse). The problem may be formulated as

Minimize $8x_{11} + 9x_{12} + 11x_{13} + 16x_{14} + 12x_{21} + 7x_{22} + 5x_{23} + 8x_{24}$
$+ 14x_{31} + 10x_{32} + 6x_{33} + 7x_{34}$

subject to
$$x_{11} + x_{12} + x_{13} + x_{14} = 50$$
$$x_{21} + x_{22} + x_{23} + x_{24} = 80$$
$$x_{31} + x_{32} + x_{33} + x_{34} = 120$$
$$x_{11} + x_{21} + x_{31} = 90$$
$$x_{12} + x_{22} + x_{32} = 70$$
$$x_{13} + x_{23} + x_{33} = 40$$
$$x_{14} + x_{24} + x_{34} = 50$$
$$x_{ij} \geq 0; i = 1, 2, 3; j = 1, 2, 3, 4$$

The foregoing model may be solved directly by the general simplex method. However, streamlined simplex procedures are available that offer the three benefits described earlier in this chapter. Charnes and Cooper developed the stepping-stone method, which was one of the first specialized simplex procedures for transportation problems. Later, Dantzig developed the *modified distribution*, or *MODI, method*, which remains the best approach for solving transportation problems. Computational researchers have further refined the MODI method so that really significant computational savings can be achieved. For instance, transportation problems that have 1,000 plants and 1,000 warehouses (that is, 1 million decision variables) have been solved in 17 seconds or so on a CDC 6600 computer. Problems of this size are not even solvable without using special-purpose algorithms.

modified distribution (MODI) method

We can generalize transportation problems to include more than plants and warehouses. We may so interpret any situation in which a homogeneous product is available in the amounts $a_1, a_2, \ldots a_m$ at m sources $1, 2, \ldots, m$, respectively. Furthermore, demands $b_1, b_2, \ldots, b_n$ are present at n destinations $1, 2, \ldots, n$, respectively. The transportation cost per unit from the ith source to the jth destination is a known constant, c_{ij}, and directly proportional to the amount shipped. Letting x_{ij} again represent the amount shipped from source i to destination j, we obtain the general transportation model

Minimize $$\sum_{i=1}^{m} \sum_{j=1}^{n} c_{ij} x_{ij}$$

[7.1]

subject to $$\sum_{j=1}^{n} x_{ij} = a_i, i = 1, 2, \ldots, m,$$

$$\sum_{i=1}^{m} x_{ij} = b_j, j = 1, 2, \ldots, n,$$

$x_{ij} \geq 0$ for $i = 1, 2, \ldots m; j = 1, 2, \ldots, n$

It is assumed that total supply equals total demand; that is

$$\sum_{i=1}^{m} a_i = \sum_{j=1}^{n} b_j.$$

We shall find that this assumption can easily be circumvented by adding a dummy source or destination.

[Solving transportation problems heuristically]

In this section, we shall consider two heuristics methods as well as the MODI optimization method for the transportation problem. The heuristics we discuss in this section are intuitive; hopefully, they will give you some insight into possible approaches to other types of problems. The heuristics are also helpful in providing a starting point for the calculations in the MODI method.

ROW MINIMUM METHOD

The row minimum heuristic is a very quick way to obtain a feasible solution to the transportation problem. Computational investigations have shown that it is one of the best heuristics with which to start the MODI method for optimizing. That is, the row minimum heuristic coupled with the MODI method can solve transportation problems faster than any other procedures.

To explain the row minimum procedure, we need a transportation tableau. A table of this type is helpful in solving transportation problems, just as the simplex tableau is helpful in solving LP problems. Tableau 7.1 illustrates a transportation tableau for the Faze Linear problem. The usual practice in these tableaus is to list the sources as rows and the destinations as columns. The available supply for each source is listed in the far right column, and the required demands at each destination are summarized in the bottom row. The per-unit transportation cost for shipping from source to destination is found in the upper left-hand corner of the square

Tableau 7.1   Transportation tableau for Faze Linear

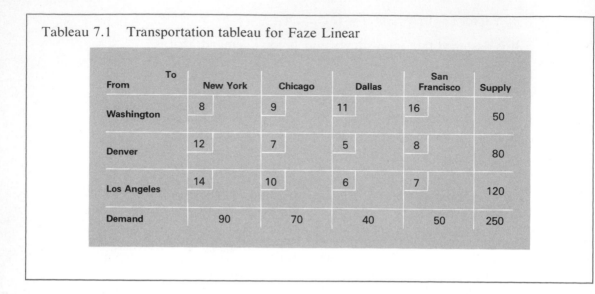

From \ To	New York	Chicago	Dallas	San Francisco	Supply
Washington	8	9	11	16	50
Denver	12	7	5	8	80
Los Angeles	14	10	6	7	120
Demand	90	70	40	50	250

in the row associated with the source and the column associated with the destination. For example, the per-unit transportation cost from the Los Angeles source to the Chicago destination is $10.

cells The 12 squares (or *cells*) formed by the three sources and four destinations correspond to direct routes over which shipments can take place. In any feasible solution, the sum of the shipments across any row must not exceed the supply available, and the sum of the shipments down any column must satisfy the demand required.

Unlike some other "quick and dirty" transportation heuristics, the row minimum rule does not ignore the costs of the various shipments. As the name implies, the row minimum heuristic proceeds by trying to assign shipments to the minimum-cost cell in each row. The process starts in row 1, continues to row 2, and so on, until all supply is exhausted and all demand is satisfied. To summarize the procedure:

1 Find the minimum-cost cell in row 1. If there is a tie, make an arbitrary choice. Allocate as much supply as possible to this cell. The maximum allocation is determined by the supply available and the demand required by the source and destination associated with this minimum-cost cell.

2 Delete the row (or column) whose supply (or demand) has just been exhausted by the allocation in the previous step.

3 Proceed to the next row that has not been deleted and find the minimum-cost cell. Again, make an allocation and delete the appropriate row or column.

4 Repeat step 3 until all supply is exhausted and all demand is satisfied. Whenever the last row in the tableau is reached, the process returns to the first row in the tableau for the next execution of step 3.

For the Faze Linear problem, the row minimum solution is shown in Tableau 7.2. The number added to a cell represents the shipment to be made from the associated source to destination. In this example, the row minimum procedure started in row 1 and made an allocation of 50 to the minimum-cost cell (1,1). We shall use the notation (i,j) to denote the cell associated with source i and destination j. Row 1 has its supply exhausted and is deleted. Proceeding to the second row, we find that cell (2,3), with a cost of 5, is minimal. Thus, 40 units is allocated to cell (2,3), and column 3 is deleted. Proceeding to the third row, we find cell (3,3), at a cost of 6, is minimal, but it is not available since column 3 has been deleted. Thus we allocate 50 units to the next minimal-cost cell (3,4). Since row 1 is deleted, we return to row 2 and allocate 40 units to cell

Tableau 7.2   Row minimum solution for Faze Linear

To (j) From (i)	New York		Chicago		Dallas		San Francisco		Supply
Washington	8	50	9		11		16		50
Denver	12		7	40	5	40	8		80
Los Angeles	14	40	10	30	6		7	50	120
Demand		90		70		40		50	250

(2,2). This deletes row 2, and we again proceed to row 3, allocating 30 units to cell (3,2) and then 40 units to cell (3,1). This deletes all three rows and also satisfies all required demand. The cost of the row minimum solution is found by multiplying each shipment by its per-unit transportation cost. The row minimum cost is 8(50) + 7(40) + 5(40) + 14(40) + 10(30) + 7(50) = \$2,090.

VOGEL'S APPROXIMATION METHOD (VAM)

Vogel's approximation heuristic is generally (though not always) more accurate than the row minimum rule. However, more calculations are involved, and thus more total computation time is required when VAM is used with the MODI method to obtain an optimal solution. VAM can be used when the decision maker is satisfied with obtaining a good heuristic solution that is not necessarily optimal.

VAM is an interesting heuristic that can be applied to problems other than transportation problems. The basic idea in VAM is to avoid shipments that have a high cost. The row minimum method is somewhat shortsighted in that it simply assigns to the lowest-cost cell available *in a particular row;* this can cause high costs to be incurred in other rows. VAM looks at the opportunity cost of not assigning to the minimum-cost cell in a row or column of the transportation tableau. The *opportunity cost* is conservatively esti- opportunity mated to be the difference in cost between the lowest- and next cost lowest-cost cells in that particular row or column. Then, assignment is made to the minimum-cost cell in the row or column that has the highest potential opportunity loss. If we view the opportunity cost as a possible penalty, the idea is to avoid a high penalty. This assignment then avoids incurring the highest opportunity loss. The details of VAM are presented as follows:

1 For each row, calculate the potential opportunity loss as the difference between the minimum-cost cell and the next lowest-cost cell in that row.

2 For each column, calculate the potential opportunity loss as the difference between the minimum-cost cell and the next lowest-cost cell in that column.

3 Find the highest potential opportunity loss from among all rows and columns, and find the minimum-cost cell associated with that row or column. If a tie exists in opportunity losses among rows and columns, break the tie arbitrarily.

4 Allocate the maximum possible amount of supply to the minimum-cost cell in step 3; this will delete a row or column. Reduce the supplies and demands appropriately.

5 If a row has been deleted, recalculate the column opportunity losses. If a column has been deleted, recalculate the row opportunity losses.

6 If all allocations have been made, stop. Otherwise, begin another iteration by returning to step 3.

Let's apply the VAM procedure to the Faze Linear distribution problem. The VAM heuristic begins by calculating the potential opportunity losses of not assigning to the lowest-cost cell in each row and column. The beginning calculations are shown in Tableau 7.3. There you see that the highest opportunity loss is 4, which is associated with column 1. This means that if we do not ship in the least-cost cell in this row ($8 per unit), we will have to ship in a cell that has a cost of at least $4 per unit more. In fact, the additional cost would be either $4 or $6 per unit. Thus, we

Tableau 7.3   Initial VAM calculations for Faze Linear

Row opportunity costs	From \ To	New York	Chicago	Dallas	San Francisco	Supply
Column opportunity costs		4	2	1	1	
1	Washington	8 50	9	11	16	50
2	Denver	12	7	5	8	80
1	Los Angeles	14	10	6	7	120
	Demand	90 40	70	40	50	250

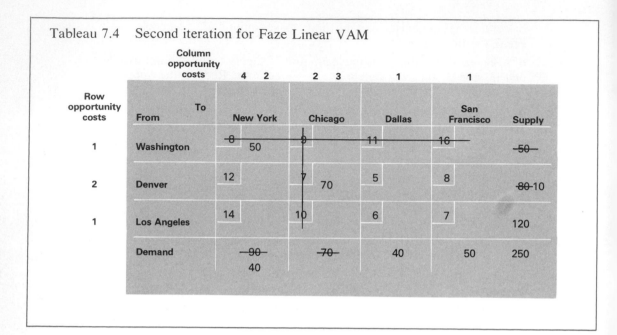

Tableau 7.4   Second iteration for Faze Linear VAM

Column opportunity costs		4 2	2 3	1	1	
Row opportunity costs	From \ To	New York	Chicago	Dallas	San Francisco	Supply
1	Washington	-8- 50	-9-	-11-	-16-	-50-
2	Denver	12	-7- 70	5	8	-80- 10
1	Los Angeles	14	10	6	7	120
	Demand	-90- 40	-70-	40	50	250

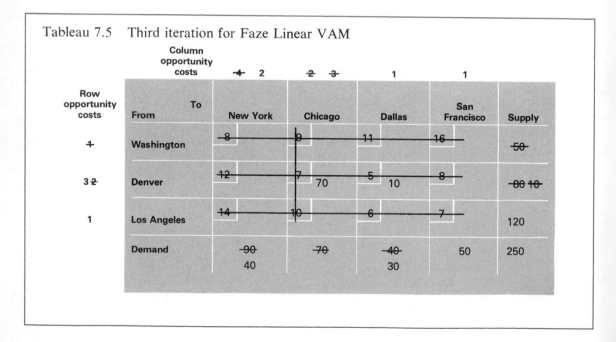

Tableau 7.5   Third iteration for Faze Linear VAM

Column opportunity costs		-4- 2	-2- -3-	1	1	
Row opportunity costs	From \ To	New York	Chicago	Dallas	San Francisco	Supply
-1-	Washington	-8-	-9-	-11-	-16-	-50-
3 2	Denver	-12-	-7- 70	-5- 10	-8-	-80- 10
1	Los Angeles	-14-	-10-	-6-	-7-	120
	Demand	-90- 40	-70-	-40- 30	50	250

allocate all the supply possible, which is 50 units, to cell (1,1), which has the minimum cost of $8. The supply for row 1 is exhausted; so we draw a line through the costs in row 1 as a reminder that these costs are no longer usable in calculating opportunity losses.

Tableau 7.4 shows the results we get when we recalculate the column opportunity losses for the next iteration. The highest opportunity loss is now 3 and is associated with column 2. Thus we allocate all we can to the lowest-cost cell (2,2); this allocation is 70 units, which is all the demand that is required in column 2. We adjust the supplies and demands, delete column 2 by drawing a line through its costs, and update the row opportunity losses in Tableau 7.5.

This time, the largest opportunity loss is the 3 associated with row 2. Allocating the available 10 units deletes row 2 and leaves only row 3 with available supply. Three more iterations are required to reach the final VAM solution. The final tableau is shown in Tableau 7.6.

Tableau 7.6   Final Solution for Faze Linear VAM

Row opportunity costs	From \ To	New York	Chicago	Dallas	San Francisco	Supply
Column opportunity costs		~~4~~ ~~2~~ 0	~~2~~ ~~3~~	~~+~~ 0	~~+~~ 0	
~~+~~	Washington	8 \ 50	9	11	16	~~50~~
~~3~~ ~~2~~	Denver	12	7 \ 70	5 \ 10	8	~~80~~ ~~10~~
~~7~~ ~~+~~	Los Angeles	14 \ 40	10	6 \ 30	7 \ 50	~~120~~ ~~90~~ 40
	Demand	~~90~~ ~~40~~	~~70~~	~~40~~ ~~30~~	~~50~~	250

The distribution cost of the VAM solution is 8(50) + 7(70) + 5(10) + 14(40) + 6(30) + 7(50) = \$2,030, which is \$60 lower than the row minimum solution. Usually, VAM provides at least as good a solution as row minimum, though not always.

[Solving transportation problems by the MODI method]

Even though the VAM solution to the Faze Linear problem is better than the row minimum solution, it is still not optimal. The MODI method can be used to take any basic feasible solution to a transportation problem and determine an optimal solution from it. MODI is a streamlined version of the simplex method that takes advantage of the special mathematical structure of the transportation model.

One advantage of the MODI method is that it does not require the use of slack or artificial variables to get a starting feasible solution. It can also take advantage of the advanced starting feasible solutions provided by row minimum or VAM. The calculations in the MODI method are aimed at making successive improvements in a feasible solution until the optimal solution is reached. The method parallels the simplex method in that the following steps are executed:

1 A variable is found that can reduce transportation costs when brought into solution.

2 This variable's maximum allowable value is determined.

3 The variable that must leave the solution is determined, then all other variables in solution are updated.

Fortunately, it is not necessary to store and update a large number of entries in a simplex tableau as you must do in the general simplex method. The corresponding amount of storage space and computation is thus eliminated.

Consider the row minimum heuristic solution to the Faze Linear distribution problem that we restate in Tableau 7.7. Notice that there are six cells in which shipments occur. For a transportation problem that has m sources and n destinations, a basic feasible

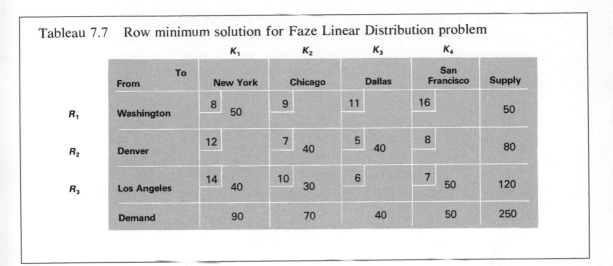

Tableau 7.7 Row minimum solution for Faze Linear Distribution problem

From	To	K_1 New York	K_2 Chicago	K_3 Dallas	K_4 San Francisco	Supply
R_1	Washington	8 50	9	11	16	50
R_2	Denver	12	7 40	5 40	8	80
R_3	Los Angeles	14 40	10 30	6	7 50	120
	Demand	90	70	40	50	250

solution always involves $m + n - 1$ cells. Even though there are $m + n$ functional constraints, one of them is redundant since all the constraints are equalities and it is assumed that total supply equals total demand. This can be illustrated by showing that a demand constraint equals the sum of all the supply constraints minus the sum of the remaining demand constraints. In using any starting solution from the row minimum or VAM heuristics, we must be sure that the solution contains $m + n - 1$ cells.

In order to improve any feasible transportation solution by means of the MODI method, we need to determine which cells need to have their shipments increased and which need to have their shipments decreased. As in the regular simplex method, we make these improvements one variable at a time. Thus, initially, we need to find a cell whose shipments we can increase and, by doing so, reduce transportation costs.

In the regular simplex method, cost-reducing variables are recognized by having a negative $c_j - z_j$ value. The same $c_j - z_j$ indicators are used in the MODI method but are calculated in a much easier way. The first step in determining $c_j - z_j$ values for all nonbasic cells (those that have no shipments) is to assign row and column indicators to each row and column of the transportation tableau. In our example, we let R_1, R_2, and R_3 represent row indicator values and K_1, K_2, K_3, and K_4 represent column indicator values. Refer to Tableau 7.7 to see these indicators associated with their appropriate rows or columns. For those of you who have already studied Chapter 6, these indicators are simply the dual variables of the dual problem.

In general, for an $m \times n$ transportation problem we let

R_i = indicator value assigned to row i, $i = 1, 2, ..., m$
K_j = indicator value assigned to column j, $j = 1, 2, ..., n$

As we have stated previously, x_{ij} represents the shipment from source i to destination j, and c_{ij} represents the associated per-unit transportation cost.

In order to compute values for the R_i and K_j indicators, we use a result from duality theory that states

$$R_i + K_j = c_{ij} \qquad \text{whenever } x_{ij} > 0 \tag{7.2}$$

Thus $R_i + K_j = c_{ij}$ for any cell (i,j) in which a positive shipment occurs. Since we have m supply constraints and n demand constraints for a total of $m + n$ constraints, we might expect to have $m + n$ basic cells. However, since one constraint is always redundant in transportation models, we actually have $m + n - 1$ cells with positive shipments in any nondegenerate solution. Thus, condition 7.2 yields $m + n - 1$ equations, which we can solve to determine the R_i and K_j values. In Tableau 7.7, the cells (1,1), (2,2), (2,3), (3,1), (3,2), and (3,4) have positive shipments. Thus we obtain the following six equations:

$$R_1 + K_1 = c_{11} = 8 \tag{7.3}$$
$$R_2 + K_2 = c_{22} = 7 \tag{7.4}$$
$$R_2 + K_3 = c_{23} = 5 \tag{7.5}$$
$$R_3 + K_1 = c_{31} = 14 \tag{7.6}$$
$$R_3 + K_2 = c_{32} = 10 \tag{7.7}$$
$$R_3 + K_4 = c_{34} = 7 \tag{7.8}$$

Notice that we have six equations in seven unknowns. Since we have one more unknown than equation, we have one degree of freedom and can set any one of the R_i or K_j equal to an arbitrary value. It is simplest to set R_1 equal to zero and then to solve for the other indicator values. Solving such a system of equations may sound tedious, but the special structure of the transportation problem makes the system of equations trivial to solve. This system of equations is triangular once R_1 is set equal to zero, and the other R_i and K_j may be determined without any calculations.

For example, once $R_1 = 0$, then in equation 7.3 we have

$$R_1 + K_1 = 8 \qquad\qquad [7.3]$$
$$0 + K_1 = 8$$
$$K_1 = 8$$

Now that $K_1 = 8$, in 7.6 we have that

$$R_3 + K_1 = 14 \qquad\qquad [7.6]$$
$$R_3 + 8 = 14$$
$$R_3 = 6$$

And now that $R_3 = 6$, we have

$$R_3 + K_2 = 10 \qquad\qquad [7.7]$$
$$6 + K_2 = 10$$
$$K_2 = 4$$
$$R_3 + K_4 = 7 \qquad\qquad [7.8]$$
$$6 + K_4 = 7$$
$$K_4 = 1$$

With $K_2 = 4$, equation 7.4 becomes

$$R_2 + K_4 = 7 \qquad\qquad [7.4]$$
$$R_2 + 4 = 7$$
$$R_2 = 3$$

And finally, given $R_2 = 3$

$$R_2 + K_3 = 5 \qquad\qquad [7.5]$$
$$3 + K_3 = 5$$
$$K_3 = 2$$

We have solved the entire system of equations by merely setting $R_1 = 0$ and substituting for the remaining R_i and K_j values. Even though the R_i and K_j values are all nonnegative in this example, they may be positive, negative, or zero.

Recall that our purpose in calculating the R_i and K_j values was to determine which variables (cells), if any, can have their shipments increased and thereby reduce transportation costs. In the regular simplex method discussed in Chapter 5, we used the $c_j - z_j$ indicators to measure potential improvements. We can use precisely the same approach in the MODI method because the sum of $R_i + K_j = z_{ij}$ for any transportation variable x_{ij}. Thus, we can calculate the opportunity cost of increasing the shipments through any nonbasic cell (those with no shipments) as

$$c_{ij} - (R_i + K_j) \tag{7.9}$$

Since we are trying to minimize costs, we achieve the optimal solution whenever all the $c_{ij} - (R_i + K_j)$ are zero or positive. We indicate the value of each $c_{ij} - (R_i + K_j)$ in the lower right-hand part of each nonbasic cell. See Tableau 7.8 for the R_i and K_j values for the initial row minimum solution of the Faze Linear distribution problem. Notice the $c_{ij} - (R_i + K_j)$ values in the enclosed portion of each empty nonbasic cell. (The $c_{ij} - (R_i + K_j)$ numbers were derived as shown in Table 7.2.) The only nonbasic cell that reduces transportation cost is cell (3,3). This is so because it is the only cell that has a negative opportunity cost. For each unit that we can ship through cell (3,3) (that is, from Los Angeles to Dallas),

Tableau 7.8   Initial transportation tableau with R_i and K_j values for Faze Linear

From \ To	New York $K_1 = 8$	Chicago $K_2 = 4$	Dallas $K_3 = 2$	San Francisco $K_4 = 1$	Supply
Washington $R_1 = 0$	8 — 50	9 — 5	11 — 9	16 — 15	50
Denver $R_2 = 3$	12 — 1	7 — 40	5 — 40	8 — 4	80
Los Angeles $R_3 = 6$	14 — 40	10 — 30	6 — −2	7 — 50	120
Demand	90	70	40	50	

Table 7.2 $c_{ij} - (R_i + K_j)$ values for Faze Linear second solution

Nonbasic cell	$c_{ij} - (R_i + K_j)$		Opportunity cost
(1,2)	$9 - (0 + 4)$	$=$	5
(1,3)	$11 - (0 + 2)$	$=$	9
(1,4)	$16 - (0 + 1)$	$=$	15
(2,1)	$12 - (3 + 8)$	$=$	1
(2,4)	$8 - (3 + 1)$	$=$	4
(3,3)	$6 - (6 + 2)$	$=$	-2

we can reduce the total transportation cost by \$2. This assumes that some of the existing shipment determinations we have made already will be reduced appropriately.

Increasing the shipments through cell (3,3) actually causes a chain reaction in some of the other shipments from sources to destinations. For instance, if we increase the shipment through cell (3,3) by, say, 10 units, then we must reduce the sum of the previous shipments out of source 3 by 10 units. This is true since source 3 (that is, Los Angeles) has only 120 units available. Likewise, if we ship 10 units through cell (3,3) into destination 3 (Dallas), we must decrease the sum of the previous shipments into destination 3 by 10 units. The overall chain reaction is illustrated in Figure 7.2.

The black lines in Figure 7.2 represent shipments that currently exist; the dotted brown line represents the upcoming shipment through cell (3,3). The solid brown lines indicate the shipments that are affected by the chain reaction caused by increasing shipments through cell (3,3). The brown lines, including the dotted one, form a *closed loop*. It is only around the closed loop that adjustments need to be made when the shipment from Los Angeles to Dallas is increased. Thus, if we increase the shipment through cell (3,3), we must decrease the shipment through cell (2,3), increase the shipment through cell (2,2), and, finally, decrease the shipment through cell (3,2). These adjustments meet all demands without exceeding any of the supply available.

It is easier to determine the chain reaction that occurs whenever a nonbasic cell's shipments are increased by finding the closed

closed
loop

Figure 7.2   Graph of current solution for Faze Linear problem

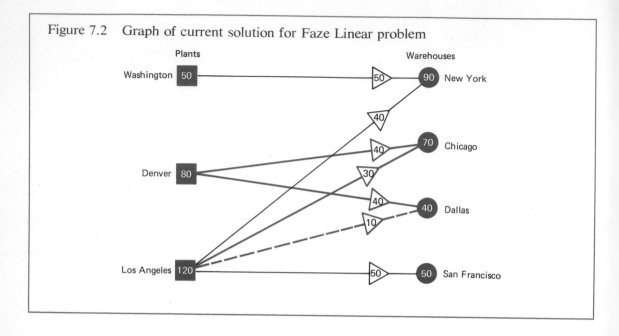

loop in the transportation tableau itself. This closed loop is established by a labeling process that assigns plus and minus signs to the appropriate cells. The general idea is to leave the nonbasic cell and make a rook's tour of the basic cells, creating a closed loop that returns to the nonbasic cell. For those of you who do not play chess, a rook's tour consists of only horizontal and vertical movements.

Only one closed loop exists in the tableau, and it can be determined and labeled by the following process: Begin by placing a plus sign (+) in the empty nonbasic cell that is to have its shipments increased. Trace a closed path consisting of basic cells (those with positive shipments) back to the nonbasic cell. The path may skip over some basic cells, but corners of the closed path must occur only at basic cells. After placing a plus sign in the nonbasic cell, alternate minus and plus signs in the basic cells that comprise the closed loop. Only label the basic cells necessary to complete the loop. Skip over any other basic cells. The number of labeled cells is always an even number.

To illustrate the process of identifying and labeling the closed loop, refer to Tableau 7.9, in which the closed loop for cell (3,3) is shown. The loop was determined by placing a plus sign in cell (3,3), a minus sign in cell (3,2), a plus in cell (2,2), and finally a minus in cell (2,3). Notice that the plus and minus signs are placed only in basic cells.

Once the closed loop has been traced, it is necessary to determine the amount of supply that can be shipped through cell (3,3). The labels on the closed loop indicate the chain reaction caused by increasing the shipment through cell (3,3). Thus, increasing shipments in cell (3,3) also increases shipments in cell (2,2) but decreases shipments through cells (2,3) and (3,2). Since no shipment can be negative, we can increase the shipment in cell (3,3) no more than the minimum of shipments in the negatively labeled cells (2,3) and (3,2). The shipment of 30 units in cell (2,3) is the smaller; thus, we can increase the shipment through cell (2,3) by 30 units.

The new solution and adjustments in shipments is shown in Tableau 7.10. Notice how the shipments in the cell labeled with pluses have been increased by 30 and the shipments in the cells labeled with minuses have been decreased by 30. Effectively, variable x_{33} has entered the solution at a value of 30, and variable x_{23} has become

Tableau 7.9   Closed loop for cell (3,3)

From	To	New York $K_1 = 8$	Chicago $K_2 = 4$	Dallas $K_3 = 2$	San Francisco $K_4 = 1$	Supply
$R_1 = 0$	Washington	8 50	9	11	16	50
$R_2 = 3$	Denver	12	7 40	5 40	8	80
$R_3 = 6$	Los Angeles	14 40	10 − 30	6 +	7 50	120
	Demand	90	70	40	50	250

Tableau 7.10   Second solution for Faze Linear based on closed-loop adjustments

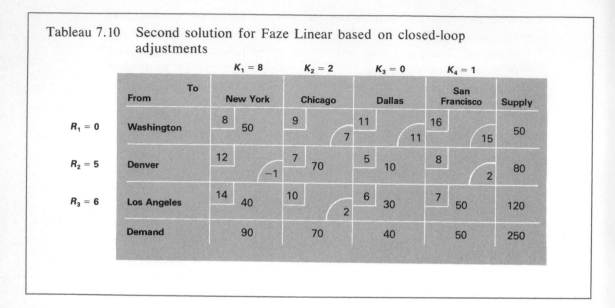

a nonbasic variable and left the solution. The total cost of the original row minimum solution was \$2,090. The total cost of the second solution obtained by the MODI method is calculated in Table 7.3. Its total cost, \$2,030, represents a savings of \$60. Coincidentally, this second solution is the same as the solution obtained by the VAM heuristic. This solution is not optimal; another iteration of the MODI method is required before optimality is achieved.

Table 7.3   Total cost of second solution

Route	Shipment	Cost per unit (\$)	Total cost (\$)
Washington/New York	50	8	400
Denver/Chicago	70	7	490
Denver/Dallas	10	5	50
Los Angeles/New York	40	14	560
Los Angeles/Dallas	30	6	180
Los Angeles/San Francisco	50	7	350
			2,030

To see where further improvements can be made, we must calculate new values of the R_i and K_j indicators. These values must satisfy equations based on the general statement in [7.2] for the new solution. Since cells (1,1), (2,2), (2,3), (3,1), (3,3), and (3,4) are basic, we obtain the system

$$R_1 + K_1 = 8$$
$$R_2 + K_2 = 7$$
$$R_2 + K_3 = 5$$
$$R_3 + K_1 = 14$$
$$R_3 + K_3 = 6$$
$$R_3 + K_4 = 7$$

Setting R_1 equal to zero and substituting, we obtain $K_1 = 8$, $R_3 = 6$, $K_3 = 0$, $K_4 = 1$, $R_2 = 5$, and $K_2 = 2$ as the solution to the foregoing system of equations.

Now we can use the R_i and K_j values with expression 7.9 to calculate the opportunity cost of increasing the shipment in any nonbasic cell. The calculations of the $c_{ij} - (R_i + K_j)$ values are shown in Table 7.4, as are the R_i and K_j values and opportunity costs. Since nonbasic cell (2,1) is the only cell with negative opportunity costs, we must increase shipments through it to make any improvements.

The next step is to determine the closed loop for cell (2,1) so that the appropriate shipment adjustments can be made. Tableau 7.11 shows the part of the second-solution tableau that contains the closed loop. The loop was traced by assigning a plus to cell

Table 7.4 $c_{ij} - (R_i + K_j)$ values for Faze Linear third solution

Nonbasic cell	$c_{ij} - (R_i + K_j)$		Opportunity cost
(1,2)	$9 - (0 + 2)$	=	7
(1,3)	$11 - (0 + 0)$	=	11
(1,4)	$16 - (0 + 1)$	=	15
(2,1)	$12 - (5 + 8)$	=	−1
(2,4)	$8 - (5 + 1)$	=	2
(3,2)	$10 - (6 + 2)$	=	2

Tableau 7.11   Closed loop for cell (2,1)

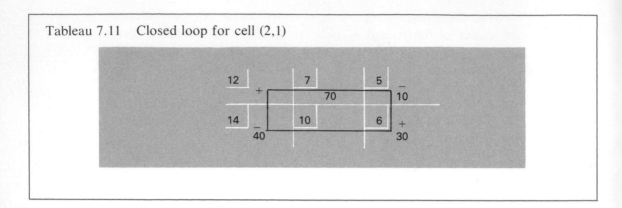

(2,1), skipping basic cell (2,2) because it is not needed, assigning a minus to cell (2,3), a plus to cell (3,3), and finally a minus to cell (3,1). The smallest shipment in a cell with a minus label is 10 units in cell (2,3). Thus, we adjust the labeled cells by 10 units and obtain the third solution in Tableau 7.12.

To find out whether this third solution is optimal, again we calculate the R_i and K_j indicators. Since cells (1,1), (2,1), (2,2), (3,1), (3,3), and (3,4) are basic, we obtain the equations

Tableau 7.12   Third solution (optimal) for Faze Linear problem

		$K_1 = 8$ New York	$K_2 = 3$ Chicago	$K_3 = 0$ Dallas	$K_4 = 1$ San Francisco	Supply
	From \ To					
$R_1 = 0$	Washington	8 50	9	11	16	50
$R_2 = 4$	Denver	12 10	7 70	5	8	80
$R_3 = 6$	Los Angeles	14 30	10	6 40	7 50	120
	Demand	90	70	40	50	250

Table 7.5 $c_{ij} - (R_i + K_j)$ values for Faze Linear optimal solution

Nonbasic cell	$c_{ij} - (R_i + K_j)$		Opportunity cost
(1,2)	$9 - (0 + 3)$	=	7
(1,3)	$11 - (0 + 0)$	=	11
(1,4)	$16 - (0 + 1)$	=	15
(2,3)	$5 - (4 + 0)$	=	−1
(2,4)	$8 - (4 + 1)$	=	3
(3,2)	$10 - (6 + 3)$	=	1

$$R_1 + K_1 = 8$$
$$R_2 + K_1 = 12$$
$$R_2 + K_2 = 7$$
$$R_3 + K_1 = 14$$
$$R_3 + K_3 = 6$$
$$R_3 + K_4 = 7$$

Setting R_1 equal to zero and backsubstituting, we obtain $K_1 = 8$, $R_2 = 4$, $K_2 = 3$, $R_3 = 6$, $K_3 = 0$, and $K_4 = 1$.

Again, we use expression 7.9 to determine the $c_{ij} - (R_i + K_j)$ opportunity costs (see Table 7.5). Since none of the opportunity costs is negative, no further improvement can be made and the third solution is optimal. Its minimum cost is calculated as $8(50) + 12(10) + 7(70) + 14(30) + 6(40) + 7(50) = \$2,020$. The optimal shipping pattern is shown in Figure 7.3.

[Summary of MODI method]

1 Generate a starting feasible solution by using a heuristic such as the row minimum rule or VAM. Make sure that the starting feasible solution contains $m + n - 1$ basic cells.

2 Compute the R_i and K_j indicator values for the current solution by using the formula $R_i + K_j = c_{ij}$ for each basic cell (i,j). Solve

Figure 7.3   Optimal shipping pattern for Faze Linear

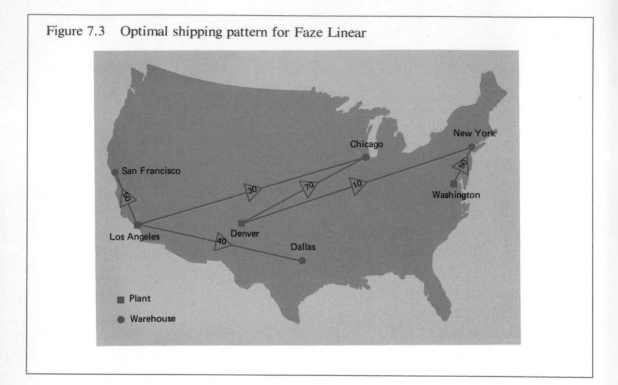

the resulting $m + n$ equations by setting R_1 equal to zero and backsubstituting for the remaining R_i and K_j values.

3 Calculate the opportunity costs of increasing shipments through each nonbasic (unused) cell using the formula $c_{ij} - (R_i + K_j) =$ opportunity cost for nonbasic cell (i,j).

4 Select the nonbasic cell with the most negative $c_{ij} - (R_i + K_j)$ value. If no nonbasic cell has a negative $c_{ij} - (R_i + K_j)$, stop, for the solution is optimal.

5 Trace the closed path for the nonbasic cell that has the most negative $c_{ij} - (R_i + K_j)$ value. Place a plus sign in this nonbasic cell and subsequently alternate minus and plus signs in labeling the basic cells around the closed loop.

6 Determine the smallest shipment Δ (the delta symbol, Δ, usually represents amount of change) in all cells with a minus label. Adjust the shipments around the closed loop by subtracting Δ from minus-labeled cells and adding Δ to all plus-labeled cells.

7 Return to step 2.

It should be noted that the MODI method can be used to maximize transportation models as well as to minimize them. The modification is the same as in the simplex method for general LP. In order to maximize, we can change the signs of the objective function and minimize, or we can choose the nonbasic cell with the most positive c_{ij} — $(R_i + K_j)$ to enter the solution; all other steps remain the same.

[Total supply and demand not equal]

In using the MODI method, we assume that total supply and demand are equal. This is generally not the case in real-world transportation applications. Usually, the problems are unbalanced in that supply exceeds demand, or vice versa. However, unbalanced transportation problems are easily balanced for the MODI method by simply adding a fictitious source or destination to absorb the excess demand or supply.

SUPPLY EXCEEDS DEMAND

Whenever supply exceeds demand, we simply add a fictitious, or *dummy*, destination whose demand equals the excess supply. Doing so artifically balances the transportation problem. To illustrate the technique, consider the Faze Linear problem with an additional 20 units of supply at the Washington plant. This makes total supply equal to 270 units, whereas total demand equals 250. Adding an additional destination is analogous to adding a slack variable in the simplex method. The cost of all shipments to the dummy destination must be zero. This is obviously the case since these shipments are never actually made. In developing a transportation tableau with excess supply, we add a dummy column with zero

dummy
destination

Tableau 7.13   Balanced tableau when supply exceeds demand

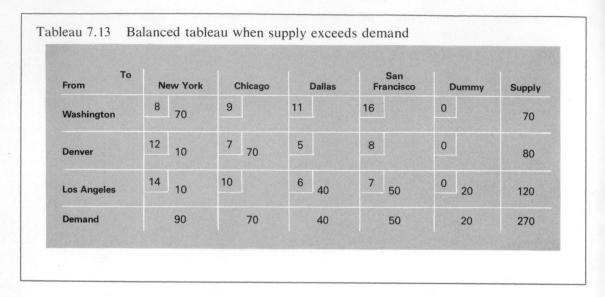

From \ To	New York	Chicago	Dallas	San Francisco	Dummy	Supply
Washington	8 — 70	9	11	16	0	70
Denver	12 — 10	7 — 70	5	8	0	80
Los Angeles	14 — 10	10	6 — 40	7 — 50	0 — 20	120
Demand	90	70	40	50	20	270

per-unit transportation costs. The optimal tableau for the Faze Linear problem with excess supply is shown in Tableau 7.13.

The solution to a transportation problem that has a dummy destination is obtained by the exact same MODI procedures. The only difference is in interpreting the optimal solution. In Tableau 7.13, we find that 20 units are allocated to cell (3,5). This simply means that these 20 units are not shipped from Los Angeles. Thus, Los Angeles is the plant that stores the excess supply. We have determined not only the optimal shipping pattern but also which plant is not utilized at full capacity.

DEMAND EXCEEDS SUPPLY

Whenever demand exceeds supply, it is, of course, impossible to meet all demand requirements. The question becomes, Which destinations shall receive shipments in order to minimize distribution of the supply that is available? The trick is similar to the case in which supply exceeds demand, except that a *dummy source* is added. Consider the Faze Linear problem with 20 additional units of demand at Dallas. Adding the dummy source to absorb the 20 extra units of demand requires an additional row in the transportation

dummy source

tableau. See Tableau 7.14 for the optimal tableau for the Faze Linear problem with excess demand.

In making accommodations for demand exceeding supply, more than one destination might fail to have all its demand requirements met. In this case, we can see in Tableau 7.14 that the 20 fictitious units at the dummy source are assigned to New York. This means that only 70 of the 90 units in demand at New York are shipped. However, the solution does allocate the 250 units of available supply at minimum transportation cost.

[Degeneracy]

Recall from Chapter 5 that degeneracy occurs whenever a basic variable assumes a zero value. In the regular simplex method, degeneracy causes no problem, but it can in the MODI method if not handled properly. The MODI method, with m sources and n destinations, requires $m + n - 1$ basic cells. If fewer than m

Tableau 7.14   Balanced tableau when demand exceeds supply

From \ To	New York	Chicago	Dallas	San Francisco	Supply
Washington	8 50	9	11	16	50
Denver	12 10	7 70	5	8	80
Los Angeles	14 10	10	6 60	7 50	120
Dummy	0 20	0	0	0	20
Demand	90	70	60	50	270

+ $n - 1$ cells are designated as basic, then the R_i and K_j values cannot be calculated and closed loops do not exist. Degeneracy is easily handled by always maintaining $m + n - 1$ basic cells even though some may have zero shipment and be degenerate. Degeneracy can arise in the following situations:

1 In determining a feasible starting solution, fewer than $m + n - 1$ cells are used.

2 In working toward optimality, the MODI method may have more than one basic cell leave the solution at an iteration. This results in fewer than $m + n - 1$ cells being basic.

In the first situation, degeneracy is easily handled by never deleting a row and a column of the transportation tableau at the same time. For instance, in using either row minimum or VAM, we may assign to a cell whose associated source has 50 units of supply and associated destination has 50 units of demand. Allocating the maximum amount (50 units) to this cell would delete its row and column at the same time. However, $m + n - 1$ cells can be preserved if the associated row is not deleted but rather has its supply adjusted to be zero! That is, we delete the column but not the row and actually allocate the zero units of supply to another cell at another step in the heuristic. This results in some cell's receiving a zero shipment, but the trick preserves the necessary number of $m + n - 1$ cells.

In the second case, degeneracy arises whenever there is more

Tableau 7.15   Degeneracy in the MODI method

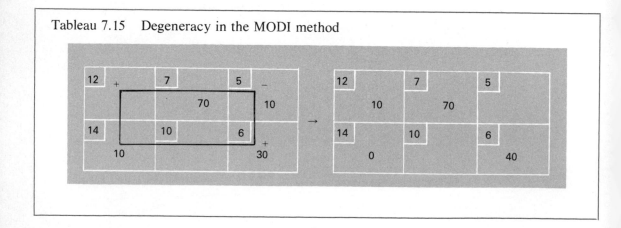

than one basic cell in the closed loop that is minus-labeled and has the minimum shipment amount. In this situation, care must be taken to delete only one of these cells. For example, consider Tableau 7.15, which is an altered version of Tableau 7.11. Both cells (2,3) and (3,1) have shipments of 10 units and are labeled with minus signs. In making the shipment adjustments, we can maintain $m + n - 1$ cells if we only delete one of these two cells, either (2,3) or (3,1). Arbitrarily deleting one and placing a zero shipment in the other maintains $m + n - 1$ basic cells. This same procedure extends to cases where more than two minus-labeled cells in the loop have the same minimal shipment.

[Further applications of transportation models]

The utility of the transportation problem is that it may be applied to more than just transportation and distribution problems. Other fruitful areas of application are production scheduling and inventory storage problems. For illustrative purposes, let us consider the following case of the El Paso Slacks Company.

[Example] The El Paso Slacks Company produces a particular pair of pants that is subject to demand fluctuations throughout the year. In order to smooth production costs, the company produces some excess during seasons when demand volume lessens and stores the pants as inventory for the season when demand is high. The production capacity is 120,000 pairs of pants per season except summer, when employee vacations reduce production capacity to 110,000 pairs. The marketing department has forecast sales for each season; figures are shown in Table 7.6. There are two types of cost, production and inventory storage. The per-unit production cost is $5 per pair of pants during the first two seasons, but inflation is expected to raise production cost to $6 in fall and winter. As inventory, the pants can be stored for several months. However, it costs $1 per quarter to store them, and due to style changes, all pants should be delivered to retailers by the end of the year. No backlogging is allowed. The company is planning ahead and

Table 7.6   El Paso slacks sales forecast data (in thousands)

Season	Forecast demand	Production capacity
Spring	110	120
Summer	90	110
Fall	140	120
Winter	115	120
	455	470

wants to know which production schedule minimizes combined production and inventory costs for the year.

The problem is legitimately modeled as a transportation problem, and the particulars are shown in Tableau 7.16. The rows of the tableau indicate quarterly production capacity, and the columns indicate quarterly demand. The costs in each cell indicate per-unit production costs plus whatever unit storage costs apply. For instance, in cell (1,4), which represents spring production for winter consump-

Tableau 7.16   El Paso Slacks Company problem

Season	Spring	Summer	Fall	Winter	Excess capacity	Production capacity
Spring	5	6	7	8	0	120
Summer		5	6	7	0	110
Fall			6	7	0	120
Winter				6	0	120
Demand	110	90	140	115	15	470

tion, the cost is $8 = $5 production cost + $3 storage cost (for three quarters). Cell (3,3) has a cost of $6 = $6 production cost + 0 storage cost. The crossed-out cells are impermissible cells because consumption cannot possibly precede production.

Solving this transportation model yields an optimum production and inventory storage schedule for the El Paso Slacks Company. The solution would be rendered in production and storage amounts rather than shipments from sources to destinations.

[The assignment problem]

The assignment problem is another special LP problem. It has a wide range of applications and, like the transportation problem, is solvable by a special-purpose algorithm that is much more efficient than the regular simplex method.

The assignment problem is closely related to the transportation problem; in fact, it is a special case of the transportation problem. However, the basic idea is to assign n single elements rather than many units from each source to destination. Some typical applications of the assignment problem include the least-cost or least-time assignment of jobs to machines, workers to tasks, salesmen to territories, and contracts to contractors. The assignment method is also used to solve subproblems of even larger and more involved management science models.

To illustrate the assignment problem, let us consider the Ace Machine Shop problem, whose data are presented in Table 7.7.

Table 7.7 Cost data ($) for assigning jobs to machines

	Machine		
Job	A	B	C
1	57	42	65
2	39	48	46
3	43	72	53

Tableau 7.17   Optimal solution for Ace Machine Shop problem

	Machine		
Job	A	B	C
1	57	**42**	65
2	39	48	**46**
3	**43**	72	53

Three jobs (1, 2, and 3) must be processed by the machine shop. Any of the three jobs can be processed on any of the three machines. However, each job is to be processed on only one machine, and each machine can be assigned only one job. Thus a solution will define a one-to-one correspondence between jobs and machines. The processing costs vary from machine to machine, as indicated in Table 7.7. The optimal solution is shown in Tableau 7.17. As indicated by the white, boldface numbers in Tableau 7.17, the least-cost solution is to assign job 1 to machine B, job 2 to machine C, and job 3 to machine A. The total cost of the assignment is $42 + 46 + 43 = \$131$.

The Ace Machine Shop problem illustrates the characteristics of assignment problems. Notice in Tableau 7.17 that precisely one assignment occurs in each row and each column. Also, the problem is square in that there are an equal number of rows and columns. We can describe the assignment model as a transportation model with an equal number of sources and destinations and all supplies and demands equal to 1.

In general, if we have n jobs to be assigned to n machines, we can state the mathematical model of the assignment problem as:

$$\text{Minimize} \quad \sum_{i=1}^{n} \sum_{j=1}^{n} c_{ij} x_{ij} \qquad [7.10]$$

subject to $\displaystyle\sum_{j=1}^{n} x_{ij} = 1, \quad i = 1,1,\ldots, n$

$$\sum_{i=1}^{n} x_{ij} = 1, \quad j = 1,2,\ldots, n$$

$x_{ij} \geq 0 \qquad$ for all i and j

where c_{ij} equals the cost of assigning job i to machine j. In solving the assignment model, n of the x_{ij} variables are in solution at a value of 1 and all other x_{ij} equal 0.

The assignment model is a special case of the transportation model; this can be seen by comparing systems 7.1 and 7.10. The assignment problem can be solved by using a transportation method such as the MODI method. However, the resulting solution would be highly degenerate (it would contain $n - 1$ degenerate cells), and even faster and more efficient techniques are available for solving assignment problems.

THE HUNGARIAN METHOD

The Hungarian method for solving the assignment problem is named in honor of the Hungarian mathematician, D. König, who proved a theorem required for its development. Our version of this method can be calculated by hand, and it may seem rather simplistic. But properly executed, the Hungarian method yields optimal solutions to the assignment problem. Our procedure is based on a mathematically proven algorithm for arriving at an optimal solution.

The method is founded upon the concept of opportunity losses. You have encountered opportunity losses before in calculations for the VAM heuristic. In the assignment method, the optimal solution incurs zero opportunity loss. Any other solution with a higher cost incurs an opportunity loss that is equal to its increase in cost over the minimum cost obtainable in the optimal solution. The basic idea in the Hungarian method is to avoid opportunity losses.

A fundamental principle underlying the Hungarian method is that a constant may be subtracted from any row or column in the assignment cost tableau without changing the optimal assignments. Changing the costs in such a manner changes the cost of the solution, of course, but not the actual assignments.

To develop the Hungarian method, let us consider the 4 $\times$ 4

Tableau 7.18   Contract bid amounts (in thousands of dollars) for Research & Development Corporation

	Project			
Bidder	1	2	3	4
A	20	36	31	17
B	24	34	40	12
C	22	40	38	18
D	36	39	35	16

assignment problem of the Research & Development Corporation, which is subcontracting four energy-related projects to four independent bidders. For political reasons, each of the bidders has been promised one project. The management at Research & Development wants to minimize the total expenditure for contracts. In Tableau 7.18, the bid amounts are indicated.

The Hungarian method has three basic steps: The first is to calculate an assignment tableau of opportunity losses; the second step is to determine whether an optimal assignment can be made. If an optimal assignment cannot be made, then we must revise the opportunity loss tableau and return to the second step. We repeat steps 2 and 3 until an optimum is achieved.

In solving the 4 × 4 assignment problem for the Research & Development Corporation, we must first calculate the opportunity loss tableau. We make use of the principle that subtracting a constant from any row or column does not change the location of the optimal assignments. In calculating the total opportunity loss tableau, we first calculate row opportunity losses, then column opportunity losses. The row opportunity losses are calculated by subtracting the least cost in each row from all other costs in that row. For instance, in Tableau 7.18, the lowest cost in row 1 is 17. Thus, making an assignment in cell (1,4) incurs zero opportunity loss.

Tableau 7.19   Row reduction of Research & Development tableau

	Project				Least cost subtracted from row
Bidder	1	2	3	4	
A	3	19	14	0	17
B	12	22	28	0	12
C	4	22	20	0	18
D	20	23	19	0	16

However, since cell (1,1) has a cost of 20, an assignment in cell (1,1) incurs an opportunity loss of $20 - 17 = 3$. Subtracting the lowest cost in a particular row from the other costs in that row yields at least one zero-cost cell in each row. This step is called a row reduction and is shown in Tableau 7.19. The row reduction does not change the solution to the problem, only the costs in the assignment tableau.

The next step is to perform a column reduction. This involves subtracting the lowest number in each column from all other numbers in that column. For example, Research & Development Corporation incurs a zero opportunity loss in assigning project 1 to bidder A. Referring to Tableau 7.19, we can see that the opportunity loss is $12 - 3 = 9$ if the assignment is made to cell (2,1) (that is, if project 1 is assigned to bidder B). Performing the column reduction for each column from Tableau 7.19, we obtain the total opportunity loss tableau in Tableau 7.20.

The total opportunity loss tableau has the same assignment solution as the original problem, and it also has a zero in each row and each column. The zero-cost cells show where an assignment can be made that incurs no opportunity loss. An optimal solution is found whenever all assignments can be made in unique cells that have zero opportunity losses. Sometimes this is possible after determining the total opportunity loss tableau. However, this is

Tableau 7.20   Total opportunity loss tableau for Research &
Development Corporation

Bidder	Project 1	2	3	4	
A	0	0	0	0	
B	9	3	14	0	
C	1	3	6	0	
D	17	4	5	0	Least cost
	3	19	14	0	subtracted ← from column

not the case in Tableau 7.20, for only two assignments can be
made in zero-cost cells.

We need a systematic procedure for determining whether an
optimal solution has been found. One such procedure entails crossing
out all zero costs by drawing as few horizontal and vertical lines
as possible through the assignment tableau. If the number of lines
necessary to accomplish this is less than the number of rows or
columns in the assignment tableau, the problem is not optimal and
the total opportunity cost tableau must be revised further. If,
however, n lines in an $(n \times n)$ assignment problem are required
to cross out all zero costs, then the problem is solved and optimal
assignments can be made. The only weakness in this procedure
is that it depends upon human judgment for determining the minimum
number of lines.

This test for optimality is applied to the total opportunity loss
tableau (Tableau 7.20). Only two lines are required (as is shown
in Tableau 7.21) to cover all zero costs. Since the problem has
four rows, an assignment is not yet possible.

The next step is to revise the opportunity loss tableau in order
to generate more zero-cost cells without altering the solution to
the original problem. We do this in the following way: (1) We select

Tableau 7.21   Crossing out all zero costs with only two lines

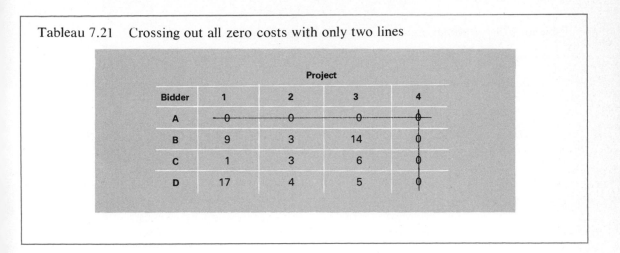

Bidder	Project 1	Project 2	Project 3	Project 4
A	0	0	0	0
B	9	3	14	0
C	1	3	6	0
D	17	4	5	0

the smallest number in the tableau not covered by a straight line and subtract this number from each number not covered by a straight line; (2) we add this smallest number to each cost that lies at the intersection of two straight lines. Note that costs covered by only one line are unchanged by this procedure.

In Tableau 7.21, we find that the smallest number not covered by a straight line is 1. Subtracting 1 from each cost not covered by a line and adding 1 to the point of intersection gives us the situation shown in Tableau 7.22.

Tableau 7.22   Revised opportunity loss tableau

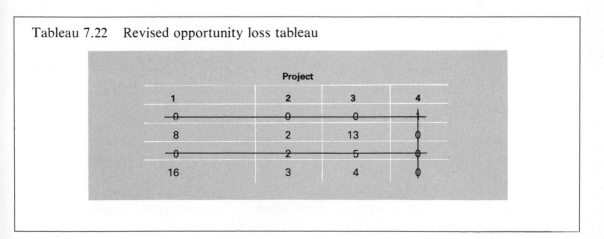

Project 1	Project 2	Project 3	Project 4
0	0	0	1
8	2	13	0
0	2	5	0
16	3	4	0

Tableau 7.23 Optimal opportunity loss tableau

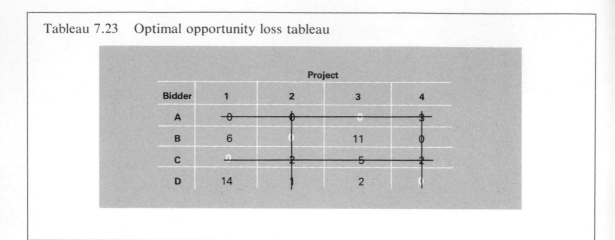

It is possible to cross out all zero costs in Tableau 7.22 with only three lines; thus, we must revise the opportunity loss tableau further. The smallest cost not covered is a 2; subtracting this from each cost not covered by a line and adding it to each point of intersection, we obtain the facts of Tableau 7.23.

Since four lines are required to cross out all zero costs, we can make an optimal assignment. The optimal assignment is to assign project 1 to bidder C, 2 to B, 3 to A, and 4 to D. The solution is indicated by the white, boldface numbers in Tableau 7.23. To calculate the total cost of the optimal solution, we refer to the original costs from Tableau 7.18 and calculate that data shown in Table 7.8.

Although we have determined that an optimal assignment can be made, it may not be obvious where these assignments should occur. A systematic approach to making the assignments is called for. One procedure is to find a row or column with only one zero-cost cell and no previous assignments. An assignment must be made in this cell. For example, column 3 in Tableau 7.23 has only one zero; it appears in cell (A,3). Since no more assignments can be made in column 3 or row A, we draw a line through column 3 and row A. Then, we again seek a row or column with a single zero and find row D. We make an assignment in cell (D,4) and

Table 7.8   Cost (in thousands of dollars) of Research &
Development Corporation optimal solution

Assignment	Cost ($)
1 to C	22
2 to B	34
3 to A	31
4 to D	16
Total cost	103

draw lines through column 4 and row D. The procedure is repeated until all assignments are made. If the remaining rows or columns all have two or more zero-cost cells, an assignment can be made in any zero-cost cell that has not been covered by a straight line.

SUMMARY OF THE HUNGARIAN METHOD

1 Determine the total opportunity loss tableau:

a Select the least cost in each row and subtract it from each cost in that row.

b Using the row-reduced cost tableau that has been generated, select the least cost in each column and subtract it from every cost in that column.

2 Determine whether an optimal assignment can be made by drawing the minimum number of horizontal and vertical lines through the total opportunity loss tableau that will cover all zero-cost cells. If the number of lines required is less than the number of rows (columns), go to step 3. Otherwise, stop and make the optimal assignments.

3 Revise the total opportunity loss tableau:

a Select the smallest number not covered by a line and stubtract this number from every number not covered by a line.

b Add this same number to any number at the intersection of two lines. Go to step 2.

Note that the Hungarian method can also be used to maximize objectives in assignment problems. To accomplish this, we simply change the signs of the profit coefficients and minimize; or, alternatively, we may calculate the total opportunity loss tableau based on the largest profit, rather than the lowest cost, in each row or column.

[Summary]

Network models are very important to, and have widespread applications among, management science techniques. Transportation and assignment models are linear network models with a special structure that considerably simplifies their computation.

Transportation problems can be solved by heuristics methods, such as row minimum or VAM (Vogel's approximation method), that are fast and yield good, but not necessarily optimal, solutions. The MODI method can be used to take a starting feasible solution from row minimum or VAM and improve it to optimality. Degeneracy is easily handled in the MODI method by ensuring that the tableau has $m + n - 1$ basic cells at all times. An important characteristic of transportation-type models is that integer (whole number) data yield integer solutions. Applications other than physical distribution exist for transportation models; among these are production scheduling and inventory storage problems.

The assignment problem is a special case of the transportation problem. The Hungarian method is an efficient procedure for determining optimal solutions to assignment problems. With minor modifications, the Hungarian method can be used to maximize, as well as minimize, assignment objectives.

[Bibliography]

Charnes, Abraham and W. W. Cooper, *Management Models and Industrial Applications of Linear Programming*, Vol. 1. New York: John Wiley & Sons, Inc., 1961.

Daellenbach, Hans G., and Earl J. Bell, *Users' Guide to Linear Programming*. Englewood Cliffs, N.J.: Prentice-Hall, Inc., 1970.

Gupta, Skiv K. and John M. Cozzolino, *Fundamentals of Operations Research for Management*. San Francisco, Calif.: Holden-Day, Inc., 1975.

Hillier, Frederick S. and Gerald J. Lieberman, *Introduction to Operations Research*. San Francisco, Calif.: Holden-Day, Inc., 1974.

Hu, T. C., *Integer Programming and Network Flows*. Reading, Mass.: Addison-Wesley Publishing Co., Inc., 1969.

Kwak, N. K., *Mathematical Programming with Business Applications*. New York: McGraw-Hill Book Company, 1973.

Loomba, N. P. and E. Turban, *Applied Programming for Management*. New York: Holt, Rhinehart, & Winston, Inc., 1974.

Di Roccaferrera, Giuseppe M., *Introduction to Linear Programming Processes*. Cincinnati, Ohio: South-Western Publishing Company, 1967.

Wagner, Harvey M., *Principles of Management Science: With Application to Executive Decisions*. Englewood Cliffs, N.J.: Prentice-Hall, Inc., 1975.

[Review questions]

1 Explain why transportation and assignment models are part of the category of network models.

2 What are the advantages of using special-purpose algorithms to solve transportation and assignment problems?

3 What are the advantages and disadvantages of using heuristics versus optimization techniques?

4 Why would you expect VAM usually to yield a better heuristic solution than the row minimum method?

5 Briefly discuss the theoretical basis of VAM.

6 List some applications of transportation models other than distribution of a commodity from plant to market.

7 Specifically, how does the assignment math model differ from the transportation math model?

8 How is degeneracy handled in the MODI method?

9 Discuss whether the Hungarian method is a heuristic or an optimization technique.

10 List some applications of the assignment model.

[Problems]

7.1 The P & R Company distributes its product from three plants to four regional warehouses. The monthly supplies and demands along with per-unit transportation costs are given below. Using the row minimum heuristic, find a feasible shipping pattern and total transportation cost.

From plant	To warehouse 1	2	3	4	Supply
1	2	12	6	10	20
2	14	6	2	12	10
3	18	8	10	8	25
Demand	11	13	17	14	55

7.2 Use VAM to solve problem 7.1.

7.3 Use the row minimum starting solution and the MODI method to determine an optimal solution to problem 7.1.

7.4 The Reasor Department Store chain has excess stock of a particular product at two stores, and shortages at four others. The objective is to redistribute the stock at minimum transportation cost. Given the following stock and cost information, find the optimal distribution pattern at minimum cost.

Store	Excess	Shortage
1	50	
2	75	
3		20
4		30
5		45
6		30

Cost data($)

	To store			
From store	3	4	5	6
1	7	3	5	8
2	6	4	2	9

7.5 Solve the El Paso Slacks Company's production scheduling problem in Tableau 7.15 by the MODI method.

7.6 The Continental Trailer Rental Company has a problem in trying to relocate rented trailers. Currently, its supply exceeds the demand, and it is necessary to relocate trailers at minimum transportation cost. There are surplus trailers at locations 1, 2, 3, and 4 whereas trailers are in demand at locations 5, 6, and 7. The relevant data are given below. Determine the optimum relocation of trailers.

	Location						
Trailer status	1	2	3	4	5	6	7
Surplus	6	7	8	3			
Shortage					5	4	9

Cost ($) per trailer transported

	To		
From	5	6	7
1	8	11	8
2	12	10	6
3	15	7	9
4	12	12	7

7.7 Consider a variation of the production/distribution example of Chapter 3. In this problem, it is necessary to address production, as well as transportation, costs in the transportation model. Assume that two plants have production capacities of 2,600 and 1,800, respectively. The three warehouses have demands of 1,500 2,000, and 900. The product is produced at plant 1 at a per-unit cost of $1.50, whereas the per-unit cost at plant 2 is $2. Transportation costs are given in the table. Set up and solve a transportation model that determines the amount to produce at each plant and the resulting shipping pattern.

From plant	To warehouse 1	To warehouse 2	To warehouse 3	Supply
1	$.30	$.50	$.80	2,600
2	$.70	$.20	$.40	1,800
Demand	1,500	2,000	900	4,400

7.8 The American Products Corporation must decide on its production schedule for the next four months. It has contracted to supply a special part for the months of October, November, December, and January at the rates of 12,000, 10,000 15,000, and 17,000 units, respectively. American can produce each part at a cost of $6 during regular time or $9 during overtime. Each month, American has a production capacity of 10,000 units during regular time and 6,000 units during overtime. The part can be stored at a cost of $2 per month; however, there is zero inventory on hand at the beginning of October and there must be zero inventory at the end of January. American can thus overproduce in some months and store the excess to help meet future demand in other months. Construct a transportation model (tableau) to solve American's production scheduling and inventory storage problem. *Hint*: Define the sources as the modes of production in each month, and define the destinations as the demand required during each month.

7.9 Three jobs must be processed. There are three machines available, but each job must be done on only one machine. Jobs may not be split between machines. The cost of processing each job on each machine is given in the table that follows. Determine the minimum-cost assignment for each job.

Job	X	Machine Y	Z
1	10	16	8
2	8	6	4
3	16	12	8

7.10 Is it actually possible to ship more for less? Assuming no quantity discounts and the same transportation costs, is there ever a situation in which shipping more units will lower costs? Consider the following 3 × 4 transportation problem with optimal solution as shown in the first tableau. Suppose we add an additional unit of supply to source 2 and an additional unit of demand to destination 1. The results are shown in the second tableau.

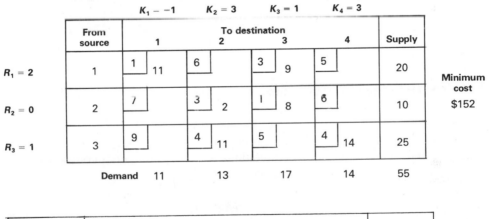

First tableau: $K_1 = -1$, $K_2 = 3$, $K_3 = 1$, $K_4 = 3$

From source	1	2	3	4	Supply
1 ($R_1 = 2$)	1 / 11	6	3 / 9	5	20
2 ($R_2 = 0$)	7	3 / 2	1 / 8	6	10
3 ($R_3 = 1$)	9	4 / 11	5	4 / 14	25
Demand	11	13	17	14	55

Minimum cost $152

Second tableau:

From source	1	2	3	4	Supply
1	1	6	3	5	20
2	7	3	1	6	11
3	9	4	5	4	25
Demand	12	13	17	14	56

Mimimum cost $151?

Obviously, shipping the additional unit through cell (2,1) raises costs by $7. Without solving the problem from scratch, can you find an alternative shipping schedule that will lower costs?

7.11 The Missan Sports Car Company produces several lines of automobiles, among which is its super racer, the 290Z. These specialty cars are hand-assembled at each of four plants, in Boston, Cleveland, Denver, and Detroit. Missan currently has custom orders for one 290Z at Chicago, Wichita, Tulsa, and Dallas. Each plant currently has one model ready for shipping. The transportation cost data are given in the table.

    a Which method is best for solving this problem?
    b Determine the optimal solution.

	Transportation cost ($) per 290Z			
From	To Chicago	Wichita	Tulsa	Dallas
Boston	130	240	250	300
Cleveland	40	210	220	270
Denver	150	110	115	125
Detroit	35	190	200	250

7.12 The Concrete Construction Company has requested bids for subcontracts on five different projects. Five companies have responded; their bids are represented below. Determine the minimum cost assignment of subcontracts to bidders, assuming that each bidder can receive only one contract. If each bidder could receive any number of contracts, then what would be the optimal assignment?

	Bid amount ($)				
Bidder	1	2	Project 3	4	5
1	41,000	72,000	39,000	52,000	25,000
2	22,000	29,000	49,000	65,000	81,000
3	27,000	39,000	60,000	51,000	40,000
4	45,000	50,000	48,000	52,000	37,000
5	29,000	40,000	45,000	26,000	30,000

7.13 The TDW Production Company is unable to meet its increased yearly demand because of production capacities. It is thinking about building a new factory to meet this new demand and also decrease transportation cost. The current production and distribution system is summarized below. The costs in the table indicate per-unit transportation costs. The proposed new factory, C, would have a capacity of 2,000 and would have transportation costs of $3, $2.50, $4, and $2 to warehouses 1, 2, 3, and 4, respectively.

| Factory | Warehouse | | | | Factory capacity |
	1	2	3	4	
A	$2.90	$2.60	$3.50	$4.00	2,500
B	3.10	3.30	3.70	3.00	1,500
					4,000
Demand	1,000	1,500	2,000	500	5,000

The company is currently losing $20 per unit on unsatisfied demand, since this is the profit they net on each unit that is sold (not including transportation costs). However, the new factory would cost $21,000 per year over the life of the factory. Evaluate TDW's proposal to add the new factory.

7.14 The Psychological Testing Agency has recently tested seven applicants for five jobs that are available at the Coldman Company. Each job has a primary skill, and Coldman's objective is to pick the five applicants whose aptitude test scores will maximize total performance. Only one worker can be assigned to only one job. The aptitude test scores are listed below. Determine the five best applicants for the five jobs.

| Applicant | Job | | | | |
	1	2	3	4	5
1	95	110	103	115	98
2	89	95	100	87	92
3	120	132	118	128	121
4	107	119	112	108	96
5	75	83	99	100	85
6	113	115	98	111	120
7	102	73	95	70	94

[South American Airways case]

South American Airways is a nonscheduled cargo airline that operates in five cities in the United States and throughout Central and South America. The airline operates a fleet of 12 aircraft consisting of four C-46s, two DC-4s, and six DC-6s. These aircraft are used to pick up and deliver cargo whenever orders are received from customers.

One of the major problems facing the traffic manager of South American Airways is that of scheduling the pick-up and delivery of cargo. On a particular day, the traffic manager receives the information in Table 1 showing the present location, final destination and weight (in pounds) of 12 customer orders that are to be shipped by the airline within the next 24 hours.

Table 1 Customer order data

Present location	Final destination	Weight (in pounds)
Atlanta	San Juan	25,000
Caracas	Santiago	10,000
Havana	Miami	10,000
Houston	San Juan	15,000
Mobile	Rio de Janeiro	10,000
Monterrey	Mexico City	15,000
New Orleans	Quito	20,000
Rio de Janeiro	New Orleans	15,000
San Salvador	New Orleans	10,000
Sao Paulo	Buenos Aires	10,000
Santiago	Caracas	10,000
Tampa	Guatemala City	20,000

From *Introduction to Linear Programming: Methods and Cases* by Thomas H. Naylor, Eugene T. Byrne, and John M. Vernon. © 1971 by Wadsworth Publishing Company, Inc., Belmont, California 94002. Reprinted by permission of the publisher.

The location of each of the airline's 12 aircraft, by type, is shown below in Table 2.

Table 2   Aircraft location

City	Type of aircraft
Bogota	C–46
Buenos Aires	DC–6
Caracas	C–46
Guatemala City	DC–4
Mexico City	DC–4
Miami	DC–6
New Orleans	C–46
New Orleans	DC–6
Rio de Janeiro	C–46
Rio de Janeiro	DC–6
San Juan	DC–6
San Salvador	DC–6

Table 3 indicates for each of the cargo loads available the maximum ranges (in miles) that can be flown before refueling is required on each of the three different types of aircraft. The data indicates that the maximum loads for the C–46, DC–4, and DC–6 are 15,000 pounds, 20,000 pounds, and 25,000 pounds respectively.

Table 3   Aircraft range per cargo weight

Cargo weight (lb)	C–46	DC–4	DC–6
Empty	1,200	2,800	3,200
10,000	900	2,800	3,200
15,000	200	2,800	3,200
20,000	—	1,200	3,200
25,000	—	—	1,000

The optimum cruising speeds for the airline's aircraft are shown in Table 4.

Table 4   Optimum cruising speed

Aircraft	Optimum speed
C–46	170 mph
DC–4	200 mph
DC–6	300 mph

Table 5 indicates (1) the approximate distances (in miles) between the present location of aircraft and the present location of cargo orders, and (2) the approximate distances between the present locations of cargo orders and the final destination of cargo.

The 21 airports mentioned in Table 5 can accommodate all types of piston-engine aircraft including the three types of aircraft that South American Airways presently uses. In addition to these airports there are eight other airports in the Latin American area the airline serves that have runways of sufficient lengths for the company's aircraft to land and take off safely. These are: San Jose, Managua, Panama, Teguci, Lima, Kingston, Ciudad Trujillo, and Belem. Any of these 27 airports may be used for intermediate stops or flights requiring refueling operations. Although DC–4s and DC–6s can land only at the aforementioned airports, C–46s can land almost anywhere, provided there is at least 2,000 feet of runway. Hence, the number of possibilities for C–46 intermediate landings is extremely large. (Intermediate airports may be determined from a world atlas or from material published by the Civil Aeronautics Board.)

The airline has computed the average operating costs per hour for each of its three types of aircraft. These data are tabulated in Table 6 for fully loaded aircraft.

The operating costs for an empty aircraft are identical to those of a loaded aircraft with the exception of the costs of fuel and oil (see Table 7).

Landing charges vary rather widely among airports and are usually a function of the weight of the particular aircraft in conjunction

Table 5 Present location and destination distance data (in miles)

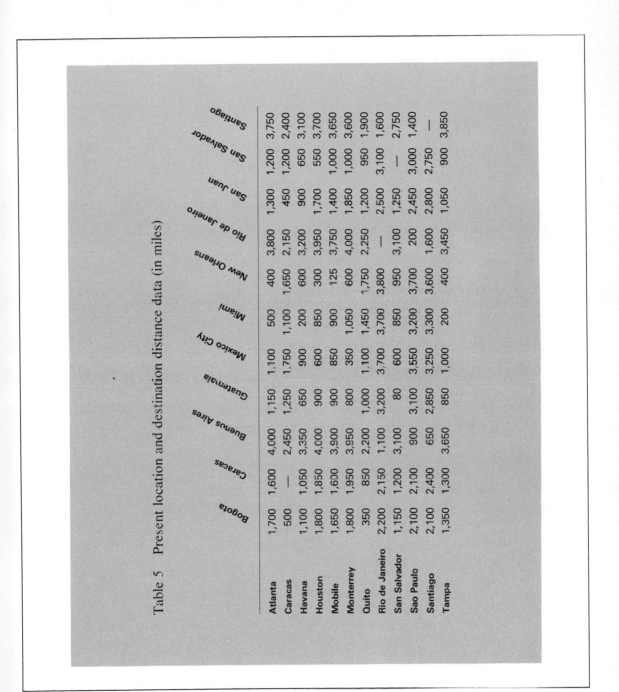

	Bogota	Caracas	Buenos Aires	Guatemala	Mexico City	Miami	New Orleans	Rio de Janeiro	San Juan	San Salvador	Santiago
Atlanta	1,700	1,600	4,000	1,150	1,100	500	400	3,800	1,300	1,200	3,750
Caracas	500	—	2,450	1,250	1,750	1,100	1,650	2,150	450	1,200	2,400
Havana	1,100	1,050	3,350	650	900	200	600	3,200	900	650	3,100
Houston	1,800	1,850	4,000	900	600	850	300	3,950	1,700	550	3,700
Mobile	1,650	1,600	3,900	900	850	900	125	3,750	1,400	1,000	3,650
Monterrey	1,800	1,950	3,950	800	350	1,050	600	4,000	1,850	1,000	3,600
Quito	350	850	2,200	1,000	1,100	1,450	1,750	2,250	1,200	950	1,900
Rio de Janeiro	2,200	2,150	1,100	3,200	3,700	3,700	3,800	—	2,500	3,100	1,600
San Salvador	1,150	1,200	3,100	80	600	850	950	3,100	1,250	—	2,750
Sao Paulo	2,100	2,100	900	3,100	3,550	3,200	3,700	200	2,450	3,000	1,400
Santiago	2,100	2,400	650	2,850	3,250	3,300	3,600	1,600	2,800	2,750	—
Tampa	1,350	1,300	3,650	850	1,000	200	400	3,450	1,050	900	3,850

Table 6   Average operating costs ($) per hour

Costs	C–46	DC–4	DC–6
Crew salaries	23	23	30
Crew expenses	3	3	3
Fuel	40	50	80
Oil	2	2	3
Hull insurance	2	4	8
Liability insurance	1	1	1
Maintenance			
Labor	20	30	45
Materials	5	10	15
Engine overhaul	20	25	40
Air frame overhaul	3	5	10

with a multiplicity of other variables. The approximate landing charges[1] for the major airports in Latin America are shown in Table 8 for each of the airline's three types of aircraft. The average landing fee for C–46 aircraft in Latin America (including airports whose runways are less than 3,000 feet in length) is around $20.

[Case problems]

1 Assuming that the cost data supplied are correct, how would you propose to assign the 12 aircraft to the 12 cargo flights?

2 Assuming you had an atlas at your disposal, how would you develop each entry in the matrix of transportation costs?

3 Using data that have been supplied by your instructor or the data you have developed yourself, determine an optimal solution to the South American Airways problem.

[1] Although these landing charges are fictitious, they do reflect the approximate range of actual landing charges.

Table 7   Fuel and oil costs ($)

Costs	C–46	DC–4	DC–6
Fuel	35.00	45.00	75.00
Oil	2.00	1.75	2.50

Table 8   Landing charges ($)

Airports	C–46	DC–4	DC–6
Atlanta	25	40	75
Belem	15	30	50
Bogota	20	30	35
Caracas	30	35	50
Ciudad Trujillo	40	55	70
Buenos Aires	30	40	60
Guatemala City	45	65	90
Havana	45	65	90
Houston	20	20	30
Kingston	25	35	50
Lima	25	30	40
Managua	30	50	60
Mexico City	15	20	25
Miami	20	30	40
Mobile	20	25	35
Monterrey	10	15	20
New Orleans	30	45	80
Panama	15	20	30
Quito	10	10	15
Rio de Janeiro	30	35	50
San Juan	15	25	25
San Jose	20	25	25
San Salvador	20	20	30
Santiago	20	30	40
Sao Paulo	25	25	35
Tampa	30	40	65
Teguci	25	30	45

[Bay Area Bakery Company case]

PROPOSAL TO BUILD A NEW BAKERY

Bay Area Bakery Company[1] was a regional baker and distributor of bread, and operated six bakeries shown on the map in Figure 1. The manager of transportation and customer service for Bay Area Bakery Company was asked to prepare a report outlining the effect of the proposed San Jose, California, baking facility on the company's physical distribution system. The problem centered around the fact that marketing territories served by the Santa Cruz and Stockton bakeries had increased rapidly in population, necessitating consideration for locating and equipping a new baking plant at San Jose.

Varying costs of labor, ingredients, and operation affected the total cost of baking a standard quantity of bread at each of the locations. This average cost for each of the bakeries is shown in Table 1, along with the daily capacity at each location. The full line of the company's goods was baked at each of the six locations.

Bay Area sold its products at an average delivered price of $3.00 per cwt. and maintained uniform delivered prices on comparable quantity orders throughout its marketing territory. Average daily sales from each bakery for each major center of consumption are shown in Table 2.

To control physical distributing costs closely and to maintain tight control over the freshness of baked items, Bay Area operated its own fleet of privately owned local delivery trucks and over-the-road

James L. Heskett, Lewis M. Schneider, Robert M. Ivie, and Nicholas A. Glaskowsky, Jr., *Case Problems in Business Logistics.* Copyright © 1973 by The Ronald Press Company, New York.

[1] Names have been disguised.

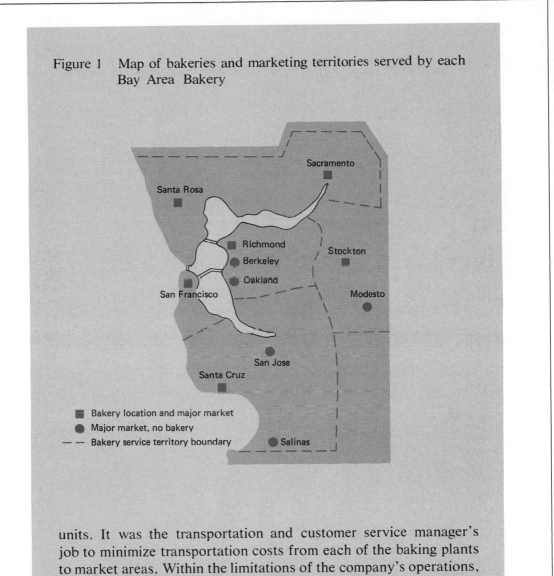

Figure 1   Map of bakeries and marketing territories served by each Bay Area Bakery

units. It was the transportation and customer service manager's job to minimize transportation costs from each of the baking plants to market areas. Within the limitations of the company's operations, he had achieved levels of costs shown in Table 2. He had also prepared an analysis of projected delivery costs between all company

Table 1 Baking costs and capacities, Bay Area Bakery Company bakeries

Location	Baking cost (per cwt.)	Daily baking capacity (in cwt)*
Santa Rosa	$19	500
Sacramento	$17	1,000
Richmond	$16	2,700
San Francisco	$17	2,000
Stockton	$18	500
Santa Cruz	$21	800

*Current value of each plant was roughly estimated at $300 per unit of daily capacity (cwt.).

Table 2 Current average daily sales, production costs, and transportation costs, Bay Area Bakery Company (by bakery and major market)*

Major market	Bakery of origin	Quantity (in cwt)	Production costs ($)	Transportation costs ($)
Santa Rosa	Santa Rosa	300	5,700	600
Sacramento	Sacramento	500	8,500	750
Richmond	Richmond	600	9,600	600
Berkeley	Richmond	400	6,400	400
Oakland	Richmond	1,100	17,600	1,320
San Francisco	San Francisco	1,300	22,100	1,300
San Jose	Santa Cruz	600	12,600	1,260
Santa Cruz	Santa Cruz	100	2,100	200
Salinas	Santa Cruz	100	2,100	280
Stockton	Stockton	400	7,200	600
Modesto	Stockton	100	1,800	260
	Total	5,500	95,700	7,570

*Bakeries operated approximately 300 days per year.

Table 3   Estimated delivery costs* ($) between bakeries and customers, Bay Area Bakery Company (per cwt)

	Plants						
	Santa Rosa	Sacramento	Richmond	San Francisco	Stockton	Santa Cruz	San Jose†
Santa Rosa	2.00	4.40	3.20	3.20	4.20	4.80	4.20
Sacramento	3.90	1.50	2.90	3.60	2.50	4.50	3.90
Richmond	2.00	2.40	1.00	1.40	2.60	2.60	2.00
Berkeley	2.00	2.40	1.00	1.40	2.60	2.60	2.00
Oakland	2.20	2.60	1.20	1.20	2.60	2.40	1.80
San Francisco	2.20	2.80	1.40	1.00	2.80	2.60	2.00
San Jose	3.70	3.90	2.50	2.50	2.90	2.10	1.50
Santa Cruz	4.80	5.00	3.60	3.60	4.00	2.00	2.60
Salinas	5.60	5.60	4.20	4.40	4.60	2.80	3.20
Stockton	3.70	2.50	3.10	3.10	1.50	3.50	2.90
Modesto	4.80	3.60	4.00	4.00	2.60	4.20	3.60

*Delivery costs are influenced primarily by (1) the distance of the market area from the bakery, and (2) the distance between deliveries in the market area.
†Proposed plant.

baking facilities and market areas, as shown in Table 3. Included in this projection were those costs of delivery which could be expected between the proposed plant at San Jose and other market areas.

A major reason for the suggested new baking plant at San Jose was the especially rapidly growing market which the area represented. It was expected that this market would double in the next 5 years, compared to an expected 10 percent increase in other markets (except less than 10 percent in San Francisco) during the same period. Also, the inefficiencies involved in serving San Jose from the Santa

Table 4   Five-year   projected   supply   pattern,   Bay   Area   Bakery
              Company

Major market	Bakery of origin	Daily quantity (in cwt)
Santa Rosa	Santa Rosa	330
Sacramento	Sacramento	500
Richmond	Richmond	660
Berkeley	Richmond	440
Oakland	Richmond	1,210
San Francisco	San Francisco	1,300
San Jose	San Jose	1,200
Santa Cruz	Santa Cruz	110
Salinas	Santa Cruz	110
Stockton	Stockton	390
Stockton	Sacramento	50
Modesto	Stockton	110

Cruz bakery could be relieved by the construction of a more efficient bakery in the growing San Jose market.

A bakery with daily capacity of 1,200 cwt. was planned. It was estimated that a facility of this size would cost $4 million fully equipped, and would be able to turn out bakery products at an average cost of $17 per hundred pounds. With the expected 5-year increase in demand, the supply pattern shown in Table 4 was projected for 5 years into the future.

[Case problems]

1 As manager of transportation and customer service for Bay Area Bakery Company, would you agree with the proposal to build a new baking facility in San Jose? In order to support your opinion, assume that you have a computer code at your disposal that will optimize transportation problems. What method of financial analysis would you use? Make any necessary assumptions regarding inflation and future building and production costs.

2 If you do not agree with the proposal, what action would you recommend for consideration by other members of the company's top management group? Is the current distribution pattern optimal?

3 If we project similar market growth for 10 years, what effect will this have on the decisions about whether and when to build a new plant?

4 What additional factors would have to be taken into consideration before reaching a final decision in this matter?

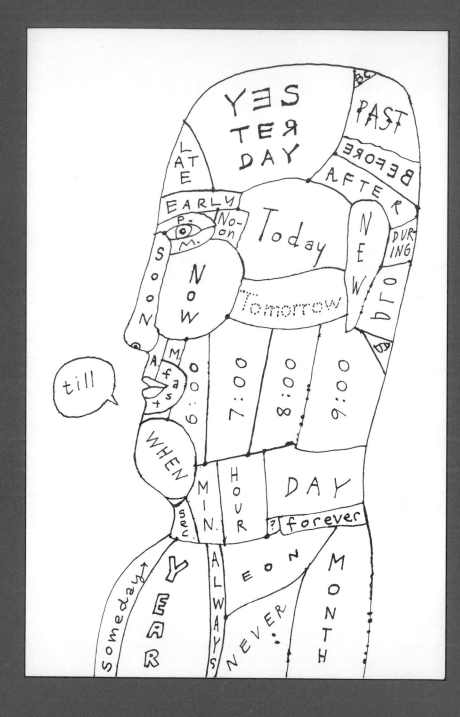

8

$$\left[\ \text{Project scheduling}\ \right]$$

Project scheduling is one of the few applications of management science that is widely accepted among both large and small organizations. Project managers must know how long a specific project will take to finish, what the critical tasks are and, very often, what the probability is of completing the project within a given time span. In addition, it is often important to know the effect on the total project of delays at individual stages. For these and other reasons, several techniques have been created upon which project managers rely. This chapter examines how the manager can integrate the use of a work breakdown structure (WBS), Gantt charts, and project evaluation and review technique (PERT) to solve the problems of scheduling and controlling projects.

The scheduling techniques we discuss in this chapter can be applied to a wide variety of projects. Government contractors are almost always required to use scheduling techniques such as PERT for projects of even moderate size. Construction companies often use these techniques for scheduling moderate to large-scale projects. One construction company, for example, applies PERT to all projects with a cost greater than $150,000. Designers of computerized information systems are using analytical scheduling techniques more and more. In short, almost any project is a likely candidate because the cost of using these techniques is often outweighed by the benefit.

[Work breakdown structure]

When confronted with the task of scheduling and controlling a project of significant size and scope, you must identify each of the tasks involved. In addition, time estimates for each task must be developed, and the necessary resources, both human and nonhuman, must be identified. In order to accomplish this primary task, it is often desirable to use a WBS. WBS is actually a graphical representation of the tasks involved in a particular project. This technique constitutes a way to classify individual tasks by a natural breakdown of

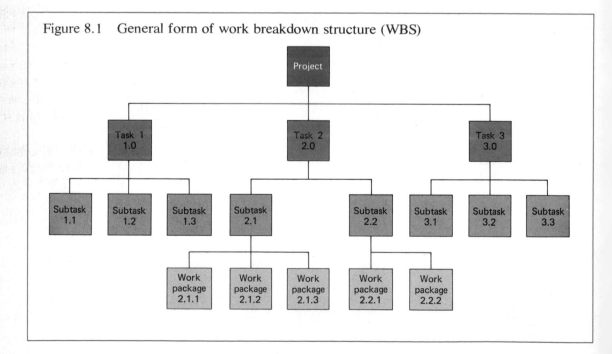

Figure 8.1   General form of work breakdown structure (WBS)

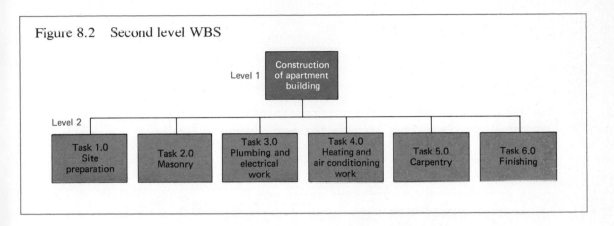

Figure 8.2 Second level WBS

the project in a manner analogous to an organization chart. Indeed, WBS is the organizational structure of the project. It starts with a word description of the project and then breaks the project down into major tasks. These major tasks are reduced to tasks, then to minor tasks, and so on. Finally, the smallest element in the work package WBS, the *work package*, is defined in detail. Each work package

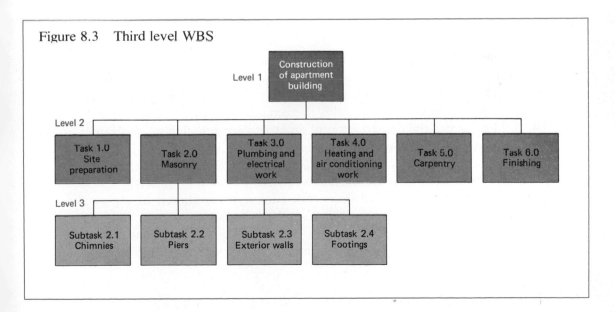

Figure 8.3 Third level WBS

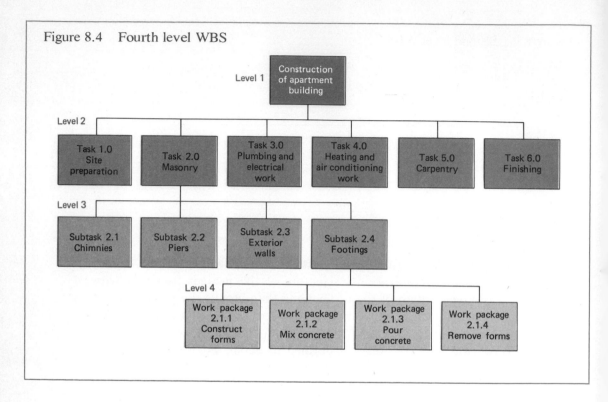

Figure 8.4   Fourth level WBS

identifies the resources and time it requires, all important precedent relationships, and the individual who is responsibile for that work package. When all work packages are completed, the project is complete. Figure 8.1 illustrates the general form of the WBS.

Let us use the construction of an apartment building to illustrate the use of WBS. As you can see in Figure 8.2, the entire project can be broken down into six major tasks. These major tasks can then be broken into subtasks, as shown in Figure 8.3. Finally, these subtasks can be broken into work packages, as shown in Figure 8.4. It should be emphasized that WBS is not a solution to the project-scheduling problem but rather a preliminary, structured approach to collecting the data necessary for use with one of the more sophisticated techniques, such as PERT. Once the project has been broken down using WBS, the next step is to choose a way to schedule and control the project.

[Gantt charts]

For relatively small projects, a simple Gantt milestone chart, or a series of them, may be the best scheduling tool. A Gantt chart is simply a bar chart that plots tasks against time. Once the project manager has created the WBS for a project, the *Begin* and *Finish*

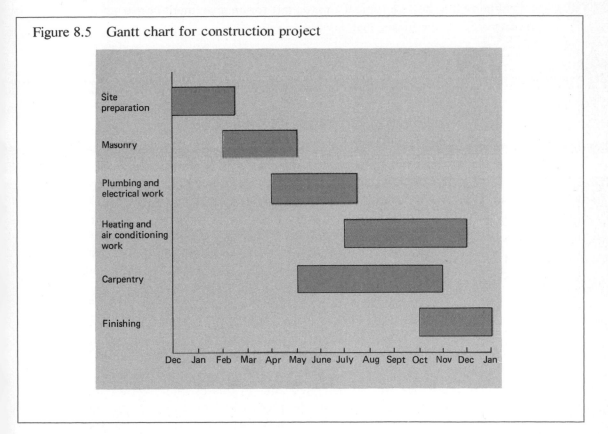

Figure 8.5   Gantt chart for construction project

dates for the various tasks, subtasks, and work packages can then be scheduled. A single Gantt chart for major tasks and subtasks might be designed for management review, but any real scheduling must be done at the lowest level in the WBS. Each work package must have beginning and ending dates.

A relatively small project, such as building a house, might be effectively scheduled and controlled by means of a Gantt chart. Ordinarily, however, Gantt charts are primarily record-keeping tools for monitoring projects. They are limited in that they cannot generate information about the interrelationships among various tasks nor about the minimum possible completion times for various tasks. Figure 8.5 shows a typical Gantt chart for an apartment construction project at the major task level.

[Deterministic PERT]

PERT (project evaluation and review technique) evolved from Gantt charts in the late 1950s and was first applied to the U.S. Navy's Polaris submarine project. This project was so large that it was actually a necessity to create a planning and control technique such as PERT. The Polaris project, for instance, had more than 3,000 contractors, many of whom were performing multiple functions. Because of PERT's success in this and subsequent programs, major federal contracting agencies, such as the Department of Defense and NASA, require contractors to utilize PERT in scheduling and controlling their projects.

What, specifically, can PERT do for the project manager? PERT can be used as a planning tool as well as a controlling tool. In its planning function, PERT can be used to compute the total expected time needed to complete a project, and it can identify "bottleneck" activities that have a critical effect on the project completion date. Stochastic PERT, to be discussed later in this chapter, allows the project manager to estimate the probability of meeting project deadlines. One of PERT's greatest benefits is that it forces the project manager to plan the project in explicit detail.

Once a project has been scheduled using PERT, you might think that the technique is of no further use. This is not the case; PERT is typically used throughout the project as a control technique. Used periodically during the project, PERT monitors progress and calls attention to any delays that threaten the success of the project as a whole. In addition, PERT and similar techniques such as the *critical path method (CPM)* can be used to evaluate and make decisions concerning time and cost tradeoffs of specific project activities.

Before we examine PERT as a methodology for scheduling and controlling a project, it is important for you to know certain terminology that we shall relate to a specific example.

activity   An *activity* is a task the project requires. Because of the nature of PERT, an activity corresponds to the smallest task in the WBS, namely, the work package. Each activity must have associated with

time   it a *time estimate*, and any *precedence relationships* must be defined.   precedence
estimate Table 8.1 depicts this pertinent information for a small project.   relationships

As these data show you, work on activities A and E can begin immediately. Activities B and C cannot be started until activity A has been completed. Activities B, C, and F must be completed before activity D can be started.

One of the problems that PERT addresses is the determination of the minimum time required to complete the project. In order to analyze our project more completely, a *network diagram*, or   network
PERT chart, is introduced. The PERT chart (Figure 8.6) is a graphical   diagram
representation of the entire project. An arrow represents an activity   or PERT
chart

event   and a circle represents an *event*, which is defined as the completion

Table 8.1   Project table

Activity	Immediate predecessor	Time estimate (in days)
A	—	3
B	A	4
C	A	5
D	B, C, F	7
E	—	3
F	E	6

Figure 8.6   PERT chart showing critical path E–F–D

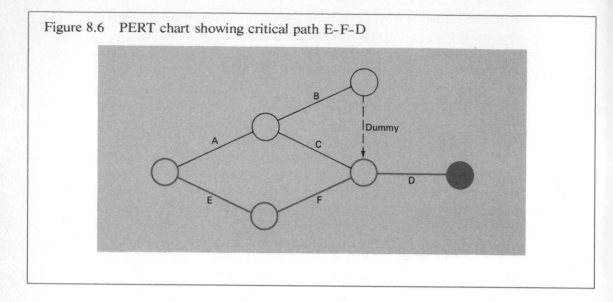

of an activity. The network depicts the precedence relationships involved in the project. As the project table states, the PERT chart shows graphically that it is necessary to finish activity A before beginning activities B and C. The *dummy activity* depicted in Figure 8.6 is a way to indicate diagrammatically that both B and C must be finished before D can be started. A *path* through a PERT network is a sequence of connected activities. In our example, there are three paths, A–B–D, A–C–D, and E–F–D. The length of each path can be computed by adding the times for each activity on the path. Thus, the length of path A–B–D is 3 + 4 + 7 = 14 days, and the lengths of paths A–C–D and E–F–D are 15 and 16 days, respectively. The longest path through the network is called the *critical path*. The length of the critical path corresponds to the minimum time required to complete the project; thus the critical nature of the longest path. The activities on the critical path are *critical activities* because a delay in any of these results in a delay of the entire project. In other words, there is no slack time in the activities on the critical path. *Slack time* is defined as the latest time an activity can be completed without delaying the project minus the earliest time the activity can be completed. In other words,

dummy activity

path

critical path

critical activities

slack time

slack time is the amount of time an activity can be delayed without delaying the entire project.

Returning to our example, it is a simple process to identify the critical path by comparing the lengths of each path. Path E–F–D has a length of 16 days. Hence, the minimum time in which the project can be completed is 16 days from the start of the project; delay of activities E, F, or D will delay the entire project. Path A–B–D has a total of 2 days of slack time, and path A–C–D has 1 day of slack time.

As the number of activities increases, drawing a chart and finding the critical path by inspection or complete enumeration becomes more and more impractical. Therefore, we need an algorithm (a systematic approach) to find the critical path. To explain the algorithm, four variables must be defined. Let

ES_i = the earliest start time for activity i assuming all predecessor activities started at their earliest start time

EF_i = the earliest finish time for activity i

   = $ES_i + t_i$ where t_i is the time estimated for activity i

LF_i = the latest finish time for activity i without delaying the project

LS_i = the latest start time for activity i without delaying the project

   = $LF_i - t_i$

Let us return to our example to illustrate how these four variables are calculated and how the critical path is identified. The algorithm to find the critical path is basically a three-step process. The first step is to calculate the earliest starting time (ES_i) and the earliest finish time (EF_i). The second step is to calculate the latest start time (LS_i) and latest finish time (LF_i) for each activity. Finally, the slack time is calculated for each activity, and the critical path is the sequence of activities that has zero slack time.

To calculate the earliest start time, let all activities that don't have any predecessors start at time zero. To calculate the earliest finish time for these initial activities, merely add the time it takes to complete the activities. Hence, the earliest start time for activities A and E of our example is zero, and the earliest finish time for both activities is $LS_i + t_i$, or $0 + 3$. To calculate the earliest start and earliest finish times for the other activities, it is necessary to add the largest earliest finish time of all immediate predecessor activities to the time for that activity. In our example, activity A has to be finished before B and C are started. Therefore, the earliest start time for activities B and C is 3 (which is the earliest finish time for predecessor A). The earliest finish time for B is $ES_B + t_B$, or $3 + 4 = 7$. Similarly, the earliest finish time for C is 8, and the earliest finish time for F is 9. Consequently, because activity D cannot be started until B, C, and F are finished, the earliest start time for D is 9 (the largest earliest finish time of all immediate predecessors).

Calculating the latest finish times and latest start times is a similar procedure, but to do it we must start at the other end of the PERT network. For all ending activities, set the latest finish time equal to the largest earliest finish time. In our example, there is only one ending activity; hence, the latest finish time is equal to the earliest finish time for activity D. Subtracting the end activity's time from its latest finish time yields the latest start time. The latest finish time for the other activities is equal to the smallest latest start time for all immediate successor activities. Therefore, the latest finish time for activities B, C, and F is 9. The latest start time for activity B is $9 - 4 = 5$.

The latest start time for activity C is $9 - 5 = 4$. Activity A has two successor activities, B and C. Remember, activity A's latest finish time is the minimum latest start time for its successor activities. Hence, the latest time activity A can finish is 4. If activity A finishes after the fourth day, the project will be delayed.

Once the four times have been calculated for each activity, it

Table 8.2   Data for PERT algorithm

Activity	Immediate predecessor	Time	ES	EF	LS	LF	Slack
A	—	3	0	3	1	4	1
B	A	4	3	7	5	9	2
C	A	5	3	8	4	9	1
D	B, C, F	7	9	16	9	16	0
E	—	3	0	3	0	3	0
F	E	6	3	9	3	9	0

Figure 8.7   Evaluated PERT chart

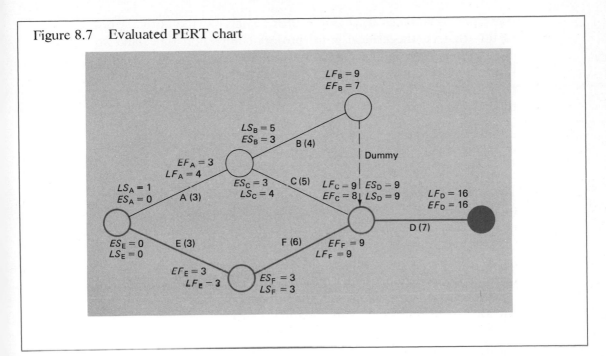

is a simple procedure to identify the critical path. Slack time is calculated by subtracting the earliest finish time from the latest finish time. Activities with zero slack time are on the critical path. In other words, a delay in any activity on the critical path results in a delay of the entire project. Table 8.2 indicates that the critical path is comprised of activities E-F-D. (See Figure 8.7 for the graphical representation of this situation.) Any activity that has a nonzero slack time is not critical and can be delayed as much as the slack time without delaying the project.

[Stochastic PERT]

Until now, we have treated PERT as a deterministic technique in which all activity times are known with certainty. It is obvious that for most projects these activity times are random variables. If these random times take on values significantly different from those point estimates used in the PERT analysis, the output from PERT (that is, the critical path, project completion time, and so on) is rendered invalid. To compensate for the lack of certainty in many of the time estimates, the project manager is often asked to give three subjective time estimates for each activity. These time estimates are

a_i = the most optimistic time required for activity i
m_i = the most likely time required for activity i
b_i = the most pessimistic time required for activity i

These three time estimates are used to define a probability distribution of time for each activity. The distribution used almost exclusively
beta distribution is the *beta distribution*. There is no rigorous mathematical proof that the beta distribution is most appropriate, but three properties make the beta a logical choice. First, it is a continuous probability distribution; second, it is not necessarily symmetrical; and finally, it has a bounded range of values. In addition, empirical investigations support the use of the beta distribution for PERT times.

The mean of the distribution, the expected time for an activity, is calculated using the following function:

$\bar{t}_i = (a_i + 4m_i + b_i)/6$
where $\bar{t}_i$ = the expected time for activity i

The standard deviation of the beta distribution can be approximated using

$\sigma_i = (b_i - a_i)/6$

Suppose, for example, the three time estimates for activity 5 are $a_5 = 2$ days, $m_5 = 6$ days, and $b_5 = 10$ days. Then the expected time for activity 5 is $\bar{t}_5 = (2 + 24 + 10)/6 = 6$ days. The standard deviation of time required for activity 5 is $\sigma_5 = (10 - 2)/6 = 8/6 = 1.33$.

The reason for calculating the standard deviation is to provide a means of computing the probability of completing the project on or before the scheduled completion date. To explain how this probability is computed, let's look at a stochastic version of our original problem. The first step is to calculate the expected time and standard deviation for each activity using the formulas specified

Project scheduling

Table 8.3   Stochastic PERT table

Activity	Immediate predecessor	a_i	m_i	b_i	$\bar{t}_i$	σ_i	σ_i^2
A	—	1	3	5	3.00	.67	.45
B	A	1	4	5	3.67	.67	.45
C	A	3	5	7	5.00	.67	.45
D	B, C, F	3	7	12	7.16	1.50	2.25
E	—	2	3	4	3.00	.33	.11
F	E	2	6	9	5.83	1.17	1.37

by the beta distribution. This is accomplished in Table 8.3. The next step is to find the *expected critical path*. (Since the calculated critical path may not, in fact, be the actual critical path, we can only refer to it as an expected critical path.) Finding the expected critical path is done by using the algorithm previously developed for deterministic PERT. The only difference is that in this situation you use the expected activity time instead of the single time estimate. As you can see in Table 8.4, the expected critical path is E–F–D.

expected critical path

Once the expected critical path has been identified, it is often useful to know the probability of completing the expected critical path within a given length of time. For example, what is the probablity that the tasks on the expected critical path will all be complete by the end of the project's seventeenth day? In order to compute

Table 8.4   Data for stochastic PERT algorithm

Activity	Immediate predecessor	Time	ES	EF	LS	LF	Slack
A	—	3.00	0	3.00	0.83	3.83	0.83
B	A	3.67	3.00	6.67	5.16	8.83	2.16
C	A	5.00	3.00	8.00	3.83	8.83	0.83
D	B, C, F	7.16	8.83	15.99	8.83	15.99	0
E	—	3.00	0	3.00	0	3.00	0
F	E	5.83	3.00	8.83	3.00	8.00	0

a probability of this type, it is necessary to calculate the variance (σ_i^2) for each activity's time. This is done by simply squaring the standard deviation. If we assume that the activities on a given path are independent (that is, that the duration of one task has no effect on the length of time necessary to complete another task), then the variance related to an entire path's length is the sum of the variances of the individual activities on that path. Therefore, assuming independence, the variance for path E–F–D is .11 + 1.37 + 2.25 = 3.73. In addition, if there are many activities on a given path (that is, more than 30), the distribution of the total time of the path is often assumed to be normally distributed.

Given the mean and variance of a normally distributed random variable (path length), it is possible to determine the probability of completing that path within a certain length of time. For example, what is the probability of completing path E–F–D within 17 days? The standard deviation of the total time that it takes to complete path E–F–D is $\sqrt{3.73}$, or 1.93, and the mean is 15.99. Given these facts, the distribution of times necessary to complete path E–F–D is shown in Figure 8.8. The probability of completing path E–F–D within 17 days is represented by the shaded portion of the normal curve in Figure 8.9.

Figure 8.8 Normal distribution of days necessary to complete path E–F–D

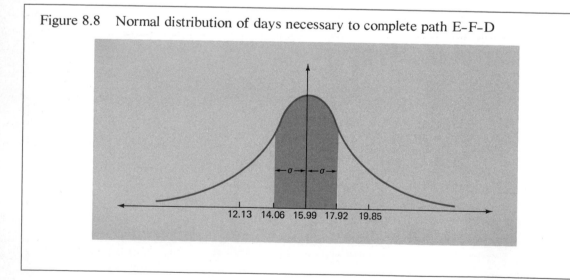

12.13   14.06   15.99   17.92   19.85

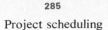

Figure 8.9   Normal distribution showing probability of completing E–F–D within 17 days

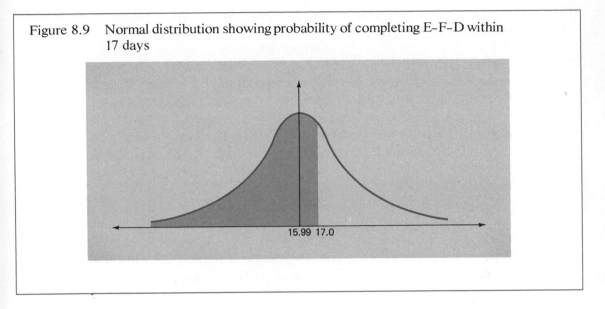

15.99 17.0

To compute this probability, it is necessary to transform our normal distribution into the standard normal with a mean of 0 and a standard deviation of 1. This is done by using the following Z transformation:

$Z = (x - \mu)/\sigma$

where μ = the mean of the nonstandard normal

σ = the standard deviation of the nonstandard normal

x = the nonstandardized normal variate

Therefore, the probability of completing path E–F–D is calculated by first calculating Z. Thus, $Z = (17 - 15.99)/1.93 = .5233$. Once Z has been computed, finding the probability of $Z \leq .5233$ is accomplished by using a standard normal table such as the one in the back of this book. The probability that path E–F–D will be finished within 17 days is approximately .699. (To find this, you look up $Z \leq .5233$ in the table. Be sure to verify it for yourself.) In other words, $P(x \leq 17) = P(Z \leq .5233) = .699$. It is important to remember that the normality assumption postulates the existence of a large number of random variables (that is, activities on a path). For rough approximations, 30 random variables is usually acceptable;

for more rigorous applications, however, an n closer to 100 is preferable.

Having computed the probability of completing the expected critical path within 17 days, can you then conclude that this probability is the probability of completing the project in 17 days or less? The answer is no. Since activity times are random variables, it is possible that a path different from the expected critical path might cause the project to last longer than 17 days. To illustrate this idea, let's consider path A–C–D. The expected time for path A–C–D (t_{A-C-D}) is $3 + 5 + 7.16 = 15.16$, and the standard deviation for path A–C–D is $\sqrt{.45 + .45 + 2.25} = 1.775$. Thus $Z = (17 - 15.16)/1.775 = 1.037$. Therefore, $P(t_{A-C-D} \le 17) = P(Z \le 1.037) \cong .849$. Similarly, the probability of completing path A–B–D within 17 days is approximately .963. Now, if we assume the length of the paths are independent random variables, we can compute the probability of completing the project within 17 days as the joint probability of completing each path within 17 days. In other words, P(project time ≤ 17 days) = P(path A–B–D ≤ 17 and path A–C–D < 17 and path E–F–D ≤ 17). If independence is assumed, P(project time ≤ 17) = $(.963)(.849)(.699) = .5715$.

If the various assumptions necessary to compute the probability of project completion cannot be made (that is, if the individual paths are not independent or do not have a large number of activities), *discrete digital simulation* is often used to estimate the probability of project completion within a specific time period. For each activity, the computer merely samples from a beta distribution for which the parameters have been established as previously described. On each iteration, a project completion time is computed and is added to a frequency distribution of project lengths. Given enough iterations, it is reasonable to use this frequency distribution to describe the probabilities of various project durations.

[Evaluating time-cost trade-offs]

So far, we have discussed two variations of PERT that emphasize time factors in project evaluation. Deterministic PERT is useful when a project's time parameters are known with a good degree of certainty. Stochastic PERT, on the other hand, allows uncertain times to be estimated so that probabilities concerning such activities' duration and completion can be computed. In a third technique, critical path method (CPM), cost was introduced as a companion factor to time for project evaluation.

In their early use, PERT and CPM actually differed in two ways. First, PERT allowed for stochastic times, using the three-point estimate discussed in the preceding section. CPM, however, assumed that times are known with certainty. This distinction is still valid to some extent. When a project is rather uncertain in nature (as, for example, a research project or an out-of-the-ordinary undertaking), PERT is the logical technique to use for planning and control. For more common projects, such as certain construction projects in which the times necessary to complete individual tasks can be closely estimated, deterministic PERT or CPM may be more desirable.

As we have mentioned, the second distinction between PERT and CPM lay in the area of project costs. CPM made use of a dual perspective, namely, time and cost. You should realize, however, that this difference between PERT and CPM has faded as both techniques have evolved. In fact, most PERT software packages now include provisions for evaluating time-cost trade-offs. For that reason, the discussion of time and cost factors that follows refers to using "versions of PERT and CPM," because, in fact, both methods have been used to make valid analyses of the kind to be discussed.

Until now, we have talked about these project-evaluating techniques primarily as descriptive and predictive tools. Versions of PERT and CPM, however, are used to make decisions concerning how best to shorten a project's completion time. A project manager often has the prerogative of increasing resource allocation to specific tasks so that the project can be finished at an earlier date. In other words, a project manager may have such options as hiring additional workers or working personnel overtime to expedite the completion of a task. To give you an idea of how these time-cost trade-off decisions are made, let's consider our previous deterministic example. Table 8.5 reflects the costs of feasible reductions in each activity's completion time.

The crash time estimate in Table 8.5 represents the amount of time it would take to complete an activity if management wished

critical path method (CPM)

Table 8.5 Time-cost trade-off data

Activity	Normal time estimate (days)	Crash time estimate (days)	Incremental cost of crash time ($)
A	3	2	150
B	4	3.5	100
C	5	4	200
D	7	5	300
E	3	3	—
F	6	5	75

to allocate additional resources to that activity. The incremental cost of crashing an activity is also reflected in Table 8.5. Remember that there were three paths in the PERT network of our original problem. These paths are summarized in Table 8.6.

In terms of shortening the total project, it is clear that to shorten paths A–B–D or A–C–D without shortening path E–F–D does no good. Remember, the minimum length of the project is the length of the longest individual path. Therefore, we must look at path E–F–D to determine how to expedite the completion of the total project. Table 8.7 indicates that we have two alternatives for shortening path E–F–D. Because of the lower per day cost, it seems logical to add resources to activity F (that is, activity F is crashed) so that the length of the project is reduced from 16 days to 15 days at a cost of $75.

In order to shorten the project further, both paths A–C–D and E–F–D must be shortened. Since D is the only activity that can

Table 8.6 PERT paths

Path	Length (days)
A–B–D	14
A–C–D	15
E–F–D	16

Table 8.7   Alternatives for shortening E-F-D

Activity	Days saved by crashing	Cost of crash per day ($)	Cost of crash ($)
E	0	—	—
F	1	75	75
D	2	150	300

still be shortened on path E-F-D, there is no alternative. Fortunately, D is common to all three paths, and a reduction in D results in shortening all three paths. For $300, D can be reduced from 7 days to 5 days, and each path can be reduced 2 days. Therefore, paths E-F-D and A-C-D would take 13 days and path A-B-D would take 12 days. Further reduction in paths A-B-D or A-C-D would not be fruitful because the length of path E-F-D cannot be reduced. To summarize, we can reduce the project schedule from 16 days to 13 days at a cost of $375.

[Summary]

The major advantage of WBS, Gantt charts, PERT, and CPM is that each of these techniques forces the project manager to explicitly plan and schedule his project in great detail. WBS is a necessary first step in planning a project in that the output from the WBS analysis is the input for any utilization of PERT or CPM. PERT or CPM can then be utilized to identify critical tasks and to estimate project completion times with various degrees of confidence. If the normality and independence assumptions of stochastic PERT cannot be accepted, the project manager can always use digital simulation to find the probabilities associated with various completion deadlines. You should also keep in mind that more sophisticated versions of PERT exist that can answer such questions as how to shorten the project schedule with the least additional cost and what to do about various resource constraints.

[Bibliography]

Bierman, Harold, Jr., Charles P. Bonini, and Warren H. Hausman, *Quantitative Analysis for Business Decisions*, 4th ed. Homewood, Ill.: Richard D. Irwin, Inc., 1973.

Buffa, Elwood S., *Operations Management: The Management of Productive Systems*. New York: John Wiley & Sons, Inc., 1976.

Evarts, Harry F., *Introduction to PERT*. Boston, Mass.: Allyn and Bacon, Inc., 1964.

Levin, Richard I., and Charles A Kirkpatrick, *Planning and Control with PERT/CPM*. New York: McGraw-Hill Book Company, 1966.

Murdick, Robert G., and Joel E. Ross, *Information Systems for Modern Management*. Englewood Cliffs, N.J.: Prentice-Hall, Inc., 1971.

Wiest, J., and F. K. Levy, *Management Guide to PERT/CPM*. Englewood Cliffs, N.J.: Prentice-Hall, Inc., 1969.

[Review questions]

1 Distinguish between Gantt charts and PERT.

2 What are the basic elements in a work package?

3 What is the basic purpose of using WBS?

4 On what kinds of project would you use deterministic PERT rather than stochastic PERT?

5 What can PERT do for the project manager?

6 Define *critical path*.

7 How is slack time computed?

8 Why is the beta distribution used for PERT times?

9 Why compute σ_i?

10 What assumptions are made in order to make probabilistic statements about project completion schedules?

11 Explain in your own words how and why simulation is used with PERT.

[Problems]

8.1 Prepare the WBS for a project with which you are familiar. In addition to identifying each task and subtask, prepare the necessary work packages.

8.2 Draw Gantt charts for the various task levels of the WBS prepared for problem 8.1.

8.3 Consider the information in the table below.

Task	Immediate predecessor	Estimated time (days)
A	—	5
B	—	4
C	A	3
D	B	7
E	C	2
F	D, E	1

    a Draw the PERT network diagram for this project.
    b Use the PERT algorithm for finding the critical path.
    c What is the minimum project completion time?
    d Would the critical path change if F were to take 5 days rather than 1? Explain.

8.4 Consider the project information in the table.

Task	Immediate predecessor	Estimated time (days)
A	—	5
B	—	6
C	A	4
D	B	3
E	B	5
F	C, D	2
G	E	2
H	E	4
I	F, G	3
J	H	2
K	I, J	5

a Draw the PERT network diagram for the project.
b Use the PERT algorithm for finding the critical path.
c What is the minimum project completion time?

8.5 Consider the project information in the table.

Task	Immediate predecessor	a_i	m_i	b_i
		Estimated time (days)		
A	—	3	5	6
B	A	3	4	7
C	A	1	3	5
D	B	2	4	7
E	C	2	5	8
F	D	1	2	4
G	E	2	3	4

a Draw the PERT network diagram for this project.
b Compute the mean and variance in time for each activity.
c Find the critical path by inspection.
d What is the expected length of the expected critical path?
e Assume that the time required to complete a path is normally distributed. What is the probability of completing the critical path in less than or equal to 15 days?
f Again assuming normality and path independence, what is the probability of completing the entire project in less than or equal to 15 days?
g If you wanted to be at least 95 percent sure of completing the project on time, what schedule would you quote?

8.6 Consider the information in the table.
a Draw the PERT network diagram for this project.
b Compute the mean and variance in time for each activity.
c Find the critical path using the PERT algorithm.
d What is the expected length of the expected critical path?
e Assuming that the time required to complete a path is normally distributed, what is the probability of completing the critical path in less than or equal to 50 days?
f Again assuming normality and path independence, what is the probability of completing the entire project in less than or equal to 50 days?
g If you wanted to be at least 95 percent sure of completing the project on time, what schedule would you quote?

Task	Immediate predecessor	Estimated time (days)		
		a_i	m_i	b_i
A	—	4	5	7
B	—	5	9	11
C	A	5	10	15
D	A	4	5	8
E	A	5	7	12
F	D, C	3	4	7
G	D, C	2	3	4
H	D	7	12	18
I	B, E	6	11	14
J	F	5	6	9
K	G	5	7	9
L	H, I	2	3	5
M	J, K	7	8	9
N	L	1	3	4
O	M, N	15	17	22

8.7 State University is planning a holiday basketball tournament and has decided to use PERT to schedule the project. The tasks and time estimates have been identified as set forth in the table.

a Draw the PERT diagram and identify the expected critical path.

b If the tournament is to be held starting December 27, when should team selection begin to assure 98 percent certainty that the tournament will be held as scheduled?

Task	Description	Immediate predecessors	Estimated time (days)		
			a_i	m_i	b_i
A	Team selection	—	1	3	5
B	Mail out invitations and receive acceptances	A	4	5	10
C	Arrange accommodations	—	8	10	15
D	Plan promotional strategy	B	2	3	5
E	Print tickets	B	4	5	8
F	Sell tickets	E	15	15	15
G	Complete arrangements	B, C	7	8	10
H	Develop practice schedules	C	2	3	4
I	Practice sessions	H	2	2	2
J	Conduct tournament	F, I	3	3	3

8.8 Consider the project in problem 8.3. Assume crash times and crash costs as set forth in the table below.

Activity	Normal time estimate (days)	Crash time Estimate (days)	Incremental cost of crash time ($)
A	5	4	100
B	4	3.5	100
C	3	2.5	150
D	7	5	400
E	2	2	—
F	1	1	—

a What is the shortest time in which the project can be completed?
b What is the total incremental cost of achieving the shortest completion time?
c What is the minimum incremental cost of completing the project in 10 days?

8.9 Consider the project in problem 8.4. Assume the crash times set forth in the table.

Activity	Normal time estimate (days)	Crash time estimate (days)	Incremental cost of crash time ($)
A	5	4	100
B	6	4	400
C	4	3.5	100
D	3	3	—
E	5	4	100
F	2	1.5	150
G	2	2	—
H	4	3	175
I	3	2	125
J	2	2	—
K	5	2	500

a What is the shortest time the project can be completed?
b What is the total incremental cost of achieving the shortest completion time?
c What is the incremental cost of completing the project in 18 days?

[Construction Associates, Inc. Case]

Construction Associates of Syracuse, New York, did general construction work. In April of 1965, the company had three jobs in progress: a six-family apartment house, a gas station, and a four-store addition to a shopping center.

The owner of the shopping center, Mr. Mahara, had recently returned from Akron, Ohio, where he had discussed with the executives of a large tire company the possibility of opening a tire sales and service shop in his shopping center. Mr. Mahara decided that a tire shop would be a profitable addition to his shopping center and on the morning of April 2, 1965, he decided to proceed at once to arrange for the construction of a suitable building to house the tire shop in one corner of the shopping center parking lot. He then called Mr. Heitman, the president of Construction Associates, to arrange a meeting to discuss plans for the building. During their meeting Mr. Mahara and Mr. Heitman agreed that a suitable building for the new tire shop would be a one-story frame structure somewhat similar in exterior design to the gas station that Construction Associates had under construction at that time.

Although the time was short Mr. Mahara was anxious to have the tire shop building completed by the time the addition to the shopping center was completed. He felt that the grand opening of the tire shop should be tied in with the opening of the four stores in the new addition. The construction schedule for the addition, which was easily being met, indicated that the shopping center addition would be completed in 51 working days after April 2.

Following his meeting with the shopping center owner, Mr. Heitman spoke with Mr. Bevis, Construction Associates' planning specialist. Realizing time was short, Mr. Heitman asked Mr. Bevis to plan immediately the construction schedule for the tire shop building. Mr. Bevis was instructed to use the plans and costs of the gas station under construction as guidelines for his preliminary planning of the tire shop.

In his initial analysis of the problem Mr. Bevis noted the following construction relationships generally observed in construction of this type:

1 A preliminary set of specifications would have to be completed before work could begin on the set of blueprints and before the foundation excavation could begin. After the excavation was completely finished the foundation could be poured.

2 The preparation of a bill of materials would have to be deferred until the final set of blueprints was prepared. When the bill of materials was completed it would be used to prepare order invoices for lumber and other items. Construction of the frame could not begin until the lumber had arrived at the construction site and the foundation had been poured.

3 After the frame was completed, electric work, erection of laths, plumbing, installation of millwork, and installation of siding could begin.

4 Painting of the interior walls could not start until the electric work, plastering of the walls, and plumbing were completed. Plastering of the walls could not begin until the laths were erected.

5 The final interior decorating work could not begin until the interior walls were painted and the trim installed. Installation of trim could not begin until the millwork was completely installed.

6 Painting of the building's exterior could not proceed until the windows and exterior doors were installed. Installation of the windows and doors, in turn, could not start until the siding was in place.

After studying the plans and construction schedule of the gas station under construction, Mr. Bevis developed an estimate of the time required to complete each step of the building of the tire shop (see Table 1). The estimates were, in most cases, developed from the figures given Mr. Bevis by the foremen on the gas station job. Mr. Bevis had found in the past that figures of this type were usually quite accurate. One exception to this was the figures obtained from the carpenter foreman, who was sometimes a little too pessimistic about his estimates.

As he studied the time estimates he had put together for the tire

Table 1   Time and cost estimates for tire shop construction project steps

Project step	Estimated Time required to execute step (days, under optimal cost conditions)	Reduction (days)	Cost ($)
A Prepare preliminary specifications	10	2	10
		3	120
B Excavate foundation	5	1	200
C Pour foundation	6	1	180
D Electric work	5	2	200
E Lath work	2	1	20
F Plumbing	6	2	80
G Plaster walls	4	1	40
		2	100
H Paint interior walls	5	1	70
		2	150
I Millwork installation	10	2	200
		3	350
J Trim installation	8	2	90
		3	150
K Erect frame and roof	15	2	1,000
		4	2,500
L Final interior decoration	8	2	100
		4	800
M Installation of siding	7	1	100
		3	600
N Paint exterior	7	1	50
		2	150
O Blueprints finalized	5	2	70
		3	120
P Prepare bill of materials and order Invoices	3	1	50
		2	170
Q Time required to receive lumber after order is sent	8	2	100
		4	290
R Window and exterior door installation	6	1	100

Table 2   Tentative construction plan for tire shop

Step	Planned duration (days)	Step	Planned duration (days)	Step	Planned duration (days)
A	8	G	3	M	7
B	5	H	4	N	6
C	5	I	7	O	3
D	3	J	5	P	2
E	1	K	15	Q	6
F	4	L	6	R	6

shop job, Mr. Bevis realized that some of the steps would have to be rushed in order to complete the job in 51 days. To provide more usable information on the effects of rushing some of the construction steps, Mr. Bevis estimated the extra cost of reducing the normal time required for each step by one or more days (Table 1). These costs would increase the cost of the tire shop over what might be called the cost under "optimal conditions," (that is, the cost incurred if each step could be performed at normal pace without undue rushing, overtime, and so on). Realizing that any extra costs should be kept to an absolute minimum, Mr. Bevis tried to develop a construction schedule which rushed only those activities where the extra cost was not too high. After several hours of work Mr. Bevis devised the tentative construction plan shown in Table 2.

Deciding the plan needed further work, Mr. Bevis put all his notes on the tire shop job into his briefcase to do further work at home that evening. He also put a booklet, *The Management Implications of PERT*, published by a management consulting firm, into his briefcase.

[Case Problems]

1 What is the critical path assuming no reductions in the time required to execute a step?

2 What is the length of the critical path?

3 Is it feasible to cut the length of the time to complete the project to 51 days?

4 What is the least-cost plan for reducing the project length to 51 days?

5 What is the minimum cost of crashing the project to 51 days?

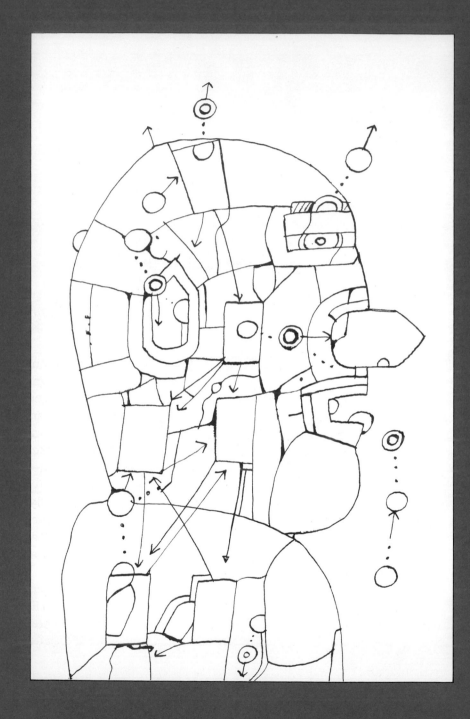

9

$$\left[\ \text{Queuing models}\ \right]$$

Queue is another name for a waiting line, and a *queuing system* is simply a system that involves a waiting line. *Queuing theory* is a branch of management science that enables the analyst to describe the behavior of queuing systems.

It is clear that each of us comes in contact with many queuing systems every day. If you have ever taken a trip by airplane, you have been a member of many queues by the time the trip is over. First, you waited to obtain the services of a ticket agent. Then, the agent joined a queue to find out if the flight you wanted was full. After buying your ticket, you had to wait in line to check in at the gate where the flight was boarding. Next, you waited to board; and once on board, your plane became a member of the queue of planes waiting to use the runway for takeoff. Eventually, the plane was circling the destination airport, waiting to land. Once on the ground, the plane may have had to wait for an unloading gate; and then, you had to wait to deplane. Finally, there was the wait for luggage and, possibly, a taxi.

The point is that the occasions for applying queuing theory are numerous and varied. When people who design systems that contain queues use queuing theory or digital simulation to estimate expected waiting times, queue lengths, and so on, members of the queue, (or *calling units*) spend less time waiting in line.

The queuing analysis we shall undertake in this chapter is different

queuing system

queuing theory

calling units

in nature from some of the optimization techniques, such as linear programming, that you have already studied. Queuing theory does not address optimization problems directly. Rather, it uses elements of statistics and mathematics for the construction of models that describe the important descriptive statistics of a queuing system. This statistical description of the operation of the queuing system then becomes part of the data upon which optimization decisions are based. The queuing system descriptive statistics include such factors as the expected waiting time of the calling units, the expected length of the line, and the percentage of idle time for the *service facility* (the source of goods or services for which the calling units wait). service facility

When queuing theory is applied, management's objective is usually to minimize two kinds of costs: those associated with providing service and those associated with waiting time. After queuing theory has generated its statistical interpretation of the queuing system, the analyst assesses the various costs of providing service versus the costs of customer waiting in order to design the system that best meets the objectives of the organization.

[The queuing system]

As you can see in Figure 9.1, there are four parts of any queuing system—the calling population, the queue, the service facility, and the served calling units. Three of these entities have certain properties

Figure 9.1　Queuing system

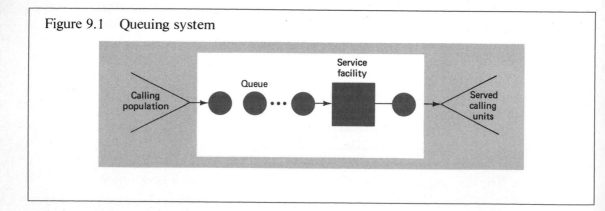

and characteristics that must be considered before appropriate modeling schemes can be formulated. We shall describe the calling population, the queue, and the service facility in some detail. In general, served calling units merely leave, or exit, the system.

CHARACTERISTICS OF THE CALLING POPULATION

The calling population, often referred to as the *input source*, has three characteristics that are important to consider when deciding on what type of queuing model to apply:

1 The size of the calling population

2 The pattern of arrivals at the queuing system

3 The attitude of the calling units

Size of the calling population This factor has a dramatic effect on the choice of queuing models. (Compare the number of alternatives associated with infinite versus finite calling populations in Figure 9.2.) Queuing systems in which the calling population can be considered *infinite* in size are generally more likely to be amenable to analytical modeling. Examples of infinite calling populations in queuing systems are cars on a toll road and patients at the emergency room of a hospital. It is much more difficult to derive queuing models that can be applied to systems in which the calling populations are very limited. Examples of *finite*, or *limited-source, queuing systems* include three in-house computers that must be serviced by a custom engineer if they break down and students who may take advantage of a professor's office hours for help in a specific course.

infinite calling population

finite calling population

The key to determining whether you can assume an infinite calling population is whether the probability of an arrival is significantly changed when a member or members of the population are receiving service and thus cannot arrive to the system. If there are only three calling units in a calling population and one is receiving service, the probability of another arrival is significantly reduced because the size of the calling population is cut by 33.3 percent. In general, a calling population greater than 200 in size is treated as infinite in queuing applications.

Figure 9.2   A representative sample of elementary queuing models

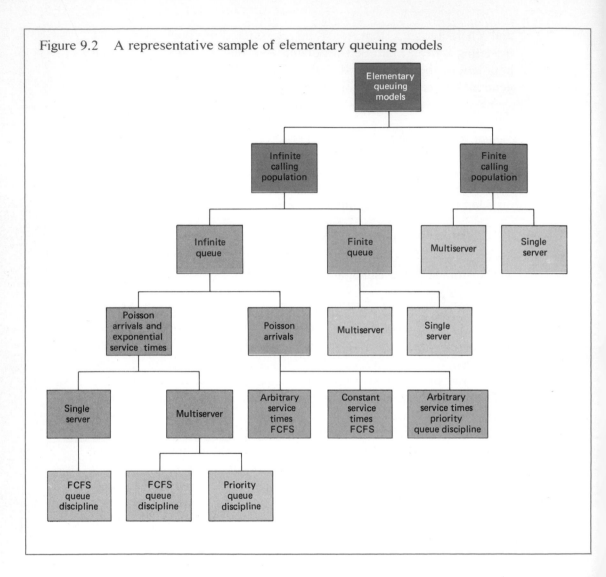

Pattern of arrivals   Calling units arrive at the queuing system either according to some predetermined schedule or in a *random* fashion. If arrivals are scheduled, such as patients at a dentist's office, analytical queuing models are usually inappropriate. If arrivals are random, it is necessary to determine the probability distribution of the time between arrivals. It has been shown mathematically

random arrivals

that if the probability density function of the interarrival times is exponential, calling units arrive according to a so-called *Poisson process*. Poisson arrivals are very common in queuing systems. They generally exist in situations where the number of arrivals during a certain time interval is independent of the number of arrivals that have occurred in previous time intervals. This basic property states that the conditional probability of any future event depends only on the present state of the system and is independent of previous states of the system. The *Poisson probability density function* gives the probability of *n* arrivals in time period *t*. The mathematical form of the Poisson probability function is

$$P_n(t) = \frac{e^{-\lambda t}(\lambda t)^n}{n!} \qquad n = 0, 1, 2, \ldots$$

where $n =$ is the number of arrivals

$t -$ size of the time interval

$\lambda =$ mean arrival rate per unit of time

Poisson process

Poisson probability density function

Although many queuing systems have random arrivals that behave according to a Poisson process, it is possible for the interarrival times to be distributed in a nonexponential fashion. Therefore, it is necessary to determine the distribution and parameters of the interarrival time statistically before deciding on how to approach any queuing problem. How to determine the probability distribution of a random variable such as interarrival time is covered in Chapter 10.

Attitude of the calling units   The final characteristic of the calling population that must be considered is the attitude of the calling unit. In other words, can you assume that a calling unit will enter the queuing system regardless of the state of the system? For example, does everybody who wants to buy gas at a particular service station stop at that station if there are 15 cars waiting for service? Then, too, can you assume that a calling unit will remain in the system until served? A customer may tire of waiting and leave. Generally, most analytical queuing models assume a very patient calling unit.

THE PROPERTY OF QUEUE LENGTH

limited
unlimited
This characteristic of queues is related in a sense to calling population size and, sometimes, to calling population attitude. In applying models, the queue is characterized by its maximum length, which can be *limited* or *unlimited*. Limitation is usually attributable either to customer attitude or to the space available for the queue. There are few choices for queuing systems that have finite queues. Generally, if you can assume that calling units join the queue regardless of its length, the probability of applying an analytical queuing model is greatly increased.

CHARACTERISTICS OF THE SERVICE FACILITY

The three basic properties of the service facility that we analyze are:

1 The structure of the queuing system
2 The distribution of service times
3 The service discipline

Queuing system structure This characteristic is classified in part as single phase or multiphase. A *single-phase* system is one in which single phase the calling unit receives service from only one type of server. A pay telephone, for example, is a single-phase queuing system. A multiphase *multiphase* system exists when the calling unit must obtain the services of several different types of server. Imagine a freighter pulling into the harbor to unload its cargo: First, that freighter must obtain the services of a tugboat; then, it must obtain a berth; then be unloaded; and after having been unloaded, the tug's services are needed again for the freighter's return to the open water.

In addition to multiphase versus single-phase structure, queuing systems can also be described as single channel or multichannel. single channel A *single-channel* system is a system with only one server. A multichannel *multichannel* system, on the other hand, has more than one server performing the same service. A drive-in bank facility is a single-channel system when there is only one teller on duty and a multichannel system when more than one teller is working. Obvious-

Figure 9.3   A representative sample of elementary queuing system
characteristics

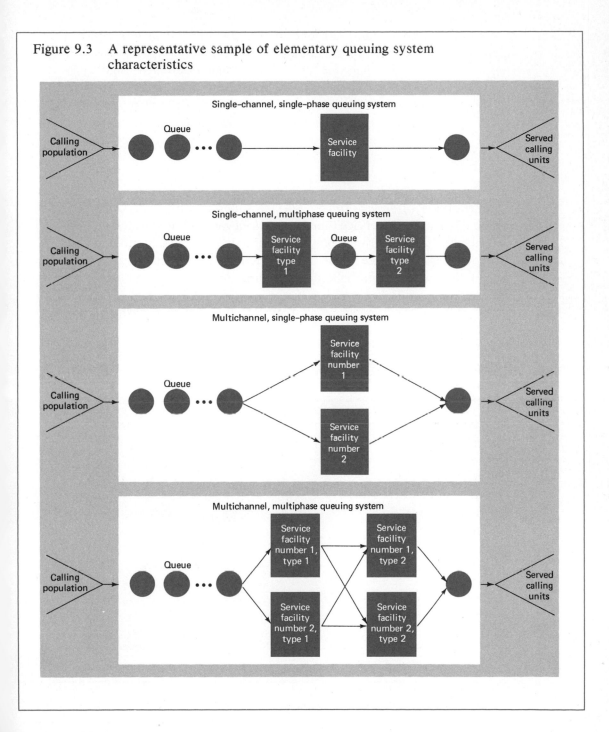

ly, queuing systems can represent any combination of phases and channels. An example of a multiphase, multichannel system is a harbor that has more than one tug and more than one berth. Figure 9.3 depicts schematics of several different queuing structures.

The great majority of queuing models are single-phase models. It is possible, nonetheless, to view a multiphase system as separate, single-phase systems in which the output from one server becomes the input for another server.

Distribution of service times   Service times can be *constant* or constant random in nature. If service time is a *random* variable, it is necessary random for the analyst to determine how that random variable is distributed. In many cases, service times are exponentially distributed; when this is the case, the probability of finding an applicable model is increased.

As you can see in Figure 9.4, if service times are *exponentially* exponential

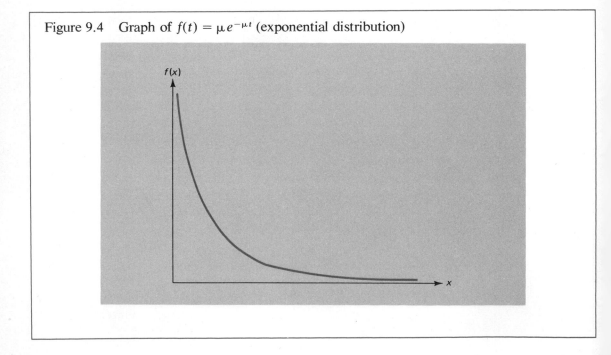

Figure 9.4   Graph of $f(t) = \mu e^{-\mu t}$ (exponential distribution)

distributed, the probability of relatively long service times is small. For example, the length of telephone calls has been shown to be exponentially distributed.

The important point is that you should not make assumptions concerning either the service times of the various servers in the system or, equally important, about the arrival pattern of calling units without using the appropriate nonparametric statistical tests.

Service discipline This characteristic is the decision rule that determines which calling unit in the queuing system receives service. A service discipline, (or *queue discipline*, as it is sometimes called), can be classified in one of two ways:

1 First come, first served (FCFS)
2 Priority

Most queuing systems that involve people operate with FCFS service discipline, even though it has been shown to be somewhat inefficient, simply because people usually do not tolerate other systems. Priority disciplines can be divided into two categories—preemptive priority and nonpreemptive priority. *Preemptive priority* disciplines allow calling units that arrive at the queuing system to replace units already receiving service. For example, consider an emergency room of a hosptial when only one doctor is on duty. Obviously, if that doctor is treating a patient whose condition is not critical at the time a critically ill patient arrives, the patient who was being served is preempted because a calling unit has arrived to the system with a higher priority.

preemptive priority

Nonpreemptive priority simply causes the units in the queue to be arranged so that, when a service facility becomes available, the calling unit with the highest priority receives service first. There is no displacement of units in service. Computer systems frequently use priority scheduling.

nonpreemptive priority

It is also possible for a queuing system to have no formal queue discipline, in which case the server selects calling units at random. *Random selection* often exists at the candy and popcorn counter in a movie theater.

random selection

DESCRIPTIVE STATISTICS OF A QUEUING SYSTEM

Now that we have described certain properties of its major components, the calling population, the queue, and the service facility, you should have a good notion of the nature of the queuing system itself. Before we go on to the specific subject of queuing models, you should be aware that almost all such mathematical models reveal information about the operating characteristics of a queuing system in a *steady state*. The steady-state condition exists when a system's behavior is not a function of time. Typically, a queuing system goes through a stage in which queuing statistics do not reflect long-term expected values (that is, the system does not exhibit the values you would expect it to show over the long run). This stage often occurs at a system's "start." For example, when a grocery store opens its doors in the morning, no customers are present in the system; therefore, there is a period of time when a statistic such as the expected time spent waiting in line would be understated.

steady
state

[Elementary queuing models]

In this section, we get down to defining some of the queuing models you first saw in Figure 9.2, and to showing the functions that describe various queuing statistics. Because the mathematics necessary to derive most queuing models is beyond the scope of this text, we have omitted model derivations. The emphasis, instead, is on identifying the assumptions of each model and on explaining how these models are used.

NOTATION AND DEFINITIONS

In order to help you understand the specific queuing statistics that are available from most queuing models, we must first define certain queuing terms and introduce a limited amount of notation. You should become familiar with the following list of notations and definitions before you read further in this chapter.

L_q = expected or mean length of the queue (number of calling units in the queue)

L_s = expected number of calling units in the system (number in the queue plus number being served)

W_q = expected or mean time spent waiting in line

W_s = expected or mean time spent in the system (including waiting time and service time)

λ = mean arrival rate (number of calling units per unit of time)

μ = mean service rate (number of calling units served per unit of time)

$1/\mu$ = mean service time for a calling unit

s = the number of parallel (equivalent) service facilities in the system

$P(n)$ = the probability of having n units in the system

ρ = server utilization factor (that is, the proportion of time the server can be expected to be busy)

MODELS THAT HAVE AN INFINITE CALLING POPULATION

All queuing models can be classified as either infinite source models or finite source models. Infinite source models are much more numerous and varied than models with finite calling populations. All models described in this text assume that μ is independent of the number of calling units in the system. Moreover, all queuing statistics given are steady-state statistics.

The basic single-server model The assumptions of this model are:

1 Poisson arrival process

2 Exponential service times

3 Single server

4 FCFS service discipline

5 Infinite source

6 Infinite queue

In order to give you some sense of the way that queuing models are derived, this simplest of queuing models is partially derived mathematically in the appendix at the end of this chapter. The basic queuing statistics are as follows:

$$P(0) = 1 - (\lambda/\mu)$$
$$P(n) = P(0)(\lambda/\mu)^n$$
$$\rho = \lambda/\mu$$
$$L_s = \lambda/(\mu - \lambda)$$
$$L_q = \lambda^2/[\mu(\mu - \lambda)]$$
$$W_s = 1/(\mu - \lambda)$$
$$W_q = \lambda/[\mu(\mu - \lambda)]$$

[Example]   To illustrate these results, consider the following application. A particular toll road has one attendant at an exit lane. Cars arrive at that toll gate in a Poisson fashion at a rate of 120 cars per hour, and it takes the attendant, on the average, 15 seconds to service a car. Service times are exponentially distributed. Assumptions of an infinite calling population and an infinite queue are reasonable. What are the basic queuing statistics for this very simple system?

First, it is necessary to determine the units of time for λ and μ. Obviously, λ and μ must be expressed in the same time units. Let's choose minutes. Therefore, λ = 2 cars per minute and μ = 4 cars per minute. Thus we have

$$P(0) = 1 - (\lambda/\mu) = 1 - (2/4)$$
$$= .5 \quad \text{(probability of an empty system)}$$
$$\rho = \lambda/\mu = 2/4 = .5 \quad \text{(proportion of time the server is busy)}$$
$$L_s = \lambda/(\mu - \lambda) = 2/(4 - 2)$$
$$= 1 \quad \text{(expected number of cars in the system)}$$
$$L_q = \lambda^2/[\mu(\mu - \lambda)] = 2^2/[4(4 - 2)] = 4/8$$
$$= .5 \quad \text{(expected number of cars waiting in the queue)}$$
$$W_s = 1/(\mu - \lambda) = 1/(4 - 2) = .5 \text{ minutes}$$
$$= 30 \text{ seconds} \quad \text{(expected total time in the system for each customer)}$$
$$W_q = \lambda/[\mu(\mu - \lambda)] = 2/[4(4 - 2)] = 2/8 = .25 \text{ minutes}$$
$$= 15 \text{ seconds} \quad \text{(expected waiting time for each customer)}$$

Given these steady-state queuing statistics, it appears unnecessary to employ two attendants at the tollgate. In other words, a half-minute wait is probably not unreasonable; and therefore, the cost of another attendant could not be justified.

Multiserver model with Poisson arrivals and exponential service times   The assumptions of this model are identical to those of the basic single-server model described previously except that the number of servers is assumed to be greater than one. There is an additional assumption: All servers have the same rate of service. For this and the remaining models presented, derivation of the results is omitted. You will find the various proofs in several of the references at the end of this chapter.

$$P(0) = \cfrac{1}{\displaystyle\sum_{n=0}^{s-1} \frac{(\lambda/\mu)^n}{n!} + \frac{(\lambda/\mu)^s}{s!} \left(1 - \frac{\lambda}{s\mu}\right)^{-1}}$$

$$P(n) = \frac{(\lambda/\mu)^n}{n!} P(0) \qquad \text{for } 0 \leq n \leq s$$

$$= \frac{(\lambda/\mu)^n}{s!\,s^{n-s}} P(0) \qquad \text{for } n \geq s$$

$$\rho = \lambda/s\mu \qquad \text{(assuming each server has the same mean service rate of } \mu \text{ units per time period)}$$

$$L_q = \frac{P(0)(\lambda/\mu)^s \rho}{s!(1-\rho)^2}$$

$$W_q = L_q/\lambda$$

$$W_s = W_q + (1/\mu)$$

$$L = L_q + (\lambda/\mu)$$

For computational convenience, a table of $P(0)$ can be found in the back of the book.

[Example]   Consider the toll road example again, but let's assume that the arrival rate has increased to 600 cars per hour and that three attendants are on duty rather than one.

$$\lambda = 10 \text{ cars per minute}$$
$$\mu = 4 \text{ cars per minute}$$
$$s = 3$$

$$P(0) = \cfrac{1}{\displaystyle\sum_{n=0}^{2} \frac{(10/4)^n}{n!} + \frac{(10/4)^3}{3!} \cdot \frac{1}{1 - (10/12)}}$$

$$= \cfrac{1}{1 + \dfrac{10}{4} + \dfrac{25/4}{2} + \dfrac{1,000/64}{6} \cdot \dfrac{1/1}{6}}$$

$$= 64/1,424 = .04494$$

$$L_q = \frac{.04494(10/4)^3(10/12)}{3![1 - (10/12)]^2}$$

$$= 3.51124 \text{ cars}$$

$$W_q = 3.51124/10 = .35112 \text{ minutes per car}$$

$$W = .351124 + .25 = .601124 \text{ minutes per car}$$

$$L = 3.51124 + (10/4) = 6.01124 \text{ cars}$$

Given these queuing statistics, three attendants would constitute a very tolerable service facility from a driver's point of view. However, for a more complete analysis, queuing statistics for two attendants should be computed to see if the degradation in service with fewer attendants is worth the decrease in cost. Obviously, since the value of driver waiting time is very vague, a value judgment must be made. The utility of the queuing model is that the value judgment you make after using it is more informed and generally should result in a better decision.

Single-server model with arbitrary service times If the analyst has determined that arrivals to the system are Poisson-distributed but cannot accept the hypothesis that service times are exponentially distributed, it is quite possible that a valid model does exist. Specifically, the assumptions of this model are:

1 Poisson arrival process

2 Infinite calling population

3 Infinite queue

4 FCFS queue discipline

5 Single server

6 The distribution of service time is unknown, but it has a mean, $1/\mu$, and a variance, σ^2. These parameters are known.

The steady-state results are:

$$L_q = (\lambda^2 \sigma^2 + \rho^2)/[2(1 - \rho)]$$
$$\rho = \lambda/\mu$$
$$L_s = \rho + L_q$$
$$W_q = L_q/\lambda$$
$$W_s = W_q + (1/\mu)$$
$$P(0) = 1 - \rho$$

It is interesting to note that as σ^2 increases L_q, L_s, W_q, and W_s all increase. This means that the performance of the queuing system is not solely dependent on mean service time but on the variance in service time as well. Consequently, a server with a higher mean service time may still be the more productive if it is also the more consistent.

When service times are constant, as might be the case in a process such as a car wash, the foregoing model can be applied. The only difference is that the variance σ^2 is equal to zero. Therefore, $L_q = \rho^2/[2(1 - \rho)]$. The other relationships remain unchanged.

[Example] A savings and loan association is opening a branch in a nearby suburb. This branch is expected to need one savings counselor, but management wants to have descriptive queuing statistics to confirm an intuition that only one savings counselor is actually necessary. Plans are to transfer one savings counselor from the main office. Data concerning this particular counselor's time spent with a customer have been collected, but goodness-of-fit tests indicate that these service times are not exponentially distributed. It is further estimated that the mean service time is 15 minutes and variance is 10 minutes. Customers are expected to arrive in a Poisson manner at a rate of two per hour.

$$\lambda = 2 \text{ customers per hour}$$
$$\mu = 4 \text{ customers per hour}$$
$$\sigma^2 = 1/6 \text{ hour}$$
$$L_q = \frac{4(1/6) + (1/2)^2}{2[1 - (1/2)]}$$
$$= \frac{11/12}{1} = 11/12 = .9166 \text{ customers}$$

$$\rho = 2/4 = 1/2$$
$$L_s = 1/2 + 11/12 = 17/12 = 1.4166 \text{ customers}$$
$$W_q = \frac{11/12}{2} = 11/24 \text{ hours} = 27.5 \text{ minutes}$$
$$W_s = 11/24 + 6/24 = 17/24 \text{ hours} = 42.5 \text{ minutes}$$
$$P(0) = 1 - 1/2 = 1/2$$

The foregoing queuing statistics suggest that either the savings and loan customers are going to have to be very patient or the firm will lose savings customers if it carries out its plan to have only one savings counselor.

[Example] The manager of a small, coin-operated car wash is thinking about adding a vacuum to the business so that customers can vacuum the inside of their automobiles. Service time for the vacuum is constant at 5 minutes, and arrivals are Poisson at a rate of 10 per hour. For this example, assume an infinite queue and calling population. Before investing in the vacuum, the manager wishes to know what to expect with respect to customers waiting for the vacuum.

$$\lambda = 10 \text{ customers per hour}$$
$$1/\mu = 1/12 \text{ hour per customer}$$
$$\sigma^2 = 0$$
$$\mu = 12 \text{ customers per hour}$$
$$\rho = 5/6 = .833$$
$$L_q = \frac{(5/6)^2}{2(1/6)} = 2.08 \text{ customers}$$
$$L_s = 5/6 + 25/12 = 2.92 \text{ customers}$$
$$W_q = \frac{25/12}{10} = .208 \text{ hours} = 12 \text{ minutes}$$
$$W_s = 12 + 5 = 17 \text{ minutes}$$

With these results, the manager might want to seriously consider two vacuums since the probability of a customer's joining the queue when there are two or more cars waiting is low.

Single-server model with arbitrary service times and a priority queue discipline Only limited results exist for queuing models that do not have an FCFS queue discipline. The model described in this section uses a nonpreemptive priority queue discipline and makes no assumption about the service time distribution. The explicit assumptions of this model are the following:

1 Poisson arrival process.

2 Infinite calling population.

3 Infinite queue.

4 The queue discipline divides calling units into classes, and service is FCFS within each priority class.

5 Single server.

6 The service time distribution for each priority class is unknown, but the mean service time and variance are known for each priority class.

The steady-state queuing statistics are given by the following expressions:

$$W_q^k = \frac{\sum_{i=1}^{m} \lambda_i [(1/\mu_i)^2 + \sigma_i^2]}{2(1 - S_{k-1})(1 - S_k)}$$

where W_q^k = the expected waiting time for a calling unit in priority
class k

λ_i = arrival rate of priority class i

μ_i = service rate of priority class i

σ_i^2 = variance in service time of priority class i

$S_k = \sum_{i=1}^{k} \rho_i < 1, \ k = 1, 2, \dots m$

$S_0 = 0$

m = number of priority classes

$\rho_k = \lambda_k / \mu_k$

$L_q^k = \lambda_k W_q^k$

$W_s^k = W_q^k + (1/\mu_k)$

$L_s^k = L_q^k + \rho_k$

$W_q = \sum_{k=1}^{m} \frac{\lambda_k}{\lambda} W_q^k$

Where $\lambda = \sum_{k=1}^{m} \lambda_k$

Introduction to management science

W_q = expected waiting time for any customer

$$W_s = \sum_{k=1}^{m} \frac{\lambda_k}{\lambda} W_s^k$$

= expected time spent in the system for any customer

[Example] Jobs to be run on a computer system are of two types and hence two different priorities. Only one job can run at one time. Both types of job arrive according to a Poisson process, but service time distributions are normal, with means of 5 minutes and 15 minutes. Variances for the two priority classes are 5 minutes and 2.5 minutes, respectively. Type I jobs arrive at a rate of three per hour and type II jobs arrive at a rate of two per hour. What are the steady-state queuing statistics?

$\rho_1 = 3/12 = .25$
$\rho_2 = 2/4 = .50$
$S_1 = .25$
$S_2 = .25 + .50 = .75$
$\lambda_1 = 3$ jobs per hour
$\lambda_2 = 2$ jobs per hour
$\mu_1 = 12$ jobs per hour
$\mu_2 = 4$ jobs per hour
$\sigma_1^2 = 1/12$ hour
$\sigma_2^2 = 1/24$ hour

$$W_q^1 = \frac{3[(1/12)^2 + (1/12)] + 2[(1/4)^2 + (1/24)]}{2(1 - 0)[1 - (3/12)]}$$

$= .47916/1.5$ hours $= .31944$ hours $= 19.17$ minutes

$$W_q^2 = \frac{3[(1/12)^2 + (1/12)] + 2[(3/12)^2 + (1/24)]}{2[1 - (3/12)][1 - (3/12 + 2/4)]}$$

$$= \frac{(39/144) + (30/144)}{(18/12)(3/12)} = 23/18 \text{ hours} = 1.278 \text{ hours}$$

$= 76.6$ minutes

$L_q^1 = 3(.31944) = .95832$ jobs
$L_q^2 = 2(1.278) = 2.556$ jobs
$W_s^1 = 19.17 + 5 = 24.17$ minutes
$W_s^2 = 76.6 + 15 = 91.6$ minutes
$L_s^1 = .95832 + .25 = 1.20832$ jobs

$$L_s^2 = 2.556 + .5 = 3.056 \text{ jobs}$$
$$W_q = (3/5)(19.17) + (2/5)(76.6) = 42.14 \text{ minutes}$$
$$W_s = .6(24.17) + .4(91.6) = 51.14 \text{ minutes}$$

This model might be used to evaluate the desirability of a priority queue discipline as opposed to an FCFS queue discipline. How might you accomplish such a comparison?

Single-server model with a finite queue Often, queue length constitutes a constraint on the queuing system. If queue length is limited either by customer attitude or the physical facilities, it is not possible to use any of the models previously described. The model we present in this section has assumptions identical to the first basic single-server model we developed in this chapter *except that* the restriction of an infinite queue length can be dropped. The steady-state results that have been derived are as follows:

$$P(0) = \frac{1 - (\lambda/\mu)}{1 - (\lambda/\mu)^{M+1}}$$

where M = maximum number of calling units in the system and the maximum queue length is $M - 1$

$$P(n) = P(0)(\lambda/\mu)^n \quad \text{for } n = 0, 1, \dots M$$
$$L_s = \frac{\lambda/\mu}{1 - (\lambda/\mu)} - \frac{(M+1)(\lambda/\mu)^{M+1}}{1 - (\lambda/\mu)^{M+1}}$$
$$L_q = L_s + P(0) - 1$$
$$W_q = \frac{L_q}{\lambda[1 - P(M)]}$$
$$W_s = W_q + 1/\mu$$

The foregoing results require that $\lambda < \mu$.

[Example] A basic programming course includes a lab at which a student "consultant" is on duty to help students debug their programs. It can be assumed that no student will get in line for help if there are more than three other students waiting. Students arrive at the lab according to a Poisson process at an average rate of four per hour. Service times are exponential, and the mean service time is 10 minutes. Because the class is large, an infinite calling population can be assumed. What are the steady-state queuing statistics?

$$M = 4$$
$$\lambda = 4$$
$$\mu = 6$$
$$P(0) = \frac{1 - (2/3)}{1 - (2/3)^5} = .384$$
$$P(4) = .384(4/6)^4$$

= probability of a full system so that a student refuses to join the queue

= .076

$$L_s = \frac{2/3}{1 - (2/3)} - \frac{5(2/3)^5}{1 - (2/3)^5}$$
$$= 2 - .757 = 1.243 \text{ students}$$
$$L_q = 1.243 + .384 - 1 = .627 \text{ students}$$
$$W_q = .627/[4(1 - .076)] = .17 \text{ hours, or } 10.2 \text{ minutes}$$
$$W_s = .17 + 1/6 = .336 \text{ hours, or } 20.2 \text{ minutes}$$

Given these queuing statistics, it is probable that university administrators are quite satisfied with the lab system because there is only a 7.6 percent chance of a student's not being serviced, and those that choose to wait wait, on the average, only 10.2 minutes.

There is a multiserver extension of this model, which is beyond the scope of this text.

Models that have a finite calling population In some queuing systems, the size of the calling population is so small that to assume it to be infinite would seriously degrade the usefulness of a queuing model. Some results that have been derived for a limited source model are presented in this section. The model described next assumes a Poisson arrival process and exponentially distributed service times. It can be applied to a multiserver queuing system or a single-server system whose queue discipline is FCFS. The steady-state descriptive statistics are:

$$P(0) = \frac{1}{\left[\sum_{n=0}^{s-1} \frac{N!}{(N - n)!\, n!} \left(\frac{\lambda}{\mu}\right)^n + \sum_{n=s}^{N} \frac{N!}{(N - n)!\, s!\, s^{n-s}} \left(\frac{\lambda}{\mu}\right)^n \right]}$$

where N = the number of calling units in the calling population
λ = mean arrival rate for *each* individual unit

$$P(n) = \begin{cases} P(0) \dfrac{N!}{(N-n)!\, n!} \left(\dfrac{\lambda}{\mu}\right)^n & \text{for } 0 \le n \le s \\[2ex] P(0) \dfrac{N!}{(N-n)!\, s!\, s^{n-s}} \left(\dfrac{\lambda}{\mu}\right)^n & \text{for } s \le n \le N \\[2ex] 0 & \text{for } n > M \end{cases}$$

$$L_s = \sum_{n=1}^{N} nP(n)$$

$$W_s = L_s / \lambda_e$$

where $\lambda_e = \lambda(N - L_s)$

$$W_q = W_s - (1/\mu)$$

$$L_q = \lambda_e W_q$$

[Example] In a certain computer facility, three central processing units (CPUs) are serviced by two customer engineers. Each CPU breaks down in a Poisson manner on the average of every 4 hours. Repair times are exponentially distributed, with a mean of 3 hours. Determine the steady-state queuing statistics.

λ = .25 per hour
μ = .33 per hour

$$P(0) = 1 \Big/ \left[\frac{3!}{(3-0)!\,0!} \cdot \left(\frac{25}{33}\right)^0 + \frac{3!}{(3-1)!\,1!} \cdot \left(\frac{25}{33}\right)^1 \right.$$
$$\left. + \frac{3!}{(3-2)!\,2!\,2^0} \cdot \left(\frac{25}{33}\right)^2 + \frac{3!}{(3-3)!\,2!\,2^1} \cdot \left(\frac{25}{33}\right)^3 \right]$$
$$= .177095$$

$$P(1) = .177095 \cdot \left(\frac{3!}{2!\,1!}\right)\left(\frac{25}{33}\right)^1 = .402489$$

$$P(2) = .177095 \cdot \left(\frac{3!}{1!\,2!}\right)\left(\frac{25}{33}\right)^2 = .304916$$

$$P(3) = .177095 \left(\frac{3!}{0!\,2!\,2^1}\right)\left(\frac{25}{33}\right)^3 = .115498$$

L_s = .402489 + 2(.304916) + 3(.115498) = 1.3588 CPUs
λ_e = .25(3 − 1.3588) = .4103
W_s = 1.3588 / .4103 = 3.31172 hours
W_q = 3.31172 − 3.0 = .31172 hours, or 18.7 minutes
L_q − .4103(.31172) = .127899 CPUs

An economic analysis of this queuing system would be possible since the cost of waiting could conceivably be computed, as could the cost of additional repairmen. Consequently, the queuing model could be used to make a very rational decision regarding the optimal number of repairmen.

[Application of queuing theory]

So far in this chapter, we have described the structure and characteristics of queuing systems and have defined several representative queuing models. By now, it is obvious to you that before a queuing model can be applied, the actual queuing system must be carefully analyzed.

Such an analysis of the queuing system should include the identification and verification of the system characteristics we described earlier in this chapter. Once the system has been analyzed, the analyst must identify the decision variables. In simple queuing systems these variables are usually the number of servers and, often, the type of server. The queue discipline often constitutes another controllable variable. Having identified decision variables, each of which is generally discrete in nature, the analyst must determine the criteria for a good set of decision variables. These criteria are usually economic in nature. The cost of the queuing system must be weighed against the waiting time of the calling units.

Two approaches to the problem of applying queuing theory to making decisions are common. One approach is to explicitly define the cost of one calling unit waiting one unit of time and then minimize an objective function such as

$$Z = C_q + C_w$$
where C_q = cost of the queuing system
C_w = cost of waiting

This approach is best if the cost of waiting can be explicitly defined; however, it is often very difficult to do so. If you are trying to decide on how many teller windows to have open in a bank or how many checkout counters to have open in a supermarket, the loss of goodwill caused by long lines and long waits is difficult to measure. If, however, you are trying to decide on the number of repairmen to have available to fix your productive machinery, these costs can be reasonably estimated.

The second approach to applying queuing theory is to seek to minimize a cost function subject to a set of constraints about the line length and expected waiting times. Although this approach is not so clear-cut nor objective as explicitly estimating the cost of waiting, it is often more acceptable to management.

Once the queuing system has been analyzed and the criteria for decision making have been defined, the analyst must then decide on the solution methodology. Either an analytical queuing model, such as one of the models presented in this chapter, can be applied or a computer simulation model can be written. The advantages of using an analytical model as opposed to a simulation model are computational efficiency and the absence of sampling error. Although queuing theory has advanced considerably in recent years and many models have been derived, real-world queuing systems often do not have a mathematical counterpart. Rather than force a real queuing system to fit a mathematical model by simplifying the assumptions about system properties, computer simulation should be used. This relatively new tool is discussed in detail in the next chapter. In addition to having the flexibility to model any queuing system, simulation is not restricted to a few steady-state operating characteristics. For example, the frequency distribution of waiting times can be determined, not just the mean or expected value of waiting time.

Regardless of whether an analytical or simulation model is used to evaluate the different sets of decision variables, you should realize that determining the "best" set of decision variables is a trial-and-error process. Queuing theory is not an optimization technique; it is a descriptive tool.

$$\lceil\text{Derivation of basic single-server}\rceil$$
$$\lfloor\quad\text{queuing model appendix}\quad\rfloor$$

In order to derive expressions for typical queuing statistics, it is first necessary to derive expressions for $P(n)$ and $P(0)$. Let

Introduction to management science

Δt = a time interval small enough such that only one event* can occur

A = an event such that at time t there are n units in the system and at time $t + \Delta t$ there are still n units in the system because there were no arrivals or departures during Δt

B = an event such that at time $t + \Delta t$ there are n units in the system as a result of one arrival and no departures during Δt and at time t there were $n - 1$ units in the system

C = an event such that at time $t + \Delta t$ there are n units in the system as a result of no arrivals and one departure during Δt and at time t there were $n + 1$ units in the system

D = an event such that at time $t + \Delta t$ there are n units in the system as a result of one arrival and one departure during Δt and at time t there were n units in the system

$P_{t + \Delta t}(n)$ = probability of n units in the queuing system at time $t + \Delta t$

Because events A, B, C, and D are mutually exclusive and represent an exhaustive set, $P_{t+\Delta t}(n) = P(A) + P(B) + P(C) + P(D)$.

Now we must develop expressions for $P(A)$, $P(B)$, and $P(C)$. First, we have that P(one arrival during $\Delta t) = \lambda \Delta t$. Because of our definition of Δt, P(no arrivals during $\Delta t) = 1 - \lambda \Delta t$. Then, P(one departure during $\Delta t) = \mu \Delta t$. Because of our definition of Δt, P(no departure during $\Delta t) = 1 - \mu \Delta t$. Thus,

$$P(A) = P_t(n)(1 - \lambda \Delta t)(1 - \mu \Delta t)$$
$$= [P_t(n) - P_t(n) \lambda \Delta t](1 - \mu \Delta t)$$
$$= P_t(n) - P_t(n)\lambda \Delta t - \mu \Delta t P_t(n) + \lambda \mu \Delta t^2 P_t(n)$$
$$P(B) = P_t(n - 1)(\lambda \Delta t)(1 - \mu \Delta t)$$
$$= P_t(n - 1) \lambda \Delta t - P_t(n - 1) \lambda \mu \Delta t^2$$
$$P(C) = P_t(n + 1)(1 - \lambda \Delta t)\mu \Delta t$$
$$= P_t(n + 1) \mu \Delta t - P_t(n + 1) \lambda \mu \Delta t^2$$
$$P(D) = 0$$

since, by definition, only one event can occur during Δt.

$$P_{t + \Delta t}(n) = P_t(n) - P_t(n)\lambda \Delta t - \mu \Delta t P_t(n)$$
$$+ P_t(n - 1)\lambda \Delta t + P_t(n + 1)\mu \Delta t\dagger$$

*An *event* in a queuing system of this type constitutes either an arrival or a departure.

† All terms containing Δt^2 have been dropped because as $\Delta t \rightarrow 0$ these terms would be sufficiently small to disregard.

$$P_{t+\Delta t}(n) - P_t(n) = -P_t(n)\lambda\Delta t - P_t(n)\mu\Delta t + P_t(n-1)\lambda\Delta t$$
$$+ P_t(n+1)\mu\Delta t$$

$$\frac{P_{t+\Delta t}(n) - P_t(n)}{\Delta t} = -P_t(n)\lambda - P_t(n)\mu + P_t(n-1)\lambda$$
$$+ P_t(n+1)\mu - P_t(n)(\lambda+\mu) + P_t(n-1)\lambda$$
$$+ P_t(n+1)\mu$$

$$\lim_{\Delta t \to 0} \frac{P_{t+\Delta t}(n) - P_t(n)}{\Delta t} = \frac{d[P(n)]}{dt}$$

$$\therefore \frac{d[P(n)]}{dt} = -P_t(n)(\lambda+\mu) + P_t(n-1)\lambda + P_t(n+1)\mu$$

Since it is impossible to have fewer than zero units in the system and since it is also impossible to have a unit depart an empty system, $d[P(0)]/dt = -\lambda P_t(0) + \mu P_t(1)$.

At steady state, $P_t(n)$ is not a function of t by definition and therefore, $d[P(n)]/dt - 0$. Consequently, $\lambda P(0) = \mu P(1)$ and $P(1) = \lambda P(0)/\mu$. Remember, $d[P(n)/dt = -P_t(n)(\lambda+\mu) + P_t(n-1)\lambda + P_t(n+1)\mu$ for $n > 0$.

We let $n = 1$ and thus $-P(1)(\lambda+\mu) + P(0)\lambda + P(2)\mu = 0$ and $P(2) = [P(1)(\lambda+\mu) - P(0)\lambda]/\mu$. Substituting $\lambda P(0)/\mu$ for $P(1)$, we have

$$P(2) = \frac{(\lambda P(0)/\mu)(\lambda+\mu) - P(0)\lambda}{\mu}$$
$$= \frac{(\lambda^2 P(0)/\mu) + \lambda\mu P(0) - P(0)\lambda}{\mu}$$
$$= \lambda^2 P(0)/(\mu^2)$$
$$= (\lambda/\mu)^2 P(0)$$

Similarly

$$P(3) = (\lambda/\mu)^3 P(0)$$

By mathematical induction, therefore,

$$P(n) = (\lambda/\mu)^n P(0)$$

Having derived an expression for $P(n)$ in terms of $P(0)$, it is necessary now to find $P(0)$ as a function of λ and μ.

$$\sum_{n=0}^{\infty} P(n) = 1$$
$$P(0) + P(1) + \ldots = 1$$

$$P(0) + \frac{\lambda P(0)}{\mu} + \left(\frac{\lambda}{\mu}\right)^2 P(0) + \ldots = 1$$

$$P(0)\left[1 + \frac{\lambda}{\mu} + \left(\frac{\lambda}{\mu}\right)^2 + \ldots\right] = 1$$

$$\frac{1}{P(0)} = 1 + \frac{\lambda}{\mu} + \left(\frac{\lambda}{\mu}\right)^2 + \ldots$$

Since $\lambda/\mu < 1$

$$\sum_{n=0}^{\infty} \left(\frac{\lambda}{\mu}\right)^n = \frac{1}{[1 - (\lambda/\mu)]} \qquad \text{(limit of a geometric series)}$$

$$P(0) = 1 - (\lambda/\mu)$$

Because it has been proven‡ that $L_s = \lambda W_s$, $L_q = \lambda W_q$, and $W_s = W_q + (1/\mu)$, all that remains is to derive an expression for one of these queuing statistics:

L_s = expected number of calling units in the queuing system

$$L_s = \sum_{n=0}^{\infty} nP(n)$$

$$L_s = 0 \cdot P(0) + 1 \cdot P(1) + 2 \cdot P(2) + \ldots$$

$$= \frac{\lambda P(0)}{\mu} + \left(\frac{\lambda}{\mu}\right)^2 P(0) + \ldots$$

$$= P(0)\left[\frac{\lambda}{\mu} + 2\left(\frac{\lambda}{\mu}\right)^2 + 3\left(\frac{\lambda}{\mu}\right)^3 + \ldots\right]$$

$$\left(\frac{\lambda}{\mu}\right)L_s = P(0)\left[\left(\frac{\lambda}{\mu}\right)^2 + 2\left(\frac{\lambda}{\mu}\right)^3 + 3\left(\frac{\lambda}{\mu}\right)^4 + \ldots\right]$$

$$L_s - \left(\frac{\lambda}{\mu}\right)L_s = P(0)\left[\frac{\lambda}{\mu} + \left(\frac{\lambda}{\mu}\right)^2 + \left(\frac{\lambda}{\mu}\right)^3 + \ldots\right]$$

$$= \frac{P(0)\lambda}{\mu}\left[1 + \frac{\lambda}{\mu} + \left(\frac{\lambda}{\mu}\right)^2 + \ldots\right]$$

$$= \frac{P(0)\lambda}{\mu}\left[\frac{1}{1 - (\lambda/\mu)}\right]$$

‡John D. Little, "A Proof for the Queueing Formula: $L = \lambda W$," *Operations Research*, 9, no. 3 (May–June, 1961), 383–387.

Since $P(0) = 1 - (\lambda/\mu)$,

$$L_s\left(1 - \frac{\lambda}{\mu}\right) = \left(1 - \frac{\lambda}{\mu}\right)\left(\frac{\lambda}{\mu}\right)\left[\frac{1}{1 - (\lambda/\mu)}\right]$$

$$L_s = \frac{\lambda}{\mu}\left[\frac{1}{1 - (\lambda/\mu)}\right]$$

$$= \frac{\lambda/\mu}{1 - (\lambda/\mu)} = \frac{\lambda}{\mu - \lambda}$$

$$L_s = \lambda W_s$$

$$\therefore W_s = \frac{L_s}{\lambda} = \frac{\lambda/(\mu - \lambda)}{\lambda}$$

$$= 1/(\mu - \lambda)$$

$$W_s = W_q + (1/\mu)$$

$$W_q = W_s - \frac{1}{\mu} = \frac{1}{\mu - \lambda} - \frac{1}{\mu}$$

$$= \frac{\mu - \mu + \lambda}{\mu(\mu - \lambda)} = \frac{\lambda}{\mu(\mu - \lambda)}$$

$$L_q = \lambda W_q$$

$$= \lambda^2/[\mu(\mu - \lambda)]$$

Summarizing the results, we have

$$P(0) = 1 - (\lambda/\mu)$$

$$P(n) = P(0)(\lambda/\mu)^n$$

$$\rho = \lambda/\mu$$

$$L_s = \lambda/(\mu - \lambda)$$

$$L_q = \lambda^2/[\mu(\mu - \lambda)]$$

$$W_s = 1/(\mu - \lambda)$$

$$W_q = \lambda/[\mu(\mu - \lambda)]$$

[Bibliography]

Cox, David R., and Walter L. Smith, *Queues*. Agincourt, Ont.: Methuen Publications, 1961.

Hillier, Fredrick S., and Gerald J. Lieberman, *Introduction to Operations Research*, 2nd ed. San Francisco, Calif.: Holden-Day Inc., 1974.

Morse, Philip M., *Queues, Inventories and Maintenance.* New York: John Wiley & Sons, Inc., 1958.

Saaty, Thomas L., *Elements of Queueing Theory.* New York: McGraw-Hill, Inc., 1961.

Taha, Hamdy A., *Operations Research: An Introduction.* New York: MacMillan Publishing Corp., 1971.

Trueman, Richard E., *An Introduction to Quantitative Methods for Decision Making.* New York: Holt, Rinehart & Winston, Inc., 1974.

[Review questions]

1 What are the three basic properties of a calling population?

2 What is meant by "customers arrive according to a Poisson process?"

3 What is meant by *queue discipline*?

4 How would you classify the structure of a hospital's emergency room?

5 Distinguish between preemptive and nonpreemptive priority queue disciplines.

6 What is meant by the statement that queuing theory is *not* an optimization technique?

7 List three reasons you might choose to use digital simulation rather than queuing theory.

[Problems]

9.1 Analyze the following queuing systems by describing their various system properties:
   a Barber shop
   b Bank
   c Machine repairman
   d Traffic light
   e Grocery store checkout counter

f Tugs in a harbor
g Airport runway
h Computer system
i Hospital emergency room
j Gas station
k Car wash
l Tool crib
m Laundromat

9.2 A large department store is preparing for the Christmas season. Last year, the store had two Santas for the children to talk to. Lines were long, and the store is trying to decide how many Santas to employ this year. Describe this problem as a queuing problem. Be sure to identify all pertinent characteristics. Include a representative schematic of the system.

9.3 Consider a tool crib in a large factory. At the present time, one worker operates the tool crib, but the vice president of production has noticed rather long lines of workers waiting for tools. Factory employees arrive to the tool crib at a rate of 25 per hour. Service times are exponential, with a mean of 2 minutes. The arrival process is Poisson. Analyze the desirability of adding a second tool crib clerk.

9.4 The Toll Road Authority wants to know how many toll booths to design into its Main Road exit. Naturally, an objective is to minimize cost, but there is also a stipulation that the expected line length during peak hours should not exceed five cars. From data taken from other toll road exits, it has been determined that interarrival times and service times are exponentially distributed. The peak arrival rate is expected to be ten cars per minute. The average service time is 15 seconds. How many toll booths should be designed into the system?

9.5 At Disneyland, plans are being made to install a new ride. Management would like to get a feel for the length of lines and the expected waiting times for this ride so that a decision can be made whether to have one or two such installations. People arrive in a Poisson manner, but the time the ride takes is constant. Estimates are that people will arrive at a rate of one every 2 minutes. The ride takes 1.75 minutes. Analyze the queuing system.

9.6 Consider a one-chair barbershop. At the present location, a barber has, on the average, 10 customers per day. The average haircut takes 20 minutes. Cutting time has been shown to be exponentially distributed.

It has been this barber's experience that customers do not wait for a haircut if two people are already waiting. A move to a new location is possible. The new location would probably increase the number of customers per day to 15. Analyze the present system and the proposed system by computing the queuing statistics for each system. Make a recommendation concerning the proposed move.

9.7 A certain professor holds office hours two hours each day. Three types of people need to see this professor: female students, other faculty, and male students. Many students complain that the queue discipline is not FCFS but a priority discipline with the priority scheme as follows: (1) female students, (2) other faculty members, and (3) male students. The conference time has been analyzed using historical data and has been found to be normal, with a mean of 5 minutes and a standard deviation of 2 minutes. People arrive at the professor's office in a Poisson manner (that is, no appointments are allowed during office hours). The arrival rate for female students is three per hour. The arrival rates for faculty members and male students are two and four per hour, respectively. What would be the effect on the queuing statistics if the professor changed to FCFS queue discipline? Assume an infinite queue and calling population.

9.8 The local supermarket has the policy that checks are cashed by the store manager only. Customers wishing to cash checks arrive in a Poisson manner at an average rate of 45 customers per hour. The manager takes, on the average, 1 minute to cash a check. This service time has been shown to be exponentially distributed. Accomplish the following:

    a Compute the percentage of time that the manager spends cashing checks.

    b Compute the average time a customer is expected to wait.

    c Compute the number of customers waiting to get checks cashed.

    d Compute the probability of the manager attending to some other function assuming that check cashing is the manager's first priority.

    e Explain to the manager how you would analyze the effect of adding the assistant manager to the check-cashing function.

9.9 Two lawyers are in partnership. Each lawyer has a secretary. Jobs arrive to each secretary in a Poisson manner at a rate of three per hour, on the average. It takes either secretary an average of 15 minutes to accomplish each individual job. This service time is exponentially distributed.

a Assuming that each secretary does only the work of one lawyer, what is the expected waiting time for each job?

b What would be the effect of pooling the secretaries?

9.10 A certain aerospace company has five identical, numerically controlled milling machines. Each machine fails on the average of three times per week, and it takes a technician on the average 2.5 hours to fix the machine. Historical data indicate a Poisson arrival process and exponential service times. Because of serious scheduling consequences, management does not want a machine down for more than 3 hours. For this reason, it has been decided that expected waiting time should not exceed $1/2$ hour. Assume the plant operates the equipment only during the prime shift.

a What are the expected times a machine will have to wait with one technician on duty? with two technicians on duty?

b What is your recommendation to management?

c What options do you think management has in addition to the number of technicians?

[G–H Company Ltd. case]

The G–H Company Ltd.[1] had operated in Kovia, an African country, as an importer of a variety of goods and machinery for 14 years. One of their major sources of revenue was the importation and sale of Land Rovers. Their Land Rover service department (which did occasional work on other makes and models at the descretion of the service manager) consisted of 72 employees. Forty-five of these were classified as mechanics of three different grades. There were about 12 Class I fitters[2] whose average wage was $K.\$1$[3] an hour, 18 Class II fitters at an average wage of $K.\$.80$ an hour, and the remainder in Class III at an average wage of $K.\$.50$ an hour. The other 27 were working in less skilled jobs such as "helpers," "cleaners," "tire changers," and so on. Their average hourly wage was $K.\$.40$ an hour.

The company's spare-parts service for mechanics consisted of two employees. One was a well-qualified parts specialist whose wage was $K.\$.90$ an hour. The other was a helper whose work consisted mainly of unloading, unpacking, and running errands. He did not fill parts orders.

Mechanics requisitioned replacement parts by bringing the service work order to the parts department, which was next to the workshop. The "public" and outside workshops purchased Land Rover parts from a counter at the opposite end of the parts department, near the street entrance. The spare-parts specialist serving outside clientele did not service mechanics' requisitions, due to a different set of pricing and invoicing procedures and different cash control procedures.

The two parts specialists reported to the head of the automotive purchasing department who in turn reported to the Automotive General

---

This case was prepared by Professor James A. Lee, Ohio University, Athens, Ohio, and was reprinted with his permission.

[1] This case has been disguised.

[2] Mechanics

[3] One Kovian dollar = U.S. $.50 = $K.\$1$.

Manager. For some time the automotive purchasing department head had been attempting to persuade his superior of the need for an additional parts specialist for the workshop service section. His arguments were mainly that mechanics complained of wasting time waiting for service at the counter. Unable to convince his superior of the need for an additional parts specialist for the mechanics' counter, he undertook, on the advice of a friend who had just studied operations management in the U.S., a study of the queuing problem at the counter. He personally timed the arrival of each mechanic requesting service and the time taken to service him. These data are given in Table 1.

After gathering his data, he wondered how they should be analyzed to help him convince his superior of the need for an extra parts service specialist. He also wondered if these data might not prove that his superior was right in refusing his request.

Table 1   Sample arrival and service times on Wednesday, March 18, 1973 from 8 A.M. to 11 A.M.

Mechanics' arrival times	Time to service each mechanic (min)	Mechanics' arrival times	Time to service each mechanic (min)	Mechanics' arrival times	Time to service each mechanic (min)
8:05	7	8:48	5	9:58	1
8:06	2	9:01	2	10:11	4
8:10	2	9:08	2	10:11	2
8:13	3	9:19	5	10:11	1
8:14	4	9:19	4	10:27	2
8:25	5	9:20	3	10:43	1
8:31	2	9:36	3	10:45	3
8:31	4	9:39	2	10:45	6
8:35	6	9:40	1	10:49	2
8:37	3	9:45	4	10:56	4

[Case problem]

1 Use the appropriate queuing models to analyze the problem and make recommendations concerning an extra parts service specialist. *Hint*: Your analysis should include the economic justification for your recommendation.

[The Engel Bag Tie Company case]

The Engel Company was founded in Cincinnati in 1967 by Mr. Abraham M. Engel, an engineer, for the purpose of developing, building, and marketing machinery to be used in the manufacture of paper-covered wire ties of the type used with plastic garbage bags. Near the end of development work on the prototype machine, however, Mr. Engel concluded that manufacture of the ties would be a far more profitable venture than sale of the machines. The ensuing years had proven this judgment to be sound, and the firm prospered. Bag ties were sold at an average price of $3 per thousand to manufacturers of blown polyethylene bags and to firms employing such bags for packaging of bakery products. By early 1973 the firm employed 125 people and had recorded profits in 14 consecutive quarters. Several promising new products had been added to the Engel Company's line in recent years, but the bag ties still accounted for over 90 percent of sales and close to 98 percent of profits.

In February of 1973, Mr. Engel observed that his firm was becoming too large for him to personally supervise all of the functional areas as he had in the past. After considerable thought, he decided that if he could hire a competent production manager, he would be taking a step toward freeing himself from the day-to-day routine, which should allow him to devote more time to the other functions of management. With this in mind, Mr. Engel placed advertisements in several leading daily newspapers and, at length, hired a young man named Brian Maxwell.

Maxwell had graduated from a prominent southern technical university with a degree in industrial engineering and had six years of industrial experience, the last three as production supervisor for a large chemical company. Mr. Engel decided that he would suggest that Brian look into the maintenance function of the bag tie machines as a way of getting his feet on the ground.

THE BAG TIE PRODUCTION OPERATION

Bag ties were produced at a rate of 500 per minute on each of 24 identical machines which were currently being operated on a three-shift, 5-day-week basis. Each shift was punctuated by two 10-minute breaks and a 30-minute lunch period during which the machines were not running. Every machine was tended by an operator who maintained raw material supplies, cleared jam-ups, packed finished goods, and monitored the quality of the finished product. The machines had been designed by Mr. Engel, who had incorporated a series of modular subsystems for ease of maintenance. Each machine consisted of a framework, an electric motor, and several mechanical modules that could be removed and interchanged with a like module on any other machine. When a machine breakdown occurred, the operator would signal the maintenance crew by means of a red light mounted on the machine. Each shift was served by three maintenance men whose only responsibility was to repair the breakdowns of the bag tie machines. Service of breakdowns was on a first-come-first-served basis to avoid long delays in returning a machine to service. Repair usually consisted of replacement of one of the modules or adjustment of feeds. When a module had to be removed from a bag tie machine, it was sent to the company machine shop for overhaul and was subsequently returned to the pool of spare modules for eventual reuse. Mr. Engel felt that the use of modules in the design of the machine had been a prime factor in achieving an exceptionally low downtime rate which, in turn, was considered to be instrumental to the overall success of the company.

The choice of having Mr. Maxwell study the bag tie maintenance function as an initial assignment was motivated not only by the conviction that the project would provide a means to acquaint him with the operations of the plant. The bag tie business was still expanding rapidly and lately the lack of production capacity had been a limiting factor, causing Mr. Engel to refuse some potentially attractive contracts. Three new machines were being built in the company machine shop and further additions were being contemplated. Mr. Engel knew that eventually he would have to add another maintenance man to each shift but he was uncertain as to when he should do so. He intuitively felt that he should have one mechanic for every ten machines or so, but his observation of the bag tie department often made him uneasy about this judgment. He knew that the mechanics were frequently idle for considerable periods, but he had also seen the department at times when as many as ten red lights were on at once. Since the work rules of the union labor agreement prohibited the operators from performing maintenance themselves, they usually congregated in the coffee break area when their machines were waiting for a mechanic to complete a previous job. During periods when there were few breakdowns, the mechanics were often seen reading popular magazines.

Table 1 Engel Bag Tie Company income statement for 1972 (in thousands of dollars)

Sales	$8,776
Cost of sales	
Direct labor	889
Material	3,636
Gross margin	4,251
General selling and administrative expenses	1,996
Depreciation	85
Miscellaneous expenses	679
Profit before tax	2,291
Tax (52%)	1,192
Profit after tax	1,099
Dividends	250
Retained	849

Table 2 Standard cost data for 3-inch bag tie

Item		Cost ($ per 1,000 ties)
Material costs		
Wire		.7954
Paper		.4779
Direct labor at $7.50 per hour	7.500	
plus 10% waste	.750	
	8.250	
plus 11.12% nonproductivity	.923	
	9.173	
times .0333		.3058
Packaging material		.0500
Total		1.6291

In an attempt to determine what to do about this situation, Mr. Engel suggested that it was a problem area of some importance to the new production manager, Mr. Maxwell. Mr. Engel gave Maxwell the Engel Company income statement for 1972 and the standard cost sheets for the most popular product, the 3-inch bag tie, as background information. (See Tables 1 and 2).

MR. MAXWELL'S STUDY

As an industrial engineer by training, Maxwell felt that the problem was subject to analysis by use of a waiting-line model. Gathering the data to use as inputs to such a model was a rather time-consuming process that he hoped to avoid if at all possible. After some thought, he got the idea of having the mechanics report the details of each maintenance call on a simple form. He discussed the project with the first shift lead mechanic, Ray Jeffries, and was given a cooperative reaction since Jeffries felt that the results of such a study would show the need for at least one additional mechanic on each shift.

Maxwell had several small pads of a reporting form (Figure 1) printed

Figure 1   Mechanic's report form

Machine number _____

Start time _____

End time _____

and distributed to the mechanics. He determined that the recording of service calls should begin at noon on Tuesday and end at noon on Thursday. Brian explained the recording scheme to each mechanic individually and he was sure that each man understood his task. The reporting was carried out only on the daytime shift in order that he and Mr. Engel could observe the men and determine that the data

Table 3   Distribution of service times

Service time (min)	Number of occurrences	Service time (min)	Number of occurrences
1	1	13	1
2	5	15	25
3	14	20	11
4	9	21	1
5	69	22	1
6	4	25	1
7	7	30	2
8	6	40	2
9	1	50	1
10	36	60	1
12	1	105	1

Total service time: 1,967 min
Total occurrences: 200

collection was being carried out conscientiously. At noon on Thursday, Maxwell collected the completed forms and, by that afternoon, he had tabulated the data, as shown in Table 3. He was somewhat disturbed to find that the data clustered around "convenient" numbers, but he felt that the data were usable if he could assume that the mean value of the data was close to the mean value of the actual service times.

Maxwell went to one of his old engineering textbooks to review queuing theory. He found that, although the mathematical basis for the theory was quite complex, the essence of the difficult calculations was captured by several simple charts and tables. The formulas and tables (Tables 4 and 5) for application of queuing theory in this situation seemed fairly straightforward, and Brian anticipated no difficulty in analyzing the problem.

ANALYSIS OF THE SYSTEM

Mr. Maxwell studied the queuing theory formulas intently (Table 4). It was obvious that N, the number of machines, equaled 24 currently

Table 4   Queuing theory parameters and formulas*

N = number of machines in system
T = average service time
U = average time between calls for service (one machine)
M = number of service channels (mechanics)
X = percent of time spent in service = $T/(T + U)$
D = probability of delay
B = percent of time spent in waiting line = $(1 - F)/F$
F = efficiency factor
Lq = mean number in waiting line = NBF
Wq = mean waiting time = $(T + U)B$
H = mean number of units being serviced = FNX
J = mean number of units running = $NF(1 - X)$

*D, F, and B are derived with the aid of a computer from a very complex set of formulas by imputing values for M and X. Lq, Wq, H, and J are found by doing simple calculations using N, T, U, F, and B as indicated above.

and that N could be varied so that the expanded system could be modeled. The average service time, T, for the period studied was the total service time divided by the number of service calls, $1.967/200$, or about 9.8 minutes. Maxwell reasoned that this average would be independent of the number of machines and also independent of the number of mechanics. Therefore, this figure would not change as the number of mechanics or the number of machines was varied. U, the mean time between service calls for an individual machine, was more difficult for Maxwell to derive. It finally became apparent, however, that that number must be the total number of minutes available to run divided by the total number of service calls. Since there were 480 minutes in a shift and 50 of those minutes were nonrunning minutes anyway (for lunch and scheduled operator breaks), there must be 10,320 minutes available for machine running per shift (430 minutes times

Table 5   Finite queuing data

N = 24 X = .094				N = 26 X = .094			
M	D	F	B	M	D	F	B
5	.065	.998	.002	6	.028	.999	.001
4	.193	.991	.009	5	.090	.997	.003
3	.474	.964	.037	4	.245	.989	.011
2	.875	.831	.203	3	.554	.953	.049
				2	.926	.790	.265

N = 28 X = .094				N = 30 X = .094			
M	D	F	B	M	D	F	B
6	.040	.999	.001	6	.055	.999	.001
5	.119	.996	.004	5	.153	.994	.006
4	.302	.985	.015	4	.363	.980	.020
3	.633	.938	.066	3	.709	.921	.086
2	.961	.747	.339	2	.982	.704	.420

Derived from Peck, L. G. & Hazelwood, R. M., *Finite Queuing Tables*, John Wiley & Sons, Inc., New York, 1958.

24 machines). Reducing this figure by the time spent in maintenance, 983 minutes per shift, gave 9,437 minutes available for running, and dividing that by 100 breakdowns per shift gave an average of about 94.4 running minutes between breakdowns for a single machine.

Since the mean time between service calls, U, was the characteristic of an individual machine, it also was independent of the number of mechanics or the number of machines. Because T and U were both independent of the effects of changes in mechanic manning level or machine population, X, the ratio of the average service time to the sum of the average service time and the average running time, must have also been a single value independent of changes in these factors. Therefore, X must have been equal to $9.8/(94.4 + 9.8) = .094$ for any number of mechanics serving any number of machines.

Turning to the finite queuing data (Table 5), Maxwell saw that S, M, and N were needed to identify a value for F, the efficiency factor, and B, the percent of total time spent in the waiting line. Once F and B were known, the problem was merely to compute values for the remaining elements and compare the costs of the various mechanic alternatives for different machine population situations. Since it had gotten late, Maxwell put the analysis in his drawer and went home feeling that he could easily complete the study the next morning. On his way out of the office he stopped by the personnel desk and found that maintenance men were paid $9 per hour, including fringe benefits.

[Case problems]

1 As Mr. Engel adds more machines, when should he add another mechanic?

2 At what level of mechanic absenteeism would you recommend hiring an additional mechanic as a buffer?

3 If you were Mr. Engel, how would you feel about Maxwell's approach to the problem?

4 Is there another way to approach this problem? Would you need any additional information?

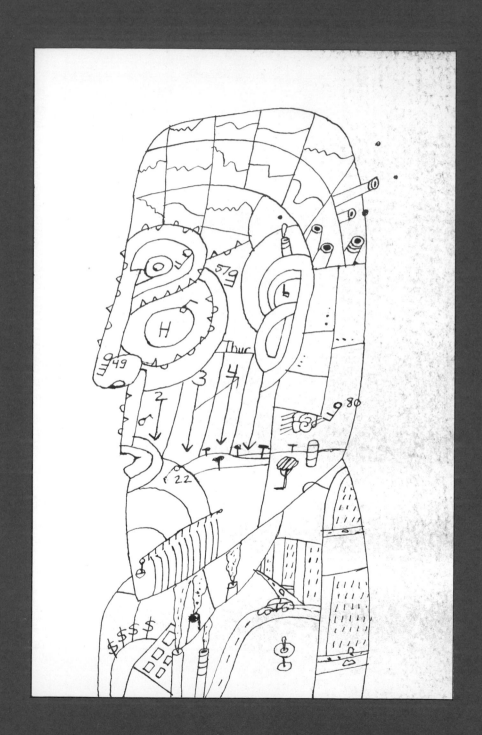

10

$$\Big[\ \text{Discrete digital simulation}\ \Big]$$

According to recent surveys, LP is the only management science technique that approaches computer simulation's extent of application. One noted management scientist whose specialty is simulation contends that simulation should be used as a last resort and only if no other management science technique can be applied to the problem. He goes on to say that that still leaves 99 percent of all applications.

DEFINITION

Monte Carlo simulation

In this chapter, we describe discrete digital simulation, which is often referred to as *Monte Carlo simulation*. In general, simulation is a descriptive, rather than an optimization, technique that involves developing a model of some real phenomenon and then performing experiments on that model. This broad definition applies to types of simulation other than discrete digital simulation. A spacecraft simulator, a wind tunnel, a model airplane, and an analog simulation of some continuous process are all examples of simulations that differ fundamentally from the discrete digital simulation used in management science. To be more specific, discrete digital simulation is a numerical technique that involves modeling a stochastic system on a digital computer with the intention of predicting the system's behavior. Experiments on the simulation model are, in effect, similar to observing the system over a significant period of time.

REASONS FOR USING SIMULATION

The many reasons why a management scientist uses simulation to solve a problem can be clustered into two major categories.

Experimentation with the real system may be impractical or impossible A software systems programmer might find it rather difficult to convince the director of computer operations to allow experimentation with job-scheduling algorithms on the real computer system. Then, too, it is impossible to experiment with a system still in the process of being designed. For example, American Airlines' computerized baggage transportation system at the Dallas-Fort Worth International Airport was simulated before the airport was built.

The real system may be too complex to permit mathematical representation or model solution For example, as we mentioned in the preceding chapter, many queuing systems exist for which closed-form mathematical solutions cannot be, or have not been, derived. Some systems are simply too complex to model mathematically.

SIMULATION APPLICATIONS

The following list indicates the power of simulation to solve a wide range of problems.

Queuing systems As you have seen in Chapter 9, many complex queuing systems exist in the real world that cannot be modeled analytically. Simulation has been used to experiment with different configurations of communications systems, airports, hospitals, and many other complex queuing systems.

Urban systems Simulation has been used to solve some of the urgent problems of today's cities, including how to cope with snow emergencies, how to schedule municipal courts, and where to deploy ambulances.

Industrial systems   Simulation has been used to dictate inventory levels, design distribution systems, determine machine maintenance schedules, and identify the best scheduling algorithms in a job shop.

Financial systems   Simulation has been used to produce pro forma statements to enable the financial manager to anticipate the short-term effects of certain decisions. Decisions concerning capital budgeting can also be made using simulation.

Military systems   Large-scale military battles as well as individual weapon systems have been simulated to aid in the design both of weapon systems and of strategic and tactical operations.

Economics systems   Econometric simulators have been used to predict the outcome of various macroeconomic policy decisions.

Agricultural systems   Simulation has been used to make decisions about equipment on a sugar plantation as well as to predict the pollution of rivers given the use of various chemical fertilizers and pest control agents.

The literature contains a wealth of diverse applications. Can you think of unusual applications of simulation described in the mass media recently?

[Manual simulation]

In order to give you some sense of the technique of computer simulation, let's analyze a very simple problem. Dr. Smith has the appointment schedule reflected in Table 10.1 for Monday morning.

Based on his past experience, Dr. Smith's estimate of arrival times are:

10% chance that patient will be 15 minutes early.

Table 10.1   Dr. Smith's appointment schedule

Appointment time	Patient	Expected appointment duration
9:00	Dupont	20
9:15	Williams	30
9:45	Stratman	20
10:00	Schmidt	30
10:30	Gwyn	30
11:00	Newlin	30
11:30	Gilbert	20
11:45	Edwards	20

25% chance that patient will be 5 minutes early.

40% chance that patient will be on time.

15% chance that patient will be 10 minutes late.

5% chance that patient will be 20 minutes late.

5% chance that patient will not show up.

The duration of each patient's appointment is a stochastic variable that, from past experience, is estimated to be distributed as follows:

10% chance that it will take 80% of the expected time.

10% chance that it will take 90% of the expected time.

40% chance that it will take 100% of the expected time.

30% chance that it will take 110% of the expected time.

5% chance that it will take 120% of the expected time.

5% chance that it will take 130% of the expected time.

Dr. Smith is due in surgery at 1:30 P.M. and must leave the office by 12:15 in order to make it. Dr. Smith would like to know the probability of not canceling any appointments and being on time for surgery.

In order to use simulation to solve this problem, several system properties must be decided upon. For example, let's assume that

Dr. Smith gets to the office at 9:00 A.M. and that patients are taken on a first come, first served basis.

The first step in developing the simulation is to develop a way of generating the two stochastic variables in the system, arrival times and appointment durations. This is done using numbers from a uniform distribution whose parameters are 0 and 1. Remember that a uniform probability distribution is one in which the random variable is defined over a range from a to b. If the parameters of the uniform distribution are 0 and 1, then random $P(x \leq .25)$, for example, is equal to 0.25, and $P(.25 \leq x \leq .75) = .5$. Figure 10.1 depicts the uniform distribution in graphic form.

The process of generating stochastic variables is basic to computer simulation; it is accomplished by defining a function that relates a uniformly distributed random variable to a random variable distributed in another manner. Remember that once this function,

process generator

known as a *process generator*, has been developed, it is easy to sample from a uniform distribution and transform that uniformly distributed random variate into an arrival time or appointment duration. In our problem, both stochastic variables are treated as discrete variables. The function describing arrival times and appointment durations can be found by defining the cumulative probability distributions of the two variables and relating that distribution to

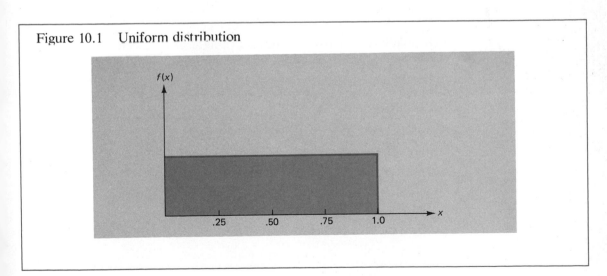

Figure 10.1   Uniform distribution

Table 10.2   Arrival function

Uniform random variable	Arrival variable
0–.10	15 minutes early
.10–.35	5 minutes early
.35–.75	On time
.75–.90	10 minutes late
.90–.95	20 minutes late
.95–1.00	Fail to arrive

a uniform random variable between 0 and 1. Because a number chosen from a uniform distribution with parameters 0 and 1 will fall in the range of 0 to .1 ten percent of the time, ten percent of the patients generated according to the function described in Table 10.2 will arrive 15 minutes early. Similarly, 25 percent of the patients generated will arrive 5 minutes early, and so forth. You must remember, however, that we are describing a random process, and it would take a large number of patient arrivals for these percentages to be considered very accurate. In other words, if only 50 arrivals were generated it would not be unreasonable for 6 or 7 to be 15 minutes early due to the random nature of the arrival process.

Having defined the system and the process generators, we are now ready to simulate Dr. Smith's Monday morning. For each patient, it is necessary to generate an arrival time and an appointment duration

Table 10.3   Appointment duration function

Uniform random variable	Appointment duration (%)
0–.10	80
.10–.20	90
.20–.60	100
.60–.90	110
.90–.95	120
.95–1.0	130

Table 10.4   Simulation iteration

Name	First random number	Second random number	Arrival time	Appointment duration (min)	In	Out
Dupont	.71	.80	9:00	22	9:00	9:22
Williams	.61	.84	9:15	33	9:22	9:55
Stratman	.01	.18	9:30	18	9:55	10:13
Schmidt	.57	.29	10:00	30	10:13	10:43
Gwyn	.94	.57	10:50	30	10:50	11:20
Newlin	.24	.06	10:55	24	11:20	11:44
Gilbert	.85	.61	11:40	22	11:44	12:06
Edwards	.63	.12	11:45	18	12:06	12:24

(see Table 10.3). Let us assume that the random numbers needed to generate arrival and service times are as shown in Table 10.4. In a manual simulation, numbers are obtained from a random number table. In a computer simulation, the computer generates pseudorandom numbers by means of a subroutine or function.

We shall let the first random number column in Table 10.4 correspond to arrivals and the second random number column to appointment duration. Because .71 is between .55 and .75, you can refer back to Table 10.2 to see that patient Dupont is simulated to arrive on time at 9:00. Because .80 is between .60 and .90, this appointment duration is 110 percent of the expected time with the doctor, or 22 minutes (see Table 10.3). You should verify each number in Table 10.4 to be sure that you understand how the simulation is progressing through time.

Based on this one trial, it appears that Dr. Smith can expect to be about 9 minutes late for surgery. Obviously, the sampling error in one sample is too great for us to accept the results of only one iteration. However, if the iteration process is repeated a number of times with different random numbers, it is possible to get a more reliable expected value of Dr. Smith's office departure time. It is also possible to generate a probability distribution relating probabilities to various departure times. Such a simulation model can then suggest possible changes in the system. In our case, Dr. Smith might consider coming to the office at 8:45 in order to take an early patient.

[Steps in a simulation study]

Dr. Smith's situation introduced you to simulation as an idea and a technique. In the rest of this chapter, we shall reinforce this intuitive understanding by describing the various stages or tasks in a simulation study. These steps are essentially the same as those in a management science project. First, you formulate the problem, then collect and analyze the data. Then, you formulate a model, submit it to computer processing, and analyze the results.

PROBLEM FORMULATION

It's difficult to arrive at the right answer if you are working on the wrong problem. Therefore, the first step is to formulate the problem properly. Often, the manager has only a vague idea of what the problem is. It is the job of the management scientist to translate this vague idea into an explicit, written statement of the objectives of the study. The explicit original statement of the problem should not be considered sacrosanct, however, for this reason: As the simulation study progresses, the management scientist becomes more knowledgeable about the system being simulated and about the objectives of the organization. Consequently, it is sometimes necessary to modify the objectives as the nature of the problem becomes clearer. Usually, the statement of objectives takes the form of questions to be answered, hypotheses to be tested, and effects to be estimated. Obviously, it is also necessary to identify the criteria to be used to evaluate these questions.

DATA COLLECTION

The second task, and possibly the most time-consuming step in a simulation study, is the job of collecting data. Quantitative data are necessary for several reasons. First, data are required to describe the system being simulated. If you don't understand the real system thoroughly, it isn't very likely that you will simulate the system properly. Second, data must be gathered as the foundation for generating the various stochastic variables in the system. For example, in a simple queuing system, real data concerning arrivals and service times must be gathered and analyzed to determine the proper probability distributions and their parameters. Finally, data are necessary to test and validate the model. In order to use a simulation model to make decisions, the decision maker must be confident that the real-world phenomenon has been adequately and accurately represented. Often, the best way to accomplish this validation is to compare simulator output with historical data.

DATA ANALYSIS

Once the data have been collected, they must be analyzed and the proper generating functions must be developed. In the Dr. Smith example, the stochastic variables—patient arrival times and appointment durations—were generated using cumulative probability distributions. These were estimated subjectively by Dr. Smith. Actually, subjective probability distributions are somewhat atypical; probability distributions based on empirical data usually yield more reliable simulation results and thus are preferable.

Two basic tasks must be accomplished in order to generate random variables. First, the raw data of a stochastic variable must be analyzed to determine how that random variable is distributed. Then, a function must be derived to generate the stochastic variable using a uniformly distributed random number between 0 and 1. The following procedure is typically used to determine how a random variable is distributed:

1 The data are grouped into a frequency distribution.

2 This frequency distribution is depicted graphically either as a histogram or a frequency polygon.

3 From the shape of the histogram, a probability distribution is hypothesized.

4 Probability distribution parameters are estimated using sample statistics.

5 The hypothesis is tested using one of several statistical tests such as the *chi-square* or *Kolmogorov-Smirnov test*.

chi-square and Kolmogorov-Smirnov tests

6 If the hypothesis is rejected, distribution parameters can be *perturbed*, or changed slightly, and the new hypothesis tested.

7 If no known probability distribution can be found to fit the sampled data, the management scientist is often forced to use the cumulative probability distribution of the sample data.

Let us illustrate these steps by a simple example. The following service times at a gas station were collected during one day: 3.4, 5.4, 4.2, 5.5, 7.9, 0.6, 9.5, 0.0, 9.5, 5.1, 6.7, 1.6, 6.2, 0.5, 1.9, 9.6, 7.9, 6.9, 4.2, 2.7, 5.5, 4.8, 1.8, 9.0, 3.5, 3.9, 6.5, 0.5, 8.8, 3.6, 8.9, 2.4, 0.4, 4.7, 0.8. The frequency distribution for these raw data is reflected in Table 10.5 and a graphical representation is shown in Figure 10.2.

From the shape of the histogram in Figure 10.2, let us hypothesize that the random variable (gas station service times) is uniformly distributed with parameters 0 and 10. Therefore,

Ho : Sample is drawn from a uniformly distributed population with
$a = 0$ and $b = 10$
$H\alpha$: Population is not uniformly distributed with $a = 0$ and $b = 10$

To test this null hypothesis, either a standard chi-square test or the Kolmogorov-Smirnov, a generally more powerful test, can be used. The latter entails the following steps:

1 Formulate the null hypothesis and the alternative hypothesis.

2 Establish the theoretical probability for each class by taking the definite integral of the hypothesized probability density function.

Table 10.5   Frequency distribution

Class	Frequency of observations
0–2	9
2–4	6
4–6	8
6–8	6
8–10	6

Discrete digital simulation

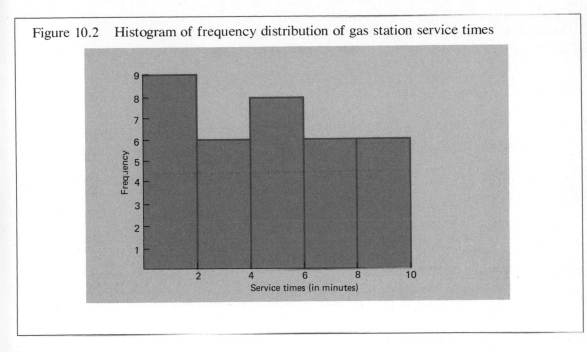

Figure 10.2 Histogram of frequency distribution of gas station service times

3 Calculate the relative frequency for each class by dividing the number of observations in a class by the sample size.

4 Compute the cumulative probability distribution of the sample data by successively adding the relative frequencies of each class. (This is also called the *observed cumulative distribution, or OCD.*)

5 Establish the cumulative probability distribution of the theoretical distribution that has been hypothesized by successively adding the theoretical probabilities of each class. (This is also called the *theoretical cumulative distribution, or TCD.*)

6 Compute the absolute difference between the observed cumulative distribution and the theoretical cumulative distribution for each class in the frequency distribution by subtracting the TCD from the OCD. This operation gives you the *absolute difference.*

7 Compare the absolute difference for each class interval with the critical value found in a standard Kolmogorov-Smirnov table. If the critical value exceeds every absolute difference then the null hypothesis cannot be rejected.

The results of submitting the gas station data to this procedure are shown in Table 10.6. Because the critical Kolmogorov-Smirov

Table 10.6 Kolmogorov-Smirnov test applied to gas station data

Class	Theoretical probability	Relative frequency	Theoretical cumulative distribution	Observed cumulative distribution	Absolute difference
0–2	.2	.257	.2	.257	.057
2–4	.2	.171	.4	.428	.029
4–6	.2	.229	.6	.657	.057
6–8	.2	.171	.8	.828	.029
8–10	.2	.171	1.0	.999*	.001
	1.0	.999*			

*Failure to sum to 1.0 is due to truncation error.

value with a level of significance of .05 is equal to .23, the null hypothesis cannot be rejected. (Verify these values in the Kolmogorov-Smirnov table at the end of the book.)

The next step in analyzing the data is to develop the functions necessary to generate a nonuniformly distributed random variable from a uniform random number between 0 and 1. If the random variable is discrete, it is easy to use the cumulative probability distribution, as we did in the manual simulation of Dr. Smith's appointment schedule. For example, let x be the number of arrivals at an emergency room in one hour. Let us assume that this random variable, x, is distributed in a Poisson manner with a mean of 1.

Table 10.7 Poisson distribution with mean = 1

Number of arrivals	Probability	Cumulative probability
0	.3679	.3679
1	.3679	.7358
2	.1839	.9197
3	.0613	.9810
4	.0153	.9963
5	.0031	.9994
6	.0005	.9999
7	.0001	1.000

Table 10.8   Poisson generating function

Random number	x
0–.3679	0
.3679–.7358	1
.7358–.9197	2
.9197–.9810	3
.9810–.9963	4
.9963–.9994	5
.9994–.9999	6
.9999–1.000	7

This probability distribution is shown in Table 10.7. It is then a simple matter to generate a uniform random number between 0 and 1 and use this random number to determine the value of x. For example, if the random number is .63278, x takes on the value of 1. If the random number is less than .3679, no arrivals occurred during that hour. The generating function is as shown in Table 10.8.

To derive a generating function for continuous random variables, you must use the integral calculus, but the basic idea is the same. The object is to define the stochastic variable in terms of a uniformly distributed random number. For example, the process generator for a random variable distributed according to a negative exponential distribution is

$$x = -\frac{1}{\lambda} \, ln(r)$$

where x = an exponentially distributed random variable
r = uniform random number between 0 and 1

See the appendix at the end of this chapter for the derivation of an exponential process generator.

FORMULATE THE MODEL

A simulation model is an abstraction—usually mathematical—of some real phenomenon or system. Model building is a very difficult step in the simulation process because the model builder must strike a balance between model realism and the cost of developing that model. If a crucial variable or functional relationship is omitted, the model does not accurately predict the behavior of the real system. If the model is too close to the real-world system, it can easily be too expensive to collect data for or to program and execute. The goal of the model builder is to build a model that adequately describes the real system at a minimum cost of human, and computer, resources. You can imagine that model building is an art rather than a science.

WRITE AND TEST THE PROGRAM

Most management science studies require the use of the computer, but for simulation the management scientist has no alternative. The computer is an absolute necessity. The computer language you use is, therefore, a matter of some consequence.

Computer programming languages can actually be thought of in a hierarchy. The assembler languages of the various computer manufacturers are at the lowest level, but they are almost never used in simulation studies. For one thing, they are machine dependent, which means that an assembler language program will not run on a machine other than the model for which it was created. An IBM 370 assembler language program, for example, can only be run on an IBM 360 or IBM 370 series computer. Then, too, it is excessively complex to write a simulation program in assembler language. A simple, single-channel queuing simulator might take as many as 5,000 assembler language instructions.

Compiler languages, the next level of programming languages, are used for simulation. FORTRAN, BASIC, PL1, and ALGOL are the most popular of these for simulation. Compiler languages are machine independent, and because they are more sophisticated than assembler languages, a programmer has far less detail to be concerned with; so the programming effort is reduced.

Special-purpose simulation languages, such as SIMSCRIPT, GPSS, DYNAMO, and GASP, simplify programming even more. This advantage is graphically demonstrated in Figures 10.3 and 10.4. The manual simulation we performed in the Dr. Smith problem is coded in FORTRAN in Figure 10.3 and in GPSS in Figure 10.4.

In view of these illustrations, you can readily see why the

Figure 10.3 FORTRAN printout for Dr. Smith problem

```
C         FORTRAN BY    SHARON WILSON        11-1-73
          DIMENSION X(15),Y(15),A(16),B(16),EVENT(15,20),ITEMP(20)
          DIMENSION C(15),D(15),E(20),F(20),IT(20)
    1 READ(5,10,END=1000)NUMBER,ISET,ITIME,IFREQ,N
   10 FORMAT(10I5)
          WRITE(6,11)NUMBER,ITIME,IFREQ,N
   11 FORMAT('1',////'     * * * * THIS PROGRAM WILL CALCULATE',I5,' SIMUL
         1ATIONS STARTING AT',I5,' HOURS',/,3X,'WITH ONE ARRIVAL EVERY',I5,
         2' MINUTES AND',I5,' TOTAL NUMBER OF ARRIVALS.',////)
          READ(5,20)(X(I),I=1,15)
   20 FORMAT(15F5.0)
          DO 21 I=1,15
          IF(X(I).EQ.0.0)GO TO 22
   21 CONTINUE
   22 LX=I-1
          WRITE(6,23)(X(I),I=1,LX)
   23 FORMAT('0 PROBABILITIES FOR INCOMING EVENTS',/,15F8.4)
          IF(ISET.EQ.0)GO TO 40
C
          READ(5,20)(Y(I),I=1,15)
          DO 31 I=1,15
          IF(Y(I).EQ.0.0)GO TO 32
   31 CONTINUE
   32 LY=I-1
          WRITE(6,33)(Y(I),I=1,LY)
   33 FORMAT('0 PROBABILITIES FOR OUT GOING EVENTS',/,15F8.4)
   40 CONTINUE
          SUM=0.0
          DO 41 I=1,LX
   41 SUM=SUM+X(I)
   50 IF(ISET.EQ.0)GO TO 55
          SUM=0.0
          DO 51 I=1,LY
   51 SUM=SUM+Y(I)
   55 IX=9
          LXX=LX
          LYY=LY
          IX=LX+1
          LY=LY+1
          TIME = ITIME
          READ(5,20)(C(I),I=1,LXX)
          WRITE(6,24)(C(I),I=1,LXX)
   24 FORMAT('0 EARLY TIME ARRIVALS',/,15F8.1)
          IF(ISET.EQ.0) GO TO 54
          READ(5,20)(D(I),I=1,LYY)
          WRITE(6,25)(D(I),I=1,LYY)
   25 FORMAT('0 DURATION TIME',/,15F8.1)
   54 CONTINUE
          A(1)=0.0
          DO 57 I=1,LX
   57 A(I+1)=A(I)+X(I)
          IF(ISET.EQ.0)GO TO 60
          B(1)=0.0
          DO 56 I=1,LY
   56 B(I+1)=B(I)+Y(I)
   60 DO 500 IJ=1,NUMBER
          WRITE(6,61)IJ
   61 FORMAT('1',29X,'* * * * * * * * * * * * * * * *',/,' ',
         129X,'* * * S I M U L A T I O N ',I5,' * * *',/,' ',29X,
         2'* * * * * * * * * * * * * * * *',////)
          CALL MOVE(0,EVENT,0,1200)
          DO 70 J=1,N
          CALL RANDNO(IX,IY,RAND)
          RAND=ABS(RAND)
          IX=IY
          IF        (RAND.LT.0.0.OR.RAND.GT.1.0)RAND=0.0
          DO 71 I=1,LX
          IF(A(I).LE.RAND.AND.RAND.LE.A(I+1))GO TO 73
   71 CONTINUE
          GO TO 70
   73 EVENT(I,J)=1.
   70 CONTINUE
          IF(ISET.EQ.0)GO TO 100
          DO 80 J=1,N
          CALL RANDNO(IX,IY,RAND)
          RAND=ABS(RAND)
          IX=IY
          IF(RAND.LT.0.0.OR.RAND.GT.1.0)RAND=0.0
          DO 81 I=1,LY
          IF(B(I).LE.RAND.AND.RAND.LE.B(I+1))GO TO 83
   81 CONTINUE
          GO TO 80
   83 EVENT(I,J)=EVENT(I,J)+2.
   80 CONTINUE
  100 CONTINUE
          DO 110 I=1,N
  110 E(I)=IFREQ*(I-1)
          WRITE(6,150)
  150 FORMAT(12X,'PROBABILITY',14X,'ARRIVAL NUMBER',/,11X,74('-'))
          DO 175 I=1,LXX
          K=1
          DO 160 J=1,N
          IF(EVENT(I,J).EQ.1.0.OR.EVENT(I,J).EQ.3.0)GO TO 159
          GO TO 160
  159 ITEMP(K)=J
          K=K+1
  160 CONTINUE
          K=K-1
          IF(K.EQ.0) GO TO 170
          WRITE(6,165)I,A(I),A(I+1),(ITEMP(KK),KK=1,K)
```

```
  165 FORMAT(' EVENT ',I2,2X,'!',F5.3,'-',F5.3,'!',20(I2,'/'))
          GO TO 175
  170 WRITE(6,165)I,A(I),A(I+1)
  175 CONTINUE
          WRITE(6,180)
  180 FORMAT(11X,74('-'))
          IF(ISET.EQ.0)  GO TO 300
          WRITE(6,250)
  250 FORMAT(///,12X,'PROBABILITY',14X,'DEPARTURE NUMBER',/,11X,74('-'))
          K=1
          DO 275 I=1,LYY
          K=1
          DO 260 J=1,N
          IF(EVENT(I,J).EQ.2.0.OR.EVENT(I,J).EQ.3.0) GO TO 259
          GO TO 260
  259 ITEMP(K)=J
          K=K+1
  260 CONTINUE
          K=K-1
          IF(K.EQ.0) GO TO 270
          WRITE(6,165)I,B(I),B(I+1),(ITEMP(KK),KK=1,K)
          GO TO 275
  270 WRITE(6,165)I,B(I),B(I+1)
  275 CONTINUE
          WRITE(6,180)
  300 CONTINUE
          WRITE(6,600)
  600 FORMAT(//,24X,'**************',/,24X,'***SCHEDULE***',/,24X,
         1'**************')
          WRITE(6,601)
  601 FORMAT('0',12X,'    ARRIVAL        ARRIVAL       DEPARTURE',/,14X,
         1'    NUMBER        TIME          TIME    ',/,12X,
         2'                   IN HOURS     IN HOURS',/,12X,40('-'))
          DO 650 J=1,N
          DO 640 I=1,LXX
          IF(EVENT(I,J).EQ.1.0.OR.EVENT(I,J).EQ.3.0) GO TO 639
          GO TO 640
  639 IT(J)=J
          E(J)=E(J)+C(I)
  640 CONTINUE
  650 CONTINUE
          CALL ORDER(N,E,IT)
          IF(ISET.EQ.0) GO TO 775
          DO 750 J=1,N
          DO 740 I=1,LYY
          IF(EVENT(I,J).EQ.2.0.OR.EVENT(I,J).EQ.3.0) GO  TO 739
          GO TO 740
  739 F(J)=D(I)
  740 CONTINUE
  750 CONTINUE
  775 CONTINUE
          INDEX=IT(1)
          IF(ISET.EQ.0) GO TO 780
          TEMPO=((E(1)+F(INDEX))/60.)+TIME
  780 TEMP1=(E(1)/60.)+TIME
          IF(ISET.EQ.0) WRITE(6,800) INDEX,TEMP1
          WRITE(6,800)INDEX,TEMP1,TEMPO
  800 FORMAT(12X,I7,6X,2(F10.3,3X))
          DO 900 ICHEAT=2,N
          INDEX=IT(ICHEAT-1)
          IF(ISET.EQ.0) F(INDEX)=0.
          IF(E(ICHEAT).GE.(E(ICHEAT-1)+F(INDEX)))GO TO 875
          FUDGE=E(ICHEAT-1)+F(INDEX)-E(ICHEAT)
          E(ICHEAT)=E(ICHEAT)+FUDGE
          INDEX=IT(ICHEAT)
          IF(ISET.EQ.0) GO TO 850
          TEMPO=((E(ICHEAT)+F(INDEX))/60.)+TIME
  850 TEMP1=(E(ICHEAT)/60.)+TIME
          IF(ISET.EQ.0) WRITE(6,800) INDEX,TEMP1
          WRITE(6,800)INDEX,TEMP1,TEMPO
          GO TO 900
  875 INDEX=IT(ICHEAT)
          IF(ISET.EQ.0) GO TO 880
          TEMPO=((E(ICHEAT)+F(INDEX))/60.)+TIME
  880 TEMP1=(E(ICHEAT)/60.)+TIME
          IF(ISET.EQ.0) WRITE(6,800) INDEX,TEMP1
          WRITE(6,800)INDEX,TEMP1,TEMPO
  900 CONTINUE
  500 CONTINUE
          GO TO 1
 1000 CONTINUE
          CALL END
          STOP
          END
          SUBROUTINE ORDER(LX,X,IT)
          DIMENSION X(2),IT(2)
          K=0
          DO 20 J=1,LX
          K=K+1
          INDEX=K
          DO 10 I=K,LX
   10 IF(X(INDEX).GT.X(I))INDEX=I
          XMIN=X(INDEX)
          IMIN=IT(INDEX)
          X(INDEX)=X(J)
          IT(INDEX)=IT(J)
          X(J)=XMIN
   20 IT(J)=IMIN
          RETURN
          END
          SUBROUTINE RANDNO(IX,IY,YFL)
          IY=IX*65539
          IF(IY)5,6,6
```

Figure 10.4   GPSS printout for Dr. Smith problem

```
        INITIAL    MH1(1,1),540/MH1(2,1),555
        INITIAL    MH1(3,1),585/MH1(4,1),600/MH1(5,1),630
        INITIAL    MH1(6,1),660/MH1(7,1),690/MH1(8,1),705
        INITIAL    MH1(1,2),20/MH1(2,2),30/MH1(3,2),20
        INITIAL    MH1(4,2),30/MH1(5,2),30/MH1(6,2),30
        INITIAL    MH1(7-8,2),20
     1  VARIABLE   P1+FN$ARRIV
     2  VARIABLE   P2#FN$TIME/100
     1  MATRIX     H,8,2
  ARRIV FUNCTION   RN2,D6
.1,-15/.35,-5/.75,0/.9,10/.95,20/1.0,999
   TIME FUNCTION   RN2,D6
.1,80/.2,90/.6,100/.9,110/.95,120/1.0,130
        GENERATE   ,,,8,,3,H
        SAVEVALUE  1+,1,H
        ASSIGN     1,MH1(XH1,1)    ASSIGN ARRIVAL TIME
        ASSIGN     2,MH1(XH1,2)    ASSIGN APPOINTMENT DURATION
        ASSIGN     3,V1
        TEST NE    P3,999,TERM
        ADVANCE    P3     TIME BEFORE ARRIVAL
        QUEUE      LINE   JOIN THE QUEUE
        SEIZE      DOC
        DEPART     LINE   LEAVE THE QUEUE
        ADVANCE    V2     APPOINTMENT DURATION
        RELEASE    DOC    RELEASE THE DOCTOR
   TERM TERMINATE  1   LEAVE THE OFFICE
        START      8
```

management scientist should use a special-purpose simulation language to write a simulation program. The reason for the obvious reduction in programming effort with a simulation language like GPSS is that each GPSS statement or block can be thought of as a FORTRAN subroutine (a small program in itself); and such things as the simulation clock and next-event logic are preprogrammed into the GPSS software. An additional benefit is that the probability of creating a valid program is increased.

Why, then, are most simulators written in compiler languages such as FORTRAN and BASIC? One reason is that special-purpose simulation languages such as GPSS and SIMSCRIPT are not so widely available as the compiler languages. All but the very smallest computers have FORTRAN, COBOL, or BASIC compilers in their software packages. Often, a simulation language such as GPSS is not used because the management scientist conducting the simulation study may not know a special-purpose language and may be unwilling to invest the time needed to learn one. Clearly, an organization that uses management science techniques to aid in its decision process should consider acquiring a simulation processor such as GPSS or SIMSCRIPT, and then train its staff in the use of the simulation language.

VALIDATING THE SIMULATION MODEL

Perhaps the most difficult step in a simulation study is validating the simulation model. It is foolish to use simulation results in the decision-making process unless you are quite confident that the simulation model represents the real-world situation accurately. Absolute validation is probably unattainable, but it is possible to gain confidence in a simulation model by making certain verifications.

Program testing   One aspect of a simulation that must be validated is whether the programmer has instructed the computer properly. It is possible that a simulation model is valid as designed but invalid as implemented on the computer. Standard program-testing techniques should be employed to insure congruence between simulator design and simulator program. These techniques include manual calculations, program traces, and so on. It is necessary to verify the absence of programming errors when you are validating a simulation, but this step alone is not sufficient. The program can be perfect and the simulation model may still be totally invalid.

Variable generation test   Earlier in this chapter we applied nonparametric goodness-of-fit tests to hypotheses concerning the distributions of the various stochastic variables. These same tests should be applied to the output from the various generating functions to insure that the real-world variables and simulated variables are distributed in the same manner. For example, if the interarrival time in a real queuing system is normally distributed with a mean of 5 minutes and a standard deviation of 2 minutes, then the random variable of interarrival times being generated in the simulation program should also be normally distributed with $\mu = 5$ and $\sigma = 2$.

Subjective validation   The design as well as the output of the simulation model ought to be reviewed by the people who are most familiar with the real system. This subjective validation should properly be done by people not directly involved in the simulation study.

Historical validation   If the simulator is designed to simulate an existing system, it is often possible to simulate the system as it is presently configured and then compare actual historical data to simulation output. For example, if the real system is a harbor operation, vital statistics such as the average wait time of a vessel and the average time a vessel spends in the harbor should be compared to the distribution of various output variables. The absence of significant differences between simulated results and historical results may tend to validate the simulator; but it does not guarantee that the simulator will accurately predict the behavior of the real system under different conditions.

Confidence in the validity of a simulation model is crucial to the successful use of simulation. For this reason, the management scientist should leave no stone unturned when performing the validation step of a simulation study.

EXPERIMENTAL DESIGN

Once a simulation model has been implemented and validated, it can be used for its original purpose, experimentation. Simulation, you will recall, is a means of providing information necessary for decision making when a real-world system cannot be sufficiently manipulated. A simulation model synthetically gathers the information necessary to describe the system under study. The object is to gather the information necessary for decision making—at the lowest possible cost. Usually, real-world experiments are more costly than simulation experiments, and thus the management scientist can experiment with a greater number of alternatives when using a simulation model. For example, if the system under study is a harbor and the decision variables are the number of tugs, the number of berths, and the queue discipline, by means of simulation the management scientist can experiment with many combinations of decision variables to determine the optimal harbor configuration. If, however, experiments were made on the real system, far fewer alternatives could be evaluated.

The questions of the length of simulation runs, initialization periods, sample sizes, and optimization procedures are beyond the scope of this text. Many of the answers are contained in the traditional literature concerning experimental design.

ANALYSIS OF SIMULATION RESULTS

If the simulation model is valid and the simulation experiments have been designed properly, analysis of simulation output is fairly straightforward. It is the function of the management scientist to interpret simulation results and make the appropriate inferences necessary for rational decision making. Often, certain statistical techniques, such as analysis of variance, can be helpful in analyzing simulation results.

[When to simulate]

Once the problem has been formulated, the management scientist must decide whether or not to attempt to solve the problem using discrete digital simulation. This decision process is depicted in Figure 10.5.

As we said earlier in this chapter, the problem should be formulated explicitly in terms of hypotheses to be tested and questions to be answered. After the problem has been formulated, a solution technique other than simulation is often judged to be more appropriate. The important point is that choosing a solution methodology must succeed, not precede, the problem formulation phase of any management science study. If an analytical technique or model is available or can be adapted to the problem, it should probably be used. If an analytical technique such as classical inventory theory

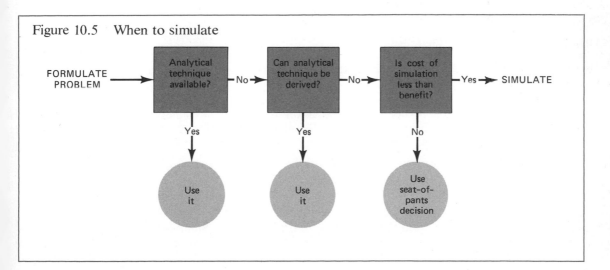

Figure 10.5   When to simulate

or queuing theory cannot be applied, then the management scientist must make the decision between simulating or making an intuitive, seat-of-the-pants decision. This judgment, in turn, depends on the nature of the individual decision. In other words, is the decision important enough to justify the estimated cost of developing, validating, and experimenting with a simulation model?

ADVANTAGES OF SIMULATION

In deciding whether or not to simulate, the management scientist must weigh the advantages of the technique.

1 The greatest advantage is that simulation allows the management scientist to model complex and dynamic phenomena that otherwise could not be dealt with in a scientific way.

2 Simulation permits experimentation that might be impossible or infeasible otherwise. "What if" questions can be asked using simulation.

3 By simulating the system, the management scientist gains valuable insight into the system and into the relative importance of the different variables.

4 Simulation allows for the compression of real time. To predict the behavior of a system over the period of a year may take only a few seconds or minutes using computer simulation.

5 Simulation is often used to test a proposed analytical solution.

DISADVANTAGES OF SIMULATION

Naturally, there are some significant disadvantages to using discrete digital simulation to solve management decision-making problems.

1 Simulation is not an optimization technique. Typically, different system configurations are experimented with to find a good, but *not* guaranteed best, solution.

2 Simulation is an expensive way to solve a problem. In addition to the cost of building and validating a simulation model, experimentation using computer simulation can be quite costly.

3 Because of the nature of simulation, sampling error exists in all output from simulation models. Of course, this sampling error can be reduced by increasing the sample size or by lengthening the computer run time.

4 A real disadvantage is that simulation is often misused because many people who are qualified to write a simulation program are not qualified to perform a total simulation study. In other words, many programmers do not possess the necessary statistical background.

5 Probably the most serious shortcoming of simulation is that it is a tool of solution evaluation and thus does not generate problem solutions. Therefore, the decision maker has to develop proposed solutions; then, simulation can be used to test the relative desirability of those solutions.

THE FUTURE OF SIMULATION

At the beginning of this chapter, we said that simulation was the most commonly used management science technique. There are four major reasons why discrete digital simulation will continue to expand into almost every imaginable area of application.

1 Simulation is probably the most powerful of management science techniques. Many different kinds of problems can be solved using simulation.

2 The cost of computing has been decreasing and will continue to do so at a very rapid rate. It has been projected that 1980 computer cost will be only 10 percent of 1970 cost.[1]

3 Simulation languages will continue to evolve and, indeed, to be invented, thus making it less expensive and less time-consuming to solve problems by means of this technique.

4 Finally, as more managers are made aware of the power of simulation as a tool for the decision-making process, the more popular simulation will become.

[Derivation of an exponential process generator appendix]

The probability density function of an exponentially distributed random variate is given by

$$f(x) = \lambda e^{-\lambda x} \qquad 0 < x < \infty \tag{10.1}$$
where $\lambda = 1/\mu$

---

[1] Stanley Rothman and Charles Mosmann, *Computers and Society* (Chicago, Ill.: Science Research Associates, Inc., 1972), p. 307.

The first step is to integrate the density function to get an expression for the cumulative distribution

$$F(x) = \int_{o}^{x} \lambda e^{-\lambda t}\, dt \qquad\qquad [10.2]$$

$$= 1 - e^{-\lambda x} \qquad\qquad [10.3]$$

Now if we let $r = F(x)$ and solve for x in terms of r, we have

$$r = 1 - e^{-\lambda x} \qquad\qquad [10.4]$$
$$1 - r = e^{-\lambda x} \qquad\qquad [10.5]$$

Taking the natural log of both sides, we get

$$-\lambda x = ln(1 - r) \qquad\qquad [10.6]$$

$$x = -\frac{1}{\lambda}\, ln(1 - r) \qquad\qquad [10.7]$$

Since $1 - r$ and r are identically distributed, equation 10.7 can be simplified to

$$x = -\frac{1}{\lambda}\, ln(r) \qquad\qquad [10.8]$$

Equation 10.8, then, is the process generator of an exponential distributed random variate with parameter λ. To illustrate the use of this function, suppose service times are exponentially distributed, with a mean of 2 minutes. If the random number chosen is .6, then $x = -2\, ln(.6) = 1.02$ minutes.

[Bibliography]

Gordon, Geoffrey, *System Simulation.* Englewood Cliffs, N.J.: Prentice Hall, Inc. 1969.

————, *The Application of GPSS V to Discrete System Simulation.* Englewood Cliffs, N.J.: Prentice-Hall, Inc., 1975.

Martin, Francis F., *Computer Modeling and Simulation.* New York: John Wiley & Sons, Inc., 1968.

Naylor, Thomas H., et al., *Computer Simulation Techniques.* New York: John Wiley & Sons, Inc., 1966.

Schriber, Thomas J., *Simulation Using GPSS.* New York: John Wiley & Sons, Inc., 1974.

Schmidt, J. W., and Richard E. Taylor, *Simulation and Analysis of Industrial Systems*. Homewood, Ill.: Richard D. Irwin, Inc., 1970.

Shannon, Robert E., *Systems Simulation: The Art and Science*. Englewood Cliffs, N.J.: Prentice-Hall, Inc., 1975.

[Review questions]

1 Define *discrete digital simulation*.

2 How does simulation differ from LP?

3 Discuss two major reasons for using simulation for solving decision problems.

4 Why is a computer necessary when simulating a real system?

5 What are the major phases in a simulation study?

6 What is a Kolmogorov-Smirnov test used for?

7 What is a process generator?

8 What are uniform random numbers used for in simulation?

9 Why aren't assembler languages used to code simulation models?

10 Why is FORTRAN the most popular language used for simulation?

11 Why should a management scientist use a special-purpose simulation language?

12 List two advantages GPSS has over FORTRAN as a simulation language.

13 Why is validation an important step in any simulation study?

14 How does historical validation differ from subjective validation?

15 List three advantages of using simulation.

16 List three disadvantages of using simulation.

17 Why is the application of simulation likely to increase significantly in the near future?

[Problems]

10.1 The Page Milk Company has a large, gallon-bottling machine that occasionally breaks down due to bearing failure. The machine has two bearings of this type. In order to replace one of the bearings, the machine must be shut down. This machine shutdown costs the company approximately $30 per hour. The bearings are relatively inexpensive, at $5 per bearing. At the present, a bearing is replaced only when it fails. The time between bearing failures is distributed as shown in the first table. The time it takes to replace a bearing

Hours between bearing failures	Probability
20	.05
40	.07
60	.13
70	.35
80	.30
90	.07
100	.03

is fairly deterministic at 1 hour. An employee has suggested that, since it is as easy to replace both bearings as one, the company should try a new policy of replacing both bearings when either one fails. Limited experience with similar bearings has yielded the following probability distribution of bearing failures when both bearings are replaced:

Hours between bearing failures	Probability
40	.05
75	.10
100	.15
125	.25
150	.20
180	.15
200	.10

Use manual or computer simulation to solve this policy problem. If you simulate manually, simulate for the period of 1 month. Assume a 24-hour work day and a 7-day work week.

10.2 The following times have been collected at the local harbor. How are these two random variables distributed?

Discrete digital simulation

Docking times (min)				Unloading times (min)			
8.59	9.62	9.29	11.34	47.78	17.55	23.82	5.58
13.84	12.89	13.52	12.02	11.93	4.40	18.06	11.16
13.59	13.99	14.87	11.03	48.10	53.61	45.82	12.32
9.29	8.79	13.13	13.86	54.90	43.57	29.43	7.61
12.79	11.03	10.00	13.41	56.65	3.25	36.63	11.24
9.89	13.32	11.62	13.98	23.00	38.50	27.78	58.47
14.14	9.44	13.58	9.57	25.65	15.94	9.77	12.15
13.08	13.89	12.29	8.69	29.76	103.05	7.92	9.88
10.86	13.86	16.66	13.38	27.62	3.00	66.32	34.73
11.39	12.62	14.23	10.73	88.40	59.47	8.79	26.62
12.71	12.03	11.67	8.73	9.40	11.36	21.46	13.29
10.70	9.63	9.56	12.47	2.75	4.21	45.32	57.50
9.20	10.12	13.71	12.78	3.28	89.12	2.38	67.63
11.49	11.24	10.66	11.18	53.67	21.62	17.70	35.54
14.90	16.95	11.76	11.22	1.07	23.51	120.14	3.40
10.09	13.06	11.43	12.27	65.01	30.41	70.32	15.82
12.62	10.21	11.96	13.53	40.49	80.90	23.95	19.19
10.92	9.21	12.56	12.57	19.32	59.24	5.36	4.76
12.70	9.77	12.86	10.17	6.03	44.61	.97	29.71
7.77	12.88	10.75	13.54	51.45	67.02	37.99	17.87
12.26	13.14	12.63	11.91	9.86	14.91	.64	1.08
10.01	14.44	9.98	10.54	10.73	11.32	32.70	5.68
16.45	13.03	10.36	11.03	9.97	13.42	47.02	37.98
15.85	13.26	8.75	12.09	136.41	12.20	44.65	42.04
9.68	13.99	13.28	11.53	14.89	42.75	22.21	1.85

10.3 The Checkmate Barbershop presently has only one barber. Business is quite good, and the proprietor is trying to decide whether to hire an additional barber. Customers arrive to the barbershop in a Poisson manner at a rate of three per hour (interarrival times are distributed exponentially, with a mean of 20 minutes). The time it takes to give a haircut is exponentially distributed, with a mean of 15 minutes. The barber has noticed that when two customers are waiting for a haircut, a new customer generally will not join the queue. Haircuts cost $4, and a new barber would cost the shop $100 per week plus $1 for each haircut. Use simulation to help in the decision of whether or not to hire the additional barber.

[Synergistic Systems Corporation case]

Mr. Norman Jenkins, manager of office equipment at Synergistic Systems Corporation, one of the top seven government contractors, was reasoning with Mr. George Wilson, manager of the contract typing pool. "George, I can't approve your request for a third copying machine just because you say you see typists waiting in line practically every time you're near your two machines. Back in 1966, I could have approved without question, but this is 1970. You know that we aren't doing as well these days due to the government cutbacks in aerospace spending. The word has come down from upstairs that we have to cut expenses wherever possible.

"As a matter of fact, we have been running a survey on usage of the machines in the building, hoping to reduce costs by eliminating unnecessary machines. Let me show you our results for your machines, George. This first table (Table 1) shows that you average 16.17 pages per contract. This second table (Table 2) shows that the average time between users arriving at the machines is 16.48 minutes.

Table 1   Pages per contract

Pages	Percentage of contracts	Pages	Percentage of contracts	Pages	Percentage of contracts
6	1	13	6	20	7
7	1	14	8	21	5
8	2	15	9	22	3
9	2	16	11	23	2
10	2	17	12	24	1
11	3	18	11	25	1
12	4	19	9		

Table 2   Time between arrivals

Time since last arrival	Percentage of arrivals	Time since last arrival	Percentage of arrivals	Time since last arrival	Percentage of arrivals
0	17	20	3	40	2
2	8	22	3	42	1
4	7	24	3	44	1
6	6	26	2	46	1
8	6	28	2	48	1
10	5	30	2	50	1
12	5	32	2	52	1
14	4	34	2	54	1
16	4	36	2	56	1
18	3	38	2	58	1
				60	1

"Previous surveys have shown that it takes one minute to make the required twenty copies of each contract page. Therefore, the average user should be on a machine 16.17 minutes. Since secretaries arrive to use the machine an average of 16.48 minutes apart, but only use the machine an average of 16.17 minutes, one machine should be adequate for your copying needs. Each machine costs us $110 per month or $5 per working day. How can I approve your request for a third machine with these facts in front of me? In fact, I was thinking of taking away one of your machines."

George Wilson puzzled over the tables a bit and then asked, "Why are all the times even numbers? Don't the users arrive 3 minutes apart, or 5 minutes apart?"

"Yes, but we found that it was convenient and accurate enough to record the information to the nearest two minutes. Anything up to 1 minute was recorded a zero, anything from 1 to 3 minutes was

Figure 1   Data sheet

Time of arrival	Number of pages	Number of copies	Machine 1		Machine 2		Machine 3	
			Time on	Time off	Time on	Time off	Time on	Time off

recorded as 2, etc. By the way here's the form we used to record the results," he added, showing Mr. Wilson the form shown in Figure 1. "We just used two of the machine columns in your case since you only had two machines, and we recorded 20 all the time in the number of copies column. We fitted a smooth curve to what we recorded on both the pages and time between arrivals."

"Well, I don't really care how you recorded that data," said Mr. Wilson, "The important point is that secretaries are waiting in line and that's costing us money.

"You're familiar with our system of assigning each typist to only one contract at a time and having her make her own copies when she finishes the typing. The worst drawback of our present system is that the time anyone spends waiting to use a machine is wasted time, and women who type with the speed and accuracy that we need don't work for peanuts. The 15 secretaries who work for me cost us about $5 an hour each, including variable overhead, and that's $40 per working day. That's why I worry when I see them waiting in line at the machine.''

Mr. Jenkins asked, "Why don't you hire someone just to make copies? You ought to be able to get someone to do that for only $2 an hour. You would save the time your typists spend making copies, and eliminate all waiting time, and still get by with only one machine.''

"I fought that battle last year with Bob Johnson in Security. He agreed that we could save money by hiring someone just to run the copying machines, but he won't allow it. Most of the contracts are classified Secret or Top Secret, and he's scared stiff of what the government security inspectors will say about any procedure where extra personnel handle the documents,'' Mr. Wilson replied. "Now the problem is worse. With the aerospace spending cuts, we've got a hiring freeze. We wouldn't be allowed to hire a Xerox operator, even if we thought it was desirable.''

"George, I understand your concerns, but I just can't help you when the numbers show that I should take a machine away from you rather than give you another one. Take this copy of our survey with you. If you can show me that I'm wrong, you'll get your machine.''

Mr. Wilson folded the copy of the survey, put it in his shirt pocket and walked out dejectedly.

[Case problems]

1 Using the data as collected, determine if another machine can be economically justified by simulating 1 day for each machine configuration. Use the random numbers in Table 3.

2 What are the simulated costs for two machines and three machines?

Discrete digital simulation

Table 3   Random numbers

20	84	27	38	66	19	60	10	51	20	11	79	34	46	41	3	75	58	9	43
35	16	74	58	72	79	98	9	47	7	40	55	20	60	59	56	51	99	15	72
98	82	69	63	23	70	80	88	86	23	9	8	45	0	14	82	61	62	56	71
94	67	94	34	3	77	89	30	49	51	1	21	91	48	89	65	89	29	13	23
4	54	32	55	94	82	8	19	20	73	99	77	42	88	66	88	19	85	69	11
11	25	66	8	79	68	19	37	82	73	87	59	80	1	30	32	32	11	7	19
0	63	79	77	41	17	6	67	18	33	47	49	88	71	62	82	13	90	11	27
51	51	54	44	64	13	51	92	10	37	61	31	50	81	45	20	43	6	63	21
49	72	73	93	29	39	37	94	42	66	14	87	47	14	63	30	6	42	45	82
77	9	20	5	20	77	47	58	96	5	87	1	64	52	98	93	84	79	42	94
16	45	77	65	20	11	65	65	56	36	63	55	83	79	34	93	61	2	35	40
51	63	28	55	12	23	72	99	4	41	27	32	86	78	52	12	20	93	8	1
64	46	55	58	78	96	52	43	23	5	59	15	57	31	37	35	42	34	44	62
37	75	41	57	2	14	88	79	97	9	45	87	79	21	70	43	12	10	25	5
55	36	70	34	66	58	63	90	6	37	65	32	35	32	36	20	13	3	35	14
99	10	23	74	53	13	59	59	36	71	4	31	7	45	16	48	26	95	56	70
53	80	84	57	47	60	60	70	69	95	43	67	78	45	94	10	35	70	72	57
99	29	37	69	30	83	48	5	88	91	67	25	32	14	52	89	23	10	64	58
21	41	63	90	85	65	7	46	75	43	58	86	51	34	74	69	73	99	17	56
1	97	45	5	95	88	19	78	14	32	98	34	18	89	43	32	68	19	13	33
23	81	67	97	42	36	67	83	87	43	72	51	16	62	41	61	90	54	34	73
68	77	12	47	11	92	34	43	78	58	61	20	28	36	51	39	23	85	65	58
21	66	62	39	83	37	4	42	69	60	48	24	37	93	56	48	49	97	87	72
64	31	1	57	42	56	58	62	43	31	17	47	26	17	39	72	52	72	84	97
48	57	11	82	70	31	79	87	83	56	50	71	77	89	83	94	14	92	38	17
52	24	74	98	51	46	52	99	72	16	31	78	74	94	71	96	18	42	33	13
62	18	75	88	67	82	58	81	93	94	42	53	0	15	86	62	47	3	51	69
94	19	96	34	2	23	81	17	29	74	66	77	37	33	11	74	84	59	76	69
31	12	20	20	37	52	3	89	63	39	86	34	68	32	28	16	12	92	89	94
55	79	29	29	57	51	8	79	77	70	85	6	76	95	21	69	14	86	75	28
50	3	7	42	43	5	78	72	55	52	46	77	45	5	72	18	72	23	16	54
97	66	37	44	80	94	96	50	80	67	52	30	57	45	65	45	71	87	95	54
82	53	1	17	49	4	45	95	33	98	85	47	94	97	81	32	91	59	94	11
85	46	83	44	34	15	8	91	0	28	29	10	41	45	5	63	18	24	97	9
90	27	65	8	18	12	68	20	61	40	66	5	79	71	19	21	32	64	87	31
80	79	30	92	83	77	8	66	0	17	80	12	92	58	6	89	18	62	47	58
38	87	62	79	12	93	10	11	1	41	53	15	63	90	49	49	58	0	59	75
47	31	42	52	89	43	59	39	45	96	68	97	74	49	31	85	35	63	6	64
90	96	55	93	97	10	35	32	16	64	9	40	8	18	34	79	32	31	72	7
49	65	82	85	17	77	24	72	97	29	57	29	49	80	42	14	32	90	39	89

11

[Inventory systems]

An inventory is a stock of goods that is held for the purpose of future production or sales. Raw materials, work in progress, and finished goods can all be classified as inventory items, and the decisions about them as inventory are similar. Obviously, such decisions often have a critical effect on the health of the firm. Organizations carry inventories for a number of the following reasons.

Smooth production   Often, the demand for an item fluctuates widely due to a number of factors such as seasonality and production schedules. For example, 50 percent of all the toys manufactured in 1 year may be sold in the 3 weeks before Christmas. If toy manufacturers were to try to produce 50 percent of a year's output in 3 weeks, they would need a tremendous influx of labor as well as huge manufacturing facilities. Instead, firms find it more economical to produce goods over a longer, slower schedule and store them as inventory. Thus, they keep the labor force fairly stable, and expenditures for capital equipment are lower.

Product availability   Most retail goods and many industrial goods are carried in inventory to insure prompt delivery to customers. Not only does a good inventory provide a competitive edge, it often means the difference between success and failure. If a firm gains a reputation for constantly being out of stock, it may lose a significant number of customers.

Advantages of producing or buying in large quantities Most production runs involve machine set-up time and production time. If set-up time is significant, real savings can be achieved by producing in large lots. In addition, most firms offer quantity discounts for buying in large quantities.

Hedge against long or uncertain lead times The time between ordering and receiving goods is known as *lead time.* Firms don't want to stop manufacturing or selling goods during lead time; so it is necessary to carry inventory.

lead time

Inventory models, like the ones to be discussed in this chapter, seek to minimize the total cost of the inventory system. These costs fall into three basic categories: ordering costs, carrying costs, and shortage costs.

ordering costs

Ordering costs are the costs involved in ordering and receiving inventory. These costs typically consist largely of salaries in the purchasing and accounting departments and wages in the receiving area; they also include purchase and transportation charges. If a firm produces its own inventory instead of purchasing from an outside source, production set-up costs are analogous to ordering costs. Ordering costs are usually expressed by a dollar amount per order.

carrying, or holding, costs

Carrying costs, also referred to as *holding costs*, are the costs that holding inventory entails. Components of carrying costs are both direct and indirect, including:

1 Interest on the money invested in inventory

2 Storage or warehousing costs, including rent, electricity, wages, insurance, security, data processing, and so on

3 Obsolescence (If the good is held too long in inventory, its value may decrease substantially.)

Carrying costs are typically calculated as a percentage of inventory value or a dollar value per unit of inventory.

The third category of inventory costs is *shortage*, or *stock-out, costs.* If demand for an off-the-shelf good exists and a firm does

shortage, or stock-out, costs

not have the good in inventory, there is an inevitable loss of customer good will as well as loss of the profit from the sale. The dollar value of this loss of good will is, at best, difficult to measure. If you had to assess it, relevant questions would include: Will the firm lose the sale? Will the firm lose the customer? What are the probabilities of these losses? What is the dollar value of that particular customer?

If the inventory is being carried for internal use (that is, production), a stock-out can have very serious effects. A stock-out can shut down an assembly line, and to shut down a typical automobile assembly line, for example, can cost as much as $20,000 per minute. The shortage cost is typically expressed as dollar cost per unit of inventory per unit of time.

The objective of any inventory model is to minimize total inventory cost. Minimizing just one of the three components of inventory cost is easy, and of little value. For example, to minimize carrying cost, a firm can simply stop carrying any inventory. This action, however, can be expected to create unreasonable stock-out or order costs. The actual process for minimizing total inventory costs entails two basic decisions: how much, and when, to order. Understandably, these are the two decision variables that inventory models use in optimizing an inventory system.

[Analyzing inventory systems]

In this section, we discuss the four essential steps in analyzing inventory systems: determining system properties; formulating and developing the appropriate inventory model; solving or manipulating the model; and performing sensitivity analysis on the model.

DETERMINING SYSTEM PROPERTIES

Inventory system properties can be classified in four categories: demand properties, replenishment properties, cost properties, and constraints. In order to prevent the misapplication of an inventory model, it is extremely important for you to identify and consider each property of an inventory system properly.

Demand properties These characteristics include the size of demand, the rate of demand, and the pattern of demand. The *size* size of of demand can be constant or variable depending on the nature demand of the good. A constant demand merely means that, for each time period, the quantity of goods demanded is constant. The size of demand for a good can be deterministic or stochastic. Given a production schedule, for example, it may be a simple calculation to determine demand for a particular period of time. However, the demand of many inventory items cannot be predicted with any degree of certainty; hence, the problem is a stochastic or probabilistic problem rather than a deterministic one.

rate of   The *rate* of demand is the size of demand over a particular unit demand of time. For example, Worldwide Widgets has a total demand for the year of 600 widgets, and its records verify that the monthly demand rate is $600/12$, or 50 units per month. Clearly, demand rate can be variable or constant, deterministic or stochastic.

demand   The *pattern* of demand refers to the manner in which units are pattern drawn from inventory. Some items may be drawn from inventory at the beginning of the time period, others at the end, still others at a uniform rate during the period. Many variations of demand pattern are possible, and it is important to try and identify the demand pattern of the inventory item in question. Figure 11.1 shows some common demand patterns.

Replenishment properties When you analyze replenishment properties, it is necessary to define the *scheduling period*. The scheduling scheduling period is the length of time between decisions concerning period replenishments. This time period can be prescribed or variable. For example, the local supermarket orders fresh lettuce twice a week (prescribed), whereas canned kidney beans are ordered when the inventory reaches a certain reorder point (variable). Variable scheduling periods require a continuous accounting for inventory. In most medium and large firms, an inventory accounting system is, or should be, totally computerized.

lead time   *Lead time*, you will recall, is the time between ordering a

Figure 11.1   Demand patterns

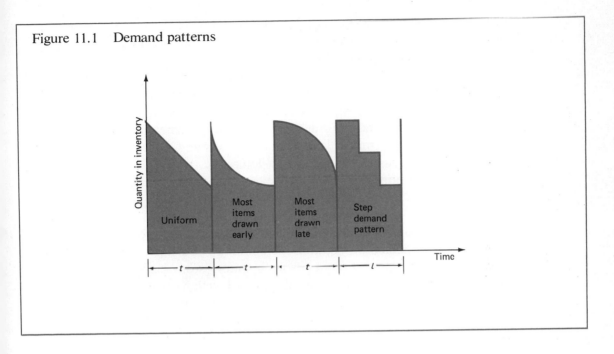

replenishment of inventory and actually receiving the goods into inventory. Lead time can be either a deterministic constant or variable, or a stochastic variable. If lead time is known with a high degree of certainty, its existence is easily treated in inventory modeling. On the other hand, if lead time is stochastic with a large variance, the difficulty in finding an appropriate inventory model is greatly increased.

replenishment, or lot, size Like demand, the *size of replenishment* can also be stochastic. In other words, the quantity ordered may not be the same as the quantity received. Replenishment size is often called *lot size.*

replenishment period The *replenishment period* is the time during which units of a particular order are added to inventory. In a purchasing situation, the replenishment period may be insignificant; but in a production environment, units are added to inventory over a period of time (that is, as they are produced). If a significant replenishment period exists, then units are added to inventory according to some *replenish- * *replenishment pattern* *ment pattern.* Replenishment patterns are similar to demand patterns except the flow of goods is going in the opposite direction.

Often, instead of specifying the lot size, an inventory policy
order specifies an *order level*. An order level is the quantity that will
level be in inventory after replenishment.

Cost properties   Earlier in this chapter, we said that inventory
systems were systems comprised of three types of cost: ordering
cost, holding cost, and shortage cost. These parameters of an
inventory model are rarely known with certainty. Consequently,
the management scientist usually must determine the sensitivity of
the optimal solution to small and reasonable changes in these
parameters.

System constraints   In addition to determining system properties,
before you can decide on solution methodology you must analyze
system constraints. For example, if the inventory storage area holds
only 100 units, an optimal order quantity of 1,000 units is irrelevant.
Similarly, if working capital is severely limited and the optimal
inventory policy calls for carrying a huge inventory, the optimal
policy may not be feasible. Typical inventory system constraints
are listed following:

1 *Space* The amount of storage space may put limits on the order
quantity.

2 *Scheduling period* If the scheduling period is prescribed, many
inventory models cannot be used.

3 *Shortage* Management may make a decision that stock-outs cannot
be allowed. On the other hand, shortages may be allowed and may
or may not result in lost sales.

4 *Dependent demand* In most inventory models, demand is considered
independent of the demand of the preceding period. When independent
demand is not characteristic of a particular inventory system, it is
generally more difficult to optimize the system.

5 *Continuous nature of inventory units* Most analytical models used
for optimizing inventory systems depend on the calculus for their
derivation. Consequently, if inventory units are not, or cannot be
considered, continuous in nature, a majority of the analytical optimization models cannot be applied. Usually, when large quantities are
involved, the assumption of continuousness is not damaging.

Determining system properties is crucial to analyzing inventory systems. If we expect to find or develop an appropriate model of the inventory system in question, we must analyze the system properties and characteristics in depth.

FORMULATING THE MODEL

The second step in analyzing inventory systems is to discover or derive the appropriate inventory model to solve the particular inventory problem. Basically, there are two types of inventory model: deterministic models and stochastic models. The parameters of deterministic inventory models are assumed to be known with certainty. For example, demand is assumed to be perfectly predictable. Stochastic inventory models contain uncontrollable variables, such as demand or lead time, that are probabilistic in nature. Generally, stochastic inventory models are mathematically more difficult to derive and solve. As the number of stochastic variables increases, it becomes increasingly difficult to derive an analytical optimization model. In addition, if a stochastic variable is not distributed according to a known probability density function, the likelihood of finding or deriving an analytical inventory model is drastically reduced. When an analytical model cannot be developed to model a particular inventory system adequately, simulation can usually be used to determine a good inventory policy. The decision of whether to simulate an inventory system hinges on the cost / benefit of the simulation.

SOLVING THE MODEL

The third step in the analysis of inventory systems is to solve the analytical model or run the simulation model. This is typically the easiest part of the process if the first two steps have been performed properly. Because the solution of analytical inventory models is not an iterative process, a computer is not considered an absolute necessity. If a computer is used, very few computer resources (core, time) are necessary to solve analytical inventory models.

An analytical model is preferable to a simulation model for two reasons. First, the cost in computer resources is considerably less. Second, an analytical model yields an optimal solution, whereas a simulation model can only search for a good solution. In short, analytical inventory models cost *much* less than simulation models to find the *best* answer. This is not to say, however, that a real system should be modeled using an analytical model whose assumptions do not adequately fit the real system properties. This is a common error in practice, and it is for this reason that we state explicitly the assumptions of each model we present in this chapter.

PERFORMING SENSITIVITY ANALYSIS

Some models yield order quantities that are extremely sensitive. In other words, slight changes in the order quantity cause significant changes in the total cost of the inventory system. In addition, it is usually helpful to the decision maker to know the relative sensitivity of such inventory variables as demand, lead time, and replenishment quantity. Unlike LP, inventory models cannot easily determine the sensitivity of the system's various parameters and decision variables. Instead, the parameter or variable in question is perturbed, and the effect of the change is observed.

[Analytical models]

In this chapter, we are going to consider several deterministic analytical models and one stochastic model. These models represent only a small sampling of the inventory models that have been developed and used since the first one was introduced in 1915.

BASIC ECONOMIC ORDER QUANTITY MODEL (EOQ)

Before examining it, we must identify the assumptions of the basic EOQ model so that you will know under what conditions to apply it. If the following assumptions cannot be accepted, thereby indicating that the real-world inventory system may not be adequately represented by the basic EOQ model, it is inappropriate to use this particular model.

1 *Deterministic demand* It must be possible to predict demand with a high degree of confidence.

2 *Constant rate of demand* Not only is it necessary to know the total demand, but units must be drawn from inventory at a uniform rate. For example, if 365 units are used each year, these items must be drawn 1 per day during the year to strictly satisfy this assumption.

3 *No shortages* Inventory replenishments are made whenever the inventory level reaches zero. Shortages are not allowed to occur. This assumption implies that, of the three costs involved in an inventory system, stock-out cost does not exist in the basic EOQ model.

4 *Constant replenishment size* The replenishment size, denoted by q, is the only decision variable in the basic EOQ model. The other decision variable—when to reorder—is fixed because demand is at a constant rate and replenishments occur when the inventory level reaches zero.

5 *Zero lead time* It is assumed that no appreciable time elapses between placing an order and receiving that order. This assumption can be easily dealt with as we explain later in conjunction with Figure 11.7.

6 *Infinite replenishment rate* Replenishment rate is defined as the rate at which units are added to inventory. An infinite replenishment rate implies that inventory replenishment occurs at one time. In other words, it takes zero time to receive an order. This assumption is reasonable for most purchased goods but is often unreasonable for manufactured goods. Typically, manufactured goods are put into inventory at some finite rate.

7 *Constant inventory costs* Both costs in the basic EOQ model are constant. Ordering cost is expressed as dollars per order and holding cost is expressed as dollars per unit per time period.

These assumptions for the basic EOQ model determine the graph in Figure 11.2.

Inventory systems in which the decision variable is the order quantity have the objective function in equation 11.1.

Min $\quad C(q) = A(q) + B(q) + D(q)$ $\hfill$ [11.1]

where $\quad C(q)$ = the total cost function

$\qquad A(q)$ = a function of q that defines the holding cost

$\qquad B(q)$ = a function of q that represents the shortage cost

$\qquad D(q)$ = a function of q that defines the ordering cost

In order to determine the optimal value of q, it is necessary to develop the functions $A(q)$, $B(q)$, and $D(q)$ for the basic EOQ model:

Figure 11.2   Graphic representation of the basic EOQ model

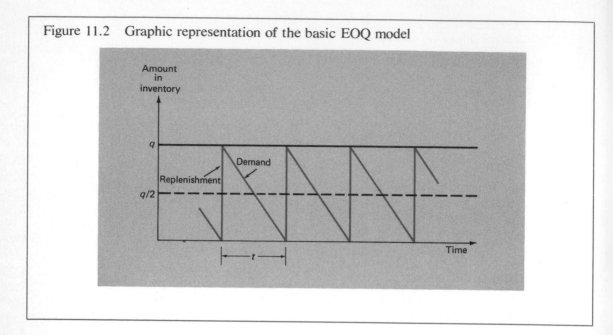

$A(q) = C_1(q/2)$
where C_1 = holding cost per unit of inventory

A look at Figure 11.2 will reveal to you that $q/2$ represents the average number of units in inventory. In other words, half the time there are more than $q/2$ units in inventory, and half the time the amount in inventory is less than $q/2$ units. Therefore, if we multiply a per-unit holding cost by the average number of units in inventory, that product is the holding cost. Since no shortages are allowed in the basic EOQ model due to the zero lead time and zero reorder point assumptions, $B(q)$ is not present in the total cost function. Ordering cost can be thought of as the cost of placing an order multiplied by the number of orders placed in a particular time period. More specifically,

$D(q) = C_3(r/q)$
where C_3 = the cost of processing one order
              r = total demand for a given period of time
            r/q = number of orders

Figure 11.3   Inventory cost basic EOQ model

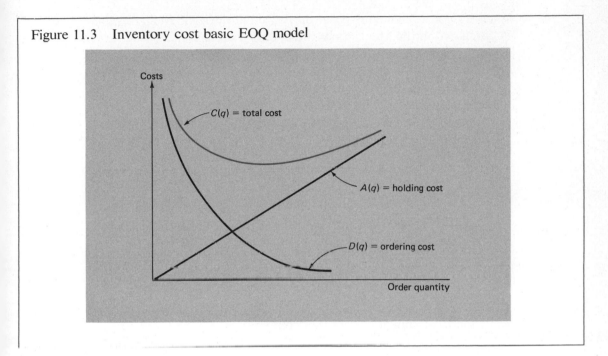

Given the preceding defined functions, the total cost function can be written as shown in equation 11.2.

$$C(q) = A(q) + D(q)$$
$$C(q) = C_1(q/2) + C_3(r/q) \qquad [11.2]$$

Remember, the question is to determine the value of q that minimizes the objective function $C(q)$. Figure 11.3 graphs the three functions $A(q)$, $C(q)$, and $D(q)$. From Figure 11.3, it is apparent that the minimum of $C(q)$ occurs at the same level of q where functions $A(q)$ and $D(q)$ intersect. It is possible, therefore, to set $A(q)$ equal to $D(q)$ and solve for q to find q^*, the optimal value of q. It must be noted that this relationship is not universally true.

$$
\begin{aligned}
A(q) &= D(q) \\
C_1(q/2) &= C_3(r/q) \\
C_1(q^2/2) &= C_3 r \\
q^2/2 &= C_3 r/C_1 \\
q^2 &= 2C_3 r/C_1 \\
q^* &= \sqrt{2C_3 r/C_1} \qquad [11.3]
\end{aligned}
$$

A more rigorous, calculus-based derivation of the basic EOQ formula is contained in the appendix at the end of the chapter.

[Example]   Now, let's look at an example of how to use the basic EOQ model. The XYZ Company uses 10,000 valves per year. Each valve costs $1. The Materials Department estimates that it costs $25 to order a shipment of valves and the Accounting Department estimates the holding cost is 12.5 percent. All the assumptions of the basic EOQ model are valid.

$$
\begin{aligned}
C_1 &= \$.125 \text{ per valve per year} \\
C_3 &= \$25 \text{ per order} \\
r &= 10{,}000 \text{ valves} \\
q^* &= \sqrt{2C_3 r / C_1} \\
&= \sqrt{2(25)10{,}000 / .125} \\
&= \sqrt{4{,}000{,}000} \\
&= 2{,}000 \text{ valves}
\end{aligned}
$$

If the XYZ Company buys 2,000 valves every time inventory reaches zero, the total annual cost of this policy is

$$
\begin{aligned}
C(q^*) &= .125(2{,}000/2) + 25(10{,}000/2{,}000) \\
&= 125 + 125 \\
&= \$250
\end{aligned}
$$

Once q^* is calculated, it is a simple matter to calculate the optimal number of orders per year and the time between each order.

$$
\begin{aligned}
N^* &= \text{optimal number of orders} \\
&= r/q^* \\
&= 10{,}000/2{,}000 \\
&= 5
\end{aligned}
$$

t^* = optimal time between orders (optimal reorder schedule)
  = Planning period $/N^*$
  = $365/5 = 73$ days

SENSITIVITY OF THE BASIC EOQ MODEL

As indicated in Figure 11.3, the shape of the total cost curve, $C(q)$, is relatively flat. Consequently, $C(q)$ is not very sensitive to small changes in q. To illustrate this fact, let us assume that the XYZ

Table 11.1   Sensitivity analysis of order quantity

Order quantity	Order cost ($)	Carrying cost ($)	Total cost ($)
100	2,500.00	6.25	2,506.25
500	500.00	31.25	531.25
750	333.33	46.88	380.21
1,000	250.00	62.50	312.50
1,250	200.00	78.13	278.13
1,500	166.65	93.75	260.40
1,750	142.85	109.38	252.23
2,000	125.00	125.00	250.00
2,250	111.10	140.63	251.73
2,500	100.00	156.25	256.25
3,000	83.33	187.50	270.83
4,000	62.50	250.00	312.50
10,000	25.00	625.00	650.00

Company orders 1,000 valves in each order instead of the optimal 2,000 valves.

$$C(1,000) = .125(1,000/2) + 25(10,000/1,000)$$
$$= 62.50 + 250$$
$$= \$312.50$$

Hence, a change of 50 percent in q resulted in only a 25 percent increase in the total inventory cost. (See Table 11.1 for a more complete sensitivity analysis.) This means that if total demand, r, is incorrectly estimated, thus causing a suboptimal q to be calculated, the consequences are not so critical as they would be if the shape of the total cost curve were more peaked.

BASIC EOQ SYSTEM WITH FINITE REPLENISHMENT RATE

Often, it is unrealistic to assume an infinite replenishment rate. If a firm is purchasing off-the-shelf items for its inventory, typically, when an order is delivered the entire replenishment quantity is

Figure 11.4 Basic EOQ system with uniform replenishment rate

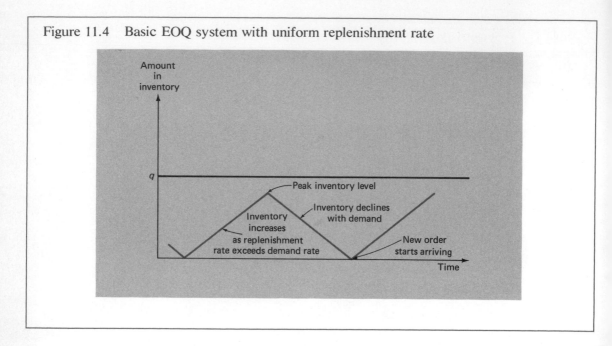

delivered at one time; hence, an infinite replenishment rate. If, however, a company is producing for inventory, units are added to inventory over a finite period of time. Therefore, the inventory system has a finite replenishment rate. If it can be assumed that this replenishment rate is uniform and all other assumptions of the basic EOQ model hold, the appropriate model is the basic EOQ system with a finite replenishment rate. The graphic representation of the model is given in Figure 11.4.

The total cost function of the inventory system depicted in Figure 11.4 is

$$C(q) = \frac{C_1 q(1 - r/p)}{2} + \frac{C_3 r}{q} \qquad [11.4]$$

Following a procedure similar to the one set forth in the appendix at chapter's end, the expression for the optimal order quantity shown in equation 11.5 can be derived.

$$q^* = \frac{\sqrt{2rC_3/C_1}}{\sqrt{1 - r/p}} \qquad [11.5]$$

where r = the total demand for a given period of time
         C_3 = the set-up cost per set-up
         C_1 = the carrying cost per unit
         p = uniform replenishment rate expressed in units per time
           period

The minimum total inventory cost is given by the following function:

$$C^* = \sqrt{2rC_1C_3}\,\sqrt{1 - r/p} \qquad\qquad [11.6]$$
where C^* = the minimum inventory cost

[Example] Let's change our previous example just slightly so that the replenishment rate changes from infinite to a uniform 500 valves per day. To restate, the XYZ Company uses 10,000 valves per year. Each valve costs $1. The Production Engineering Department estimates set-up costs at $25, and the Accounting Department estimates that the holding cost is 12.5 percent of the value of inventory.

r = 10,000 valves
C_3 = $25 per order
C_1 = $.125 per valve per year
p = 125,000 valves per year†

$$q^* = \sqrt{\frac{2rC_3/C_1}{1 - (r)/p)}}$$

$$= \sqrt{\frac{2(10,000)25/.125}{1 - (10,000/125,000)}}$$

$$= \sqrt{4,000,000/.92}$$

$$= \sqrt{4,350,000}$$

$$= 2,086$$

†It was necessary to convert the per-day production of valves to per-year production of valves because the time units must be compatible; that is, r was expressed in units per year.

Therefore, the XYZ Company should order 2,086 valves every time inventory for the valves reaches zero. The total inventory cost of this ordering policy is calculated following:

$$C^* = \sqrt{2rC_1C_3}\,\sqrt{1 - (r/p)}$$

$$= \sqrt{2(10,000).125(25)}\,\sqrt{1 - (10,000)/125,000}$$

$$= \sqrt{62,500} \sqrt{.92}$$
$$\cong \$239.75$$

Therefore, if the XYZ Company orders 2,086 valves approximately 60 times a year, inventory cost related to this particular valve is minimized at about $240 per year.

BASIC ORDER LEVEL SYSTEM

The basic order level system is very similar to the basic lot size system previously described. In fact, all properties are the same except that shortages are allowed and back-ordered and the scheduling period is prescribed. This type of system is very common in the real world when an organization places orders for certain inventory items on a regularly scheduled basis, such as once a month. An advantage of a prescribed scheduling period is that it does *not* necessitate continuous monitoring of inventory levels.

The basic order level system has the following properties:

1 Demand is deterministic.

2 The rate of demand is constant; that is, it is a linear demand function.

3 The scheduling period is prescribed.

4 The lead time is zero.

5 The replenishment rate is infinite.

6 Shortages are made up; that is, there are no lost sales.

7 The decision variable is the order level, S; that is, the decision variable is the amount of inventory after replenishment.

8 Holding cost is constant and is expressed as dollars per unit per time period.

9 Shortage cost is constant and expressed as dollars per unit per time period.

The basic order level system is depicted in Figure 11.5.

Since the scheduling period is prescribed, the only controllable inventory costs are the carrying and shortage costs. Since order level is the decision variable in this inventory model, the total cost function is a function of order level, S. It can be shown geometrically, using similar triangles, that the total cost function is

Figure 11.5   Basic order level system

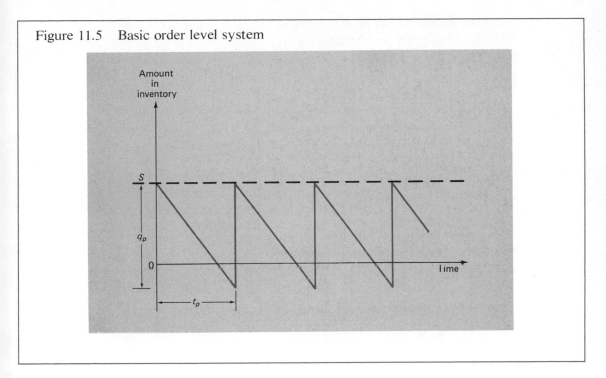

$$C(S) = C_1 S^2/2q_p + C_2(q_p - S)^2/2q_p \qquad\qquad [11.7]$$
where C_1 = carrying cost per unit
             S = order level
           q_p = prescribed lot size (rate of demand multiplied by
                  the prescribed time period)
           C_2 = shortage cost per unit

Minimizing this total cost function, the optimal order level is

$$S^* = q_p C_2/(C_1 + C_2)$$

[Example]   A local television store reviews its stock of 25-inch
color television sets every month, then orders for the next month.
Last year, it sold 120 25-inch color sets, and sales were spread
evenly throughout the year. Predictions are that this year's sales
will be approximately the same. Lead time is effectively zero, and
shortages are made up. The holding cost is $80 per set per year,

and shortage cost has been determined to be $10 per set per month. The optimal order level, therefore, is

$$S^* = 10(120)/(80 + 120)$$
$$= 6 \text{ sets}$$

To find the minimum cost of this solution, merely substitute S^* into the cost function

$$C(6) = 80[6^2/(2 \cdot 10)] + 120(10 - 6)^2/20$$
$$= \$240$$

In summary, the inventory policy of the local television store is to order 6 25-inch color TV sets whenever back orders reach 4.

Figure 11.6   Order level system with stock-outs

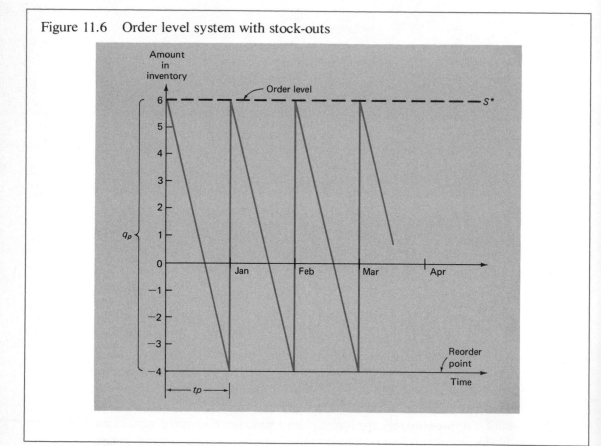

This policy costs $240 per year in inventory cost; any other policy would cost the TV store more. The graph of this inventory policy is shown in Figure 11.6.

BASIC EOQ MODEL WITH DISCRETE PRICE BREAKS

An organization may find it advantageous to procure inventories in large quantities in order to get quantity discounts. A supplier often sells a product at a price that fluctuates with the quantity purchased. Usually, the price-break scheme is discrete in nature. For example, the per-unit cost of an item might be $25 for quantities of 50 or less; $22 for quantities of less than 100 but more than 50; and $20 per unit for more than 100 units.

Buying large quantities has advantages other than merely lowering the per-unit cost of the particular inventory item. Obviously, because fewer orders are placed, ordering costs are reduced when an organization takes advantage of quantity discounts and buys in larger quantities. Transportation costs, also, are usually lower for a few large shipments rather than many small shipments. If demand is stochastic and lead time is not zero, buying in larger quantities results in fewer stock-outs.

As you have probably realized, buying in large quantities has some very important disadvantages, too. The most obvious is that, because the average amount in inventory is increased with large orders, the carrying cost of the inventory item is increased. In addition to increased carrying cost, more capital is required to buy larger quantities. For firms with limited capital, this can be a critical drawback, and sometimes it prevents taking advantage of quantity discounts. If the inventory item is perishable or has an otherwise limited life, buying in larger quantities may also be disadvantageous to a firm. High-fashion, ready-to-wear clothing is an example of such an inventory item. Even if a manufacturer is willing to give a quantity discount that would ordinarily minimize the retailer's total inventory cost, it may be wiser to buy the smaller quantity due to the potential obsolescence of the article.

The model we describe in this section is a simple, discrete price-break model. The assumptions concerning demand and replenishment properties are the same as the basic EOQ model except that in this model there exists the condition of discrete prices based on the quantity ordered. Since the cost of goods purchased is no longer constant but is a function of the price, the objective function is composed of ordering cost, carrying cost, and the cost of goods. More specifically,

$$C(q_i) = fq_i b_i /2 + (C_3 r/q_i) + rb_i \qquad\qquad [11.8]$$

where f = carrying cost fraction
           q_i = order quantity for price break i
           b_i = unit cost for price break i
           C_3 = ordering cost per order
           r = total demand

If you look carefully at the objective function in equation 11.8, you can see that it closely resembles the total cost function of the basic EOQ model. In fact, the first two terms are identical if you realize that the carrying cost (C_1) in dollars per unit per time period is simply the carrying cost fraction (f) multiplied by the unit cost (b_i). The only difference is the existence of more than one price level and the addition of the cost of goods.

Because the total cost function is noncontinuous, it is not possible to use the calculus to derive a simple formula to compute the optimal order quantity. Instead, we must develop an algorithm to do this. The first step in the algorithm is to compute the EOQ for each price level, starting at the price level that has the lowest cost per unit, until an EOQ fits in the relevant range of its price level. In other words, let q_0 be the largest EOQ for which

$$q_i \leq q_0 < q_{i+1}$$

where q_i = minimum order quantity for price level i

The next step is to compare the total cost of q_0 with the total cost of all minimum quantities for orders larger than q_0. In other words, compare $C(q_0)$ to $C(q_j)$ for $j < i$ where q_j = the minimum order quantity for price level j and i = the price level for q_0.

[Example]   A manufacturing company has planned its production schedule for the coming year based on forecast demand, back orders, and plant capacity. Instead of making a particular hydraulic pump that goes into the final product, the company has decided

Table 11.2   Victor Pumps Inc. price schedule

Quantity ordered	Unit price ($)
1–1,999	15.00
2,000–4,999	13.50
5,000–7,999	12.50
8,000–20,000	12.00
Over 20,000	11.50

to buy the pump. There are two such pumps in the end product, and the production schedule calls for producing 10,000 units of the end product. Therefore, 20,000 pumps will be needed next year. Ordering costs are estimated at $50 per order, and the carrying cost fraction for the firm is .20. A request for bids has yielded only one supplier, Victor Pumps Inc., who is approved by the Engineering Department; hence, the Purchasing Department has only one basic decision. That decision concerns the quantity to be ordered. Victor Pumps Inc. has submitted the price schedule shown in Table 11.2 along with its technical proposal.

$$EOQ_5 = \sqrt{\frac{2(20,000)50}{.2(11.50)}} \qquad b_5 = 11.50$$

$$\cong 933$$

$$EOQ_4 = \sqrt{\frac{2(20,000)50}{.2(12)}} \qquad b_4 = 12.00$$

$$\cong 913$$

$$EOQ_3 = \sqrt{\frac{2(20,000)50}{.2(12.50)}} \qquad b_3 = 12.50$$

$$\cong 894$$

$$EOQ_2 = \sqrt{\frac{2(20,000)50}{.2(13.50)}} \qquad b_2 = 13.50$$

$$\cong 861$$

$$EOQ_1 = \sqrt{\frac{2(20,000)50}{.2(15)}} \qquad b_1 = 15.00$$

$$\cong 816$$

The largest EOQ that falls in the relevant range of order quantities is $q_0 = 816$, falling between 1 and 1,999. What remains to be done is to compare the total cost of $q_0 = 816$ to order quantities equal to the minimum levels of the different price breaks. This is done by substituting the various order quantities into equation 11.7.

$$C(816) = \frac{1.2(816)15}{2} + 50\left(\frac{20,000}{816}\right) + 20,000(15)$$
$$= \$302,449.45$$

$$C(2,000) = \frac{.2(2,000)13.50}{2} + 50\left(\frac{20,000}{2,000}\right) + 20,000(13.50)$$
$$= \$273,200$$

$$C(5,000) = \frac{.2(5,000)12.50}{2} + 50\left(\frac{20,000}{5,000}\right) + 20,000(12.50)$$
$$= \$256,450$$

$$C(8,000) = \frac{.2(8,000)12}{2} + 50\left(\frac{20,000}{8,000}\right) + 20,000(12)$$
$$= \$249,725$$

$$C(12,000) = \frac{.2(20,000)11.50}{2} + 50\left(\frac{20,000}{20,000}\right) + 20,000(11.50)$$
$$= \$253,050$$

According to the foregoing analysis, the manufacturing company should order 8,000 pumps in order to minimize total inventory cost for the pump. In addition to the assumptions described for this simple price-break model, it must be noted that buying in quantities of 8,000 is going to require significantly more capital investment in inventory and, consequently, may not be the wisest choice if money in tight for the firm.

A STOCHASTIC DEMAND MODEL

Until now, we have assumed that all demand parameters of an inventory system are known with certainty. In addition, we have assumed that lead time is zero. If we loosen only this latter assumption, very little has to change except that we must order prior to running out of inventory to prevent stock-outs. (Figure 11.7 illustrates the basic EOQ system with nonzero lead time.) In

Figure 11.7   Basic EOQ with nonzero lead time, deterministic demand

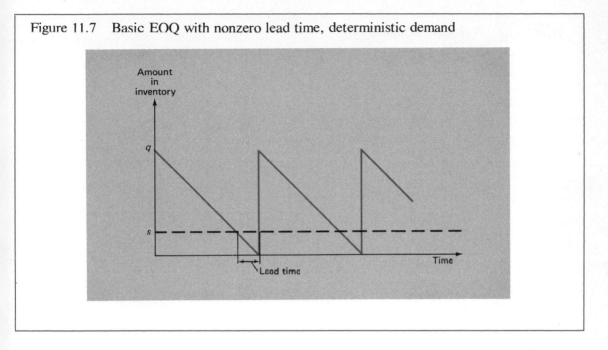

this situation, let's say, for example, that demand is 10 units per day and lead time is known to be 5 days; then the reorder point, s, is equal to 50 units. Therefore, whenever inventory reaches 50 units, an order for q units should be processed.

If we loosen the assumption of known or certain demand, then the problem of when to order becomes more complicated. As you can see in Figure 11.8, there is now the danger of stock-outs.

If an inventory system has all the properties of the basic EOQ system except that lead time is not zero and demand is not deterministic and constant, we can proceed in the following manner. The problem is still how much, and when, to order. If we assume that a reasonable estimate of the optimal order quantity can be calculated using the basic EOQ formula, then the problem reduces to merely determining the reorder point. In most real situations, using the EOQ formula when demand is not known with certainty has little effect on total inventory costs because of the relative insensitivity of total costs to moderate changes in the order quantity.

Since the order quantity is given, ordering costs should not be

Figure 11.8   Stochastic demand

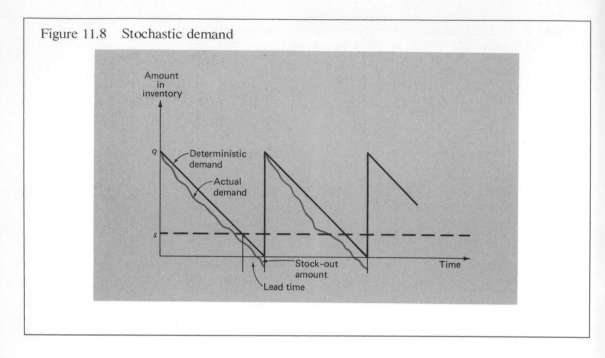

affected by changes in the reorder point. The inventory costs affected by changes in the reorder point are the carrying costs and the stock-out costs. The problem, however, is that when stock-out costs are lowered by increasing the safety stock, carrying costs are increased because the average value of inventory is increased.

To illustrate how to determine the reorder point, let us consider the following problem. A sporting goods store wants to determine the proper reorder point for a T–3000 Wilson tennis racket. Annual demand is for 1,000 rackets sold at a rate of approximately 4 per day. It takes 5 days between the day the order is placed and the receipt of the shipment from Wilson. The question is, at what point does the sporting goods store order T–3000 tennis rackets? In order to answer the question, it is necessary to have some idea of the probability distribution of the number of rackets demanded in any 5-day period. This information is summarized in Table 11.3. In order to determine a good reorder point, it is possible to look at six reorder points and calculate the expected cost of each, then

Table 11.3 Frequency distribution of 5-day demand for T–3000 tennis rackets

Demand for 5-day periods	Frequency of specified demand	Relative frequency	Cumulative relative frequency
10	5	.10	.10
15	15	.20	.40
20	20	.40	.80
25	5	.20	.90
30	4	.08	.98
35	1	.02	1.00
	50	1.00	

simply choose the reorder level with the smallest total cost. In order to determine this total cost, it is necessary to ascertain a per-unit stock-out cost. Let us assume this stock-out cost is $10 per racket. Then

$$q^0 = \sqrt{[2(1,000)(25)]/5}$$
$$= \sqrt{10,000}$$
$$= 100$$

If the sporting goods company reorders when inventory hits 10 rackets, there is a high probability (90%) of having a shortage before the shipment is received. The shortage cost associated with this policy can be calculated in the following way:

$$C_2 = \left[\sum_{i=1}^{n} x_i P(x_i) c_2 \right] (r/q) \tag{11.9}$$

where C_2 = shortage cost for year
    x_i = number short during lead time
    $P(x_i)$ = probability of being short x_i units
    c_2 = per-unit shortage costs
    r = total annual demand
    q = order quantity
    n = number of reorder points to be examined

Table 11.4   Stock-out costs

Reorder point	Stock-out costs ($)
10	1,010
15	560
20	210
25	60
30	10
35	0

Given that the reorder point is 10

$$C_2 = [0(.1)10 + 5(.2)10 + 10(.4)10 + 15(.2)10$$
$$+ 20(.08)10 + 25(.02)10](1,000/100)$$
$$= \$1,010$$

Stock-out costs for other reorder points are shown in Table 11.4.

The incremental carrying costs for the various reorder points under consideration are represented by

$$\Delta C_1 = \sum_{i=1}^{n} y_i P(y_i)c_1 \qquad [11.10]$$

where y_i = number of units in inventory at the time of replenishment

ΔC_1 = incremental carrying cost

$P(y_i)$ = probability of y_i units in inventory at the time of replenishment

c_1 = per-unit carrying cost

n = number of reorder points to be examined

Given a reorder point of 10,

$$\Delta C_1 = 0(.1)5 + 0(.2)5 + 0(.4)5 + 0(.2)5 + 0(.08)5 + 0(.02)5$$
$$= 0$$

For a reorder point of 25,

$$\Delta C_1 = 15(.1)5 + 10(.2)5 + 5(.4)5 + 0(.2)5 + 0(.08)5 + 0(.02)5$$
$$= \$27.50$$

Table 11.5　Cost of reorder point policies

Reorder point	Expected stock-out costs ($)	Expected incremental carrying costs ($)	Total costs ($) $c_2 + \Delta c_1$
10	1,010	0	1,010.00
15	560	2.50	562.50
20	210	10.00	220.00
25	60	27.50	87.50
30	10	50.00	60.00
35	0	74.50	74.50

Table 11.5 reflects total incremental costs per year based on reorder point. Since the total incremental cost of the various reorder point policies is minimized when the reorder point is 30, the optimal inventory policy for the sporting goods company is to order 100 tennis rackets 10 times a year whenever the inventory level reaches 30 rackets.

[Simulation approach]

Although there are many more inventory models than the few we have discussed in this chapter, it is very common for a real inventory system not to have an analytical counterpart. In other words, a model may not exist or be derivable mathematically that adequately describes a real inventory system. This is especially true when several properties are stochastic in nature. For example, many systems with stochastic demand, stochastic lead time, and nonconstant cost parameters have no mathematical model that can be solved analytically. As in the case of complex queuing systems, simulation can usually be applied when inventory systems become too complex to be optimized analytically. The trouble with simulation as a means

Table 11.6   Historical frequency of demand

Demand per day	Number of observations	Relative frequency
0	19	.095
1	27	.135
2	42	.210
3	49	.245
4	34	.170
5	17	.085
6	9	.045
7	2	.010
8	1	.005
	200	1.000

for solving inventory system problems is that simulation is a descriptive technique, not an optimization technique. Simulation can answer questions regarding the desirability of various inventory policies; but it cannot, by itself, assign values to the various decision variables.

[Example]   You can gain specific insight into how simulation is used to answer inventory questions by working through a simple inventory simulation. A ski shop carries a particularly popular pair

Table 11.7   Historical frequency of lead time

Lead time in days	Number of observations	Relative frequency
4	11	.22
5	7	.14
6	3	.06
7	21	.42
8	5	.10
9	2	.04
10	1	.02
	50	1.00

Table 11.8   Price schedule

Order	Price per pair of skis ($)
Less than 25	100
More than 25	95
More than 50	90
More than 100	80

of skis that sells for $120 and wishes to know how much, and when, to order. Because demand is not known with certainty (see Table 11.6) and lead time is not known with certainty (see Table 11.7), simulation appears to be a proper approach to the problem. The cost of the skis, which depends on the quantity ordered, is reflected in Table 11.8. Ordering cost is estimated at $25 per order, and the carrying cost fraction is .2. Stock-out cost is assumed to be $25 per unit.

In order to utilize simulation to solve this inventory problem, we must develop functions that can be used to generate the two stochastic variables in the problem, namely, demand and lead time. Let's assume that no known probability distribution can be fitted to the two sets of historical data and that we are forced to use these empirical distributions. Hence, the generating functions we need can be found merely by using the cumulative frequency distribution of the two stochastic variables. (See Tables 11.9 and 11.10 for these distributions.) You can refer back to Chapter 10, if necessary, for an explanation of how the two generating functions were derived.

Once we have the generating functions, the next step is to experiment with a particular inventory policy. For example, let's compare two inventory policies:

1 Order 25 pairs of skis when inventory reaches 10 pairs of skis.
2 Order 25 pairs of skis when inventory reaches 15 pairs of skis.

For illustrative purposes, we shall simulate 1 month manually. Then, using a computer, we'll simulate a number of different policies to determine a good inventory policy. Tables 11.11 and 11.12 reflect

Table 11.9 Demand generating function

Random number range	Demand per day
0–.095	0
.095–.230	1
.230–.440	2
.440–.685	3
.685–.855	4
.855–.940	5
.940–.985	6
.985–.995	7
.995–1.00	8

the results of the manual simulation for both inventory policies we established. Look at the carrying cost and the stock-out costs for the two policies simulated in Tables 11.11 and 11.12. (Ordering costs and the cost of goods are constant for the two policies.) You can see that, by increasing the reorder level five units, the stock-out cost is decreased by $150 with only a $1.50 increase in the month's carrying cost.

Obviously, other inventory policies need to be examined and the number of days simulated must be significantly increased before we can have much faith in the results of the simulation experiments. To give you some idea of what it costs to "solve" the ski inventory

Table 11.10 Lead time generating function

Random number range	Lead time in days
0–.22	4
.22–.36	5
.36–.42	6
.42–.84	7
.84–.94	8
.94–.98	9
.98–1.0	10

Inventory systems

Table 11.11   Simulation: Reorder point = 10, order quantity = 25

Day	Random number	Demand	Amount ordered (pairs)	Random number	Lead time (days)	Amount received (pairs)	Ending inventory	Carrying cost ($)	Stock-out cost ($)	Cost of goods ($)	Order cost ($)	Total cost ($)
1	.134	1					14	1.06	0	0	0	1.06
2	.909	5	25	.344	5		9	.69	0	2,375	25	2,400.69
3	.204	1					8	.61	0	0	0	.61
4	.906	5					3	.23				.23
5	.387	2					1	.08				.08
6	.045	0					1	.08				.08
7	.894	5				25	0	0	100			100.00
8	.172	1					24	1.82				1.82
9	.380	2					22	1.67				1.67
10	.390	2					20	1.52				1.52
11	.513	3					17	1.29				1.29
12	.563	3					14	1.06				1.06
13	.670	3					11	.84				.84
14	.428	2	25	.633	7		9	.68				.68
15	.589	3					6	.46				.46
16	.040	0					6	.46				.46
17	.738	4					2	.15				.15
18	.460	3					0	0	25			25.00
19	.007	0					0	0	0			0
20	.775	4					0	0	100			100.00
21	.421	2				25	23	1.73		2,375	25	2,401.78
22	.072	1					23	1.73				1.78
							Totals	$16.25	$225	$4,750	$50	$5,041.26

Table 11.12 Simulation: Reorder point = 15, order size = 25

Day	Random number	Demand	Amount ordered (pairs)	Random number	Lead time (days)	Amount received (pairs)	Ending inventory	Carrying cost ($)	Stock-out cost ($)	Cost of goods ($)	Order cost ($)	Total cost ($)
1	.134	1	25	.344	5		14	1.06		2,375	25	2,401.06
2	.909	5					9	.69				.69
3	.204	1					8	.61				.61
4	.906	5					3	.23				.23
5	.387	2					1	.08				.08
6	.045	0					1	.08				.08
7	.894	5				25	20	1.52				1.52
8	.172	1					19	1.44				1.44
9	.380	2					17	1.29				1.29
10	.390	2	25	.633	7		15	1.14		2,375	25	2,401.14
11	.513	3					12	.91				.91
12	.563	3					9	.68				.68
13	.670	3					6	.46				.46
14	.428	2					4	.30				.30
15	.589	3					1	.08				.08
16	.040	0					1	.08				.08
17	.738	4					0	0	75			75.00
18	.460	3				25	22	1.67				1.67
19	.007	0					22	1.67				1.67
20	.775	4					18	1.37				1.37
21	.421	2					16	1.22				1.22
22	.072	1					16	1.22				1.22
							Total	$17.80	$75	$4,750	$50	$4,892.80

Figure 11.9   GPSS program

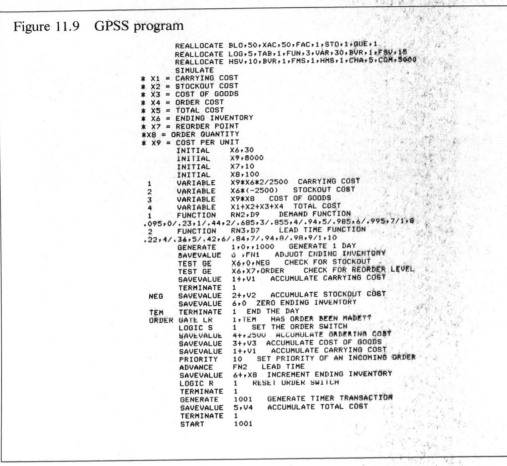

```
            REALLOCATE BLO,50,XAC,50,FAC,1,STO,1,QUE,1
            REALLOCATE LOG,5,TAB,1,FUN,3,VAR,30,BVR,1,FSV,15
            REALLOCATE HSV,10,BVR,1,FMS,1,HMS,1,CHA,5,COM,5000
            SIMULATE
 *  X1 = CARRYING COST
 *  X2 = STOCKOUT COST
 *  X3 = COST OF GOODS
 *  X4 = ORDER COST
 *  X5 = TOTAL COST
 *  X6 = ENDING INVENTORY
 *  X7 = REORDER POINT
 *X8 = ORDER QUANTITY
 *  X9 = COST PER UNIT
            INITIAL     X6,30
            INITIAL     X9,8000
            INITIAL     X7,10
            INITIAL     X8,100
 1          VARIABLE    X9*X6*2/2500   CARRYING COST
 2          VARIABLE    X6*(-2500)     STOCKOUT COST
 3          VARIABLE    X9*X8     COST OF GOODS
 4          VARIABLE    X1+X2+X3+X4    TOTAL COST
 1          FUNCTION    RN2,D9      DEMAND FUNCTION
.095,0/.23,1/.44,2/.685,3/.855,4/.94,5/.985,6/.995,7/1,8
 2          FUNCTION    RN3,D7      LEAD TIME FUNCTION
.22,4/.36,5/.42,6/.84,7/.94,8/.98,9/1,10
            GENERATE    1,0,,1000     GENERATE 1 DAY
            SAVEVALUE   6 ,FN1    ADJUST ENDING INVENTORY
            TEST GE     X6,0,NEG    CHECK FOR STOCKOUT
            TEST GE     X6,X7,ORDER     CHECK FOR REORDER LEVEL
            SAVEVALUE   1+,V1     ACCUMULATE CARRYING COST
            TERMINATE   1
 NEG        SAVEVALUE   2+,V2    ACCUMULATE STOCKOUT COST
            SAVEVALUE   6,0    ZERO ENDING INVENTORY
 TEM        TERMINATE   1   END THE DAY
 ORDER      GATE LR     1,TEM   HAS ORDER BEEN MADE??
            LOGIC S     1     SET THE ORDER SWITCH
            SAVEVALUE   4+,2500   ACCUMULATE ORDERING COST
            SAVEVALUE   3+,V3   ACCUMULATE COST OF GOODS
            SAVEVALUE   1+,V1    ACCUMULATE CARRYING COST
            PRIORITY    10    SET PRIORITY OF AN INCOMING ORDER
            ADVANCE     FN2    LEAD TIME
            SAVEVALUE   6+,X8   INCREMENT ENDING INVENTORY
            LOGIC R     1    RESET ORDER SWITCH
            TERMINATE   1
            GENERATE    1001    GENERATE TIMER TRANSACTION
            SAVEVALUE   5,V4    ACCUMULATE TOTAL COST
            TERMINATE   1
            START       1001
```

problem using computer simulation, we wrote and ran a simulation program to determine the effects of various inventory policies. The program, reflected in Figure 11.9, was written in GPSS, a special-purpose simulation language. It took approximately 2 hours to write and debug. One experiment simulating 4 years took .1214 minutes to run on a Xerox Sigma 6 computer. In all, 15 experiments were run at a total computer cost of approximately $9. As you can see in Table 11.13, the best inventory policy concerning skis is to order 100 pairs whenever inventory level reaches 25 pairs.

Table 11.13   Simulation results: Total adjusted inventory costs (including cost of goods)

Order quantity	Reorder level				
	10	15	20	25	30
25	$283,258	$276,738	$271,863	$269,611	$269,055
50	$263,589	$259,330	$256,271	$255,367	$254,937
100	$232,559	$229,395	$228,529	$227,777	$227,828

[Conclusion]

In order to implement truly effective inventory management, an organization must have an integrated management information system for the purpose of inventory control. In most organizations, inventory control is nothing more than an inventory accounting system. In other words, whether the system is computer-based or not, it merely keeps track of inventory items and alerts management when inventory levels get low. Typically, the system has little capacity for decision making about when, and how much, to order. Some progressive organizations, however, are developing or using systems that actually integrate inventory models like the ones we described in this chapter into their management information systems. These more progressive systems may be real-time or batch-oriented systems. What distinguishes the management information system from the inventory accounting system is the decision-making capability of the MIS.

Management science's primary challenge in relation to inventory theory is the successful application of existing theory. More theory is always useful, but unless organizations can be persuaded to apply the inventory theory thus far developed, the marginal utility of new theory is questionable.

To apply existing inventory theory successfully, you must beware of two pitfalls. First, you must avoid the misapplication of various inventory models by carefully examining the properties of an existing inventory system and making sure system properties adequately match model assumptions. Too many firms are using the basic EOQ model when it is inappropriate. Second, to implement a decision-making management information system, many human factors must be dealt with carefully. People naturally resist change, especially when it threatens their security or self-image. Many times, it is more effective, for example, to have the management information system suggest an order quantity rather than automatically print the purchase or production order. A major reason why management science has not progressed faster in most organizations is a failure to take into consideration the human factors connected with organizational change. Unless the people in an organization are in favor of a change, that change, regardless of its individual merits, will not succeed.

[Derivation of the basic EOQ model appendix]

From Equation 11.2,

$$C(q) = (C_1 q/2) + C_3 r/q$$

To optimize, take the first derivative with respect to q, set it equal to zero, and solve for q. Thus

$$\frac{dC(q)}{dq} = \frac{C_1}{2} - \frac{C_3 r}{q^2}$$

$$\frac{C_1}{2} - \frac{C_3 r}{q^2} = 0$$

Solve for q

$$\frac{C_1}{2} = \frac{C_3 r}{q^2}$$

$$q^2 = \frac{C_3 r}{q^2}$$

$$q^0 = \sqrt{2 C_3 r / C_1}$$

To determine whether q^0 is a maximum or a minimum, take the second derivative: If it is greater than zero, q^0 is a minimum; if $d^2 C(q)/dq^2$ is less than zero, q^0 is a maximum. Thus

$$\frac{d^2 C(q)}{dq^2} = \frac{2qC_3 r}{q^4} = \frac{2C_3 r}{q^3}$$

Since C_3, r, and q are all greater than zero, the second derivative is greater than zero. Therefore, q^0 is a minimum.

[Bibliography]

Bierman, Harold, Jr., Charles P. Bonini, and Warren H. Hausman, *Quantitative Analysis for Business Decisions,* 4th ed. Homewood, Ill.: Richard D. Irwin, Inc., 1973.

Buffa, Elwood S., *Operations Management: The Management of Productive Systems.* New York: Wiley Hamilton, 1976.

————, *Production-Inventory Systems: Planning and Control.* Homewood, Ill.: Richard D. Irwin, Inc., 1968.

Chase, Richard B. and Nicholas J. Aquilano, *Production and Operations Management: A Life Cycle Approach.* Homewood, Ill.: Richard D. Irwin, Inc., 1973.

Hadley, George, and T. M. Whitin, *Analysis of Inventory Systems.* Englewood Cliffs, N.J.: Prentice-Hall, Inc., 1963.

Levin, Richard I., and Charles A. Kirkpatrick, *Quantitative Approaches to Management,* 3rd ed. New York: McGraw-Hill Book Company, 1975.

Naddor, Eliezer, *Inventory Systems.* New York: John Wiley & Sons, Inc., 1966.

Schmidt, J. W., and R. E. Taylor, *Simulation and Analysis of Industrial Systems.* Homewood, Ill.: Richard D. Irwin, Inc., 1970.

Shore, Barry, *Operations Management.* New York: McGraw-Hill Book Company, 1973.

Wagner, Harvey M., *Principles of Operations Research,* 2nd ed. Englewood Cliffs, N.J.: Prentice-Hall, Inc., 1975.

[Review questions]

1 List four reasons for carrying an inventory.

2 What is the object of inventory models?

3 What are the two major decision variables in inventory models?

4 Describe the three components of inventory cost.

5 Briefly explain the four basic steps in analyzing an inventory system.

6 Why is the determination of system properties so important?

7 What is meant by demand patterns?

8 Define *lead time.*

9 Distinguish between stochastic demand and deterministic demand.

10 Define *replenishment period.*

11 Distinguish between order level and reorder level.

12 Why is it sometimes necessary to simulate an inventory system?

13 Why is sensitivity analysis an important step in analyzing inventory systems?

14 List the assumptions of the basic EOQ model.

15 Distinguish between finite and infinite replenishment rate.

16 What is the major difference between the basic EOQ model and the basic order level model?

17 List three benefits of taking advantage of price breaks.

18 What are two major disadvantages of using a simulation approach to inventory problems?

19 Why is simulation often used for inventory problems?

20 What distinguishes a management information system from an inventory accounting system?

21 Why haven't inventory models been more widely applied?

[Problems]

11.1 An aerospace company has a contract with the U.S. Navy to produce 120 airplanes during the next year. The plan is to produce these airplanes at a rate of 10 per month. An actuating cylinder used to move the wing flap is purchased off the shelf from a nearby supplier; no lead time is required. Since there are two wings, two cylinders are needed per airplane. The actuating cylinders cost $100. Holding cost for the cylinders is $10 per year per cylinder. In addition, it costs $75 to order these cylinders and receive them from the vendor.

a What is the optimal order quantity?

b What is the optimal number of orders per year?

c What is the optimal time between orders?

d What is the total inventory cost of ordering the optimal order quantity?

e Perform a limited amount of sensitivity analysis on the order quantity.

11.2 An automobile manufacturer plans to produce 30,000 cars in the next month. All cars planned for production use the same head lamps; therefore, demand for the headlights for the next month is known to be 60,000. The purchasing agent wants to know how many head lamps to buy at one time. Historically, head lamps have been received on the same day they were ordered. It costs $35 to order head lamps, and the carrying cost fraction used by the auto company is 15 percent. The lamps cost $.87 each.

a What is the optimal order quantity?

b What is the optimal number of orders per year?

c What is the frequency of orders?

d What is the total inventory cost of ordering the optimal order quantity?

e How sensitive is the optimal order quantity?

11.3 a Referring to problem 11.1, what should the aerospace company do if lead time is 1 month rather than zero? In other words, what should the inventory policy be?

b Does the existence of lead time change the total inventory cost of the actuating cylinders? If so, what is the total cost of the new inventory policy?

11.4 A management decision has been made to make the actuating cylinders in problem 11.1 rather than buy them from an outside vendor. The demand is for 240 cylinders for the next year, or 20 cylinders per month. To make the cylinders costs the company $90 each, and set-up time amounts to $100 per set-up. Holding cost remains at $10 per cylinder. Since these cylinders are not being bought off the shelf, replenishment of inventory is not simultaneous. In fact, the production department says it can produce 200 cylinders per month given present human and capital resources.

    a What is the optimal order quantity?

    b What is the optimal number of set-ups per year?

    c What is the optimal time between orders?

    d What is the total inventory cost of the optimal order policy?

11.5 The automobile manufacturer in problem 11.2 has decided to make the head lamps. It has been determined that 150,000 head lamps per month can be produced; but due to various resource constraints, management has decided to buy half the necessary quantity of head lamps and make the other half. It costs the company $.75 to make each head lamp, and set-up costs are $50 per set-up. Refer to problem 11.2 for the parameters of the purchasing decision.

    a What is the optimal order quantity to be purchased from the outside supplier?

    b What is the EOQ for in-house production?

    c What is the total inventory cost for the head lamps?

    d What is the optimal number of purchase orders per month?

    e What is the optimal number of production runs per month?

11.6 A mail-order, auto supply firm reviews its stock of tires each month and orders for the next month. Its most popular tire last year was the XR-100 radial. Last year, 600 sets were sold; these sales were spread evenly throughout the year. Predictions are that this year's sales will be approximately the same. Lead time from the manufacturer is effectively zero, and no sales are lost due to shortages. Instead, the tires are merely delivered 1 month later. A recent market survey revealed that 60 percent of the customers surveyed would not buy tires again from this firm if they were made to wait an extra month. Profit on a set of tires is $50. Management, therefore, has estimated stock-out cost to be .6(profit on two future sales), or $60, or $720 per set per year. Holding cost per set of tires is $75 per year.

    a What is the optimal order level?

    b What is the minimum inventory cost for the XR-100 radial tire?

    c What is the order level sensitivity?

11.7 An automobile dealer has the exclusive rights to market a foreign car. For this reason, no sales are lost if he is out of stock when a customer wants to buy. Demand for the car has been running at 20 units per month. The dealer orders one time per month and receives the order within a day or two. The dealer's subjective estimate of the cost of the loss of customer good will is $100 per month. The dealer cost on the cars is $4,000, and his carrying cost fraction is approximately 15 percent.

    a What is the optimal order level?
    b What is the minimum inventory cost for the foreign car?
    c What is the sensitivity of the order level?

11.8 A large hospital's nursery uses disposable diapers for its newborn babies at a rate of 60 cases per day. Ordering costs have been estimated at $50 per order. The hospital's Accounting Department has assigned a carrying cost fraction of .15 to the nursery supplies. All the assumptions of the basic EOQ model, such as zero lead time, are applicable. The purchasing agent for the hospital has an opportunity to take advantage of one of several quantity discounts. The pricing schedule is listed following:

Quantity ordered (cases)	Unit price ($)
0–1,999	2.50
2,000–4,999	2.45
5,000–10,000	2.40
Over 10,000	2.35

    a What is the optimal order quantity?
    b What is the minimum inventory cost?

11.9 A large restaurant sells 600 16-ounce strip steaks each week. It costs the restaurant $25 to order steaks from a local meat packer, and since the meat packer is close there is effectively no lead time involved. The restaurant's accountant has estimated the carrying cost fraction to be .2. The local meat packer has submitted the following price schedule:

Quantity ordered	Price per pound ($)
Less than 500	2.00
500–999	1.90
1,000–1,999	1.85
2,000–3,999	1.80
4,000–6,999	1.75
7,000–9,999	1.73
More than 10,000	1.70

Assume that the restaurant has ample freezing capacity.

    a What is the optimal order quantity?

    b What is the minimum total cost?

    c How much initial investment capital would it require to implement the optimal inventory policy?

    d What policy would you recommend to the restaurant manager?

11.10 A large retail chain store sells a vacuum cleaner for $150. The cost of the vacuum cleaner, including selling cost, is $120. Cost of goods is $100. Demand for this vacuum cleaner model is stochastic; past demand is reflected in the following table:

Weekly demand	Frequency
0	2
1	7
2	10
3	7
4	12
5	20
6	14
7	10
8	9
9	7
10	2
	100

Total demand for 1 year is forecast to be 260 units. Stock-out cost is assumed to be the profit lost, or $30. Lead time is 7 days. Ordering costs are $40 per order. Carrying cost is 23 percent of the inventory value.

    a What is the best inventory policy for the model LX–1002 vacuum cleaner?

    b What do the expected stock-out and incremental carrying costs of the selected inventory policy total?

11.11 Given the policy you recommended in problem 11.10, simulate manually 1 month's activity. Interpret your simulation results.

11.12 You are asked by the manager of a blood bank to study its inventory problem and make recommendations for optimizing costs using management science techniques. The manager has been taking some night courses and has been taught the following formula and wonders if it might be applied to the problem:

$$q^* = \sqrt{2C_3\,r/c_1}$$

Specifically, do the following:

a Indicate to the manager what an inventory model is meant to do.

b Discuss properties of this inventory problem.

c Recommend use of the aforementioned formula or state specific reasons why it shouldn't be used.

[Tom Newberry's dilemma]

Tom Newberry was despondent. As he worked his way slowly homeward in the bind of Boston 5 P.M. traffic on a warm September afternoon, he mulled over the day's discouraging events. After spending all summer on the first assignment of his new job he was suddenly threatened by the disheartening prospect that not only had he worked on the wrong problem but his solution to the problem he had worked on was worthless.

Newberry had received his M.B.A. the previous June from a well-known eastern business school. He had immediately begun work as assistant to Horace Davidson, the manufacturing vice-president of J.B. Koffman and Co., Inc., a Boston-based manufacturer of specialty plastics products. Davidson had asked him, as his first assignment, to conduct a review of Koffman's inventory procedures and make recommendations for improvements. Davidson had expressed the opinion that they were carrying far too much inventory of some items and not enough of others.

Koffman and Co. grouped its manufacturing operations into ten departments, segregated by type of basic manufacturing process and finishing operations. The basic manufacturing departments included five injection molding and two punch press departments. Newberry had been instructed by Davidson to look first at products manufactured in the injection molding departments.

Over the summer Newberry had familiarized himself with manufacturing operations in the various departments and begun collecting data for his study.

Newberry's assignment at Koffman was his first really close contact with manufacturing operations. Prior to attending business school, he had served for three years as a lieutenant in the army after graduating with an undergraduate degree in engineering.

In his graduate M.B.A. program he had followed a general management course of study, feeling that this would best prepare him, ultimately, for heading his own business. Although he had taken a number of elective courses dealing with manufacturing policy and small business management, his primary exposure to inventory control concepts was obtained in the production management course required of all M.B.A. candidates. The latter course had emphasized the use of the economic order quantity concept in inventory control. He had learned the types of costs involved in the calculation of EOQs and how to calculate the EOQ for individual products. Thus it was with some degree of confidence that he decided, upon learning that Koffman's inventory control procedures were not based on EOQs, to attempt to apply these concepts.

The first problem he had encountered was difficulty in obtaining reliable cost data to use in the EOQ formula. Although somewhat prepared for this from what he had learned in school, he was surprised at the amount of effort required to actually dig out cost data product by product and, more importantly, to get agreement among different people that the resulting costs were reasonably correct. He had spent the better part of 6 weeks in attempting to determine set-up costs and carrying costs for each of about 75 injection molding products he had selected as most important on the basis of an "A-B-C" analysis. He was reasonably satisfied with his figures for set-up cost. But he knew that the values of inventory holding cost he had finally arrived at, in some desperation, were still disputed in some quarters of the company.

In contrast to the development of cost data, Newberry found that estimates of annual demand for the 75 products he had selected were relatively easy to obtain. Koffman's marketing personnel had, for the past several years, been fairly accurate in their sales forecasts on these items. It had required only about 5 days for marketing personnel to provide him with new projected 1-year estimates of demand for his products. After adjusting these figures by scrap, inspection, and pilferage loss figures supplied to him by manufacturing personnel, he had what were generally agreed by all concerned to be the best possible estimates of future demand on the injection molding departments for each of the products.

The next thing Newberry had done was to determine the order quantities (run sizes) currently used for each product. These quantities were set by the department foremen and were determined in a variety of ways, depending upon the individual. Although the order quantity for particular items varied a great deal from year to year in some cases, Newberry found that the variation over the previous 4 months was relatively small for most products. He therefore took the average order size over this period as the order size currently in use. He had obtained agreement from each of the foremen concerned that these quantities were reasonably close to what they would in fact run, and had also obtained from them the amount of set-up time required for each order.

Finally, after gathering all of the various data required above—a task which had consumed most of the summer—he had sat down and calculated the EOQs for each product. The results of these calculations convinced him that his efforts had been worthwhile. For almost every product on his list the order quantities calculated by the EOQ formula were significantly lower than the order quantities currently used by the foremen. From a quick perusal of his results, he was convinced that Koffman could reduce the average inventory required on this group of products by almost 25 percent.

Before presenting his results to Horace Davidson, however, he had decided to show them to one or two of the department foremen, to get their reactions and to correct any possible mistakes he had made. To facilitate his discussions with each man, he separated the products into groups by department. Table 1, as an example, shows data on 8 items, from his list of 75, that were all produced in Injection Molding Department Number 1.

With a sense of barely concealed elation, he had, two days ago, taken the data shown in Table 1 to George Green, the foreman of the Number 1 Department. Green had listened patiently to Newberry's description of how he had calculated the new order quantities and had shown little reaction when Newberry pointed out that his results

Table 1   Eight products from Department No. 1

Product	Yearly demand units	Present order quantity	Set-up hours per order	Product unit cost ($)*‡	EOQ†
A	3,200,000	140,000	6.0	.1272	73,800
B	2,000,000	80,000	5.0	.0510	84,000
C	5,600,000	300,000	6.5	.0134	313,000
D	1,200,000	100,000	4.5	.0388	70,600
E	400,000	60,000	4.0	.1006	24,000
F	960,000	160,000	2.5	.0174	70,600
G	320,000	40,000	4.5	.0754	26,200
H	1,440,000	180,000	3.0	.0074	145,200
		1,060,000			807,400

*Figured on basis of direct labor and material costs.

†Calculated using the standard EOQ formula, with set-up cost per hour = $3.60 (same rate for all items in this department).

‡Inventory carrying cost equals 20 percent of product unit cost for all items in this department. For example, for product A

$$EOQ = \sqrt{\frac{2(3,200,000)\ 6.0(3.60)}{.20(.1272)}}$$

$$= 73,800 \text{ units}$$

indicated a reduction of almost 25 percent in the average inventory carried in these eight products. When Newberry had finished speaking, Green asked him to leave the figures with him so that he might look them over. Because something in Green's manner bothered Newberry, he decided to wait for Green's final reaction before showing his results to anyone else.

That morning shortly after he had arrived at his office George Green came in with a sheaf of calculations plus the data Newberry had left with him.

"Tom," Green said, "I've been doing some work with these numbers you showed me. I don't understand all this EOQ math, but I do know

Table 2   Calculation of set-up time for present and new order quantities shown in Table 1

Part A New order quantities (EOQ calculation)		Part B Present order quantities	
Product	Set-up hours required	Product	Set-up hours required
A	260.8	A	137.2
B	119.2	B	124.8
C	116.0	C	121.2
D	76.4	D	54.0
E	66.8	E	26.8
F	34.0	F	15.2
G	55.2	G	36.0
H	30.0	H	24.0
	758.4		539.2

Note: Yearly set-up hours = yearly demand/order quantity (set-up hour per order). For example, for item A at its present order quantity, set-up hours are 3,200,000(6.0)/140,000 − 137.2.

that I can't operate with these new order quantities of yours, no matter how you calculated them. Because most of your order sizes are smaller than what I'm now running, I'll have to make a lot more runs to get the same amount of product out. That would be okay with me except for the set-up time involved."

He pushed the set of figures in front of Newberry.

"Look, I ran off the amount of set-up time which will be required if I use your new order quantities (Table 2, part A). You can see here that it amounts to about 760 hours for these products. That's a 41 percent increase over the set-up time required with my present order sizes (Table, 2 part B). You know as well as I do that my department is already pushed to capacity. I just can't spare any more time for set-ups than what I'm currently using. Davidson would blow his top if he found out I want to increase my set-up time by 41 percent just to get the same amount of product out the door. If you want to come up with something that I can use, show me how I can cut inventory without increasing my set-up time. These EOQs don't mean a thing unless you can do that." With that, he got up and left Newberry's office.

After Green had left, Newberry sat studying Green's calculations for a long while. There was no doubt the foreman was correct—the set-up time would increase by 41 percent under the EOQ-based order sizes. Newberry was angry with himself for not having seen this, and spent several hours fruitlessly trying to figure out a way around the problem. He realized that he needed some way of showing the relationship of total lot-size inventory cost to total set-up cost.

Then, that afternoon, to make matters worse, Horace Davidson had come into his office.

"I hear you've gotten some results on your inventory study, Tom," the older man had said with a note of humor. "Mind if I have a look at them?"

Newberry had reluctantly shown Davidson a portion of his results. He suspected that Davidson already knew of the implications of his results on set-up time even though Davidson did not mention it. So he was careful to point out that his calculations were rough and needed some further work before they could be used.

Figure 1

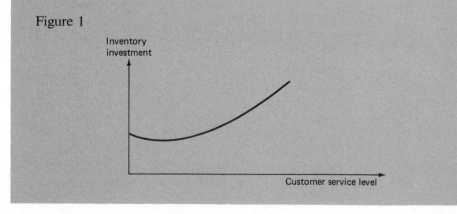

After listening to Newberry and looking over the EOQ calculations shown him, Davidson and risen to his feet and said, with a slight tone of impatience in his voice, "These EOQ calculations are okay, Tom. You've put a lot of time into developing them, and I'm sure you'll be able to adjust them so they can be used. But your EOQs don't help me much with some of the other inventory questions I've been worried about. I want to know how much unnecessary investment in inventory we're making now at our present customer service levels. And I'd like to know how much it will cost us to improve our service. What I'd really like is something like this," he said, as he quickly sketched out the diagram in Figure 1 on Newberry's desk pad.

Then as he turned to walk out the door, he had remarked, "The trouble with this EOQ approach is that it keeps you thinking about inventory on a product-by-product basis, and you end up missing the big picture. I hope you'll give some thought to that."

As Tom Newberry sat in traffic that afternoon remembering these events, he was alternately discouraged and angry. He realized that he had naturally focused on the EOQ approach because of what he had learned in his business school production course. In fact, he recalled ruefully, it was hard to remember having learned anything about inventory control *except* how to do the EOQ calculations for a particular item. The problem with set-up time that he had encountered in George Green's department seemed obvious in retrospect. But he was sure that none of his course material had covered this and no one had ever mentioned it in class discussions.

He decided that the first thing he would do that evening after dinner would be to review the calculations for George Green's department. He wanted to find some way of adjusting his order quantity calculations that would overcome Green's objections and at the same time salvage at least some of the time and effort he had invested so far.

He realized that he had to take an entirely different approach to develop the type of information that Davidson wanted. The only trouble was, he wasn't sure where to begin.

"I'll think about that tomorrow," he said to himself, as he turned into his driveway and switched off the engine.

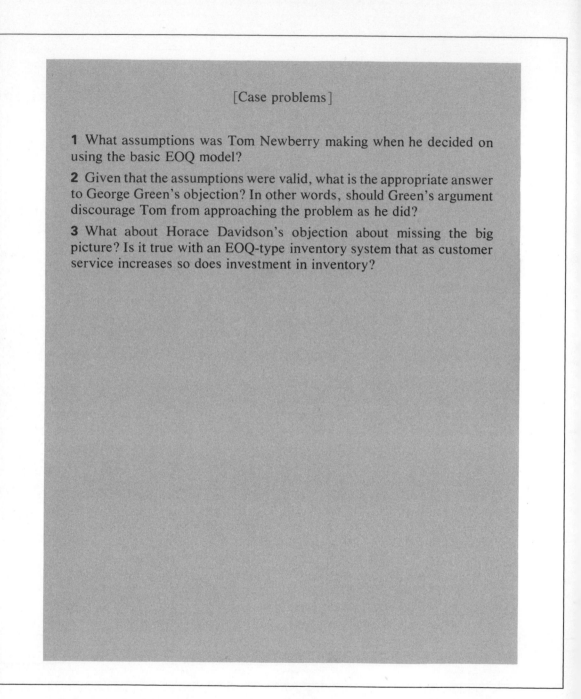

[Case problems]

1 What assumptions was Tom Newberry making when he decided on using the basic EOQ model?

2 Given that the assumptions were valid, what is the appropriate answer to George Green's objection? In other words, should Green's argument discourage Tom from approaching the problem as he did?

3 What about Horace Davidson's objection about missing the big picture? Is it true with an EOQ-type inventory system that as customer service increases so does investment in inventory?

[The Worrell Company case]

The Worrell Company was founded by John Worrell and his son, Hubert, in 1923. Originally, the firm manufactured cranes and hoists. Successful operations with these products enabled the company to move readily with changes in demand. A line of heavy earth-moving equipment was added, and acceptance of this product, its larger market, and its greater profit margin led the Worrell Company to sell its crane and hoist operations and concentrate on the earth-moving equipment. The first units produced were large off-highway trucks. This unit is still the largest line sold by the company. Crawler tractors, bottom dumps, twin scrapers, coal and log haulers, and tractor shovels were later added to the company's line of products.

In 1953 the company was purchased by one of the largest domestic corporations in the United States. The Hudson plant of the Worrell Company was built in 1959. It was designed to build crawler tractors in the $35,000 to $75,000 price range.

Within the Hudson plant, a production control department was organized. Among its principal duties is the responsibility for ordering material as needed for the production line. The method presently employed is identical to that used at the other Worrell plants. A vendor scheduling card, Figure 1, acts as a record for all transactions involving productive material. For each purchased part, a different card of this type is used. The listing of vendors in the upper left corner indicates vendors from whom the part is, or was, purchased. Generally, the vendor indicated by the higher number is the current source of supply. In the lower portion of the card material rejected as unacceptable for use, or scrapped due to damage in attempted use, is indicated by a circle. If the circle appears in the *Material received* column, the *Material scheduled* column, and the *Material ordered* column, the

Figure 1   Vendor material scheduling record

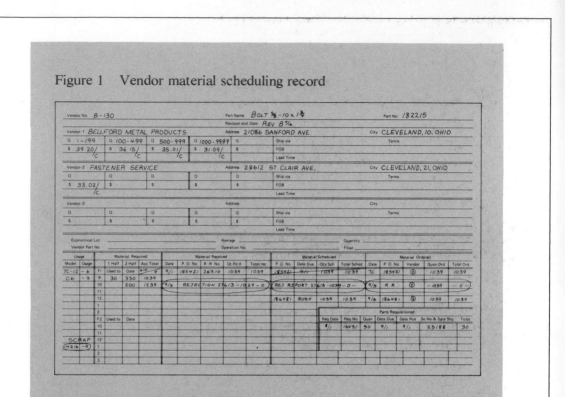

shipment is shown to have been rejected by inspection and the material is automatically placed on reorder.

Ordering is done once a month. Monthly, the production control scheduler computes the amounts to be ordered, considering price breaks or quantity discounts as established by the Purchasing Department.

Production is increasing at a rapid rate, and, with each increase in production, the system of monthly ordering becomes more and more costly and more time-consuming. Quantity discounts are not used to the best advantage. Some increase in handling charges at the plant may also be attributed to the ordering system. No attempt has been made to establish an inventory level that would eliminate stock-outs by determining and maintaining a safety stock within the inventory. This, with the system of monthly ordering, has produced the situation shown diagramatically in Figure 2. Stock-outs do occur, and storage

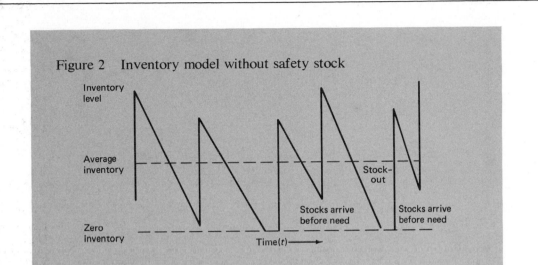

Figure 2 Inventory model without safety stock

space and other costs are increased when items arrive before they are needed.

Gayle Fedder, production control supervisor, is convinced that the problem, a troublesome one at present, will become a critical one in the near future if immediate steps are not taken to correct it. He has proposed that a quantity formula be developed and used to schedule material into the plant from the outside vendors. A preliminary survey conducted by Fedder indicated that the company incurs a processing cost of $10 in making an order, and that the cost of carrying inventory would approximate 20 percent of the value of the item on an annual basis.

Mr. Fedder has to this point been unsuccessful in gaining acceptance of his proposal. His superior, a long-time associate of the senior Worrell, can see no justification for substituting mathematical procedures for the background and experience of persons who have been making such decisions for the company for years, during which the company has prospered. The superior also feels that management has the obligation to make the decision personally as to how such factors as cost, interest, usage, cost of insurance, and taxes shall be evaluated.

Introduction to management science

Table 1 Sample of population of hardware items purchased at Hudson plant

Item	Description	Annual usage (number of pieces)	Price ($)	Annual usage ($)	Orders per year
1	Bolt $3/8$–18 $\times$ $6^1/2$	7,920	30.15/c	2,387.87	2
2	Bearing retainer	2,560	0.60 ea.	1,536.00	5
3	Bolt $5/8$–11 $\times$ 2	1,872	62.58/M	1,170.19	5
4	Stud	3,840	19.60/c	752.64	5
5	Bolt $3/4$–10 $\times$ $1^3/4$	6,120	106.47/M	649.44	3
6	Snap ring	1,280	323.55/M	420.60	3
7	Bolt $5/8$–11 $\times$ 4	3,240	10.39/c	336.00	4
8	Bolt $5/8$–18 $\times$ $1^1/2$	5,040	54.81/M	279.53	3
9	Bolt $3/4$–10 $\times$ $3/4$	1,080	18.60/c	200.88	4
10	Lockwasher $3/4$	7,920	0.02 ea.	158.40	4
11	Bolt $5/8$–11 $\times$ $3/4$	1,440	9.87/c	142.22	3
12	Bracket	1,440	0.077 ea.	110.88	2
13	Set screw	2,160	4.80/c	103.68	3
14	Bolt $5/8$–18 $\times$ 2	360	6.23/c–28/c	22.41	4
15	Nut $7/16$–14	720	1.76/c	12.67	4
16	Nut $5/16$–24	1,440	0.45/c	6.48	4
17	Screw #6–32 $\times$ $1^1/4$	720	5.83/M	3.89	5
18	Nut #6–32	720	5.07/M	3.65	4
19	Cotter pin $3/32$–$1^1/4$	1,440	1.40/M	2.05	4
20	Washer $5/16$	720	0.15/c	1.08	3
				8,300.56	74

Table 1 contains data of a sample of hardware items purchased from outside vendors. The sample was taken by Mr. Fedder as the basis for determining order quantities mathematically in the model he proposes to use to change materials programming.

[Case problems]

1 If Figure 2 accurately depicts the inventory behavior of the hardware items in Table 1, would an EOQ type of procedure be applicable? Could this be done on a periodic review basis?

2 For the sample reflected in Table 1, calculate the annual dollar savings that could be realized by switching to a basic EOQ ordering procedure.

3 In order to implement an EOQ ordering procedure, what would Mr. Fedder have to do?

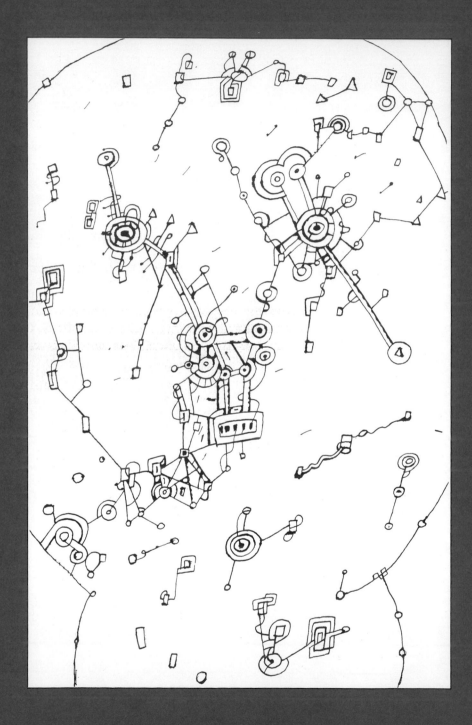

12

[Management science: present and future]

Much progress has been made in management science during the past 30 years. The growth in technical literature has been explosive. Many new procedures have been developed, and many existing techniques have been refined, extended, and improved. Perhaps the most important accomplishments are the successful applications that have been achieved by both government and industry. In spite of these advances, the field is not without its present problems and future challenges. In this last chapter, we shall examine present conditions and current trends as well as some differing points of view about new directions for management science.

One fruitful way to gain insight into the present and future of management science is to examine the discipline in relation to its prior developmental phases. John F. Magee, president of Arthur D. Little, Inc., has described management science as having progressed through three overlapping phases.[1]

The primitive stage This stage occurred from World War II through the 1950s. The emphasis during this time was on solving practical operational problems. The problems generally were well defined and small enough to be handled by the relatively unsophisiti-

---

[1] John F. Magee, "Progress in the Management Sciences," *TIMS Interfaces*, 3, (February 1973), 35–41.

cated computers of the day. Research activity focused on the development of quantitative techniques in order to get optimal solutions to clearly defined problems. The professionals in the field—far fewer than today—were drawn mostly from related disciplines such as mathematics, physics, and chemistry. Academic interest in OR/MS was limited; only three universities offered formal programs in the discipline.

The academic phase The academic phase occurred during the 1960s. It was characterized by the tremendous growth of academic interest in OR/MS. In 1962, only 6 institutions offered programs of study; by 1968, 37 did.

As a consequence of the expanding educational programs, people who had some exposure to OR/MS began to appear at the management level. These people naturally caused OR/MS to be accepted more widely, used more often, and applied more innovatively than ever before. Nonetheless, an emphasis on the development of quantitative techniques prevailed; new techniques were generated and others refined. The simultaneous development of computer hardware and software also expanded the range of operational problems that could be solved successfully. Computer manufacturers developed "canned" programs (commercial software packages) for the application of various standard techniques. Computer-based management information systems were designed during this period. The systematic approach to information utilization characteristic of management information systems also helped to supply the data necessary for OR/MS procedures. One of the more important results of the actual use of OR/MS during the sixties was that professionals gained a more realistic understanding of the strengths and limitations of management science.

Research during the sixties, however, was often academic, rather than practical, in nature. It tended to be directed at development and elaboration of technique, apparently without concern or interest for management issues. Practitioners sometimes did not understand the more esoteric developments and thought they were irrelevant to actual decision making. Emphasis was placed on developing techniques instead of on obtaining good data, understanding the behavior and values of organizations, and identifying options.

The maturing phase Some signs of the maturing phase of the 1970s were evident as early as the 1950s. The maturing phase is characterized by a better balance between theory and observation, greater attention to qualitative aspects of problem solving, and increased interest in investigating processes as well as solutions. During the maturing phase, management scientists have become more reflective about the goals and accomplishments of their discipline. The Institute of Management Sciences' (TIMS) credo states a concern for identifying, extending and unifying scientific knowledge pertaining to management. In the maturing phase, more attention has been given to real management problems. Magee's summary of the characteristics of the maturing phase is, in itself, a statement of the most worthy objectives of management science today:

1 "More realistic understanding by both managers and management scientists of what the management sciences can and cannot accomplish."

2 "More attention paid to getting the facts, describing what is going on and why, compared with development of abstract sophisticated techniques."

3 "Less attention to finding 'optimum' answers, more to developing processes and evolving successively better answers, adapted to evolving circumstances."

4 "Better integration of behavioral, functional, and quantitative analysis, fuller appreciation of the importance of values as well as arithmetic, a clearer understanding of the importance of assumptions as well as of logic."[2]

[A look at management science in organizations]

Since the 1950s, several researchers have tried to determine the status of OR/MS usage in industry and government. These investigations seek to establish whether and how OR/MS use is growing, which techniques are used, what kinds of personnel are employed, and what usage trends are evident.

[2] Magee, "Progress in the Management Sciences," pp. 35–41.

A particularly thorough investigation into the growth and development of OR/MS activities in industry and government has been carried out by a team of researchers at Northwestern University. Over a 13-year period, Radnor and associates have conducted several surveys that include the United States and 20 foreign countries. In 1968 an investigation of 66 large U.S. corporations (all but nine among *Fortune's* top 500 companies) suggested several trends and factors related to the integration and utilization of OR/MS activities in U.S. business organizations. Some of the more significant trends were:

1 "A shift in the types of OR/MS personnel away from the mathematics-science professionals toward the more generally trained and management-oriented organizationals."

2 "A movement of core OR/MS groups out of research and engineering locations toward finance-accounting and later top management or planning positions, together with an increasing degree of organizational diffusion of OR/MS skills and endeavors, and a growing interdependence between OR/MS and computer activities."

3 "A shift in work portfolios, initially away from major large-scale projects, toward a mixed portfolio containing short-run, limited projects, as well as large programs."

4 "A generally increasing, but not yet stabilized, level of integration into the organization of OR/MS activities, together with a low but increasing degree of management understanding and support."[3]

A follow-up study[4] through December 1970 extended the results of the 1968 investigation. The 1970 study was more extensive and included 108 large U.S. corporations. In general, most of the trends identified in the 1968 study were found to have continued through 1970. In brief, the study made the following observations:

1 The field of OR/MS is exhibiting signs of maturity; it is in a "success phase" in its developmental history.

2 There exists a definite trend toward the diffusion of OR/MS capabilities within the firm.

[3] M. Radnor, H. Rubenstein, and A. Bean, "Integration and Utilization of Management Science Activities in Organizations," *Operational Research Quarterly*, 19 (1968), 117–41.
[4] M. Radnor and R. Neal, "The Progress of Management-Science Activities in Large U.S. Industrial Corporations," *Operations Research*, 21 (1973), 427–50.

3 The actual process of performing an OR/MS analysis has become increasingly formalized—and increasingly routine.

4 The level of management acceptance shows a strong upward trend.

5 The data-processing or management information system function is increasingly viewed as a distinct entity, and OR/MS tends to be located or associated with the management information system function within the firm.

Based on the Radnor investigations, it appears that OR/MS functions are still in a state of change; stable or static conditions are not indicated. Thus, OR/MS activities are probably in a transitional state within the organization; but, for the most part, they seem to be undergoing steady improvement in terms of acceptance, significance, and the utilization of their outputs.

AREAS OF APPLICATION

Questionnaire surveys conducted over the past two decades can, with qualifications, give important insight into the ways corporations use OR/MS. Surveys made in the late fifties and middle sixties were followed up by the authors with a comparative survey in March 1974. The three surveys were conducted in a similar manner: They all examined OR/MS activities in large-scale U.S. corporations. In particular, the questionnaires were mailed to selected *Fortune* 500 companies. We mailed 240 questionnaires; 105 were returned. The results of the 1974 survey are based on the 84 responding companies who reported OR/MS activities.

Table 12.1 shows approximately how applications have changed during the periods of each survey. Keep in mind that the comparative estimates are rough, and each is subject to sampling error. In order to view the results of the surveys as objectively as possible, you must remember that such samples are incomplete and can involve biased responses. Given these qualifications, there is strong evidence from Table 12.1 that applications involving forecasting, transportation, capital budgeting, and plant location have grown significantly since 1958. In 1974, more than half the companies responding indicated applications in forecasting, production scheduling, inventory control, transportation, capital budgeting, and plant location.

Table 12.1   Areas of application of OR/MS techniques

Area of application	Percent of companies reporting activity		
	1958	1964	1974
Forecasting	57	73	89
Production scheduling	47	90	69
Inventory control	45	90	68
Transportation	26	54	60
Capital budgeting	11	39	58
Plant location	15	32	55
Optimum capacity studies	na	na	45
Advertising and sales research	20	27	39
Equipment replacement	15	27	31
Product development	na	na	31
Accounting procedures	16	17	27
Quality control	33	51	26
Loading and sequencing	na	na	25
Plant layout	na	na	18
Maintenance and repair	16	32	16
Routing	na	na	11
Personnel selection	na	na	11
Tax assessment analysis	na	na	8
Weapon systems analysis	na	na	8
Packaging	13	7	7
Paperwork scheduling	na	na	6

Most of the listed applications show increasing use over the course of the three surveys. (In fact, OR/MS activity in general has a healthy long-term growth pattern.) In 1958 and 1964, the percentage of companies reporting OR/MS activity was 68 and 75, respectively. In 1974, 80 percent of the respondents reported OR/MS activity.

TECHNIQUE USAGE

One question on the 1974 survey was designed to measure the degree of usage of OR/MS techniques. The results corroborated an earlier investigation that found the three most widely used techniques to be LP, computer simulation, and statistical techniques in general. Unfortunately, our survey did not examine the usage of statistical techniques. However, the many statistics/probability procedures probably make up the largest class of quantitative procedures administrative decision makers use. Some of the more common of these are forecasting techniques, multiple regression and correla-

Table 12.2   Usage of OR/MS techniques

Technique	Percent of companies reporting			
	Very frequently	Frequently	Rarely	Never
LP	37.5	32.5	25.0	5.0
Digital computer simulation	41.0	39.7	7.7	11.6
Inventory control models	24.0	38.7	28.0	9.3
Pert/CPM	12.0	41.4	37.3	9.3
Heuristics	9.9	40.8	21.1	28.2
Transportation method	6.8	20.6	47.9	24.7
Queuing theory	2.0	18.6	37.1	42.2
0-1 integer programming	2.7	17.8	37.0	42.5
Branch and bound techniques	1.4	17.4	44.9	36.3
Transhipment	1.6	18.8	20.3	59.3
Dynamic programming	4.3	14.3	31.4	50.0
Constrained nonlinear optimization	1.4	16.9	19.7	62.0
Game theory	0.0	15.6	31.3	53.1
General integer programming	1.4	11.4	38.6	48.6
Markov chains	0.0	13.9	29.2	56.9
Unconstrained nonlinear optimization	4.3	4.3	27.6	63.8
Quadratic programming	1.5	3.0	19.7	75.8

tion analysis, time series analysis, hypothesis testing, and sampling theory.

Table 12.2 displays the reported usage of prominent OR/MS techniques. The usage categories *Frequently* and *Rarely* are ambiguous, but they give you some sense of how often these techniques are employed. One important observation we can make from Table 12.2 is that the more exotic OR/MS techniques are rarely used in practice, at least among the *Fortune* 500 companies that responded to this survey. Techniques such as game theory and Markov chains apparently receive little utilization. The reasons for this may range from sampling error to a lack of knowledge on management's part to difficulty in applying these techniques to real-world problems. As OR/MS progresses, these techniques will probably be more effectively utilized. You will note, however, that the seven most widely used techniques as shown in Table 12.2 are the principal topics in this text.

EDUCATIONAL BACKGROUND OF OR/MS PERSONNEL

The educational backgrounds of an OR/MS staff are typically quite diversified. Table 12.3 compares the backgrounds of the OR/MS personnel in each of the 1958, 1964, and 1974 surveys. One noteworthy trend is the increase in personnel who actually have a degree in OR/MS. There is also a very significant increase in personnel who have a degree in business administration. The M.B.A. degree appears to be desirable for practitioners of OR/MS in industry. The Radnor and Neal study showed that the "most desired" person had a quantitative or engineering undergraduate degree, some form of computer experience, and an M.B.A. This trend reflects the emphasis in the practice of OR/MS on understanding how a business functions and on solving real-world problems.

IMPLEMENTATION OF MANAGEMENT SCIENCE

From the start, implementation has been management science's most rewarding aspect—and its most troublesome. It is one thing to build models and propose solutions, and it is quite another to implement a solution or proposed change successfully in the real world.

Table 12.3   The educational background of OR/MS personnel

Major field	B.A. (%)	M.A. (%)	Ph.D. (%)	All degrees, 1974 survey (%)	Average percentage in other surveys	
					1958	1964
OR/MS	7.0	18.0	33.3	14.0	na	na
Industrial engineering	16.1	10.2	10.8	13.0	7	14
Mathematics and statistics	21.3	18.5	23.7	20.2	27	30
Mechanical engineering	10.1	4.9	1.1	7.1	12	13
Business administration	17.1	32.8	3.2	23.2	6	8
Economics	9.4	4.4	15.1	7.6	4	7
Aeronautical engineering	3.3	2.6	2.2	2.8	10	6
Chemistry	1.8	.7	3.2	1.4	8	6
Physics	3.7	2.7	1.1	3.0	na	na
Electrical engineering	4.7	2.7	4.3	3.8	7	2
Other	5.4	2.7	2.2	3.9	19	14
Totals	100.0	100.0	100.0	100.0		

Implementation always requires some kind of change within the organization, whether of attitude, behavior, or activity. Successful implementations must overcome Murphy's law, which states that if there is any way for something to go wrong, it will, and at the most inopportune moment! Some of the most serious implementation problems involve inaccurate data or behavioral difficulties arising from management attitudes and lack of communication.

Despite continual problems, progress has been made in implementing management science in business and government organizations. In the fifties and sixties, management scientists had to justify their existence and thus spent much time trying to "sell" the discipline. Earlier, management was skeptical that there were real monetary benefits to be gained by using management science. Today, a larger percentage of top management realizes the potential contributions that management science can make. Management scientists are seldom required to justify their existence these days, but they often have to cost-justify the various projects they consider.

Several of the surveys we have discussed examined the nature of implementation problems. The Radnor and Neal study found that almost all the 105 companies surveyed had some implementation problems. However, only 13 were identified as having very serious implementation problems. Their long-term studies seem to suggest that implementation problems were less severe in 1970 than in the sixties.

In the 1974 survey, we found that 65 percent of the companies that use OR/MS reported no major implementation difficulties. (Incidentally, one of the respondents said that anyone who answered no to the question about having implementation problems was either a liar, an idiot, or could walk on water.) When asked to comment on the nature of their implementation difficulties, many respondents cited problems that typically exist between OR/MS personnel and an organization's management. The most frequently encountered problems were: poor communication between staff and user; lack of top-level management support or commitment; lack of quality data; lack of objectivity in management attitudes; and failure (often of awareness or education) on management's part to utilize the results of an OR/MS project successfully. Other problems reported by the respondents included the difficulty in selling OR/MS projects to management, interorganization politics, and project failures.

In spite of these implementation problems, occasional project failures, and in rare instances an OR staff disbandment, OR/MS is more readily accepted by top management than ever before. Radnor and Neal found several reasons for management's increased interest in OR/MS:

1 The size and complexity of the business situation is ever increasing.

2 There is a growing need for faster response times.

3 Organizations want to utilize more fully the potential of their computer facilities.

4 It is important to have more complete and rapid exchange of information about new techniques, particularly with relation to what competitors are doing.

5 It is imperative to answer on an equivalent basis the more sophisticated questions top management is being asked about its operations by customers, regulating agencies, and stockholders.

These needs were apparently well recognized by the companies that responded to our 1974 survey, for all 84 companies who reported OR/MS activity claimed that they would continue OR/MS in the future.

TOWARD MORE SUCCESSFUL IMPLEMENTATION

Management scientists have made progress toward better implementation, but there is still room for improvement. In this section, we examine certain factors relating to the success or failure of implementation. In another study on implementation in industry and government,[5] Radnor, et al. name three categories that relate to the nature of implementation problems. These categories involve the nature of the client/researcher relation, the level and kind of support from top management, and the organizational and external environment in which the research activity is pursued. Most implementation problems fall into the first two categories.

Arguments have been set forth blaming either management, the management scientist, or both for implementation problems. Often, line managers have been away from school for many years and are not familiar with current advances. This lack of familiarity often breeds their reluctance to use a tool they do not understand. In some cases, new procedures can pose a threat to job security or decision-making power. Some managers may appreciate the benefits of OR/MS but hesitate to get directly involved because they feel they lack the technical competence or understanding. Communication problems may exist between the manager and the management scientist. Management scientists have been criticized not so much for their technical approach but for their failure to take into consideration the human and organizational factors that are affected when solutions are implemented. Failure to consider political factors or the personalities of managers has sometimes led to the rejection

[5] M. Radnor, A. Rubenstein, and D. Tansik, "Implementation in Operations Research and R & D in Government and Business Organization, *Operations Research*, 18 (Nov.-Dec. 1970), 967–91.

of OR/MS projects. Management scientists have also been criticized for not having the patience nor the diplomatic skill to get their output used. Too often, it is said, they feel that their approach is scientifically sound and thus shouldn't have to be explained, interpreted, or justified.

PARTICIPATION OF MANAGEMENT

Positive steps, however, help to promote more successful implementation. Perhaps the most important of these is to effect the direct participation of management in an OR/MS project. Many OR/MS projects cut across different departments or organizational structures; consequently, they must have the support and guidance of top management. Top management is in the best position to decide whether proposed projects contribute adequately to the overall goals of the organization. The support of top management is also required to establish the credibility of a project for line managers and other operating personnel.

Operating management must also be directly involved in an OR/MS project. Lack of support at this level can lead to project failure early or late. These managers should participate in the project's formulation, administration, and evaluation. Their first-hand, comprehensive understanding of operations, limitations, and constraints is necessary input to any OR model. Moreover, operating management's confidence (or lack of it) in the project carries down to the people who are directly affected by proposed changes and who thus affect the ultimate success of the project.

It is management's responsibility to make organizational objectives clearly known. These must be translated into operational goals that serve as guidelines for project undertakings and criteria for measuring success. Organizational policies regarding external factors as well as operations must be specified. Mathematical models are useless unless they reflect the constraints pertaining to operational restrictions. OR/MS projects must take into account management's attitudes and policies in such areas as social responsibility, government regulations, pollution control standards, public relations, and employment levels. These policies clearly must be considered by any mathematical model or OR/MS project that is truly meant to benefit the organization.

In the aforementioned study on implementation, Radnor, et al. offer several suggestions for implementing an OR/MS project. These suggestions cannot guarantee success, but they certainly enhance the likelihood.

1 Make sure that there is a clear and recognized need for the results at the time the project is undertaken.

2 Involve the ultimate user of the results early in the process, and maintain communication with this person throughout the project.

3 Focus the direction or strategy of the project in an individual or small group that can review progress and, if necessary, make changes.

4 Gain enthusiastic support from top management.

5 Allow and encourage researchers to follow projects into applications and make careers there, if they so desire.

Successful implementation clearly involves a meeting of the minds, with input and cooperation from both management and OR/MS staff. Without sincere commitments from both sides, potentially successful projects will either fail or fall short of expectations.

[A look at the future]

Up to now, we have looked at management science's evolution over a period of forty-odd years. Comments about the future can only be speculative; however, if we extrapolate certain trends, we can make some forecasts.

Organizations, both private and governmental, will exist in a world that is more complex and subject to even more rapid change than today's. The term *future shock* will be ever more appropriate. The world will have more people; and at least over the short term, these people will be competing for dwindling supplies of the natural resources used at present. Standards of living will, in general, continue to move in their present directions. Underdeveloped countries will have increasing impact on international politics. Technology will grow at an ever-increasing rate and will have many positive benefits if properly managed. The new frontiers will be space and the earth's oceans. Proportionately greater effort will be directed at solving pressing societal problems. World issues such as energy, food supply, transportation, environmental control, pollution, urban development, and war will be among the most pressing problems.

Organizations will have to survive in this world of increased complexity. Institutions will become more organized and specialized. Government will play a larger role in business and society in general. People will be more demanding of their leaders and organizations. There is a strong move now toward accountability for both business and government leaders. Decision makers will need to rely further on rational means for justifying various courses of action. Consequently, OR/MS will be more widely practiced in institutions of all kinds.

That there will be a need for management science to aid in managerial decision making in this future environment is obvious. However, more and better procedures are necessary for future progress. Continual development and refinement of quantitative techniques is required if we are to tackle ever more complex problems. Such progress is typical of advancements in the past and can be expected to continue to do so. Advances have greatly increased the size of problems that can be solved by LP and other mathematical programming approaches. Future developments will be tied to computer hardware and software advances as well as to mathematical breakthroughs. Such advances will no doubt cause certain seldom used techniques such as nonlinear, dynamic, and integer programming to be utilized more often.

Advances will also be made in multicriteria decision making. In this elementary text we have focused on single objective function cirteria. In many applications, however, more than one goal may be sought. One approach to solving problems with multiple objectives is goal programming. This approach is an extension of LP that attempts to *satisfice*, or come as close as possible to satisfying, various goals and constraints. It does not attempt to optimize an objective function directly; instead, it tries to minimize the deviations from stated goals within a specified set of constraints. Goal programming and future developments of this nature should play an integral part in analyzing societal problems with their multiple objectives.

Management science must also progress in the area of increasingly difficult stochastic problems. Most developments in management science have dealt with problems that have the nice, accessible properties of certainty and well-defined objectives and constraints. Decision makers in the future will often face shorter time frames and, in some cases, increased uncertainty. In order to contribute more to actual management problems, management science will have to deal with problems that are complex, fuzzy, and loosely structured. Some signs of progress in this area have already begun to appear. Research on *fuzzy sets* and *fuzzy mathematics* is presently being applied to cognitive and decision processes.

Progress in management science is directly related to technological progress in computer hardware and software development. Second and third generation computers greatly advanced problem solving when they were introduced, and a fourth generation of computers already exists. No one knows what technological advancements subsequent computers will be capable of. Every significant computer development increases the classes of problems that can actually be solved.

Time-sharing computer facilities and management information systems have brought dramatic changes in decision making. Time-sharing facilities make it possible to monitor business transactions continuously, just as they make it simple to retrieve information for real-time decision making. Time sharing also facilitates the use of management science models in decision situations that require fast response times. More decision makers of the future will have access to computer time-sharing terminals. Successful decision making requires accurate, timely information. Management information systems are designed to provide this required information. The interfacing of management science and management information systems can make significant contributions to the art and science of decision making. You may recall that one of the impediments to implementing OR/MS is the lack of timely or quality data. Well-designed management information systems can keep crucial data virtually at hand.

[Challenges and changes]

As you can see, the future is full of challenges for the field of management science. In this section, we shall consider the views of three experienced management scientists about which new directions to take.

It is customary for each new president of The Institute of Management Sciences to make a formal statement about the past and future courses of the organization. In his message from the president, Donald Rice challenges management scientists to develop analytical methods for problems in the public sector. As Rice points out, these intractable societal problems are not amenable to straightforward, single objective analysis:

The objectives of many programs in the public sector—education, welfare, and housing, to name a few—are much more difficult to identify and to specify in terms that make it possible for the application of traditional analytical methods to help the decision maker.

Indeed, most such problems are marked by multiple and, worse yet, sometimes conflicting objectives. The nature of the constraints, as reflected in energy or other resource limitations, environmental factors, human preferences, and others, all add to the complexities involved in trying to model many public sector problems. Approaches different from those used in the past must be taken to increase theory and understanding, as well as relevant data, to deal with such problems.

Social program experiments are one recent analytical development that can help to generate relevant data for analysis and provide an opportunity to gain greater insight into these complex problem areas. But much work is needed on the theory and practice of experimentation under the conditions encountered in social problem areas.[6]

More radical changes are proposed by Milan Zeleny for the future landscape of management science. Zeleny feels that management

[6] Donald B. Rice, "Message from the President," OR/MS Today, 3 (September 1975), 5.

science has made great strides in improving man's capabilities for solving well-defined, well-structured problems of a quantitative nature. But, if the discipline "has been successful where it has improved or replaced man's analytical faculties in dealing with problems, it has been less successful in trying to approach new complex problems and has not even tried to enhance man's intuitive faculties."[7] Zeleny calls for the marriage of both analytical and intuitive aspects in the managerial decision process because "most problems are neither purely analytical nor purely intuitive; rather they combine both components in an intricate interaction."[8]

Zeleny also implies that the transition to a new management science will require a different attitude or mentality. He says, "Linear and nonlinear programming, queueing theory, inventory theory, critical path, dynamic programming, etc., all have been around right from the beginning. Nothing really new has been added to these seminal ideas and concepts , , , we need to be effective more than efficient . . . we need new ideas."[9] Zeleny feels that the biggest challenge for management science is the development of new ideas that will enhance the intuitive powers of managers. Among these will be:

1 Psychological models of the human decision-making process
2 Interactive programming
3 Management science linguistics
4 Fuzzy mathematics
5 Multiple criteria decision making
6 Qualitative management science
7 Intergroup and intragroup decision making
8 Organic systems analysis

Professor Harvey Wagner is a past president of TIMS and an experienced consultant. Wagner feels that the fundamental breakthrough for management science so far has been the "repeated demonstration that formal model building, energized by computer

---

[7] Milan Zeleny, "Notes, Ideas & Techniques New Vistas of Management Science," *Computers and Operations Research*, 2, (1975), 121.
[8] Ibid., p. 123.
[9] Ibid., p. 122.

systems, is able to improve pivotal managerial decisions." [10] However, many challenges remain. Even though many industrial applications of OR/MS have taken place, it is still a frustratingly difficult task to carry out these applications. Wagner calls for improvement in the mechanical aspects of applying OR/MS. He also claims that operations researchers and management scientists must develop better ways to diagnose the benefits that management can expect from OR/MS efforts.

Wagner also cites some progress within the discipline on large-scale programming problems, but surprisingly little progress has been made with daily operational problems. Problems of the latter kind are being tackled by systems analysts not using OR techniques. In Wagner's opinion, "a reexamination by operations researchers of the real nature of daily operating problems is vitally needed." [11]

Since quality data is such a limiting factor in OR/MS applications, Wagner suggests that more effort be directed toward a science of data collection and measurement. Such a science would consider how to obtain accurate information from managers, accountants and engineers, as well as study procedures for estimating unknown parameters.

In order to tackle the challenges of the future, contributions are needed by talented people of many different types. Wagner concludes by offering challenges to practitioners, theoreticians, and educators in OR/MS. The high-priority tasks for *practitioners* are to:

1 "Improve the mechanics of applying operations research so as to reduce the resource costs for developing, analyzing, and implementing OR models."

2 "Devise diagnostic techniques to predict accurately the economic benefits that will accrue from a proposed OR application."

3 "Expand the purview of OR into new areas of management, including formulating a corporation's growth strategy, structuring organizational responsibilities, bridging cultural gaps within a company, improving a company's profit performance, designing management information systems, and delineating the enterprise's public responsibilities."

[10] Harvey M. Wagner, "The ABC's of OR," *Operations Research*, 19, (October 1971), 1262.

[11] Ibid., p. 1266.

The challenges open to management science *theoreticians* are to:

1 "Develop insightful models that sidestep the axiom of managerial rationality."

2 "Propose analytic concepts that enable managers to deal with the future as reality."

3 "Build practical models for treating day-to-day operating problems."

4 "Find new ways to exploit the full power of computers."

5 "Explore approaches to model building that encompass principles of behavioral science."

The challenges for *educators* are that they:

1 "Assess the appropriate mix between professional and technical training to best prepare students for having a practical influence on managerial decision making."

2 "Examine the relative merits of the various approaches to OR higher education that have been in vogue for over a decade."[12]

[Summary]

Management science procedures have proved their usefulness for solving problems of many kinds. With the use of computers, management scientists have been able to deal with complicated decision problems that human intelligence alone cannot resolve. The discipline has enabled management to improve the efficiency of operations and various decision processes significantly. This, in turn, has freed management to apply its creativity to policy and other, less well-structured problems.

Management science is a dynamic field that is evolving over time. It shows trends toward the expansion and application of its techniques and procedures into problems in the social sciences, the public sector, and the environment, many of which are problems of worldwide concern. OR/MS is becoming a tool not only for industrial management but for decision makers in general.

[12] Ibid., p. 1281.

In order to help meet the demands of the future, progress is badly needed in such areas as implementation, data collection and estimation, and the interfacing of behavioral and analytical procedures. Future progress in management science will not only require effort at theoretical levels but also necessitate a concerted attempt to understand and deal with the kinds of problems real-world decision makers face.

These decision problems are mind-boggling in scope and complexity. Future decision makers must become familiar with management science and learn how to synthesize the objective information provided by OR/MS with their own insight and intuition. For the decision maker of the future, a working knowledge of management science will be a necessity. What is perceived as progressive practice today will be standard procedure tomorrow.

[Bibliography]

Grayson, C. Jackson, Jr., "Management Science and Business Practice," *Harvard Business Review*, 51, no. 4 (July-August 1973), 41-48.

Harvey, A., "Factors Making for Implementation Success and Failure," *Management Science*, 16, no. 6 (February 1970), B312-21.

Heany, Donald F., "Is TIMS Talking to Itself?" Management Science, 12, no. 4 (December 1965), B146-55.

Hertz, D. B., "The Unity of Sciences and Management," *Management Science*, 11, no. 6 (April 1965), B89-97.

Miller, David W. and Martin K. Starr, *Executive Decisions and Operations Research*, 2nd ed. Englewood Cliffs, N.J.: Prentice-Hall, Inc., 1969.

Radnor, M., A. H. Rubenstein, and A. S. Bean, "Integration and Utilization of Management Sciences Activities in Organizations," *Operational Research* Quarterly, 19, no. 6 (June 1968), 117-41.

————, A. H. Rubenstein, and D. A. Tansik, "Implementation in Operations Research, and R & D in Government and Business Organizations," *Operations Research*, 18, no. 6 (November-December 1970), 967-91.

Schumacher, C. C. and B. E. Smith, "A Sample Survey of Industrial

Operations Research Activities II,'' *Operations Research*, 13, no. 6 (November-December 1965), 1023-27.

Thierauf, Robert J. and Robert C. Klekamp, *Decision Making Through Operations Research*, 2nd ed. New York: John Wiley & Sons, Inc., 1975.

Turban, E., ''A Sample Survey of Operations Research Activities at the Corporate Level,'' *Operations Research*, 20, no. 3 (May-June 1972), 708-21.

Wagner, Harvey M., ''The ABC's of OR,'' *Operations Research*, 19, no. 6 (October 1971), 1259-81.

Wagner, Harvey M., *Principles of Management Science*, 2nd ed. Englewood Cliffs, N.J.: Prentice-Hall, Inc., 1975.

Zeleny, Milan, ''Notes, Ideas and Techniques: New Vistas of Management Science,'' *Computers and Operations Research*, 2, no. 2 (September 1975), 121-25.

[Review questions]

1 What are the three phases through which OR/MS has evolved?

2 What are the characteristics of the maturing phase?

3 To what types of problems has OR/MS been mostly successfully applied?

4 To what types of problems would management like to have better OR/MS procedures applied?

5 What gaps exist between management science theory and the practice of management science?

6 What are some of the emerging trends in management science?

7 Discuss the relationship between management science and management information systems.

8 List some of the main problems that must be overcome to achieve a successful OR/MS implementation.

9 How does management science benefit all levels of management?

10 What kinds of contributions will be required of theoreticians, practitioners, and educators in order to meet the decision-making challenges of the future?

TABLE 1

[The standard normal distribution]

z	.00	.01	.02	.03	.04	.05	.06	.07	.08	.09
0.0	.0000	.0040	.0080	.0120	.0160	.0199	.0239	.0279	.0319	.0359
0.1	.0398	.0438	.0478	.0517	.0557	.0596	.0636	.0675	.0714	.0753
0.2	.0793	.0832	.0871	.0910	.0948	.0987	.1026	.1064	.1103	.1141
0.3	.1179	.1217	.1255	.1293	.1331	.1368	.1406	.1443	.1480	.1517
0.4	.1554	.1591	.1628	.1664	.1700	.1736	.1772	.1808	.1844	.1879
0.5	.1915	.1950	.1985	.2019	.2054	.2088	.2123	.2157	.2190	.2224
0.6	.2257	.2291	.2324	.2357	.2389	.2422	.2454	.2486	.2517	.2549
0.7	.2580	.2611	.2642	.2673	.2704	.2734	.2764	.2794	.2823	.2852
0.8	.2881	.2910	.2939	.2967	.2995	.3023	.3051	.3078	.3106	.3133
0.9	.3159	.3186	.3212	.3238	.3264	.3289	.3315	.3340	.3365	.3389
1.0	.3413	.3438	.3461	.3485	.3508	.3531	.3554	.3577	.3599	.3621
1.1	.3643	.3665	.3686	.3708	.3729	.3749	.3770	.3790	.3810	.3830
1.2	.3849	.3869	.3888	.3907	.3925	.3944	.3962	.3980	.3997	.4015
1.3	.4032	.4049	.4066	.4082	.4099	.4115	.4131	.4147	.4162	.4177
1.4	.4192	.4207	.4222	.4236	.4251	.4265	.4279	.4292	.4306	.4319
1.5	.4332	.4345	.4357	.4370	.4382	.4394	.4406	.4418	.4429	.4441
1.6	.4452	.4463	.4474	.4484	.4495	.4505	.4515	.4525	.4535	.4545
1.7	.4554	.4564	.4573	.4582	.4591	.4599	.4608	.4616	.4625	.4633
1.8	.4641	.4649	.4656	.4664	.4671	.4678	.4686	.4693	.4699	.4706
1.9	.4713	.4719	.4726	.4732	.4738	.4744	.4750	.4756	.4761	.4767
2.0	.4772	.4778	.4783	.4788	.4793	.4798	.4803	.4808	.4812	.4817
2.1	.4821	.4826	.4830	.4834	.4838	.4842	.4846	.4850	.4854	.4857
2.2	.4861	.4864	.4868	.4871	.4875	.4878	.4881	.4884	.4887	.4890
2.3	.4893	.4896	.4898	.4901	.4904	.4906	.4909	.4911	.4913	.4916
2.4	.4918	.4920	.4922	.4925	.4927	.4929	.4931	.4932	.4934	.4936
2.5	.4938	.4940	.4941	.4943	.4945	.4946	.4948	.4949	.4951	.4952
2.6	.4953	.4955	.4956	.4957	.4959	.4960	.4961	.4962	.4963	.4964
2.7	.4965	.4966	.4967	.4968	.4969	.4970	.4971	.4972	.4973	.4974
2.8	.4974	.4975	.4976	.4977	.4977	.4978	.4979	.4979	.4980	.4981
2.9	.4981	.4982	.4982	.4983	.4984	.4984	.4985	.4985	.4986	.4986
3.0	.4987	.4987	.4987	.4988	.4988	.4989	.4989	.4989	.4990	.4990

TABLE 2

[The cumulative binomial probability distribution]

$$P(r \geq r \mid n, p)$$

$n = 1$

	p	01	02	03	04	05	06	07	08	09	10
r	1	0100	0200	0300	0400	0500	0600	0700	0800	0900	1000
	p	11	12	13	14	15	16	17	18	19	20
r	1	1100	1200	1300	1400	1500	1600	1700	1800	1900	2000
	p	21	22	23	24	25	26	27	28	29	30
r	1	2100	2200	2300	2400	2500	2600	2700	2800	2900	3000
	p	31	32	33	34	35	36	37	38	39	40
r	1	3100	3200	3300	3400	3500	3600	3700	3800	3900	4000
	p	41	42	43	44	45	46	47	48	49	50
r	1	4100	4200	4300	4400	4500	4600	4700	4800	4900	5000

$n = 2$

	p	01	02	03	04	05	06	07	08	09	10
r	1	0199	0396	0591	0784	0975	1164	1351	1536	1719	1900
	2	0001	0004	0009	0016	0025	0036	0049	0064	0081	0100
	p	11	12	13	14	15	16	17	18	19	20
r	1	2079	2256	2431	2604	2775	2944	3111	3276	3439	3600
	2	0121	0144	0169	0196	0225	0256	0289	0324	0361	0400
	p	21	22	23	24	25	26	27	28	29	30
r	1	3759	3916	4071	4224	4375	4524	4671	4816	4959	5100
	2	0441	0484	0529	0576	0625	0676	0729	0784	0841	0900
	p	31	32	33	34	35	36	37	38	39	40
r	1	5239	5376	5511	5644	5775	5904	6031	6156	6279	6400
	2	0961	1024	1089	1156	1225	1296	1369	1444	1521	1600
	p	41	42	43	44	45	46	47	48	49	50
r	1	6519	6636	6751	6864	6975	7084	7191	7296	7399	7500
	2	1681	1764	1849	1936	2025	2116	2209	2304	2401	2500

$n = 3$

	p	01	02	03	04	05	06	07	08	09	10
r	1	0297	0588	0873	1153	1426	1694	1956	2213	2464	2710
	2	0003	0012	0026	0047	0073	0104	0140	0182	0228	0280
	3				0001	0001	0002	0003	0005	0007	0010
	p	11	12	13	14	15	16	17	18	19	20
r	1	2950	3185	3415	3639	3859	4073	4282	4486	4686	4880
	2	0336	0397	0463	0533	0608	0686	0769	0855	0946	1040
	3	0013	0017	0022	0027	0034	0041	0049	0058	0069	0080
	p	21	22	23	24	25	26	27	28	29	30
r	1	5070	5254	5435	5610	5781	5948	6110	6268	6421	6570
	2	1138	1239	1344	1452	1563	1676	1793	1913	2035	2160
	3	0093	0106	0122	0138	0156	0176	0197	0220	0244	0270
	p	31	32	33	34	35	36	37	38	39	40
r	1	6715	6856	6992	7125	7254	7379	7500	7617	7730	7840
	2	2287	2417	2548	2682	2818	2955	3094	3235	3377	3520
	3	0298	0328	0359	0393	0429	0467	0507	0549	0593	0640

The cumulative probability distribution

n = 3

p	41	42	43	44	45	46	47	48	49	50
r 1	7946	8049	8148	8244	8336	8425	8511	8594	8673	8750
2	3665	3810	3957	4104	4253	4401	4551	4700	4850	5000
3	0689	0741	0795	0852	0911	0973	1038	1106	1176	1250

n = 4

p	01	02	03	04	05	06	07	08	09	10
r 1	0394	0776	1147	1507	1855	2193	2519	2836	3143	3439
2	0006	0023	0052	0091	0140	0199	0267	0344	0430	0523
3			0001	0002	0005	0008	0013	0019	0027	0037
4									0001	0001

p	11	12	13	14	15	16	17	18	19	20
1	3726	4003	4271	4530	4780	5021	5254	5479	5695	5904
2	0624	0732	0847	0968	1095	1228	1366	1509	1656	1808
3	0049	0063	0079	0098	0120	0144	0171	0202	0235	0272
4	0001	0002	0003	0004	0005	0007	0008	0010	0013	0016

p	21	22	23	24	25	26	27	28	29	30
1	6105	6298	6485	6664	6836	7001	7160	7313	7459	7599
2	1963	2122	2285	2450	2617	2787	2959	3132	3307	3483
3	0312	0356	0403	0453	0508	0566	0628	0694	0763	0837
4	0019	0023	0028	0033	0039	0046	0053	0061	0071	0081

p	31	32	33	34	35	36	37	38	39	40
1	7733	7862	7985	8103	8215	8322	8425	8522	8615	8704
2	3660	3837	4015	4193	4370	4547	4724	4900	5075	5248
3	0915	0996	1082	1171	1265	1362	1464	1569	1679	1792
4	0092	0105	0119	0134	0150	0168	0187	0209	0231	0256

p	41	42	43	44	45	46	47	48	49	50
1	8788	8868	8944	9017	9085	9150	9211	9269	9323	9375
2	5420	5590	5759	5926	6090	6252	6412	6569	6724	6875
3	1909	2030	2155	2283	2415	2550	2689	2831	2977	3125
4	0283	0311	0342	0375	0410	0448	0488	0531	0576	0625

n = 5

p	01	02	03	04	05	06	07	08	09	10
r 1	0490	0961	1413	1846	2262	2661	3043	3409	3760	4095
2	0010	0038	0085	0148	0226	0319	0425	0544	0674	0815
3		0001	0003	0006	0012	0020	0031	0045	0063	0086
4						0001	0001	0002	0003	0005

p	11	12	13	14	15	16	17	18	19	20
r 1	4416	4723	5016	5296	5563	5818	6061	6293	6513	6723
2	0965	1125	1292	1467	1648	1835	2027	2224	2424	2627
3	0112	0143	0179	0220	0266	0318	0375	0437	0505	0579
4	0007	0009	0013	0017	0022	0029	0036	0045	0055	0067
5				0001	0001	0001	0001	0002	0002	0003

p	21	22	23	24	25	26	27	28	29	30
r 1	6923	7113	7293	7464	7627	7781	7927	8065	8196	8319
2	2833	3041	3251	3461	3672	3883	4093	4303	4511	4718
3	0659	0744	0836	0933	1035	1143	1257	1376	1501	1631
4	0081	0097	0114	0134	0156	0181	0208	0238	0272	0308
5	0004	0005	0006	0008	0010	0012	0014	0017	0021	0024

The cumulative probability distribution

$n = 5$

p	31	32	33	34	35	36	37	38	39	40
r 1	8436	8546	8650	8748	8840	8926	9008	9084	9155	9222
2	4923	5125	5325	5522	5716	5906	6093	6276	6455	6630
3	1766	1905	2050	2199	2352	2509	2670	2835	3003	3174
4	0347	0390	0436	0486	0540	0598	0660	0726	0796	0870
5	0029	0034	0039	0045	0053	0060	0069	0079	0090	0102

p	41	42	43	44	45	46	47	48	49	50
r 1	9285	9344	9398	9449	9497	9541	9582	9620	9655	9688
2	6801	6967	7129	7286	7438	7585	7728	7865	7998	8125
3	3349	3525	3705	3886	4069	4253	4439	4625	4813	5000
4	0949	1033	1121	1214	1312	1415	1522	1635	1753	1875
5	0116	0131	0147	0165	0185	0206	0229	0255	0282	0313

$n = 6$

p	01	02	03	04	05	06	07	08	09	10
r 1	0585	1142	1670	2172	2649	3101	3530	3936	4321	4686
2	0015	0057	0125	0216	0328	0459	0608	0773	0952	1143
3		0002	0005	0012	0022	0038	0058	0085	0118	0159
4					0001	0002	0003	0005	0008	0013
5										0001

p	11	12	13	14	15	16	17	18	19	20
r 1	5030	5356	5664	5954	6229	6487	6731	6960	7176	7379
2	1345	1556	1776	2003	2235	2472	2713	2956	3201	3446
3	0206	0261	0324	0395	0473	0560	0655	0759	0870	0989
4	0018	0025	0034	0045	0059	0075	0094	0116	0141	0170
5	0001	0001	0002	0003	0004	0005	0007	0010	0013	0016
6										0001

p	21	22	23	24	25	26	27	28	29	30
r 1	7569	7748	7916	8073	8220	8358	8487	8607	8719	8824
2	3692	3937	4180	4422	4661	4896	5128	5356	5580	5798
3	1115	1250	1391	1539	1694	1856	2023	2196	2374	2557
4	0202	0239	0280	0326	0376	0431	0492	0557	0628	0705
5	0020	0025	0031	0038	0046	0056	0067	0079	0093	0109
6	0001	0001	0001	0002	0002	0003	0004	0005	0006	0007

p	31	32	33	34	35	36	37	38	39	40
r 1	8921	9011	9095	9173	9246	9313	9375	9432	9485	9533
2	6012	6220	6422	6619	6809	6994	7172	7343	7508	7667
3	2744	2936	3130	3328	3529	3732	3937	4143	4350	4557
4	0787	0875	0969	1069	1174	1286	1404	1527	1657	1792
5	0127	0148	0170	0195	0223	0254	0288	0325	0365	0410
6	0009	0011	0013	0015	0018	0022	0026	0030	0035	0041

p	41	42	43	44	45	46	47	48	49	50
r 1	9578	9619	9657	9692	9723	9752	9778	9802	9824	9844
2	7819	7965	8105	8238	8364	8485	8599	8707	8810	8906
3	4764	4971	5177	5382	5585	5786	5985	6180	6373	6563
4	1933	2080	2232	2390	2553	2721	2893	3070	3252	3438
5	0458	0510	0566	0627	0692	0762	0837	0917	1003	1094
6	0048	0055	0063	0073	0083	0095	0108	0122	0138	0156

The cumulative probability distribution

$n = 7$

$n = 7$

P r	01	02	03	04	05	06	07	08	09	10
1	0679	1319	1920	2486	3017	3515	3983	4422	4832	5217
2	0020	0079	0171	0294	0444	0618	0813	1026	1255	1497
3		0003	0009	0020	0038	0063	0097	0140	0193	0257
4				0001	0002	0004	0007	0012	0018	0027
5								0001	0001	0002

P r	11	12	13	14	15	16	17	18	19	20
1	5577	5913	6227	6521	6794	7049	7286	7507	7712	7903
2	1750	2012	2281	2556	2834	3115	3396	3677	3956	4233
3	0331	0416	0513	0620	0738	0866	1005	1154	1313	1480
4	0039	0054	0072	0094	0121	0153	0189	0231	0279	0333
5	0003	0004	0006	0009	0012	0017	0022	0029	0037	0047
6					0001	0001	0001	0002	0003	0004

P r	21	22	23	24	25	26	27	28	29	30
1	8080	8243	8395	8535	8665	8785	8895	8997	9090	9176
2	4506	4775	5040	5298	5551	5796	6035	6266	6490	6706
3	1657	1841	2033	2231	2436	2646	2861	3081	3304	3529
4	0394	0461	0536	0617	0706	0802	0905	1016	1134	1260
5	0058	0072	0088	0107	0129	0153	0181	0213	0248	0288
6	0005	0006	0008	0011	0013	0017	0021	0026	0031	0038
7					0001	0001	0001	0001	0002	0002

P r	31	32	33	34	35	36	37	38	39	40
1	9255	9328	9394	9454	9510	9560	9606	9648	9686	9720
2	6914	7113	7304	7487	7662	7828	7987	8137	8279	8414
3	3757	3987	4217	4447	4677	4906	5134	5359	5581	5801
4	1394	1534	1682	1837	1998	2167	2341	2521	2707	2898
5	0332	0380	0434	0492	0556	0625	0701	0782	0869	0963
6	0046	0055	0065	0077	0090	0105	0123	0142	0164	0188
7	0003	0003	0004	0005	0006	0008	0009	0011	0014	0016

P r	41	42	43	44	45	46	47	48	49	50
1	9751	9779	9805	9827	9848	9866	9883	9897	9910	9922
2	8541	8660	8772	8877	8976	9068	9153	9233	9307	9375
3	6017	6229	6436	6638	6836	7027	7213	7393	7567	7734
4	3094	3294	3498	3706	3917	4131	4346	4563	4781	5000
5	1063	1169	1282	1402	1529	1663	1803	1951	2105	2266
6	0216	0246	0279	0316	0357	0402	0451	0504	0562	0625
7	0019	0023	0027	0032	0037	0044	0051	0059	0068	0078

$n = 8$

P r	01	02	03	04	05	06	07	08	09	10
1	0773	1492	2163	2786	3366	3904	4404	4868	5297	5695
2	0027	0103	0223	0381	0572	0792	1035	1298	1577	1869
3	0001	0004	0013	0031	0058	0096	0147	0211	0289	0381
4			0001	0002	0004	0007	0013	0022	0034	0050
5							0001	0001	0003	0004

$n = 8$

p	11	12	13	14	15	16	17	18	19	20
r 1	6063	6404	6718	7008	7275	7521	7748	7956	8147	8322
2	2171	2480	2794	3111	3428	3744	4057	4366	4670	4967
3	0487	0608	0743	0891	1052	1226	1412	1608	1815	2031
4	0071	0097	0129	0168	0214	0267	0328	0397	0476	0563
5	0007	0010	0015	0021	0029	0038	0050	0065	0083	0104
6		0001	0001	0002	0002	0003	0005	0007	0009	0012
7									0001	0001

p	21	22	23	24	25	26	27	28	29	30
r 1	8483	8630	8764	8887	8999	9101	9194	9278	9354	9424
2	5257	5538	5811	6075	6329	6573	6807	7031	7244	7447
3	2255	2486	2724	2967	3215	3465	3718	3973	4228	4482
4	0659	0765	0880	1004	1138	1281	1433	1594	1763	1941
5	0129	0158	0191	0230	0273	0322	0377	0438	0505	0580
6	0016	0021	0027	0034	0042	0052	0064	0078	0094	0113
7	0001	0002	0002	0003	0004	0005	0006	0008	0010	0013
8									0001	0001

p	31	32	33	34	35	36	37	38	39	40
r 1	9486	9543	9594	9640	9681	9719	9752	9782	9808	9832
2	7640	7822	7994	8156	8309	8452	8586	8711	8828	8936
3	4736	4987	5236	5481	5722	5958	6189	6415	6634	6846
4	2126	2319	2519	2724	2936	3153	3374	3599	3828	4059
5	0661	0750	0846	0949	1061	1180	1307	1443	1586	1737
6	0134	0159	0187	0218	0253	0293	0336	0385	0439	0498
7	0016	0020	0024	0030	0036	0043	0051	0061	0072	0085
8	0001	0001	0001	0002	0002	0003	0004	0004	0005	0007

p	41	42	43	44	45	46	47	48	49	50
r 1	9853	9872	9889	9903	9916	9928	9938	9947	9954	9961
2	9037	9130	9216	9295	9368	9435	9496	9552	9602	9648
3	7052	7250	7440	7624	7799	7966	8125	8276	8419	8555
4	4292	4527	4762	4996	5230	5463	5694	5922	6146	6367
5	1895	2062	2235	2416	2604	2798	2999	3205	3416	3633
6	0563	0634	0711	0794	0885	0982	1086	1198	1318	1445
7	0100	0117	0136	0157	0181	0208	0239	0272	0310	0352
8	0008	0010	0012	0014	0017	0020	0024	0028	0033	0039

$n = 9$

p	01	02	03	04	05	06	07	08	09	10
r 1	0865	1663	2398	3075	3698	4270	4796	5278	5721	6126
2	0034	0131	0282	0478	0712	0978	1271	1583	1912	2252
3	0001	0006	0020	0045	0084	0138	0209	0298	0405	0530
4			0001	0003	0006	0013	0023	0037	0057	0083
5						0001	0002	0003	0005	0009
6										0001

The cumulative probability distribution

$n = 9$

p	11	12	13	14	15	16	17	18	19	20
r 1	6496	6835	7145	7427	7684	7918	8131	8324	8499	8658
2	2599	2951	3304	3657	4005	4348	4685	5012	5330	5638
3	0672	0833	1009	1202	1409	1629	1861	2105	2357	2618
4	0117	0158	0209	0269	0339	0420	0512	0615	0730	0856
5	0014	0021	0030	0041	0056	0075	0098	0125	0158	0196
6	0001	0002	0003	0004	0006	0009	0013	0017	0023	0031
7						0001	0001	0002	0002	0003

p	21	22	23	24	25	26	27	28	29	30
r 1	8801	8931	9048	9154	9249	9335	9411	9480	9542	9596
2	5934	6218	6491	6750	6997	7230	7452	7660	7856	8040
3	2885	3158	3434	3713	3993	4273	4552	4829	5102	5372
4	0994	1144	1304	1475	1657	1849	2050	2260	2478	2703
5	0240	0291	0350	0416	0489	0571	0662	0762	0870	0988
6	0040	0051	0065	0081	0100	0122	0149	0179	0213	0253
7	0004	0006	0008	0010	0013	0017	0022	0028	0035	0043
8		0001	0001	0001	0001	0002	0003	0003	0004

p	31	32	33	34	35	36	37	38	39	40
r 1	9645	9689	9728	9762	9793	9820	9844	9865	9883	9899
2	8212	8372	8522	8661	8789	8908	9017	9118	9210	9295
3	5636	5894	6146	6390	6627	6856	7076	7287	7489	7682
4	2935	3173	3415	3662	3911	4163	4416	4669	4922	5174
5	1115	1252	1398	1553	1717	1890	2072	2262	2460	2666
6	0298	0348	0404	0467	0536	0612	0696	0787	0886	0994
7	0053	0064	0078	0094	0112	0133	0157	0184	0215	0250
8	0006	0007	0009	0011	0014	0017	0021	0026	0031	0038
9				0001	0001	0001	0001	0002	0002	0003

p	41	42	43	44	45	46	47	48	49	50
r 1	9913	9926	9936	9946	9954	9961	9967	9972	9977	9980
2	9372	9442	9505	9563	9615	9662	9704	9741	9775	9805
3	7866	8039	8204	8359	8505	8642	8769	8889	8999	9102
4	5424	5670	5913	6152	6386	6614	6836	7052	7260	7461
5	2878	3097	3322	3551	3786	4024	4265	4509	4754	5000
6	1109	1233	1366	1508	1658	1817	1985	2161	2346	2539
7	0290	0334	0383	0437	0498	0564	0637	0717	0804	0898
8	0046	0055	0065	0077	0091	0107	0125	0145	0169	0195
9	0003	0004	0005	0006	0008	0009	0011	0014	0016	0020

$n = 10$

p	01	02	03	04	05	06	07	08	09	10
r 1	0956	1829	2626	3352	4013	4614	5160	5656	6106	6513
2	0043	0162	0345	0582	0861	1176	1517	1879	2254	2639
3	0001	0009	0028	0062	0115	0188	0283	0401	0540	0702
4			0001	0004	0010	0020	0036	0058	0088	0128
5					0001	0002	0003	0006	0010	0016
6									0001	0001

The cumulative probability distribution

$n = 10$

P	11	12	13	14	15	16	17	18	19	20
r 1	6882	7215	7516	7787	8031	8251	8448	8626	8784	8926
2	3028	3417	3804	4184	4557	4920	5270	5608	5932	6242
3	0884	1087	1308	1545	1798	2064	2341	2628	2922	3222
4	0178	0239	0313	0400	0500	0614	0741	0883	1039	1209
5	0025	0037	0053	0073	0099	0130	0168	0213	0266	0328
6	0003	0004	0006	0010	0014	0020	0027	0037	0049	0064
7			0001	0001	0001	0002	0003	0004	0006	0009
8									0001	0001

P	21	22	23	24	25	26	27	28	29	30
r 1	9053	9166	9267	9357	9437	9508	9570	9626	9674	9718
2	6536	6815	7079	7327	7560	7778	7981	8170	8345	8507
3	3526	3831	4137	4442	4744	5042	5335	5622	5901	6172
4	1391	1587	1794	2012	2241	2479	2726	2979	3239	3504
5	0399	0479	0569	0670	0781	0904	1037	1181	1337	1503
6	0082	0104	0130	0161	0197	0239	0287	0342	0404	0473
7	0012	0016	0021	0027	0035	0045	0056	0070	0087	0106
8	0001	0002	0002	0003	0004	0006	0007	0010	0012	0016
9							0001	0001	0001	0001

P	31	32	33	34	35	36	37	38	39	40
r 1	9755	9789	9818	9843	9865	9885	9902	9916	9929	9940
2	8656	8794	8920	9035	9140	9236	9323	9402	9473	9536
3	6434	6687	6930	7162	7384	7595	7794	7983	8160	8327
4	3772	4044	4316	4589	4862	5132	5400	5664	5923	6177
5	1679	1867	2064	2270	2485	2708	2939	3177	3420	3669
6	0551	0637	0732	0836	0949	1072	1205	1348	1500	1662
7	0129	0155	0185	0220	0260	0305	0356	0413	0477	0548
8	0020	0025	0032	0039	0048	0059	0071	0086	0103	0123
9	0002	0003	0003	0004	0005	0007	0009	0011	0014	0017
10								0001	0001	0001

P	41	42	43	44	45	46	47	48	49	50
r 1	9949	9957	9964	9970	9975	9979	9983	9986	9988	9990
2	9594	9645	9691	9731	9767	9799	9827	9852	9874	9893
3	8483	8628	8764	8889	9004	9111	9209	9298	9379	9453
4	6425	6665	6898	7123	7340	7547	7745	7933	8112	8281
5	3922	4178	4436	4696	4956	5216	5474	5730	5982	6230
6	1834	2016	2207	2407	2616	2832	3057	3288	3526	3770
7	0626	0712	0806	0908	1020	1141	1271	1410	1560	1719
8	0146	0172	0202	0236	0274	0317	0366	0420	0480	0547
9	0021	0025	0031	0037	0045	0054	0065	0077	0091	0107
10	0001	0002	0002	0003	0003	0004	0005	0006	0008	0010

The cumulative probability distribution

$n = 11$

$n = 11$

p	01	02	03	04	05	06	07	08	09	10
r 1	1047	1993	2847	3618	4312	4937	5499	6004	6456	6862
2	0052	0195	0413	0692	1019	1382	1772	2181	2601	3026
3	0002	0012	0037	0083	0152	0248	0370	0519	0695	0896
4			0002	0007	0016	0030	0053	0085	0129	0185
5					0001	0003	0005	0010	0017	0028
6								0001	0002	0003

p	11	12	13	14	15	16	17	18	19	20
r 1	7225	7549	7839	8097	8327	8531	8712	8873	9015	9141
2	3452	3873	4286	4689	5078	5453	5811	6151	6474	6779
3	1120	1366	1632	1915	2212	2521	2839	3164	3494	3826
4	0256	0341	0442	0560	0694	0846	1013	1197	1397	1611
5	0042	0061	0087	0119	0159	0207	0266	0334	0413	0504
6	0005	0008	0012	0018	0027	0037	0051	0068	0090	0117
7		0001	0001	0002	0003	0005	0007	0010	0014	0020
8							0001	0001	0002	0002

p	21	22	23	24	25	26	27	28	29	30
r 1	9252	9350	9436	9511	9578	9636	9686	9730	9769	9802
2	7065	7333	7582	7814	8029	8227	8410	8577	8730	8870
3	4158	4488	4814	5134	5448	5753	6049	6335	6610	6873
4	1840	2081	2333	2596	2867	3146	3430	3719	4011	4304
5	0607	0723	0851	0992	1146	1313	1493	1685	1888	2103
6	0148	0186	0231	0283	0343	0412	0490	0577	0674	0782
7	0027	0035	0046	0059	0076	0095	0119	0146	0179	0216
8	0003	0005	0007	0009	0012	0016	0021	0027	0034	0043
9			0001	0001	0001	0002	0002	0003	0004	0006

p	31	32	33	34	35	36	37	38	39	40
r 1	9831	9856	9878	9896	9912	9926	9938	9948	9956	9964
2	8997	9112	9216	9310	9394	9470	9537	9597	9650	9698
3	7123	7361	7587	7799	7999	8186	8360	8522	8672	8811
4	4598	4890	5179	5464	5744	6019	6286	6545	6796	7037
5	2328	2563	2807	3059	3317	3581	3850	4122	4397	4672
6	0901	1031	1171	1324	1487	1661	1847	2043	2249	2465
7	0260	0309	0366	0400	0501	0581	0670	0768	0876	0994
8	0054	0067	0082	0101	0122	0148	0177	0210	0249	0293
9	0008	0010	0013	0016	0020	0026	0032	0039	0048	0059
10	0001	0001	0001	0002	0002	0003	0004	0005	0006	0007

The cumulative probability distribution

$n = 11$

p	41	42	43	44	45	46	47	48	49	50
r 1	9970	9975	9979	9983	9986	9989	9991	9992	9994	9995
2	9739	9776	9808	9836	9861	9882	9900	9916	9930	9941
3	8938	9055	9162	9260	9348	9428	9499	9564	9622	9673
4	7269	7490	7700	7900	8089	8266	8433	8588	8733	8867
5	4948	5223	5495	5764	6029	6288	6541	6787	7026	7256
6	2690	2924	3166	3414	3669	3929	4193	4460	4729	5000
7	1121	1260	1408	1568	1738	1919	2110	2312	2523	2744
8	0343	0399	0461	0532	0610	0696	0791	0895	1009	1133
9	0072	0087	0104	0125	0148	0175	0206	0241	0282	0327
10	0009	0012	0014	0018	0022	0027	0033	0040	0049	0059
11	0001	0001	0001	0001	0002	0002	0002	0003	0004	0005

$n = 12$

p	01	02	03	04	05	06	07	08	09	10
r 1	1136	2153	3062	3873	4596	5241	5814	6323	6775	7176
2	0062	0231	0486	0809	1184	1595	2033	2487	2948	3410
3	0002	0015	0048	0107	0196	0316	0468	0652	0866	1109
4		0001	0003	0010	0022	0043	0075	0120	0180	0256
5				0001	0002	0004	0009	0016	0027	0043
6							0001	0002	0003	0005
7										0001

p	11	12	13	14	15	16	17	18	19	20
r 1	7530	7843	8120	8363	8578	8766	8931	9076	9202	9313
2	3867	4314	4748	5166	5565	5945	6304	6641	6957	7251
3	1377	1667	1977	2303	2642	2990	3344	3702	4060	4417
4	0351	0464	0597	0750	0922	1114	1324	1552	1795	2054
5	0065	0095	0133	0181	0239	0310	0393	0489	0600	0726
6	0009	0014	0022	0033	0046	0065	0088	0116	0151	0194
7	0001	0002	0003	0004	0007	0010	0015	0021	0029	0039
8					0001	0001	0002	0003	0004	0006
9										0001

p	21	22	23	24	25	26	27	28	29	30
r 1	9409	9493	9566	9629	9683	9730	9771	9806	9836	9862
2	7524	7776	8009	8222	8416	8594	8755	8900	9032	9150
3	4768	5114	5450	5778	6093	6397	6687	6963	7225	7472
4	2326	2610	2904	3205	3512	3824	4137	4452	4765	5075
5	0866	1021	1192	1377	1576	1790	2016	2254	2504	2763
6	0245	0304	0374	0453	0544	0646	0760	0887	1026	1178
7	0052	0068	0089	0113	0143	0178	0219	0267	0322	0386
8	0008	0011	0016	0021	0028	0036	0047	0060	0076	0095
9	0001	0001	0002	0003	0004	0005	0007	0010	0013	0017
10						0001	0001	0001	0002	0002

The cumulative probability distribution

n = 12

p	31	32	33	34	35	36	37	38	39	40
r 1	9884	9902	9918	9932	9943	9953	9961	9968	9973	9978
2	9256	9350	9435	9509	9576	9634	9685	9730	9770	9804
3	7704	7922	8124	8313	8487	8648	8795	8931	9054	9166
4	5381	5681	5973	6258	6533	6799	7053	7296	7528	7747
5	3032	3308	3590	3876	4167	4459	4751	5043	5332	5618
6	1343	1521	1711	1913	2127	2352	2588	2833	3087	3348
7	0458	0540	0632	0734	0846	0970	1106	1253	1411	1582
8	0118	0144	0176	0213	0255	0304	0359	0422	0493	0573
9	0022	0028	0036	0045	0056	0070	0086	0104	0127	0153
10	0003	0004	0005	0007	0008	0011	0014	0018	0022	0028
11				0001	0001	0001	0001	0002	0002	0003

p	41	42	43	44	45	46	47	48	49	50
r 1	9982	9986	9988	9990	9992	9994	9995	9996	9997	9998
2	9834	9860	9882	9901	9917	9931	9943	9953	9961	9968
3	9267	9358	9440	9513	9579	9637	9688	9733	9773	9807
4	7953	8147	8329	8498	8655	8801	8934	9057	9168	9270
5	5899	6175	6443	6704	6956	7198	7430	7652	7862	8062
6	3616	3889	4167	4448	4731	5014	5297	5577	5855	6128
7	1765	1959	2164	2380	2607	2843	3089	3343	3604	3872
8	0662	0760	0869	0988	1117	1258	1411	1575	1751	1938
9	0183	0218	0258	0304	0356	0415	0481	0555	0638	0730
10	0035	0043	0053	0065	0079	0095	0114	0137	0163	0193
11	0004	0005	0007	0009	0011	0014	0017	0021	0026	0032
12				0001	0001	0001	0001	0001	0002	0002

n = 13

p	01	02	03	04	05	06	07	08	09	10
r 1	1225	2310	3270	4118	4867	5526	6107	6617	7065	7458
2	0072	0270	0564	0932	1354	1814	2298	2794	3293	3787
3	0003	0020	0062	0135	0245	0392	0578	0799	1054	1339
4		0001	0005	0014	0031	0060	0103	0163	0242	0342
5				0001	0003	0007	0013	0024	0041	0065
6						0001	0001	0003	0005	0009
7									0001	0001

p	11	12	13	14	15	16	17	18	19	20
r 1	7802	8102	8364	8592	8791	8963	9113	9242	9354	9450
2	4270	4738	5186	5614	6017	6396	6751	7080	7384	7664
3	1651	1985	2337	2704	3080	3463	3848	4231	4611	4983
4	0464	0609	0776	0967	1180	1414	1667	1939	2226	2527
5	0097	0139	0193	0260	0342	0438	0551	0681	0827	0991
6	0015	0024	0036	0053	0075	0104	0139	0183	0237	0300
7	0002	0003	0005	0008	0013	0019	0027	0038	0052	0070
8			0001	0001	0002	0003	0004	0006	0009	0012
9								0001	0001	0002

The cumulative probability distribution

$n = 13$

p	21	22	23	24	25	26	27	28	29	30
r 1	9533	9604	9666	9718	9762	9800	9833	9860	9883	9903
2	7920	8154	8367	8559	8733	8889	9029	9154	9265	9363
3	5347	5699	6039	6364	6674	6968	7245	7505	7749	7975
4	2839	3161	3489	3822	4157	4493	4826	5155	5478	5794
5	1173	1371	1585	1816	2060	2319	2589	2870	3160	3457
6	0375	0462	0562	0675	0802	0944	1099	1270	1455	1654
7	0093	0120	0154	0195	0243	0299	0365	0440	0527	0624
8	0017	0024	0032	0043	0056	0073	0093	0118	0147	0182
9	0002	0004	0005	0007	0010	0013	0018	0024	0031	0040
10			0001	0001	0001	0002	0003	0004	0005	0007
11									0001	0001

p	31	32	33	34	35	36	37	38	39	40
r 1	9920	9934	9945	9955	9963	9970	9975	9980	9984	9987
2	9450	9527	9594	9653	9704	9749	9787	9821	9849	9874
3	8185	8379	8557	8720	8868	9003	9125	9235	9333	9421
4	6101	6398	6683	6957	7217	7464	7698	7917	8123	8314
5	3760	4067	4376	4686	4995	5301	5603	5899	6188	6470
6	1867	2093	2331	2581	2841	3111	3388	3673	3962	4256
7	0733	0854	0988	1135	1295	1468	1654	1853	2065	2288
8	0223	0271	0326	0390	0462	0544	0635	0738	0851	0977
9	0052	0065	0082	0102	0126	0154	0187	0225	0270	0321
10	0009	0012	0015	0020	0025	0032	0040	0051	0063	0078
11	0001	0001	0002	0003	0003	0005	0006	0008	0010	0013
12							0001	0001	0001	0001

p	41	42	43	44	45	46	47	48	49	50
r 1	9990	9992	9993	9995	9996	9997	9997	9998	9998	9999
2	9895	9912	9928	9940	9951	9960	9967	9974	9979	9983
3	9499	9569	9630	9684	9731	9772	9808	9838	9865	9888
4	8492	8656	8807	8945	9071	9185	9288	9381	9464	9539
5	6742	7003	7254	7493	7721	7935	8137	8326	8502	8666
6	4552	4849	5146	5441	5732	6019	6299	6573	6838	7095
7	2524	2770	3025	3290	3563	3842	4127	4415	4707	5000
8	1114	1264	1426	1600	1788	1988	2200	2424	2659	2905
9	0379	0446	0520	0605	0698	0803	0918	1045	1183	1334
10	0096	0117	0141	0170	0203	0242	0287	0338	0396	0461
11	0017	0021	0027	0033	0041	0051	0063	0077	0093	0112
12	0002	0002	0003	0004	0005	0007	0009	0011	0014	0017
13							0001	0001	0001	0001

$n = 14$

p	01	02	03	04	05	06	07	08	09	10
r 1	1313	2464	3472	4353	5123	5795	6380	6888	7330	7712
2	0084	0310	0645	1059	1530	2037	2564	3100	3632	4154
3	0003	0025	0077	0167	0301	0478	0698	0958	1255	1584
4		0001	0006	0019	0042	0080	0136	0214	0315	0441
5				0002	0004	0010	0020	0035	0059	0092
6						0001	0002	0004	0008	0015
7									0001	0002

The cumulative probability distribution

$n = 14$

p	11	12	13	14	15	16	17	18	19	20
r 1	8044	8330	8577	8789	8972	9129	9264	9379	9477	9560
2	4658	5141	5599	6031	6433	6807	7152	7469	7758	8021
3	1939	2315	2708	3111	3521	3932	4341	4744	5138	5519
4	0594	0774	0979	1210	1465	1742	2038	2351	2679	3018
5	0137	0196	0269	0359	0467	0594	0741	0907	1093	1298
6	0024	0038	0057	0082	0115	0157	0209	0273	0349	0439
7	0003	0006	0009	0015	0022	0032	0046	0064	0087	0116
8		0001	0001	0002	0003	0005	0008	0012	0017	0024
9						0001	0001	0002	0003	0004

p	21	22	23	24	25	26	27	28	29	30
r 1	9631	9691	9742	9786	9822	9852	9878	9899	9917	9932
2	8259	8473	8665	8837	8990	9126	9246	9352	9444	9525
3	5887	6239	6574	6891	7189	7467	7727	7967	8188	8392
4	3366	3719	4076	4432	4787	5136	5479	5813	6137	6448
5	1523	1765	2023	2297	2585	2884	3193	3509	3832	4158
6	0543	0662	0797	0949	1117	1301	1502	1718	1949	2195
7	0152	0196	0248	0310	0383	0467	0563	0673	0796	0933
8	0033	0045	0060	0079	0103	0132	0167	0208	0257	0315
9	0006	0008	0011	0016	0022	0029	0038	0050	0065	0083
10	0001	0001	0002	0002	0003	0005	0007	0009	0012	0017
11						0001	0001	0001	0002	0002

p	31	32	33	34	35	36	37	38	39	40
r 1	9945	9955	9963	9970	9976	9981	9984	9988	9990	9992
2	9596	9657	9710	9756	9795	9828	9857	9881	9902	9919
3	8577	8746	8899	9037	9161	9271	9370	9457	9534	9602
4	6747	7032	7301	7556	7795	8018	8226	8418	8595	8757
5	4486	4813	5138	5458	5773	6080	6378	6666	6943	7207
6	2454	2724	3006	3297	3595	3899	4208	4519	4831	5141
7	1084	1250	1431	1626	1836	2059	2296	2545	2805	3075
8	0381	0458	0545	0643	0753	0876	1012	1162	1325	1501
9	0105	0131	0163	0200	0243	0294	0353	0420	0497	0583
10	0022	0029	0037	0048	0060	0076	0095	0117	0144	0175
11	0003	0005	0006	0008	0011	0014	0019	0024	0031	0039
12		0001	0001	0001	0001	0002	0003	0003	0005	0006
13										0001

p	41	42	43	44	45	46	47	48	49	50
r 1	9994	9995	9996	9997	9998	9998	9999	9999	9999	9999
2	9934	9946	9956	9964	9971	9977	9981	9985	9988	9991
3	9661	9713	9758	9797	9830	9858	9883	9903	9921	9935
4	8905	9039	9161	9270	9368	9455	9532	9601	9661	9713
5	7459	7697	7922	8132	8328	8510	8678	8833	8974	9102
6	5450	5754	6052	6344	6627	6900	7163	7415	7654	7880
7	3355	3643	3937	4236	4539	4843	5148	5451	5751	6047
8	1692	1896	2113	2344	2586	2840	3105	3380	3663	3953
9	0680	0789	0910	1043	1189	1348	1520	1707	1906	2120
10	0212	0255	0304	0361	0426	0500	0583	0677	0782	0898
11	0049	0061	0076	0093	0114	0139	0168	0202	0241	0287
12	0008	0010	0013	0017	0022	0027	0034	0042	0053	0065
13	0001	0001	0001	0002	0003	0003	0004	0006	0007	0009
14										0001

The cumulative probability distribution

$n = 15$

$n = 15$

p	01	02	03	04	05	06	07	08	09	10
r 1	1399	2614	3667	4579	5367	6047	6633	7137	7570	7941
2	0096	0353	0730	1191	1710	2262	2832	3403	3965	4510
3	0004	0030	0094	0203	0362	0571	0829	1130	1469	1841
4		0002	0008	0024	0055	0104	0175	0273	0399	0556
5			0001	0002	0006	0014	0028	0050	0082	0127
6					0001	0001	0003	0007	0013	0022
7								0001	0002	0003

p	11	12	13	14	15	16	17	18	19	20
r 1	8259	8530	8762	8959	9126	9269	9389	9490	9576	9648
2	5031	5524	5987	6417	6814	7179	7511	7813	8085	8329
3	2238	2654	3084	3520	3958	4392	4819	5234	5635	6020
4	0742	0959	1204	1476	1773	2092	2429	2782	3146	3518
5	0187	0265	0361	0478	0617	0778	0961	1167	1394	1642
6	0037	0057	0084	0121	0168	0227	0300	0387	0490	0611
7	0006	0010	0015	0024	0036	0052	0074	0102	0137	0181
8	0001	0001	0002	0004	0006	0010	0014	0021	0030	0042
9					0001	0001	0002	0003	0005	0008
10									0001	0001

p	21	22	23	24	25	26	27	28	29	30
r 1	9709	9759	9802	9837	9866	9891	9911	9928	9941	9953
2	8547	8741	8913	9065	9198	9315	9417	9505	9581	9647
3	6385	6731	7055	7358	7639	7899	8137	8355	8553	8732
4	3895	4274	4650	5022	5387	5742	6086	6416	6732	7031
5	1910	2195	2495	2810	3135	3469	3810	4154	4500	4845
6	0748	0905	1079	1272	1484	1713	1958	2220	2495	2784
7	0234	0298	0374	0463	0566	0684	0817	0965	1130	1311
8	0058	0078	0104	0135	0173	0219	0274	0338	0413	0500
9	0011	0016	0023	0031	0042	0056	0073	0094	0121	0152
10	0002	0003	0004	0006	0008	0011	0015	0021	0028	0037
11			0001	0001	0001	0002	0002	0003	0005	0007
12									0001	0001

p	31	32	33	34	35	36	37	38	39	40
r 1	9962	9969	9975	9980	9984	9988	9990	9992	9994	9995
2	9704	9752	9794	9829	9858	9883	9904	9922	9936	9948
3	8893	9038	9167	9281	9383	9472	9550	9618	9678	9729
4	7314	7580	7829	8060	8273	8469	8649	8813	8961	9095
5	5187	5523	5852	6171	6481	6778	7062	7332	7587	7827
6	3084	3393	3709	4032	4357	4684	5011	5335	5654	5968
7	1509	1722	1951	2194	2452	2722	3003	3295	3595	3902
8	0599	0711	0837	0977	1132	1302	1487	1687	1902	2131
9	0190	0236	0289	0351	0422	0504	0597	0702	0820	0950
10	0048	0062	0079	0099	0124	0154	0190	0232	0281	0338
11	0009	0012	0016	0022	0028	0037	0047	0059	0075	0093
12	0001	0002	0003	0004	0005	0006	0009	0011	0015	0019
13					0001	0001	0001	0002	0002	0003

The cumulative probability distribution

n = 15

p	41	42	43	44	45	46	47	48	49	50
r 1	9996	9997	9998	9998	9999	9999	9999	9999	10000	10000
2	9958	9966	9973	9979	9983	9987	9990	9992	9994	9995
3	9773	9811	9843	9870	9893	9913	9929	9943	9954	9963
4	9215	9322	9417	9502	9576	9641	9697	9746	9788	9824
5	8052	8261	8454	8633	8796	8945	9080	9201	9310	9408
6	6274	6570	6856	7131	7392	7641	7875	8095	8301	8491
7	4214	4530	4847	5164	5478	5789	6095	6394	6684	6964
8	2374	2630	2898	3176	3465	3762	4065	4374	4686	5000
9	1095	1254	1427	1615	1818	2034	2265	2510	2767	3036
10	0404	0479	0565	0661	0769	0890	1024	1171	1333	1509
11	0116	0143	0174	0211	0255	0305	0363	0430	0506	0592
12	0025	0032	0040	0051	0063	0079	0097	0119	0145	0176
13	0004	0005	0007	0009	0011	0014	0018	0023	0029	0037
14			0001	0001	0001	0002	0002	0003	0004	0005

n = 16

p	01	02	03	04	05	06	07	08	09	10
r 1	1485	2762	3857	4796	5599	6284	6869	7366	7789	8147
2	0109	0399	0818	1327	1892	2489	3098	3701	4289	4853
3	0005	0037	0113	0242	0429	0673	0969	1311	1694	2108
4		0002	0011	0032	0070	0132	0221	0342	0496	0684
5			0001	0003	0009	0019	0038	0068	0111	0170
6					0001	0002	0005	0010	0019	0033
7							0001	0001	0003	0005
8										0001

p	11	12	13	14	15	16	17	18	19	20
r 1	8450	8707	8923	9105	9257	9386	9493	9582	9657	9719
2	5386	5885	6347	6773	7161	7513	7830	8115	8368	8593
3	2545	2999	3461	3926	4386	4838	5277	5698	6101	6482
4	0907	1162	1448	1763	2101	2460	2836	3223	3619	4019
5	0248	0348	0471	0618	0791	0988	1211	1458	1727	2018
6	0053	0082	0120	0171	0235	0315	0412	0527	0662	0817
7	0009	0015	0024	0038	0056	0080	0112	0153	0204	0267
8	0001	0002	0004	0007	0011	0016	0024	0036	0051	0070
9			0001	0001	0002	0003	0004	0007	0010	0015
10							0001	0001	0002	0002

p	21	22	23	24	25	26	27	28	29	30
r 1	9770	9812	9847	9876	9900	9919	9935	9948	9958	9967
2	8791	8965	9117	9250	9365	9465	9550	9623	9686	9739
3	6839	7173	7483	7768	8029	8267	8482	8677	8851	9006
4	4418	4814	5203	5583	5950	6303	6640	6959	7260	7541
5	2327	2652	2991	3341	3698	4060	4425	4788	5147	5501
6	0992	1188	1405	1641	1897	2169	2458	2761	3077	3402
7	0342	0432	0536	0657	0796	0951	1125	1317	1526	1753
8	0095	0127	0166	0214	0271	0340	0420	0514	0621	0744
9	0021	0030	0041	0056	0075	0098	0127	0163	0206	0257
10	0004	0006	0008	0012	0016	0023	0031	0041	0055	0071
11	0001	0001	0001	0002	0003	0004	0006	0008	0011	0016
12						0001	0001	0001	0002	0003

The cumulative probability distribution

$n = 16$

P	31	32	33	34	35	36	37	38	39	40
r 1	9974	9979	9984	9987	9990	9992	9994	9995	9996	9997
2	9784	9822	9854	9880	9902	9921	9936	9948	9959	9967
3	9144	9266	9374	9467	9549	9620	9681	9734	9778	9817
4	7804	8047	8270	8475	8661	8830	8982	9119	9241	9349
5	5846	6181	6504	6813	7108	7387	7649	7895	8123	8334
6	3736	4074	4416	4759	5100	5438	5770	6094	6408	6712
7	1997	2257	2531	2819	3119	3428	3746	4070	4398	4728
8	0881	1035	1205	1391	1594	1813	2048	2298	2562	2839
9	0317	0388	0470	0564	0671	0791	0926	1076	1242	1423
10	0092	0117	0148	0185	0229	0280	0341	0411	0491	0583
11	0021	0028	0037	0048	0062	0079	0100	0125	0155	0191
12	0004	0005	0007	0010	0013	0017	0023	0030	0038	0049
13		0001	0001	0001	0002	0003	0004	0005	0007	0009
14								0001	0001	0001

P	41	42	43	44	45	46	47	48	49	50
r 1	9998	9998	9999	9999	9999	9999	10000	10000	10000	10000
2	9974	9979	9984	9987	9990	9992	9994	9995	9997	9997
3	9849	9876	9899	9918	9934	9947	9958	9966	9973	9979
4	9444	9527	9600	9664	9719	9766	9806	9840	9869	9894
5	8529	8707	8869	9015	9147	9265	9370	9463	9544	9616
6	7003	7280	7543	7792	8024	8241	8441	8626	8795	8949
7	5058	5387	5711	6029	6340	6641	6932	7210	7476	7728
8	3128	3428	3736	4051	4371	4694	5019	5343	5665	5982
9	1619	1832	2060	2302	2559	2829	3111	3405	3707	4018
10	0687	0805	0936	1081	1241	1416	1607	1814	2036	2272
11	0234	0284	0342	0409	0486	0574	0674	0786	0911	1051
12	0062	0078	0098	0121	0149	0183	0222	0268	0322	0384
13	0012	0016	0021	0027	0035	0044	0055	0069	0086	0106
14	0002	0002	0003	0004	0006	0007	0010	0013	0016	0021
15					0001	0001	0001	0001	0002	0003

$n = 17$

P	01	02	03	04	05	06	07	08	09	10
r 1	1571	2907	4042	5004	5819	6507	7088	7577	7988	8332
2	0123	0446	0909	1465	2078	2717	3362	3995	4604	5182
3	0006	0044	0134	0286	0503	0782	1118	1503	1927	2382
4		0003	0014	0040	0088	0164	0273	0419	0603	0826
5			0001	0004	0012	0026	0051	0089	0145	0221
6					0001	0003	0007	0015	0027	0047
7							0001	0002	0004	0008
8										0001

P	11	12	13	14	15	16	17	18	19	20
r 1	8621	8862	9063	9230	9369	9484	9579	9657	9722	9775
2	5723	6223	6682	7099	7475	7813	8113	8379	8613	8818
3	2858	3345	3836	4324	4802	5266	5711	6133	6532	6904
4	1087	1383	1710	2065	2444	2841	3251	3669	4091	4511
5	0321	0446	0598	0778	0987	1224	1487	1775	2087	2418

$n = 17$

	p	11	12	13	14	15	16	17	18	19	20
r	6	0075	0114	0166	0234	0319	0423	0548	0695	0864	1057
	7	0014	0023	0037	0056	0083	0118	0163	0220	0291	0377
	8	0002	0004	0007	0011	0017	0027	0039	0057	0080	0109
	9		0001	0001	0002	0003	0005	0008	0012	0018	0026
	10						0001	0001	0002	0003	0005
	11										0001

	p	21	22	23	24	25	26	27	28	29	30
r	1	9818	9854	9882	9906	9925	9940	9953	9962	9970	9977
	2	8996	9152	9285	9400	9499	9583	9654	9714	9765	9807
	3	7249	7567	7859	8123	8363	8578	8771	8942	9093	9226
	4	4927	5333	5728	6107	6470	6814	7137	7440	7721	7981
	5	2766	3128	3500	3879	4261	4643	5023	5396	5760	6113
	6	1273	1510	1770	2049	2347	2661	2989	3329	3677	4032
	7	0479	0598	0736	0894	1071	1268	1485	1721	1976	2248
	8	0147	0194	0251	0320	0402	0499	0611	0739	0884	1046
	9	0037	0051	0070	0094	0124	0161	0206	0261	0326	0403
	10	0007	0011	0016	0022	0031	0042	0057	0075	0098	0127
	11	0001	0002	0003	0004	0006	0009	0013	0018	0024	0032
	12				0001	0001	0002	0002	0003	0005	0007
	13									0001	0001

	p	31	32	33	34	35	36	37	38	39	40
r	1	9982	9986	9989	9991	9993	9995	9996	9997	9998	9998
	2	9843	9872	9896	9917	9933	9946	9957	9966	9973	9979
	3	9343	9444	9532	9608	9673	9728	9775	9815	9849	9877
	4	8219	8437	8634	8812	8972	9115	9241	9353	9450	9536
	5	6453	6778	7087	7378	7652	7906	8142	8360	8559	8740
	6	4390	4749	5105	5458	5803	6139	6465	6778	7077	7361
	7	2536	2838	3153	3479	3812	4152	4495	4839	5182	5522
	8	1227	1426	1642	1877	2128	2395	2676	2971	3278	3595
	9	0492	0595	0712	0845	0994	1159	1341	1541	1757	1989
	10	0162	0204	0254	0314	0383	0464	0557	0664	0784	0919
	11	0043	0057	0074	0095	0120	0151	0189	0234	0286	0348
	12	0009	0013	0017	0023	0030	0040	0051	0066	0084	0106
	13	0002	0002	0003	0004	0006	0008	0011	0015	0019	0025
	14				0001	0001	0001	0002	0002	0003	0005
	15										0001

	p	41	42	43	44	45	46	47	48	49	50
r	1	9999	9999	9999	9999	10000	10000	10000	10000	10000	10000
	2	9984	9987	9990	9992	9994	9996	9997	9998	9998	9999
	3	9900	9920	9935	9948	9959	9968	9975	9980	9985	9988
	4	9610	9674	9729	9776	9816	9849	9877	9901	9920	9936
	5	8904	9051	9183	9301	9404	9495	9575	9644	9704	9755
	6	7628	7879	8113	8330	8529	8712	8878	9028	9162	9283
	7	5856	6182	6499	6805	7098	7377	7641	7890	8122	8338
	8	3920	4250	4585	4921	5257	5590	5918	6239	6552	6855

The cumulative probability distribution

$n = 17$

p r	41	42	43	44	45	46	47	48	49	50
9	2238	2502	2780	3072	3374	3687	4008	4335	4667	5000
10	1070	1236	1419	1618	1834	2066	2314	2577	2855	3145
11	0420	0503	0597	0705	0826	0962	1112	1279	1462	1662
12	0133	0165	0203	0248	0301	0363	0434	0517	0611	0717
13	0033	0042	0054	0069	0086	0108	0134	0165	0202	0245
14	0006	0008	0011	0014	0019	0024	0031	0040	0050	0064
15	0001	0001	0002	0002	0003	0004	0005	0007	0009	0012
16							0001	0001	0001	0001

$n = 18$

p r	01	02	03	04	05	06	07	08	09	10
1	1655	3049	4220	5204	6028	6717	7292	7771	8169	8499
2	0138	0495	1003	1607	2265	2945	3622	4281	4909	5497
3	0007	0052	0157	0333	0581	0898	1275	1702	2168	2662
4		0004	0018	0050	0109	0201	0333	0506	0723	0982
5			0002	0006	0015	0034	0067	0116	0186	0282
6				0001	0002	0005	0010	0021	0038	0064
7							0001	0003	0006	0012
8									0001	0002

p r	11	12	13	14	15	16	17	18	19	20
1	8773	8998	9185	9338	9464	9566	9651	9719	9775	9820
2	6042	6540	6992	7398	7759	8080	8362	8609	8824	9009
3	3173	3690	4206	4713	5203	5673	6119	6538	6927	7287
4	1282	1618	1986	2382	2798	3229	3669	4112	4554	4990
5	0405	0558	0743	0959	1206	1482	1787	2116	2467	2836
6	0102	0154	0222	0310	0419	0551	0708	0889	1097	1329
7	0021	0034	0054	0081	0118	0167	0229	0306	0400	0513
8	0003	0006	0011	0017	0027	0041	0060	0086	0120	0163
9		0001	0002	0003	0005	0008	0013	0020	0029	0043
10					0001	0001	0002	0004	0006	0009
11								0001	0001	0002

p r	21	22	23	24	25	26	27	28	29	30
1	9856	9886	9909	9928	9944	9956	9965	9973	9979	9984
2	9169	9306	9423	9522	9605	9676	9735	9784	9824	9858
3	7616	7916	8187	8430	8647	8839	9009	9158	9288	9400
4	5414	5825	6218	6591	6943	7272	7578	7860	8119	8354
5	3220	3613	4012	4414	4813	5208	5594	5968	6329	6673
6	1586	1866	2168	2488	2825	3176	3538	3907	4281	4656
7	0645	0799	0974	1171	1390	1630	1891	2171	2469	2783
8	0217	0283	0363	0458	0569	0699	0847	1014	1200	1407
9	0060	0083	0112	0148	0193	0249	0316	0395	0488	0596
10	0014	0020	0028	0039	0054	0073	0097	0127	0164	0210
11	0003	0004	0006	0009	0012	0018	0025	0034	0046	0061
12		0001	0001	0002	0002	0003	0005	0007	0010	0014
13						0001	0001	0001	0002	0003

The cumulative probability distribution

$n = 18$

p / r	31	32	33	34	35	36	37	38	39	40
1	9987	9990	9993	9994	9996	9997	9998	9998	9999	9999
2	9886	9908	9927	9942	9954	9964	9972	9978	9983	9987
3	9498	9581	9652	9713	9764	9807	9843	9873	9897	9918
4	8568	8759	8931	9083	9217	9335	9439	9528	9606	9672
5	7001	7309	7598	7866	8114	8341	8549	8737	8907	9058
6	5029	5398	5759	6111	6450	6776	7086	7379	7655	7912
7	3111	3450	3797	4151	4509	4867	5224	5576	5921	6257
8	1633	1878	2141	2421	2717	3027	3349	3681	4021	4366
9	0720	0861	1019	1196	1391	1604	1835	2084	2350	2632
10	0264	0329	0405	0494	0597	0714	0847	0997	1163	1347
11	0080	0104	0133	0169	0212	0264	0325	0397	0480	0576
12	0020	0027	0036	0047	0062	0080	0102	0130	0163	0203
13	0004	0005	0008	0011	0014	0019	0026	0034	0044	0058
14	0001	0001	0001	0002	0003	0004	0005	0007	0010	0013
15						0001	0001	0001	0002	0002

p / r	41	42	43	44	45	46	47	48	49	50
1	9999	9999	10000	10000	10000	10000	10000	10000	10000	10000
2	9990	9992	9994	9996	9997	9998	9998	9999	9999	9999
3	9934	9948	9959	9968	9975	9981	9985	9989	9991	9993
4	9729	9777	9818	9852	9880	9904	9923	9939	9952	9962
5	9193	9313	9418	9510	9589	9658	9717	9767	9810	9846
6	8151	8372	8573	8757	8923	9072	9205	9324	9428	9519
7	6582	6895	7193	7476	7742	7991	8222	8436	8632	8811
8	4713	5062	5408	5750	6085	6412	6728	7032	7322	7597
9	2928	3236	3556	3885	4222	4562	4906	5249	5591	5927
10	1549	1768	2004	2258	2527	2812	3110	3421	3742	4073
11	0686	0811	0951	1107	1280	1470	1677	1902	2144	2403
12	0250	0307	0372	0449	0537	0638	0753	0883	1028	1189
13	0074	0094	0118	0147	0183	0225	0275	0334	0402	0481
14	0017	0022	0029	0038	0049	0063	0079	0100	0125	0154
15	0003	0004	0006	0007	0010	0013	0017	0023	0029	0038
16		0001	0001	0001	0001	0002	0003	0004	0005	0007
17									0001	0001

$n = 19$

p / r	01	02	03	04	05	06	07	08	09	10
1	1738	3188	4394	5396	6226	6914	7481	7949	8334	8649
2	0153	0546	1100	1751	2453	3171	3879	4560	5202	5797
3	0009	0061	0183	0384	0665	1021	1439	1908	2415	2946
4		0005	0022	0061	0132	0243	0398	0602	0853	1150
5			0002	0007	0020	0044	0085	0147	0235	0352
6				0001	0002	0006	0014	0029	0051	0086
7						0001	0002	0004	0009	0017
8								0001	0001	0003

TABLE 3
[The cumulative Poisson distribution]

$P(r \leq r_0 \mid \mu)$

μ \ r_0	0	1	2	3	4	5	6	7	8	9
0.02	980	1000								
0.04	961	999	1000							
0.06	942	998	1000							
0.08	923	997	1000							
0.10	905	995	1000							
0.15	861	990	999	1000						
0.20	819	982	999	1000						
0.25	779	974	998	1000						
0.30	741	963	996	1000						
0.35	705	951	994	1000						
0.40	670	938	992	999	1000					
0.45	638	925	989	999	1000					
0.50	607	910	986	998	1000					
0.55	577	894	982	998	1000					
0.60	549	878	977	997	1000					
0.65	522	861	972	996	999	1000				
0.70	497	844	966	994	999	1000				
0.75	472	827	959	993	999	1000				
0.80	449	809	953	991	999	1000				
0.85	427	791	945	989	998	1000				
0.90	407	772	937	987	998	1000				
0.95	387	754	929	984	997	1000				
1.00	368	736	920	981	996	999	1000			
1.1	333	699	900	974	995	999	1000			
1.2	301	663	879	966	992	998	1000			
1.3	273	627	857	957	989	998	1000			
1.4	247	592	833	946	986	997	999	1000		
1.5	223	558	809	934	981	996	999	1000		
1.6	202	525	783	921	976	994	999	1000		
1.7	183	493	757	907	970	992	998	1000		
1.8	165	463	731	891	964	990	997	999	1000	
1.9	150	434	704	875	956	987	997	999	1000	
2.0	135	406	677	857	947	983	995	999	1000	
2.2	111	355	623	819	928	975	993	998	1000	
2.4	091	308	570	779	904	964	988	997	999	1000
2.6	074	267	518	736	877	951	983	995	999	1000
2.8	061	231	469	692	848	935	976	992	998	999
3.0	050	199	423	647	815	916	966	988	996	999

μ	10
2.8	1000
3.0	1000

The cumulative Poisson distribution

μ \ r_0	0	1	2	3	4	5	6	7	8	9
3.2	041	171	380	603	781	895	955	983	994	998
3.4	033	147	340	558	744	871	942	977	992	997
3.6	027	126	303	515	706	844	927	969	988	996
3.8	022	107	269	473	668	816	909	960	984	994
4.0	018	092	238	433	629	785	889	949	979	992
4.2	015	078	210	395	590	753	867	936	972	989
4.4	012	066	185	359	551	720	844	921	964	985
4.6	010	056	163	326	513	686	818	905	955	980
4.8	008	048	143	294	476	651	791	887	944	975
5.0	007	040	125	265	440	616	762	867	932	968
5.2	006	034	109	238	406	581	732	845	918	960
5.4	005	029	095	213	373	546	702	822	903	951
5.6	004	024	082	191	342	512	670	797	886	941
5.8	003	021	072	170	313	478	638	771	867	929
6.0	002	017	062	151	285	446	606	744	847	916
6.2	002	015	054	134	259	414	574	716	826	902
6.4	002	012	046	119	235	384	542	687	803	886
6.6	001	010	040	105	213	355	511	658	780	869
6.8	001	009	034	093	192	327	480	628	755	850
7.0	001	007	030	082	173	301	450	599	729	830

μ	10	11	12	13	14	15	16	17
3.2	1000							
3.4	999	1000						
3.6	999	1000						
3.8	998	999	1000					
4.0	997	999	1000					
4.2	996	999	1000					
4.4	994	998	999	1000				
4.6	992	997	999	1000				
4.8	990	996	999	1000				
5.0	986	995	998	999	1000			
5.2	982	993	997	999	1000			
5.4	977	990	996	999	1000			
5.6	972	988	995	998	999	1000		
5.8	965	984	993	997	999	1000		
6.0	957	980	991	996	999	999	1000	
6.2	949	975	989	995	998	999	1000	
6.4	939	969	986	994	997	999	1000	
6.6	927	963	982	992	997	999	999	1000
6.8	915	955	978	990	996	998	999	1000
7.0	901	947	973	987	994	998	999	1000

The cumulative Poisson distribution

r_0 / μ	0	1	2	3	4	5	6	7	8	9
7.2	001	006	025	072	156	276	420	569	703	810
7.4	001	005	022	063	140	253	392	539	676	788
7.6	001	004	019	055	125	231	365	510	648	765
7.8	000	004	016	048	112	210	338	481	620	741
8.0	000	003	014	042	100	191	313	453	593	717
8.5	000	002	009	030	074	150	256	386	523	653
9.0	000	001	006	021	055	116	207	324	456	587
9.5	000	001	004	015	040	089	165	269	392	522
10.0	000	000	003	010	029	067	130	220	333	458
10.5	000	000	002	007	021	050	102	179	279	397
11.0	000	000	001	005	015	038	079	143	232	341
11.5	000	000	001	003	011	028	060	114	191	289
12.0	000	000	001	002	008	020	046	090	155	242
12.5	000	000	000	002	005	015	035	070	125	201

	10	11	12	13	14	15	16	17	18	19
7.2	887	937	967	984	993	997	999	999	1000	
7.4	871	926	961	980	991	996	998	999	1000	
7.6	854	915	954	976	989	995	998	999	1000	
7.8	835	902	945	971	986	993	997	999	1000	
8.0	816	888	936	966	983	992	996	998	999	1000
8.5	763	849	909	949	973	986	993	997	999	999
9.0	706	803	876	926	959	978	989	995	998	999
9.5	645	752	836	898	940	967	982	991	996	998
10.0	583	697	792	864	917	951	973	986	993	997
10.5	521	639	742	825	888	932	960	978	988	994
11.0	460	579	689	781	854	907	944	968	982	991
11.5	402	520	633	733	815	878	924	954	974	986
12.0	347	462	576	682	772	844	899	937	963	979
12.5	297	406	519	628	725	806	869	916	948	969

	20	21	22	23	24	25	26
8.5	1000						
9.0	1000						
9.5	999	1000					
10.0	998	999	1000				
10.5	997	999	999	1000			
11.0	995	998	999	1000			
11.5	992	996	998	999	1000		
12.0	988	994	997	999	999	1000	
12.5	983	991	995	998	999	999	1000

The cumulative Poisson distribution

r_0 μ	0	1	2	3	4	5	6	7	8	9
13.0	000	000	000	001	004	011	026	054	100	166
13.5	000	000	000	001	003	008	019	041	079	135
14.0	000	000	000	000	002	006	014	032	062	109
14.5	000	000	000	000	001	004	010	024	048	088
15.0	000	000	000	000	001	003	008	018	037	070

	10	11	12	13	14	15	16	17	18	19
13.0	252	353	463	573	675	764	835	890	930	957
13.5	211	304	409	518	623	718	798	861	908	942
14.0	176	260	358	464	570	669	756	827	883	923
14.5	145	220	311	413	518	619	711	790	853	901
15.0	118	185	268	363	466	568	664	749	819	875

	20	21	22	23	24	25	26	27	28	29
13.0	975	986	992	996	998	999	1000			
13.5	965	980	989	994	997	998	999	1000		
14.0	952	971	983	991	995	997	999	999	1000	
14.5	936	960	976	986	992	996	998	999	999	1000
15.0	917	947	967	981	989	994	997	998	999	1000

The cumulative Poisson distribution

μ \ r₀	4	5	6	7	8	9	10	11	12	13
16	000	001	004	010	022	043	077	127	193	275
17	000	001	002	005	013	026	049	085	135	201
18	000	000	001	003	007	015	030	055	092	143
19	000	000	001	002	004	009	018	035	061	098
20	000	000	000	001	002	005	011	021	039	066
21	000	000	000	000	001	003	006	013	025	043
22	000	000	000	000	001	002	004	008	015	028
23	000	000	000	000	000	001	002	004	009	017
24	000	000	000	000	000	000	001	003	005	011
25	000	000	000	000	000	000	001	001	003	006

	14	15	16	17	18	19	20	21	22	23
16	368	467	566	659	742	812	868	911	942	963
17	281	371	468	564	655	736	805	861	905	937
18	208	287	375	469	562	651	731	799	855	899
19	150	215	292	378	469	561	647	725	793	849
20	105	157	221	297	381	470	559	644	721	787
21	072	111	163	227	302	384	471	558	640	716
22	048	077	117	169	232	306	387	472	556	637
23	031	052	082	123	175	238	310	389	472	555
24	020	034	056	087	128	180	243	314	392	473
25	012	022	038	060	092	134	185	247	318	394

	24	25	26	27	28	29	30	31	32	33
16	978	987	993	996	998	999	999	1000		
17	959	975	985	991	995	997	999	999	1000	
18	932	955	972	983	990	994	997	998	999	1000
19	893	927	951	969	980	988	993	996	998	999
20	843	888	922	948	966	978	987	992	995	997
21	782	838	883	917	944	963	976	985	991	994
22	712	777	832	877	913	940	959	973	983	989
23	635	708	772	827	873	908	936	956	971	981
24	554	632	704	768	823	868	904	932	953	969
25	473	553	629	700	763	818	863	900	929	950

	34	35	36	37	38	39	40	41	42	43
19	999	1000								
20	999	999	1000							
21	997	998	999	999	1000					
22	994	996	998	999	999	1000				
23	988	993	996	997	999	999	1000			
24	979	987	992	995	997	998	999	999	1000	
25	966	978	985	991	994	997	998	999	999	1000

TABLE 4

[The chi-square distribution]

Degrees of freedom	$\chi^2_{.995}$	$\chi^2_{.99}$	$\chi^2_{.975}$	$\chi^2_{.95}$	$\chi^2_{.05}$	$\chi^2_{.025}$	$\chi^2_{.01}$	$\chi^2_{.005}$	Degrees of freedom
				Level of significance					
1	.0000393	.000157	.000982	.00393	3.841	5.024	6.635	7.879	1
2	.0100	.0201	.0506	.103	5.991	7.378	9.210	10.597	2
3	.0717	.115	.216	.352	7.815	9.348	11.345	12.838	3
4	.207	.297	.484	.711	9.488	11.143	13.277	14.860	4
5	.412	.554	.831	1.145	11.070	12.832	15.086	16.750	5
6	.676	.872	1.237	1.635	12.592	14.449	16.812	18.548	6
7	.989	1.239	1.690	2.167	14.067	16.013	18.475	20.278	7
8	1.344	1.646	2.180	2.733	15.507	17.535	20.090	21.955	8
9	1.735	2.088	2.700	3.325	16.919	19.023	21.666	23.589	9
10	2.156	2.558	3.247	3.940	18.307	20.483	23.209	25.188	10
11	2.603	3.053	3.816	4.575	19.675	21.920	24.725	26.757	11
12	3.074	3.571	4.404	5.226	21.026	23.337	26.217	28.300	12
13	3.565	4.107	5.009	5.892	22.362	24.736	27.688	29.819	13
14	4.075	4.660	5.629	6.571	23.685	26.119	29.141	31.319	14
15	4.601	5.229	6.262	7.261	24.996	27.488	30.578	32.801	15
16	5.142	5.812	6.908	7.962	26.296	28.845	32.000	34.267	16
17	5.697	6.408	7.564	8.672	27.587	30.191	33.409	35.718	17
18	6.265	7.015	8.231	9.390	28.869	31.526	34.805	37.156	18
19	6.844	7.633	8.907	10.117	30.144	32.852	36.191	38.582	19
20	7.434	8.260	9.591	10.851	31.410	34.170	37.566	39.997	20
21	8.034	8.897	10.283	11.591	32.671	35.479	38.932	41.401	21
22	8.643	9.542	10.982	12.338	33.924	36.781	40.289	42.796	22
23	9.260	10.196	11.689	13.091	35.172	38.076	41.638	44.181	23
24	9.886	10.856	12.401	13.848	36.415	39.364	42.980	45.558	24
25	10.520	11.524	13.120	14.611	37.652	40.646	44.314	46.928	25
26	11.160	12.198	13.844	15.379	38.885	41.923	45.642	48.290	26
27	11.808	12.879	14.573	16.151	40.113	43.194	46.963	49.645	27
28	12.461	13.565	15.308	16.928	41.337	44.461	48.278	50.993	28
29	13.121	14.256	16.047	17.708	42.557	45.722	49.588	52.336	29
30	13.787	14.953	16.791	18.493	43.773	46.979	50.892	53.672	30

TABLE 5

$\left[\begin{array}{c}\text{One-tailed table of critical values for}\\\text{the Kolmogorov-Smirnov test}\end{array}\right]$

Values of $d_\alpha(N)$ such that $Pr[\max|S_N(x)-F_0(x)|>d_\alpha(N)]=\alpha$, where $F_0(x)$ is the theoretical cumulative distribution and $S_N(x)$ is an observed cumulative distribution for a sample of N.

Sample size (N)	Level of significance (α)				
	0.20	0.15	0.10	0.05	0.01
1	0.900	0.925	0.950	0.975	0.995
2	0.684	0.726	0.776	0.842	0.929
3	0.565	0.597	0.642	0.708	0.828
4	0.494	0.525	0.564	0.624	0.733
5	0.446	0.474	0.510	0.565	0.669
6	0.410	0.436	0.470	0.521	0.618
7	0.381	0.405	0.438	0.486	0.577
8	0.358	0.381	0.411	0.457	0.543
9	0.339	0.360	0.388	0.432	0.514
10	0.322	0.342	0.368	0.410	0.490
11	0.307	0.326	0.352	0.391	0.468
12	0.295	0.313	0.338	0.375	0.450
13	0.284	0.302	0.325	0.361	0.433
14	0.274	0.292	0.314	0.349	0.418
15	0.266	0.283	0.304	0.338	0.404
16	0.258	0.274	0.295	0.328	0.392
17	0.250	0.266	0.286	0.318	0.381
18	0.244	0.259	0.278	0.309	0.371
19	0.237	0.252	0.272	0.301	0.363
20	0.231	0.246	0.264	0.294	0.356
25	0.21	0.22	0.24	0.27	0.32
30	0.19	0.20	0.22	0.24	0.29
35	0.18	0.19	0.21	0.23	0.27
over 35	$\dfrac{1.07}{\sqrt{N}}$	$\dfrac{1.14}{\sqrt{N}}$	$\dfrac{1.22}{\sqrt{N}}$	$\dfrac{1.36}{\sqrt{N}}$	$\dfrac{1.63}{\sqrt{N}}$

TABLE 6

$$\left[\begin{array}{c}\text{Multiserver Poisson-exponential queuing system:}\\\text{Probability that the system is idle, } p_0\end{array}\right]$$

	Number of Channels, s								
$\dfrac{\lambda}{s\mu}$	2	3	4	5	6	7	8	10	15
.02	.9608	.9418	.9231	.9048	.8869	.8694	.85214	.81873	.74082
.04	.9231	.8869	.8521	.8187	.7866	.7558	.72615	.67032	.54881
.06	.8868	.8353	.7866	.7408	.6977	.6570	.61878	.54881	.40657
.08	.8519	.7866	.7261	.6703	.6188	.5712	.52729	.44933	.30119
.10	.8182	.7407	.6703	.6065	.5488	.4966	.44933	.36788	.22313
.12	.7857	.6975	.6188	.5488	.4868	.4317	.38289	.30119	.16530
.14	.7544	.6568	.5712	.4966	.4317	.3753	.32628	.24660	.12246
.16	.7241	.6184	.5272	.4493	.3829	.3263	.27804	.20190	.09072
.18	.6949	.5821	.4866	.4065	.3396	.2837	.23693	.16530	.06721
.20	.6667	.5479	.4491	.3678	.3012	.2466	.20189	.13534	.04979
.22	.6393	.5157	.4145	.3328	.2671	.2144	.17204	.11080	.03688
.24	.6129	.4852	.3824	.3011	.2369	.1864	.14660	.09072	.02732
.26	.5873	.4564	.3528	.2723	.2101	.1620	.12492	.07427	.02024
.28	.5625	.4292	.3255	.2463	.1863	.1408	.10645	.06081	.01500
.30	.5385	.4035	.3002	.2228	.1652	.1224	.09070	.04978	.01111
.32	.5152	.3791	.2768	.2014	.1464	.1064	.07728	.04076	.00823
.34	.4925	.3561	.2551	.1821	.1298	.0925	.06584	.03337	.00610
.36	.4706	.3343	.2351	.1646	.1151	.0804	.05609	.02732	.00452
.38	.4493	.3137	.2165	.1487	.1020	.0698	.04778	.02236	.00335
.40	.4286	.2941	.1993	.1343	.0903	.0606	.04069	.01830	.00248

.42	.4085	.2756	.1834	.1213	.0800	.0527	.03465	.01498	.00184
.44	.3889	.2580	.1686	.1094	.0708	.0457	.02950	.01226	.00136
.46	.3699	.2414	.1549	.0987	.0626	.0397	.02511	.01003	.00101
.48	.3514	.2255	.1422	.0889	.0554	.0344	.02136	.00820	.00075
.50	.3333	.2105	.1304	.0801	.049	.0298	.01816	.00671	.00055
.52	.3158	.1963	.1195	.0721	.0432	.0259	.01544	.00548	.00041
.54	.2987	.1827	.1094	.0648	.0831	.0224	.01311	.00448	.00030
.56	.2821	.1699	.0999	.0581	.0336	.0194	.01113	.00366	.00022
.58	.2658	.1576	.0912	.0521	.0296	.0167	.00943	.00298	.00017
.60	.2500	.1460	.0831	.0466	.0260	.0144	.00799	.00243	.00012
.62	.2346	.1349	.0755	.0417	.0228	.0124	.00675	.00198	.00009
.64	.2195	.1244	.0685	.0372	.0200	.0107	.00570	.00161	.00007
.66	.2048	.1143	.0619	.0330	.0175	.0092	.00480	.00131	.00005
.68	.1905	.1048	.0559	.0293	.0152	.0079	.00404	.00106	.00004
.70	.1765	.0957	.0502	.0259	.0132	.0067	.00338	.00085	.00003
.72	.1628	.0870	.0450	.0228	.0114	.0057	.00283	.00069	.00002
.74	.1494	.0788	.0401	.0200	.0099	.0048	.00235	.00055	.00001
.76	.1364	.0709	.0355	.0174	.0085	.0041	.00195	.00044	
.78	.1236	.0634	.0313	.0151	.0072	.0034	.00160	.00035	
.80	.1111	.0562	.0273	.013	.0061	.0028	.00131	.00028	
.82	.0989	.0493	.0236	.0111	.0051	.0023	.00106	.00022	
.84	.0870	.0428	.0202	.0093	.0042	.0019	.00085	.00017	
.86	.0753	.0366	.0170	.0077	.0035	.0015	.00067	.00013	
.88	.0638	.0306	.0140	.0063	.0028	.0012	.00052	.00010	
.90	.0526	.0249	.0113	.0050	.0021	.0009	.00039	.00007	
.92	.0417	.0195	.0087	.0038	.0016	.0007	.00028	.00005	
.94	.0309	.0143	.0063	.0027	.0011	.0005	.00019	.00003	
.96	.0204	.0093	.0040	.0017	.0007	.0003	.00012	.00002	
.98	.0101	.0045	.0019	.0008	.0003	.0001	.00005	.00001	

TABLE 7

[Random numbers]

04433	80674	24520	18222	10610	05794	37515
60298	47829	72648	37414	75755	04717	29899
67884	59651	67533	68123	17730	95862	08034
89512	32155	51906	61662	64130	16688	37275
32653	01895	12506	88535	36553	23757	34209
95913	15405	13772	76638	48423	25018	99041
55864	21694	13122	44115	01601	50541	00147
35334	49810	91601	40617	72876	33967	73830
57729	32196	76487	11622	96297	24160	09903
86648	13697	63677	70119	94739	25875	38829
30574	47609	07967	32422	76791	39725	53711
81307	43694	83580	79974	45929	85113	72268
02410	54905	79007	54939	21410	86980	91772
18969	75274	52233	62319	08598	09066	95288
87863	82384	66860	62297	80198	19347	73234
68397	71708	15438	62311	72844	60203	46412
28529	54447	58729	10854	99058	18260	38765
44285	06372	15867	70418	57012	72122	36634
86299	83430	33571	23309	57010	29285	67870
84842	68668	90894	61658	15001	94055	36308
56970	83609	52098	04184	54967	72938	56834
83125	71257	60490	44369	66130	72936	69848
55503	52423	02464	26141	68779	66388	75242
47019	76273	33203	29608	54553	25971	69573
84828	32592	79526	29554	84580	37859	28504
68921	08141	79227	05748	51270	57143	31926
36458	96045	30424	98420	72925	40729	22337
95752	59445	36847	87729	81679	59126	59437
26768	47323	58454	56958	20575	76740	49878
42613	37056	43636	58085	06766	60227	96414
95457	30566	65482	25596	02678	54592	63607
95276	17894	63564	95958	39750	04379	46059
66954	52324	64776	92345	95110	59448	77249
17457	18481	14113	62462	02798	54977	48349
03704	36872	83214	59337	01695	60666	97410
21538	86497	33210	60337	27976	70661	08250
57178	67619	98310	70348	11317	71623	55510
31048	97558	94953	55866	96283	46620	52087
69799	55380	16498	80733	96422	58078	99643
90595	61867	59231	17772	67831	33317	00520
33570	04981	98939	78784	09977	29398	93896
15340	93460	57477	13898	48431	72936	78160
64079	42483	36512	56186	99098	48850	72527
63491	05546	67118	62063	74958	20946	28147
92003	63868	41034	28260	79708	00770	88643
52360	46658	66511	04172	73085	11795	52594
74622	12142	68355	65635	21828	39539	18988
04157	50079	61343	64315	70836	82857	35335
86003	60070	66241	32836	27573	11479	94114
41268	80187	20351	09636	84668	42486	71303

Random numbers

48611	62866	33963	14045	79451	04934	45576
78812	03509	78673	73181	29973	18664	04555
19472	63971	37271	31445	49019	49405	46925
51266	11569	08697	91120	64156	40365	74297
55806	96275	26130	47949	14877	69594	83041
77527	81360	18180	97421	55541	90275	18213
77680	58788	33016	61173	93049	04694	43534
15404	96554	88265	34537	38526	67924	40474
14045	22917	60718	66487	46346	30949	03173
68376	43918	77653	04127	69930	43283	35766
93385	13421	67957	20384	58731	53396	59723
09858	52104	32014	53115	03727	98624	84616
93307	34116	49516	42148	57740	31198	70336
04794	01534	92058	03157	91758	80611	45357
86265	49096	97021	92582	61422	75890	86442
65943	79232	45702	67055	39024	57383	44424
90038	94209	04055	27393	61517	23002	96560
97283	95943	78363	36498	40662	94188	18202
21913	72958	75637	99936	58715	07943	23748
41161	37341	81838	19389	80336	46346	91895
23777	98392	31417	98547	92058	02277	50315
59973	08144	61070	73094	27059	69181	55623
82690	74099	77885	23813	10054	11900	44653
83854	24715	48866	65745	31131	47636	45137
61980	34997	41825	11623	07320	15003	56774
99915	45821	97702	87125	44488	77613	56823
48293	86847	43186	42951	37804	85129	28993
33225	31280	41232	34750	91097	60752	69783
06846	32828	24425	30249	78801	26977	92074
32671	45587	79620	84831	38156	74211	82752
82096	21913	75544	55228	89796	05694	91552
51666	10433	10945	55306	78562	89630	41230
54044	67942	24145	42294	27427	84875	37022
66738	60184	75679	38120	17640	36242	99357
55064	17427	89180	74018	44865	53197	74810
69599	60264	84549	78007	88450	06488	72274
64756	87759	92354	78694	63638	80939	98644
80817	74533	68407	55862	32476	19326	95558
39847	96884	84657	33697	39578	90197	80532
90401	41700	95510	61166	33757	23279	85523
78227	90110	81378	96659	37008	04050	04228
87240	52716	87697	79433	16336	52862	69149
08486	10951	26832	39763	02485	71688	90936
39338	32169	03713	93510	61244	73774	01245
21188	01850	69689	49426	49128	14660	14143
13287	82531	04388	64693	11934	35051	68576
53609	04001	19648	14053	49623	10840	31915
87900	36194	31567	53506	34304	39910	79630
81641	00496	36058	75899	46620	70024	88753
19512	50277	71508	20116	79520	06269	74173

Random numbers

24418	28508	91507	76455	54941	72711	39406
57404	73678	08272	62941	02349	71389	45605
77644	98489	86268	73652	98210	44546	27174
68366	65614	01443	07607	11826	91326	29664
64472	72294	95432	53555	96810	17100	35066
88205	37913	98633	81009	81060	33449	68055
98455	78685	71250	10329	56135	80647	51404
48977	36794	56054	50243	57361	65304	93258
93077	72941	92779	23581	24548	56415	61027
84533	26564	91583	83411	66504	02036	02922
11338	12903	14514	27585	45068	05520	56321
23853	68500	92274	87026	99717	01542	72090
94096	74920	25822	98026	05394	61840	83089
83160	82362	09350	98536	38155	42661	02363
97425	47335	69709	01386	74319	04318	99387
83951	11954	24317	20345	18134	90062	10761
93085	35203	05740	03206	92012	42710	34650
33762	83193	58045	89880	78101	44392	53767
49665	85397	85137	30106	23409	42846	94810
37541	82627	80051	72521	35342	56119	97190
22145	85304	35348	82854	55846	18076	12415
27153	08662	61078	52433	22184	33998	87436
00301	49425	66682	25442	83668	66236	79655
43815	43272	73778	63460	50083	70096	13558
14689	86482	74157	46012	97765	27552	40617
16680	55936	82453	19532	49988	13176	94219
86938	60429	01137	86168	78257	86249	46134
33944	29219	73161	46061	30946	22210	79302
16045	67736	18608	18198	10468	70358	60203
37044	52523	25627	63107	30806	80857	84383
61471	45322	35340	35132	42163	60332	98851
47422	21296	16785	66303	30249	51463	95963
24133	39719	14484	58613	88717	29289	77360
67253	67064	10748	16006	16767	57345	42285
62382	76941	01635	35829	77516	98468	51686
98011	16503	09201	03523	87192	60483	55649
37366	24386	20654	85117	74078	64120	04643
73587	83993	54176	06221	94119	20108	78101
33583	68291	50547	96085	62180	27453	18567
02878	33223	39109	49536	56199	05993	71201
91498	41673	17195	33175	04904	09879	70337
91127	19815	30219	55591	21725	43827	78862
12997	55013	18662	81724	24305	37661	18956
96098	13651	15393	69995	14762	69734	89150
97627	17837	10472	18983	28387	99781	52977
40064	47981	31484	76603	54088	91095	00010
16239	68743	71374	55863	22672	91609	51514
58354	24913	20435	30965	17453	65623	93058
52567	65085	60220	84641	18273	49604	47418
06236	29052	91392	07551	83532	68130	56970

Random numbers

94620	27963	96478	21559	19246	88097	44926
60947	60775	73181	43264	56895	04232	59604
27499	53523	63110	57106	20865	91683	80688
01603	23156	89223	43429	95353	44662	59433
00815	01552	06392	31437	70385	45863	75971
83844	90942	74857	52419	68723	47830	63010
06626	10042	93629	37609	57215	08409	81906
56760	63348	24949	11859	29793	37457	59377
64416	29934	00755	09418	14230	62887	92683
63569	17906	38076	32135	19096	96970	75917
22693	35089	72994	04252	23791	60249	83010
43413	59744	01275	71326	91382	45114	20245
09224	78530	50566	49965	04851	18280	14039
67625	34683	03142	74733	63558	09665	22610
86874	12549	98699	54952	91579	26023	81076
54548	49505	62515	63903	13193	33905	66936
73236	66167	49728	03581	40699	10396	81827
15220	66319	13543	14071	59148	95154	72852
16151	08029	36954	03891	38313	34016	18671
43635	84249	88984	80993	55431	90793	62603
30193	42776	85611	57635	51362	79907	77364
37430	45246	11400	20986	43996	73122	88474
88312	93047	12088	86937	70794	01041	74867
98995	58159	04700	90443	13168	31553	67891
51734	20849	70198	67906	00880	82899	66065
88698	41755	56216	66852	17748	04963	54859
51865	09836	73966	65711	41699	11732	17173
40300	08852	27528	84648	79589	95295	72895
02760	28625	70476	76410	32988	10194	94917
78450	26245	91763	73117	33047	03577	62599
50252	56911	62693	73817	98693	18728	94741
07929	66728	47761	81472	44806	15592	71357
09030	39605	87507	85446	51257	89555	75520
56670	88445	85799	76200	21795	38894	58070
48140	13583	94911	13318	64741	64336	95103
36764	86132	12463	28385	94242	32063	45233
14351	71381	28133	68269	65145	28152	39087
81276	00835	63835	87174	42446	08882	27067
55524	86088	00069	59254	24654	77371	26409
78852	65889	32719	13758	23937	90740	16866
11861	69032	51915	23510	32050	52052	24004
67699	01009	07050	73324	06732	27510	33761
50064	39500	17450	18030	63124	48061	59412
93126	17700	94400	76075	08317	27324	72723
01657	92602	41043	05686	15650	29970	95877
13800	76690	75133	60456	28491	03845	11507
98135	42870	48578	29036	69876	86563	61729
08313	99293	00990	13595	77457	79969	11339
90974	83965	62732	85161	54330	22406	86253
33273	61993	88407	69399	17301	70975	99129

TABLE 8

[Squares and square roots]

n	n^2	$\sqrt{n}$	$\sqrt{10n}$	n	n^2	$\sqrt{n}$	$\sqrt{10n}$
1.00	1.0000	1.000000	3.162278	1.50	2.2500	1.224745	3.872983
1.01	1.0201	1.004988	3.178050	1.51	2.2801	1.228821	3.885872
1.02	1.0404	1.009950	3.193744	1.52	2.3104	1.232883	3.898718
1.03	1.0609	1.014889	3.209361	1.53	2.3409	1.236932	3.911521
1.04	1.0816	1.019804	3.224903	1.54	2.3716	1.240967	3.924283
1.05	1.1025	1.024695	3.240370	1.55	2.4025	1.244990	3.937004
1.06	1.1236	1.029563	3.255764	1.56	2.4336	1.249000	3.949684
1.07	1.1449	1.034408	3.271085	1.57	2.4649	1.252996	3.962323
1.08	1.1664	1.039230	3.286335	1.58	2.4964	1.256981	3.974921
1.09	1.1881	1.044031	3.301515	1.59	2.5281	1.260952	3.987480
1.10	1.2100	1.048809	3.316625	1.60	2.5600	1.264911	4.000000
1.11	1.2321	1.053565	3.331666	1.61	2.5921	1.268858	4.012481
1.12	1.2544	1.058301	3.346640	1.62	2.6244	1.272792	4.024922
1.13	1.2769	1.063015	3.361547	1.63	2.6569	1.276715	4.037326
1.14	1.2996	1.067708	3.376389	1.64	2.6896	1.280625	4.049691
1.15	1.3225	1.072381	3.391165	1.65	2.7225	1.284523	4.062019
1.16	1.3456	1.077033	3.405877	1.66	2.7556	1.288410	4.074310
1.17	1.3689	1.081665	3.420526	1.67	2.7889	1.292285	4.086563
1.18	1.3924	1.086278	3.435113	1.68	2.8224	1.296148	4.098780
1.19	1.4161	1.090871	3.449638	1.69	2.8561	1.300000	4.110961
1.20	1.4400	1.095445	3.464102	1.70	2.8900	1.303840	4.123106
1.21	1.4641	1.100000	3.478505	1.71	2.9241	1.307670	4.135215
1.22	1.4884	1.104536	3.492850	1.72	2.9584	1.311488	4.147288
1.23	1.5129	1.109054	3.507136	1.73	2.9929	1.315295	4.159327
1.24	1.5376	1.113553	3.521363	1.74	3.0276	1.319091	4.171331
1.25	1.5625	1.118034	3.535534	1.75	3.0625	1.322876	4.183300
1.26	1.5876	1.122497	3.549648	1.76	3.0976	1.326650	4.195235
1.27	1.6129	1.126943	3.563706	1.77	3.1329	1.330413	4.207137
1.28	1.6384	1.131371	3.577709	1.78	3.1684	1.334166	4.219005
1.29	1.6641	1.135782	3.591657	1.79	3.2041	1.337909	4.230839
1.30	1.6900	1.140175	3.605551	1.80	3.2400	1.341641	4.242641
1.31	1.7161	1.144552	3.619392	1.81	3.2761	1.345362	4.254409
1.32	1.7424	1.148913	3.633180	1.82	3.3124	1.349074	4.266146
1.33	1.7689	1.153256	3.646917	1.83	3.3489	1.352775	4.277850
1.34	1.7956	1.157584	3.660601	1.84	3.3856	1.356466	4.289522
1.35	1.8225	1.161895	3.674235	1.85	3.4225	1.360147	4.301163
1.36	1.8496	1.166190	3.687818	1.86	3.4590	1.363818	4.312772
1.37	1.8769	1.170470	3.701351	1.87	3.4969	1.367479	4.324350
1.38	1.9044	1.174734	3.714835	1.88	3.5344	1.371131	4.335897
1.39	1.9321	1.178983	3.728270	1.89	3.5721	1.374773	4.347413
1.40	1.9600	1.183216	3.741657	1.90	3.6100	1.378405	4.358899
1.41	1.9881	1.187434	3.754997	1.91	3.6481	1.382027	4.370355
1.42	2.0164	1.191638	3.768289	1.92	3.6864	1.385641	4.381780
1.43	2.0449	1.195826	3.781534	1.93	3.7249	1.389244	4.393177
1.44	2.0736	1.200000	3.794733	1.94	3.7636	1.392839	4.404543
1.45	2.1025	1.204159	3.807887	1.95	3.8025	1.396424	4.415880
1.46	2.1316	1.208305	3.820995	1.96	3.8416	1.400000	4.427189
1.47	2.1609	1.212436	3.834058	1.97	3.8809	1.403567	4.438468
1.48	2.1904	1.216553	3.847077	1.98	3.9204	1.407125	4.449719
1.49	2.2201	1.220656	3.860052	1.99	3.9601	1.410674	4.460942

Squares and square roots

n	n^2	$\sqrt{n}$	$\sqrt{10n}$	n	n^2	$\sqrt{n}$	$\sqrt{10n}$
2.00	4.0000	1.414214	4.472136	2.50	6.2500	1.581139	5.000000
2.01	4.0401	1.417745	4.483302	2.51	6.3001	1.584298	5.009990
2.02	4.0804	1.421267	4.494441	2.52	6.3504	1.587451	5.019960
2.03	4.1209	1.424781	4.505552	2.53	6.4009	1.590597	5.029911
2.04	4.1616	1.428286	4.516636	2.54	6.4516	1.593738	5.039841
2.05	4.2025	1.431782	4.527693	2.55	6.5025	1.596872	5.049752
2.06	4.2436	1.435270	4.538722	2.56	6.5536	1.600000	5.059644
2.07	4.2849	1.438749	4.549725	2.57	6.6049	1.603122	5.069517
2.08	4.3264	1.442221	4.560702	2.58	6.6564	1.606238	5.079370
2.09	4.3681	1.445683	4.571652	2.59	6.7081	1.609348	5.089204
2.10	4.4100	1.449138	4.582576	2.60	6.7600	1.612452	5.099020
2.11	4.4521	1.452584	4.593474	2.61	6.8121	1.615549	5.108816
2.12	4.4944	1.456022	4.604346	2.62	6.8644	1.618641	5.118594
2.13	4.5369	1.459452	4.615192	2.63	6.9169	1.621727	5.128353
2.14	4.5796	1.462874	4.626013	2.64	6.9696	1.624808	5.138093
2.15	4.6225	1.466288	4.636809	2.65	7.0225	1.627882	5.147815
2.16	4.6656	1.469694	4.647580	2.66	7.0756	1.630951	5.157519
2.17	4.7089	1.473092	4.658326	2.67	7.1289	1.634013	5.167204
2.18	4.7524	1.476482	4.669047	2.68	7.1824	1.637071	5.176872
2.19	4.7961	1.479865	4.679744	2.69	7.2361	1.640122	5.186521
2.20	4.8400	1.483240	4.690416	2.70	7.2900	1.643168	5.196152
2.21	4.8841	1.486607	4.701064	2.71	7.3441	1.646208	5.205766
2.22	4.9284	1.489966	4.711688	2.72	7.3984	1.649242	5.215362
2.23	4.9729	1.493318	4.722288	2.73	7.4529	1.652271	5.224940
2.24	5.0176	1.496663	4.732864	2.74	7.5076	1.655295	5.234501
2.25	5.0625	1.500000	4.743416	2.75	7.5625	1.658312	5.244044
2.26	5.1076	1.503330	4.753946	2.76	7.6176	1.661325	5.253570
2.27	5.1529	1.506652	4.764452	2.77	7.6729	1.664332	5.263079
2.28	5.1984	1.509967	4.774935	2.78	7.7284	1.667333	5.272571
2.29	5.2441	1.513275	4.785394	2.79	7.7841	1.670329	5.282045
2.30	5.2900	1.516575	4.795832	2.80	7.8400	1.673320	5.291503
2.31	5.3361	1.519868	4.806246	2.81	7.8961	1.676305	5.300943
2.32	5.3824	1.523155	4.816638	2.82	7.9524	1.679286	5.310367
2.33	5.4289	1.526434	4.827007	2.83	8.0089	1.682260	5.319774
2.34	5.4756	1.529706	4.837355	2.84	8.0656	1.685230	5.329165
2.35	5.5225	1.532971	4.847680	2.85	8.1225	1.688194	5.338539
2.36	5.5696	1.536229	4.857983	2.86	8.1796	1.691153	5.347897
2.37	5.6169	1.539480	4.868265	2.87	8.2369	1.694107	5.357238
2.38	5.6644	1.542725	4.878524	2.88	8.2944	1.697056	5.366563
2.39	5.7121	1.545962	4.888763	2.89	8.3521	1.700000	5.375872
2.40	5.7600	1.549193	4.898979	2.90	8.4100	1.702939	5.385165
2.41	5.8081	1.552417	4.909175	2.91	8.4681	1.705872	5.394442
2.42	5.8564	1.555635	4.919350	2.92	8.5264	1.708801	5.403702
2.43	5.9049	1.558846	4.929503	2.93	8.5849	1.711724	5.412947
2.44	5.9536	1.562050	4.939636	2.94	8.6436	1.714643	5.422177
2.45	6.0025	1.565248	4.949747	2.95	8.7025	1.717556	5.431390
2.46	6.0516	1.568439	4.959839	2.96	8.7616	1.720465	5.440588
2.47	6.1009	1.571623	4.969909	2.97	8.8209	1.723369	5.449771
2.48	6.1504	1.574802	4.979960	2.98	8.8804	1.726268	5.458938
2.49	6.2001	1.577973	4.989990	2.99	8.9401	1.729162	5.468089

n	n^2	$\sqrt{n}$	$\sqrt{10n}$	n	n^2	$\sqrt{n}$	$\sqrt{10n}$
3.00	9.0000	1.732051	5.477226	3.50	12.2500	1.870829	5.916080
3.01	9.0601	1.734935	5.486347	3.51	12.3201	1.873499	5.924525
3.02	9.1204	1.737815	5.495453	3.52	12.3904	1.876166	5.932959
3.03	9.1809	1.740690	5.504544	3.53	12.4609	1.878829	5.941380
3.04	9.2416	1.743560	5.513620	3.54	12.5316	1.881489	5.949790
3.05	9.3025	1.746425	5.522681	3.55	12.6025	1.884144	5.958188
3.06	9.3636	1.749286	5.531727	3.56	12.6736	1.886796	5.966574
3.07	9.4249	1.752142	5.540758	3.57	12.7449	1.889444	5.974948
3.08	9.4864	1.754993	5.549775	3.58	12.8164	1.892089	5.983310
3.09	9.5481	1.757840	5.558777	3.59	12.8881	1.894730	5.991661
3.10	9.6100	1.760682	5.567764	3.60	12.9600	1.897367	6.000000
3.11	9.6721	1.763519	5.576737	3.61	13.0321	1.900000	6.008328
3.12	9.7344	1.766352	5.585696	3.62	13.1044	1.902630	6.016644
3.13	9.7969	1.769181	5.594640	3.63	13.1769	1.905256	6.024948
3.14	9.8596	1.772005	5.603570	3.64	13.2496	1.907878	6.033241
3.15	9.9225	1.774824	5.612486	3.65	13.3225	1.910497	6.041523
3.16	9.9856	1.777639	5.621388	3.66	13.3956	1.913113	6.049793
3.17	10.0489	1.780449	5.630275	3.67	13.4689	1.915724	6.058052
3.18	10.1124	1.783255	5.639149	3.68	13.5424	1.918333	6.066300
3.19	10.1761	1.786057	5.648008	3.69	13.6161	1.920937	6.074537
3.20	10.2400	1.788854	5.656854	3.70	13.6900	1.923538	6.082763
3.21	10.3041	1.791647	5.665686	3.71	13.7641	1.926136	6.090977
3.22	10.3684	1.794436	5.674504	3.72	13.8384	1.928730	6.099180
3.23	10.4329	1.797220	5.683309	3.73	13.9129	1.931321	6.107373
3.24	10.4976	1.800000	5.692100	3.74	13.9876	1.933908	6.115554
3.25	10.5625	1.802776	5.700877	3.75	14.0625	1.936492	6.123724
3.26	10.6276	1.805547	5.709641	3.76	14.1376	1.939072	6.131884
3.27	10.6929	1.808314	5.718391	3.77	14.2129	1.941649	6.140033
3.28	10.7584	1.811077	5.727128	3.78	14.2884	1.944222	6.148170
3.29	10.8241	1.813836	5.735852	3.79	14.3641	1.946792	6.156298
3.30	10.8900	1.816590	5.744563	3.80	14.4400	1.949359	6.164414
3.31	10.9561	1.819341	5.753260	3.81	14.5161	1.951922	6.172520
3.32	11.0224	1.822087	5.761944	3.82	14.5924	1.954483	6.180615
3.33	11.0889	1.824829	5.770615	3.83	14.6689	1.957039	6.188699
3.34	11.1556	1.827567	5.779273	3.84	14.7456	1.959592	6.196773
3.35	11.2225	1.830301	5.787918	3.85	14.8225	1.962142	6.204837
3.36	11.2896	1.833030	5.796551	3.86	14.8996	1.964688	6.212890
3.37	11.3569	1.835756	5.805170	3.87	14.9769	1.967232	6.220932
3.38	11.4244	1.838478	5.813777	3.88	15.0544	1.969772	6.228965
3.39	11.4921	1.841195	5.822371	3.89	15.1321	1.972308	6.236986
3.40	11.5600	1.843909	5.830952	3.90	15.2100	1.974842	6.244998
3.41	11.6281	1.846619	5.839521	3.91	15.2881	1.977372	6.252999
3.42	11.6964	1.849324	5.848077	3.92	15.3664	1.979899	5.260990
3.43	11.7649	1.852026	5.856620	3.93	15.4449	1.982423	6.268971
3.44	11.8336	1.854724	5.865151	3.94	15.5236	1.984943	6.276942
3.45	11.9025	1.857418	5.873670	3.95	15.6025	1.987461	6.284903
3.46	11.9716	1.860108	5.882176	3.96	15.6816	1.989975	6.292853
3.47	12.0409	1.862794	5.890671	3.97	15.7609	1.992486	6.300794
3.48	12.1104	1.865476	5.899152	3.98	15.8404	1.994994	6.308724
3.49	12.1801	1.868154	5.907622	3.99	15.9201	1.997498	6.316645

n	n^2	$\sqrt{n}$	$\sqrt{10n}$	n	n^2	$\sqrt{n}$	$\sqrt{10n}$
4.00	16.0000	2.000000	6.324555	4.50	20.2500	2.121320	6.708204
4.01	16.0801	2.002498	6.332456	4.51	20.3401	2.123676	6.715653
4.02	16.1604	2.004994	6.340347	4.52	20.4304	2.126029	6.723095
4.03	16.2409	2.007486	6.348228	4.53	20.5209	2.128380	6.730527
4.04	16.3216	2.009975	6.356099	4.54	20.6116	2.130728	6.737952
4.05	16.4025	2.012461	6.363961	4.55	20.7025	2.133073	6.745369
4.06	16.4836	2.014944	6.371813	4.56	20.7936	2.135416	6.752777
4.07	16.5649	2.017424	6.379655	4.57	20.8849	2.137756	6.760178
4.08	16.6464	2.019901	6.387488	4.58	20.9764	2.140093	6.767570
4.09	16.7281	2.022375	6.395311	4.59	21.0681	2.142429	6.774954
4.10	16.8100	2.024846	6.403124	4.60	21.1600	2.144761	6.782330
4.11	16.8921	20.27313	6.410928	4.61	21.2521	2.147091	6.789698
4.12	16.9744	2.029778	6.418723	4.62	21.3444	2.149419	6.797058
4.13	17.0569	2.032240	6.426508	4.63	21.4369	2.151743	6.804410
4.14	17.1396	2.034699	6.434283	4.64	21.5296	2.154066	6.811755
4.15	17.2225	2.037155	6.442049	4.65	21.6225	2.156386	6.819091
4.16	17.3056	2.039608	6.449806	4.66	21.7156	2.158703	6.826419
4.17	17.3889	2.042058	6.457554	4.67	21.8089	2.161018	6.833740
4.18	17.4724	2.044505	6.465292	4.68	21.9024	2.163331	6.841053
4.19	17.5561	2.046949	6.473021	4.69	21.9961	2.165641	6.848357
4.20	17.6400	2.049390	6.480741	4.70	22.0900	2.167948	6.855655
4.21	17.7241	2.051828	6.488451	4.71	22.1841	2.170253	6.862944
4.22	17.8084	2.054264	6.496153	4.72	22.2784	2.172556	6.870226
4.23	17.8929	2.056696	6.503845	4.73	22.3729	2.174856	6.877500
4.24	17.9776	2.059126	6.511528	4.74	22.4676	2.177154	6.884766
4.25	18.0625	2.061553	6.519202	4.75	22.5625	2.179449	6.892024
4.26	18.1476	2.063977	6.526868	4.76	22.6576	2.181742	6.899275
4.27	18.2329	2.066398	6.534524	4.77	22.7529	2.184033	6.906519
4.28	18.3184	2.068816	6.542171	4.78	22.8484	2.186321	6.913754
4.29	18.4041	2.071232	6.549809	4.79	22.9441	2.188607	6.920983
4.30	18.4900	2.073644	6.557439	4.80	23.0400	2.190890	6.928203
4.31	18.5761	2.076054	6.565059	4.81	23.1361	2.193171	6.935416
4.32	18.6624	2.078461	6.572671	4.82	23.2324	2.195450	6.942622
4.33	18.7489	2.080865	6.580274	4.83	23.3289	2.197726	6.949820
4.34	18.8356	2.083267	6.587868	4.84	23.4256	2.200000	6.957011
4.35	18.9225	2.085665	6.595453	4.85	23.5225	2.202272	6.964194
4.36	19.0096	2.088061	6.603030	4.86	23.6196	2.204541	6.971370
4.37	19.0969	2.090454	6.610598	4.87	23.7169	2.206808	6.978539
4.38	19.1844	2.092845	6.618157	4.88	23.8144	2.209072	6.985700
4.39	19.2721	2.095233	6.625708	4.89	23.9121	2.211334	6.992853
4.40	19.3600	2.097618	6.633250	4.90	24.0100	2.213594	7.000000
4.41	19.4481	2.100000	6.640783	4.91	24.1081	2.215852	7.007139
4.42	19.5364	2.102380	6.648308	4.92	24.2064	2.218107	7.014271
4.43	19.6249	2.104757	6.655825	4.93	24.3049	2.220360	7.021396
4.44	19.7136	2.107131	6.663332	4.94	24.4036	2.222611	7.028513
4.45	19.8025	2.109502	6.670832	4.95	24.5025	2.224860	7.035624
4.46	19.8916	2.111871	6.678323	4.96	24.6016	2.227106	7.042727
4.47	19.9809	2.114237	6.685806	4.97	24.7009	2.229350	7.049823
4.48	20.0704	2.116601	6.693280	4.98	24.8004	2.231591	7.056912
4.49	20.1601	2.118962	6.700746	4.99	24.9001	2.233831	7.063993

Squares and square roots

n	n^2	$\sqrt{n}$	$\sqrt{10n}$	n	n^2	$\sqrt{n}$	$\sqrt{10n}$
5.00	25.0000	2.236068	7.071068	5.50	30.2500	2.345208	7.416198
5.01	25.1001	2.238303	7.078135	5.51	30.3601	2.347339	7.422937
5.02	25.2004	2.240536	7.085196	5.52	30.4704	2.349468	7.429670
5.03	25.3009	2.242766	7.092249	5.53	30.5809	2.351595	7.436397
5.04	25.4016	2.244994	7.099296	5.54	30.6916	2.353720	7.443118
5.05	25.5025	2.247221	7.106335	5.55	30.8025	2.355844	7.449832
5 06	25.6036	2.249444	7.113368	5.56	30.9136	2.357965	7.456541
5.07	25.7049	2.251666	7.120393	5.57	31.0249	2.360085	7.463243
5.08	25.8064	2.253886	7.127412	5.58	31.1364	2.362202	7.469940
5.09	25.9081	2.256103	7.134424	5.59	31.2481	2.364318	7.476630
5.10	26.0100	2.258318	7.141428	5.60	31.3600	2.366432	7.483315
5.11	26.1121	2.260531	7.148426	5.61	31.4721	2.368544	7.489993
5.12	26.2144	2.262742	7.155418	5.62	31.5844	2.370654	7.496666
5.13	26.3169	2.264950	7.162402	5.63	31.6969	2.372762	7.503333
5.14	26.4196	2.267157	7.169379	5.64	31.8096	2.374868	7.509993
5.15	26.5225	2.269361	7.176350	5.65	31.9225	2.376973	7.516648
5.16	26.6256	2.271563	7.183314	5.66	32.0356	2.379075	7.523207
5.17	26.7289	2.273763	7.190271	5.67	32.1489	2.381176	7.529940
5.18	26.8324	2.275961	7.197222	5.68	32.2624	2.383275	7.536577
5.19	26.9361	2.278157	7.204165	5.69	32.3761	2.385372	7.543209
5.20	27.0400	2.280351	7.211103	5.70	32.4900	2.387467	7.549834
5.21	27.1441	2.282542	7.218033	5.71	32.6041	2.389561	7.556454
5.22	27.2484	2.284732	7.224957	5.72	32.7184	2.391652	7.563068
5.23	27.3529	2.286919	7.231874	5.73	32.8329	2.393742	7.569676
5.24	27.4576	2.289105	7.238784	5.74	32.9476	2.395830	7.576279
5.25	27.5625	2.291288	7.245688	5.75	33.0625	2.397916	7.582875
5.26	27.6676	2.293469	7.252586	5.76	33.1776	2.400000	7.589466
5.27	27.7729	2.295648	7.259477	5.77	33.2929	2.402082	7.596052
5.28	27 8784	2.297825	7.266361	5.78	33.4084	2.404163	7.602631
5.29	27.9841	2.300000	7.273239	5.79	33.5241	2.406242	7.609205
5.30	28.0900	2.302173	7.280110	5.80	33.6400	2.408319	7.615773
5.31	28.1961	2.304344	7.286975	5.81	33.7561	2.410394	7.622336
5.32	28.3024	2.306513	7.293833	5.82	33.8724	2.412468	7.628892
5.33	28.4089	2.308679	7.300685	5.83	33.9889	2.414539	7.635444
5.34	28.5156	2.310844	7.307530	5.84	34.1056	2.416609	7.641989
5.35	28.6225	2.313007	7.314369	5.85	34.2225	2.418677	7.648529
5.36	28.7296	2.315167	7.321202	5.86	34.3396	2.420744	7.655064
5.37	28.8369	2.317326	7.328028	5.87	34.4569	2.422808	7.661593
5.38	28.9444	2.319483	7.334848	5.88	34.5744	2.424871	7.668116
5.39	29.0521	2.321637	7.341662	5.89	34.6921	2.426932	7.674634
5.40	29.1600	2.323790	7.348469	5.90	34.8100	2.428992	7.681146
5.41	29.2681	2.325941	7.355270	5.91	34.9281	2.431049	7.687652
5.42	29.3764	2.328089	7.362065	5.92	35.0464	2.433105	7.694154
5.43	29.4849	2.330236	7.368853	5.93	35.1649	2.435159	7.700649
5.44	29.5936	2.332381	7.357636	5.94	35.2836	2.437212	7.707140
5.45	29.7025	2.334524	7.382412	5.95	35.4025	2.439262	7.713624
5.46	29.8116	2.336664	7.389181	5.96	35.5216	2.441311	7.720104
5.47	29.9209	2.338803	7.395945	5.97	35.6409	2.443358	7.726578
5.48	30.0304	2.340940	7.402702	5.98	35.7604	2.445404	7.733046
5.49	30.1401	2.343075	7.409453	5.99	35.8801	2.447448	7.739509

Squares and square roots

n	n^2	$\sqrt{n}$	$\sqrt{10n}$	n	n^2	$\sqrt{n}$	$\sqrt{10n}$
6.00	36.0000	2.449490	7.745967	6.50	42.2500	2.549510	8.062258
6.01	36.1201	2.451530	7.752419	6.51	42.3801	2.551470	8.068457
6.02	36.2404	2.453569	7.758866	6.52	42.5104	2.553429	8.074652
6.03	36.3609	2.455606	7.765307	6.53	42.6409	2.555386	8.080842
6.04	36.4816	2.457641	7.771744	6.54	42.7716	2.557342	8.087027
6.05	36.6025	2.459675	7.778175	6.55	42.9025	2.559297	8.093207
6.06	36.7236	2.461707	7.784600	6.56	43.0336	2.561250	8.099383
6.07	36.8449	2.463737	7.791020	6.57	43.1649	2.563201	8.105554
6.08	36.9664	2.465766	7.797435	6.58	43.2964	2.565151	8.111720
6.09	37.0881	2.467793	7.803845	6.59	43.4281	2.567100	8.117881
6.10	37.2100	2.469818	7.810250	6.60	43.5600	2.569047	8.124038
6.11	37.3321	2.471841	7.816649	6.61	43.6921	2.570992	8.130191
6.12	37.4544	2.473863	7.823043	6.62	43.8244	2.572936	8.136338
6.13	37.5769	2.475884	7.829432	6.63	43.9569	2.574879	8.142481
6.14	37.6996	2.477902	7.835815	6.64	44.0896	2.576820	8.148620
6.15	37.8225	2.479919	7.842194	6.65	44.2225	2.578759	8.154753
6.16	37.9456	2.481935	7.848567	6.66	44.3556	2.580698	8.160882
6.17	38.0689	2.483948	7.854935	6.67	44.4889	2.582634	8.167007
6.18	38.1924	2.485961	7.861298	6.68	44.6224	2.584570	8.173127
6.19	38.3161	2.487971	7.867655	6.69	44.7561	2.586503	8.179242
6.20	38.4400	2.489980	7.874008	6.70	44.8900	2.588436	8.185353
6.21	38.5641	2.491987	7.880355	6.71	45.0241	2.590367	8.191459
6.22	38.6884	2.493993	7.886698	6.72	45.1584	2.592296	8.197561
6.23	38.8129	2.495997	7.893035	6.73	45.2929	2.594224	8.203658
6.24	38.9376	2.497999	7.899367	6.74	45.4276	2.596151	8.209750
6.25	39.0625	2.500000	7.905694	6.75	45.5625	2.598076	8.215838
6.26	39.1876	2.501999	7.912016	6.76	45.6976	2.600000	8.221922
6.27	39.3129	2.503997	7.918333	6.77	45.8329	2.601922	8.228001
6.28	39.4384	2.505993	7.924645	6.78	45.9684	2.603843	8.234076
6.29	39.5641	2.507987	7.930952	6.79	46.1041	2.605763	8.240146
6.30	39.6900	2.509980	7.937254	6.80	46.2400	2.607681	8.246211
6.31	39.8161	2.511971	7.943551	6.81	46.3761	2.609598	8.242272
6.32	39.9424	2.513961	7.949843	6.82	46.5124	2.611513	8.258329
6.33	40.0689	2.515949	7.956130	6.83	46.6489	2.613427	8.264381
6.34	40.1956	2.517936	7.962412	6.84	46.7856	2.615339	8.270429
6.35	40.3225	2.519921	7.968689	6.85	46.9225	2.617250	8.276473
6.36	40.4496	2.521904	7.974961	6.86	47.0596	2.619160	8.282512
6.37	40.5769	2.523886	7.981228	6.87	47.1969	2.621068	8.288546
6.38	40.7044	2.525866	7.987490	6.88	47.3344	2.622975	8.294577
6.39	40.8321	2.527845	7.993748	6.89	47.4721	2.624881	8.300602
6.40	40.9600	2.529822	8.000000	6.90	47.6100	2.626785	8.306624
6.41	41.0881	2.531798	8.006248	6.91	47.7481	2.628688	8.312641
6.42	41.2164	2.533772	8.012490	6.92	47.8864	2.630589	8.318654
6.43	41.3449	2.535744	8.018728	6.93	48.0249	2.632489	8.324662
6.44	41.4736	2.537716	8.024961	6.94	48.1636	2.634388	8.330666
6.45	41.6025	2.539685	8.031189	6.95	48.3025	2.636285	8.336666
6.46	41.7316	2.541653	8.037413	6.96	48.4416	2.638181	8.342661
6.47	41.8609	2.543619	8.043631	6.97	48.5809	2.640076	8.348653
6.48	41.9904	2.545584	8.049845	6.98	48.7204	2.641969	8.354639
6.49	42.1201	2.547548	8.056054	6.99	48.8601	2.643861	8.360622

Squares and square roots

n	n^2	$\sqrt{n}$	$\sqrt{10n}$	n	n^2	$\sqrt{n}$	$\sqrt{10n}$
7.00	49.0000	2.645751	8.366600	7.50	56.2500	2.738613	8.660254
7.01	49.1401	2.647640	8.372574	7.51	56.4001	2.740438	8.660026
7.02	49.2804	2.649528	8.378544	7.52	56.5504	2.742262	8.671793
7.03	49.4209	2.651415	8.384510	7.53	56.7009	2.744085	8.677557
7.04	49.5616	2.653300	8.390471	7.54	56.8516	2.745906	8.683317
7.05	49.7025	2.655184	8.396428	7.55	57.0025	2.747726	8.689074
7.06	49.8436	2.657066	8.402381	7.56	57.1536	2.749545	8.694826
7.07	49.9849	2.658947	8.408329	7.57	57.3049	2.751363	8.700575
7.08	50.1264	2.660827	8.414274	7.58	57.4564	2.753180	8.706320
7.09	50.2681	2.662705	8.420214	7.59	57.6081	2.754995	8.712061
7.10	50.4100	2.664583	8.426150	7.60	57.7600	2.756810	8.717798
7.11	50.5521	2.666458	8.432082	7.61	57.9121	2.758623	8.723531
7.12	50.6944	2.668333	8.438009	7.62	58.0644	2.760435	8.729261
7.13	50.8369	2.670206	8.443933	7.63	58.2169	2.762245	8.734987
7.14	50.9796	2.672078	8.449852	7.64	58.3696	2.764055	8.740709
7.15	51.1225	2.673948	8.455767	7.65	58.5225	2.765863	8.746428
7.16	51.2656	2.675818	8.461678	7.66	58.6756	2.767671	8.752143
7.17	51.4089	2.677686	8.467585	7.67	58.8289	2.769476	8.757854
7.18	51.5524	2.679552	8.473488	7.68	58.9824	2.771281	8.763561
7.19	51.6961	2.681418	8.479387	7.69	59.1361	2.773085	8.769265
7.20	51.8400	2.683282	8.485281	7.70	59.2900	2.774887	8.774964
7.21	51.9841	2.685144	8.491172	7.71	59.4441	2.776689	8.780661
7.22	52.1284	2.687006	8.497058	7.72	59.5984	2.778489	8.786353
7.23	52.2729	2.688866	8.502941	7.73	59.7529	2.780288	8.792042
7.24	52.4176	2.690725	8.508819	7.74	59.9076	2.782086	8.797727
7.25	52.5625	2.692582	8.514693	7.75	60.0625	2.783882	8.803408
7.26	52.7076	2.694439	8.520563	7.76	60.2176	2.785678	8.809086
7.27	52.8529	2.696294	8.526429	7.77	60.3729	2.787472	8.814760
7.28	52.9984	2.698148	8.532292	7.78	60.5284	2.789265	8.820431
7.29	53.1441	2.700000	8.538150	7.79	60.6841	2.791057	8.826098
7.30	53.2900	2.701851	8.544004	7.80	60.8400	2.792848	8.831761
7.31	53.4361	2.703701	8.549854	7.81	60.9961	2.794638	8.837420
7.32	53.5824	2.705550	8.555700	7.82	61.1524	2.796426	8.843076
7.33	53.7289	2.707397	8.561542	7.83	61.3089	2.798214	8.848729
7.34	53.8756	2.709243	8.567380	7.84	61.4656	2.800000	8.854377
7.35	54.0225	2.711088	8.573214	7.85	61.6225	2.801785	8.860023
7.36	54.1696	2.712932	8.579044	7.86	61.7796	2.803569	8.865664
7.37	54.3169	2.714774	8.584870	7.87	61.9369	2.805352	8.871302
7.38	54.4644	2.716616	8.590693	7.88	62.0944	2.807134	8.876936
7.39	54.6121	2.718455	8.596511	7.89	62.2521	2.808914	8.882567
7.40	54.7600	2.720294	8.602325	7.90	62.4100	2.810694	8.888194
7.41	54.9081	2.722132	8.608136	7.91	62.5681	2.812472	8.893818
7.42	55.0564	2.723968	8.613942	7.92	62.7264	2.814249	8.899438
7.43	55.2049	2.725803	8.619745	7.93	62.8849	2.816026	8.905055
7.44	55.3536	2.727636	8.625543	7.94	63.0436	2.817801	8.910668
7.45	55.5025	2.729469	8.631338	7.95	63.2025	2.819574	8.916277
7.46	55.6516	2.731300	8.637129	7.96	63.3616	2.821347	8.921883
7.47	55.8009	2.733130	8.642916	7.97	63.5209	2.823119	8.927486
7.48	55.9504	2.734959	8.648699	7.98	63.6804	2.824889	8.933085
7.49	56.1001	2.736786	8.654479	7.99	63.8401	2.826659	8.938680

Squares and square roots

n	n^2	$\sqrt{n}$	$\sqrt{10n}$	n	n^2	$\sqrt{n}$	$\sqrt{10n}$
8.00	64.0000	2.828427	8.944272	8.50	72.2500	2.915476	9.219544
8.01	64.1601	2.830194	8.949860	8.51	72.4201	2.917190	9.224966
8.02	64.3204	2.831960	8.955445	8.52	72.5904	2.918904	9.230385
8.03	64.4809	2.833725	8.961027	8.53	72.7609	2.920616	9.235800
8.04	64.6416	2.835489	8.966605	8.54	72.9316	2.922328	9.241212
8.05	64.8025	2.837252	8.972179	8.55	73.1025	2.924038	9.246621
8.06	64.9636	2.839014	8.977750	8.56	73.2736	2.925748	9.252027
8.07	65.1249	2.840775	8.983318	8.57	73.4449	2.927456	9.257429
8.08	65.2864	2.842534	8.988882	8.58	73.6164	2.929164	9.262829
8.09	65.4481	2.844293	8.994443	8.59	73.7881	2.930870	9.268225
8.10	65.6100	2.846050	9.000000	8.60	73.9600	2.932576	9.273618
8.11	65.7721	2.847806	9.005554	8.61	74.1321	2.934280	9.279009
8.12	65.9344	2.849561	9.011104	8.62	74.3044	2.935984	9.284396
8.13	66.0969	2.851315	9.016651	8.63	74.4769	2.937686	9.289779
8.14	66.2596	2.853069	9.022195	8.64	74.6496	2.939388	9.295160
8.15	66.4225	2.854820	9.027735	8.65	74.8225	2.941088	9.300538
8.16	66.5856	2.856571	9.033272	8.66	74.9956	2.942788	9.305912
8.17	66.7489	2.858321	9.038805	8.67	75.1689	2.944486	9.311283
8.18	66.9124	2.860070	9.044335	8.68	75.3424	2.946184	9.316652
8.19	67.0761	2.861818	9.049862	8.69	75.5161	2.947881	9.322017
8.20	67.2400	2.863564	9.055385	8.70	75.6900	2.949576	9.327379
8.21	67.4041	2.865310	9.060905	8.71	75.8641	2.951271	9.332738
8.22	67.5684	2.867054	9.066422	8.72	76.0384	2.952965	9.338094
8.23	67.7329	2.868798	9.071935	8.73	76.2129	2.954657	9.343447
8.24	67.8976	2.870540	9.077445	8.74	76.3876	2.956349	9.348797
8.25	68.0625	2.872281	9.082951	8.75	76.5625	2.958040	9.354143
8.26	68.2276	2.874022	9.088454	8.76	76.7376	2.959730	9.359487
8.27	68.3929	2.875761	9.093954	8.77	76.9129	2.961419	9.364828
8.28	68.5584	2.877499	9.099451	8.78	77.0884	2.963106	9.370165
8.29	68.7241	2.879236	9.104944	8.79	77.2641	2.964793	9.375500
8.30	68.8900	2.880972	9.110434	8.80	77.4400	2.966479	9.380832
8.31	69.0561	2.882707	9.115920	8.81	77.6161	2.968164	9.386160
8.32	69.2224	2.884441	9.121403	8.82	77.7924	2.969848	9.391486
8.33	69.3889	2.886174	9.126883	8.83	77.9689	2.971532	9.396808
8.34	69.5556	2.887906	9.132360	8.84	78.1456	2.973214	9.402127
8.35	69.7225	2.889637	9.137833	8.85	78.3225	2.974895	9.407444
8.36	69.8896	2.891366	9.143304	8.86	78.4996	2.976575	9.412757
8.37	70.0569	2.893095	9.148770	8.87	78.6769	2.978255	9.418068
8.38	70.2244	2.894823	9.154234	8.88	78.8544	2.979933	9.423375
8.39	70.3921	2.896550	9.159694	8.89	79.0321	2.981610	9.428680
8.40	70.5600	2.898275	9.165151	8.90	79.2100	2.983287	9.433981
8.41	70.7281	2.900000	9.170605	8.91	79.3881	2.984962	9.439280
8.42	70.8964	2.901724	9.176056	8.92	79.5664	2.986637	9.444575
8.43	71.0649	2.903446	9.181503	8.93	79.7449	2.988311	9.449868
8.44	71.2336	2.905168	9.186947	8.94	79.9236	2.989983	9.455157
8.45	71.4025	2.906888	9.192388	8.95	80.1025	2.991655	9.460444
8.46	71.5716	2.908608	9.197826	8.96	80.2816	2.993326	9.465728
8.47	71.7409	2.910326	9.203260	8.97	80.4609	2.994996	9.471008
8.48	71.9104	2.912044	9.208692	8.98	80.6404	2.996665	9.476286
8.49	72.0801	2.913760	9.214120	8.99	80.8201	2.998333	9.481561

Squares and square roots

n	n^2	$\sqrt{n}$	$\sqrt{10n}$	n	n^2	$\sqrt{n}$	$\sqrt{10n}$
9.00	81.0000	3.000000	9.486833	9.50	90.2500	3.082207	9.746794
9.01	81.1801	3.001666	9.492102	9.51	90.4401	3.083829	9.751923
9.02	81.3604	3.003331	9.497368	9.52	90.6304	3.085450	9.757049
9.03	81.5409	3.004996	9.502631	9.53	90.8209	3.087070	9.762172
9.04	81.7216	3.006659	9.507891	9.54	91.0116	3.088689	9.767292
9.05	81.9025	3.008322	9.513149	9.55	91.2025	3.090307	9.772410
9.06	82.0836	3.009983	9.518403	9.56	91.3936	3.091925	9.777525
9.07	82.2649	3.011644	9.523655	9.57	91.5849	3.093542	9.782638
9.08	82.4464	3.013304	9.528903	9.58	91.7764	3.095158	9.787747
9.09	82.6281	3.014963	9.534149	9.59	91.9681	3.096773	9.792855
9.10	82.8100	3.016621	9.539392	9.60	92.1600	3.098387	9.797959
9.11	82.9921	3.018278	9.544632	9.61	92.3521	3.100000	9.803061
9.12	83.1744	3.019934	9.549869	9.62	92.5444	3.101612	9.808160
9.13	83.3569	3.021589	9.555103	9.63	92.7369	3.103224	9.813256
9.14	83.5396	3.023243	9.560335	9.64	92.9296	3.104835	9.818350
9.15	83.7225	3.024897	9.565563	9.65	93.1225	3.106445	9.823441
9.16	83.9056	3.026549	9.570789	9.66	93.3156	3.108054	9.828530
0.17	84.0089	3.028201	9.576012	9.67	93.5089	3.109662	9.833616
9 18	84.2724	3.020851	9.581232	9.68	93.7024	3.111270	9.838699
9.19	84.4561	3.031501	9.586449	9.69	93.8961	3.112876	9.843780
9.20	84.6400	3.033150	9.591663	9.70	94.0900	3.114482	9.848858
9.21	84.8241	3.034798	9.596874	9.71	94.2841	3.116087	9.853933
9.22	85.0084	3.036445	9.602083	0.72	94.4784	3.117691	9.859006
9.23	85.1929	3.038092	9.607289	9.73	94.6729	3.119295	9.864076
9.24	85.3776	3.039737	9.612492	9.74	94.8676	3.120897	9.869144
9.25	85.5625	3.041381	9.617692	9.75	95.0625	3.122499	9.874209
9.26	85.7476	3.043025	9.622889	9.76	95.2576	3.124100	9.879271
9.27	85.9329	3.044667	9.628084	9.77	95.4529	3.125700	9.884331
9.28	80.1184	3.046309	9.633276	9.78	95.6484	3.127299	9.889388
9.29	86.3041	3.047950	9.638465	9.79	95.8441	3.128898	9.894443
9.30	86.4900	3.049590	9.643651	9.80	96.0400	3.130495	9.899495
9.31	86.6761	3.051229	9.648834	9.81	96.2361	3.132092	9.904544
9.32	86.8624	3.052868	9.654015	9.82	96.4324	3.133688	9.909591
9.33	87.0489	3.054505	9.659193	9.83	96.6289	3.135283	9.914636
9.34	87.2356	3.056141	9.664368	9.84	96.8256	3.136877	9.919677
9.35	87.4225	3.057777	9.669540	9.85	97.0225	3.138471	9.924717
9.36	87.6096	3.059412	9.674709	9.86	97.2196	3.140064	9.929753
9.37	87.7969	3.061046	9.679876	9.87	97.4169	3.141656	9.934787
9.38	87.9844	3.062679	9.685040	9.88	97.6144	3.143247	9.939819
9.39	88.1721	3.064311	9.690201	9.89	97.8121	3.144837	9.944848
9.40	88.3600	3.065942	9.695360	9.90	98.0100	3.146427	9.949874
9.41	88.5481	3.067572	9.700515	9.91	98.2081	3.148015	9.954898
9.42	88.7364	3.069202	9.705668	9.92	98.4064	3.149603	9.959920
9.43	88.9249	3.070831	9.710819	9.93	98.6049	3.151190	9.964939
9.44	89.1136	3.072458	9.715966	9.94	98.8036	3.152777	9.969955
9.45	89.3025	3.074085	9.721111	9.95	99.0025	3.154362	9.974969
9.46	89.4916	3.075711	9.726253	9.96	99.2016	3.155947	9.979980
9.47	89.6809	3.077337	9.731393	9.97	99.4009	3.157531	9.984989
9.48	89.8704	3.078961	9.736529	9.98	99.6004	3.159114	9.989995
9.49	90.0601	3.080584	9.741663	9.99	99.8001	3.160696	9.994999

[Answers to selected problems]

2.1a $1/16$ **b** $1/16$ **c** $1/2$ **2.4** .3024 **2.6** .70
2.7 .2817 **2.9** .72 **2.12** .704 **2.16** .5491
2.17a .0993 **b** .59096 **c** .5129 **2.19a** .0455 **b** .00003
c .99994

CHAPTER 3

3.1b Cost plus 15%; EMV $31,000 **3.3c** Buy 3-dozen balls early
for an EMV equal to $301.20. **3.5b** Do the research and bet on
the team that the research indicates is going to win. EMV = $32.
3.7c Go without research. EMV = $62,500.

CHAPTER 5

5.1 $x_1 = 12$, $x_2 = 4$, max value $= 104$ **5.4** $x_1 = 35/91$, $x_2 =$
$45/13$, max value $= 2,485/91$ **5.5** $x_1 = 24/13$, $x_2 = 10/19$, min
value $= 468/13$ **5.8a** One **b** $x_1 = 1.75$, max value $= 8.75$
5.9a $x_1 = 0$, $x_2 = 1$, $x_3 = 4$, $x_4 = 0$ **b** Yes **c** No **d** No
5.12 Produce 160 sq yd plywood; profit is $48,000.

CHAPTER 6

6.3 The dual; it has fewer constraints **6.5** $x_1 = 0$, $x_2 = 2$, max
value $= 16$; $y_1 = 2$, min value $= 16$ **6.6** $y_1 = 0$, $y_2 = 0$, y_3
$= 1$, min value $= 18$; for primal yields, $x_1 = 9$, $x_2 = 0$, max value $=$
18 **6.7a** Resources 1 and 2 **b** Either resource 1 or 2; both
shadow prices are $1 **c** Resource 1 could be increased by 12;
resource 2 could be increased by 2; resource 3 could be increased to
no limit. **d** $x_1 = 1.5$, $x_2 = 10$, $S_3 = 20$; profit increased to 26.
6.11a $y_1 = .12$, $y_2 = 0$, $y_3 = .04$ **b** 6.2 **c** Decrease 30,
increase 0 **d** Range $(.12, \infty)$ **6.14** Constraints 2 and 3 are
tight. Shadow price 1 is zero.

CHAPTER 7

7.2 Two solutions are possible; min cost is 304. One solution is $x_{11} = 11$, $x_{13} = 7$, $x_{14} = 2$, $x_{23} = 10$, $x_{32} = 13$, $x_{34} = 12$.   **7.3** VAM solution in problem 7.2 is optimal.   **7.6** $x_{15} = 5$, $x_{27} = 7$, $x_{36} = 4$, $x_{47} = 2$ **7.9** Job 1 to machine 1, job 2 to machine 2, job 3 to machine 3   **7.12** If each bidder receives only one contract, subcontract 1 goes to bidder 5, 2 to 2, 3 to 1, 4 to 3, and 5 to 4; minimum cost is $155,000. If bidders could be awarded any number of contracts, the optimal assignment is 1 to 2, 2 to 2, 3 to 1, 4 to 5, and 5 to 1 for a minimum cost of $141,000.   **7.13** Total cost with two factories is $32,000 (transportation cost is $12,000); total cost with three factories is $35,750 (transportation cost is $14,750).

CHAPTER 8

8.3b Critical path is B–D–F   **c** 12 days   **8.5d** 15.833 **e** .267   **f** .093   **8.7b** November 23, assuming a 7-day work week   **8.9a** 15 days   **b** $1,275   **c** $600

CHAPTER 9

9.4 3   **9.5** $\rho = .875$; $L_q = 3.0625$; $W_s = 7.875$ minutes; $L_s = 3.9375$; $W_q = .102083$ hours   **9.8a** 75%   **b** 3 minutes and 4 minutes total expected "in-system" time   **c** 3   **d** 25% **9.10a** 2.322 hours, 1 repairman; 11.76 minutes, 2 repairmen

CHAPTER 11

11.1a 60   **b** 4   **c** 3 months   **d** $600   **11.4a** 23   **b** 10.43 set-ups per year   **c** 24 days   **d** $657.21   **11.8a** 10,000 **b** $53,337   **11.10a** Order 30 vacuum cleaners when the inventory level reaches 9 units.   **b** $96.51

[Index]

Italic page numbers signify the point of definition for key terms.

Copyright Acknowledgments

We should like to acknowledge the following sources for permission to include the tables found on pages 455 to 495 of *Introduction to Management Science:*

Table 1 The standard normal distribution From *Modern Elementary Statistics*, 4th ed., by John E. Freund (Englewood Cliffs, N.J.: Prentice-Hall, Inc., 1973). Reproduced by permission of the publisher.

Table 2 The cumulative binomial probability distribution From Robert Schlaifer, *Probability and Statistics for Business Decisions* (New York: McGraw-Hill, Inc., 1959), by specific permission of the President and Fellows of Harvard College, who hold the copyright. Reproduced from *Quantitative Techniques for Business Decisions* by Rodney D. Johnson and Bernard R. Siskin (Englewood Cliffs, N.J.: Prentice-Hall, Inc., 1976) with permission of the publisher.

Table 3 The cumulative Poisson distribution From *Statistical Quality Control*, 3rd ed., by E. L. Grant. Copyright © 1964 by McGraw-Hill, Inc. Used with permission of McGraw-Hill Book Company. Reproduced from *Quantitative Techniques for Business Decisions* by Rodney D. Johnson and Bernard R. Siskin (Englewood Cliffs, N.J.: Prentice-Hall, Inc., 1976) with permission of the publisher.

Table 4 The chi-square distribution This table is based on Table 8 of *Biometrika Tables for Statisticians*, vol. I (New York: Cambridge University Press, 1954) by permission of the *Biometrika* trustees. Reproduced from *Modern Elementary Statistics*, 4th ed., by John E. Freund (Englewood Cliffs, N.J.: Prentice-Hall, Inc., 1973) with permission of the publisher.

Table 5 One-tailed table of critical values for the Kolmogorov-Smirnov test From "The Kolmogorov-Smirnov Test for Goodness of Fit" by Frank J. Massey, Jr., *Journal of the American Statistical Association*, 46, no. 253 (March 1951), with permission of the publisher.

Table 6 Multiserver Poisson-exponential queuing system: probability that the system is idle, p_0 From *Operations Research for Managerial Decisions* by Donald R. Plane and Gary A. Kochenberger (Homewood, Ill.: Richard D. Irwin, Inc., 1972) with permission of the publisher.

Table 7 Random numbers   From *Modern Elementary Statistics*, 4th ed., by John E. Freund (Englewood Cliffs, N.J.: Prentice-Hall, Inc., 1973). Reproduced by permission of the publisher. Based on parts of *Table of 105,000 Random Decimal Digits*, Interstate Commerce Commission, Bureau of Transport Economics and Statistics, Washington, D.C.

Table 8 Squares and square roots   From *Modern Elementary Statistics*, 4th ed., by John E. Freund (Englewood Cliffs, N.J.: Prentice-Hall, Inc., 1973). Reproduced by permission of the publisher.